Boatkeeper

The Boatowner's Guide to Maintenance, Repair, and Improvement

Advice on Keeping Your Boat Shipshape
From the Columns of
MOTOR BOATING & SAILING MAGAZINE

Edited by Bernard Gladstone and Tom Bottomley

Illustrated by Fred Wolff

HEARST MARINE BOOKS / New York

Library of Congress Catalog Card Number: 84-80492

ISBN: 0-688-03565-5

Printed in the United States of America

9 10

BOOK DESIGN BY
STANLEY S. DRATE/FOLIO GRAPHICS CO. INC.

ACKNOWLEDGMENTS

Through the years the "Boatkeeper" column in *Motor Boating & Sailing* magazine has greatly benefited from the tips, advice, and information supplied by boatowners throughout the country. Below is a list of the people who have contributed to the material in this book.

LIST OF CONTRIBUTORS

Timothy Banse	Leonard Katz	Gerald L. Palmer, Jr.
Walter Bechmann	Kirk and Dorothy Kirkpatrick	Henry J. Perry
Stephanie Bernardo	D. W. Knoll	Ron A. Peterson
Tom Bottomley	Kenneth Koetzner	Douglas E. Piehler
Bill Brogdon	Sheryl S. Krawchuk	Marley Pierson
Debra Carmichael	Dennis Langlois	Bob Preston
Jerry Cartwright	Arthur R. Lee	Rod Radford
Mickey Cell	Pete Leech	Douglas Reedy
Daniel S. J. Choy	Natalie and Al Levy	Harley L. Sachs
Robert L. Coen	A. Allen Lipton	E. A. Sack
Jimmy Cornell	Ronald Lumachi	Norman G. Samet
Fred Crowe, Jr.	Dave MacLean	Alfred E. Schram
Damon Crumb	Gordon Manning	Jack Seville
Jack Dillon	Jerold Marmer	Bill Shaw
Ed Dennis	Ferenc Maté	Bill Shellenberger
Bill Draper	Ellie Mazzo	Steven Siblisky
Michael Gilboy	William A. McIntyre	Townshend S. Smith
Bernard Gladstone	D. and G. McKain	Linda Soltysik
Chuck Gneagy	C. Miller	Ted Squier
Claude Goche	William C. Miller	Fred Stearns
Jack Haigh	M. M. Mitchell	Rod Stephens
Hank Halsted	Joanne L. Mooney	Frederick E. Still
Katie and Gene Hamilton	Thomas B. Moore	Karl R. Timm
Robert R. Hamilton	Sergio Moreno	Jack Tyler
Eric S. Handford	Ed Nabb	Chris Vogler
Dorothy L. Herbert	Elsie K. Nelson	Steve Wales
Arthur Hill	Patrick Nerbonne	David Wall
Robert E. Huffman	Malcolm B. Ochs	H. J. Webb
William Immergluck	Bob O'Leary	William Weton, Jr.
Ted Jones	Dan Orfan	Eleanor G. White

CONTENTS

4. Miscellaneous Interior Maintenance and Repairs / 97

5. Tools, Materials, and Equipment / 109

6. Annual Laying Up and Fitting Out / 127

7. Electricity and Electronics / 153

8. Engines and Propulsion Gear / 169

9. Shortcuts to Save Time and Money / 201

10. Bernie Gladstone's Boatyard: Readers' Questions Answered / 213

INTRODUCTION

The "Boatkeeper" section of *Motor Boating & Sailing* magazine has long been one of its most popular and most widely read sections—not only because it is full of the kind of information boatowners are constantly on the lookout for, but also because it provides a forum through which boatowners around the country can exchange maintenance tips and suggestions for better boat care, and can question the editors on all types of boat problems.

In the years during which I have been editing this section, I have always been amazed at the interest shown by most boatowners in trying to maintain their boats in as near "like new" condition as possible. In fact, many want to even go one step further: They want to add improvements or make small changes that they feel the manufacturer should have added; in other words, they actually want to make their boats "better than new" in many cases.

The "Boatkeeper" section is an effort to supply this kind of information by helping boatowners to learn from each other's experiences. I frequently receive requests for copies of material that was printed in past issues of "Boatkeeper," something I cannot always do, so here is a book that should solve that problem. It includes the best of "Boatkeeper," as selected from the last few years' issues of *Motor Boating & Sailing*—all bound together in one handy volume.

In these pages I believe you will find the answers to most of your questions, so that you can use it as a handy reference book that you can depend on to solve many of your boatkeeping problems. Let me know if there is anything you feel should have been included, or if you have any suggestions for further ideas that can be included in future issues of the "Best of Boatkeeper."

—BERNARD GLADSTONE
"Boatkeeper" Editor

Boatkeeper

1 EXTERIOR MAINTENANCE AND REPAIRS

Those Maddening Leaks: How to Find and Fix Them

Leaks that develop around hatches, windows, cabin tops, decks and other parts of the boat's superstructure are probably No. 1 on the average boatowner's enemies list. Unlike holes below the waterline, superstructure leaks are seldom serious enough to endanger your boat, but they are often the most frustrating of all problems to solve.

Found in brand new fiberglass boats as well as in old wooden boats, cabin and deck leaks always seem to show up right over the skipper's berth, or inside a clothes locker where water can do the maximum amount of damage.

Eliminating leaks of this kind can be simply a matter of applying some caulking compound or sealant to an open seam, or it can be a time-consuming job that will require complete removal of moldings, stanchions, or other deck fittings. The real headache is finding out just where the water is actually coming from and how it is entering the boat's superstructure in the first place.

For example, if water is dripping down on your head while you are lying in your bunk, the logical thing to do is to look for a crack, hole or open seam in the deck directly overhead. Unfortunately, the problem is seldom as simple as this. The water may actually be entering through a tiny crevice that is many feet away from your bunk, then quietly seeping across overhead stringers and down through hollow spaces in the cabin's outer shell, until finally it drops down through an open joint directly over your bunk.

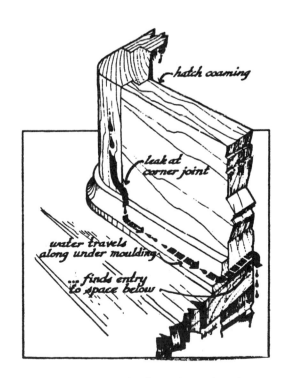

Water insinuates itself anywhere, given the opportunity.

How do you go about tracking down and then eliminating leaks of this kind? First of all, make up your mind that it will probably take time and patience, so don't expect to solve the problem quickly. Remember that water can and will flow horizontally along a stringer or structural member, but it definitely does not flow upward, so you know that your search will be limited to points of entry that are higher than, or on a level with, the place where the water shows up on the inside.

The surest way to find out how the water is entering is to track it backward from inside—ideally while the water is still dripping. This may mean pulling off the overhead lining, removing some moldings, or even ripping apart cabinets or lockers so that you can follow the path of the water back to its source. This can involve extensive repair work, so in most cases the more logical procedure is to try to locate the source of the leak from the outside.

Where to Look

To track down a leak that shows up in your cabin ceiling, start by checking the overhead deck or cabin top on the outside. Look for cracks or open seams where caulking or sealant is missing and, if the boat is wood, remember that peeling paint and other defects can also allow water to enter. Patch or fill any openings that seem even *slightly* suspicious, and be sure you probe all joints and seams with a knife blade, even though no openings are readily visible.

The next place to check is wherever a stanchion railing, cleat, or deck fitting of any kind is fastened to the boat above or alongside the area where the leak has developed. When screws and bolts penetrate wood or fiberglass there is always a

potential danger of water working its way in through the same opening. Each fixture should be sealed with bedding compound or an elastomeric caulking compound before it is installed. But workmen are sometimes careless about doing this properly, so the only solution in many cases is to play it safe and remove the fixture. Take out the screws completely, force a little silicone rubber or Thiokol-type sealant into the screw hole, then tighten. If the fixture is through-bolted, loosen the nut from underneath, pull the bolt head up part way, then work some sealant down into the hole and under the head of the bolt before replacing and re-tightening it.

A common mistake that causes leaks is overtightening the bolts and nuts that hold deck fittings in place. This not only squeezes so much of the bedding compound out that there is none left to seal out water, but it also creates stress that causes cracking and distortion of the wood or fiberglass—and this

will eventually create minute openings that allow water to enter.

To ensure a watertight seal when you use a rubber base sealant, draw the nut or bolt up just tight enough to cause most of the excess to ooze out. Then wait a few hours before finishing the tightening process. This will allow the rubber sealant to partially cure and form a sort of gasket so that when additional pressure is applied, enough compound will remain in place to maintain a watertight seal. Just be sure you have spread enough compound under the fixture so that all voids will be filled in, including the hole in which the bolt or screw fits.

Another common source of water entry is the joint where a cabin side meets the deck of the boat, or where hatches are joined to the deck or cabin top. In some cases this joint will be covered with a piece of quarter-round wood molding or with a metal cove molding, while in others it will merely be sealed with a bead of caulking.

Even if there are no obvious

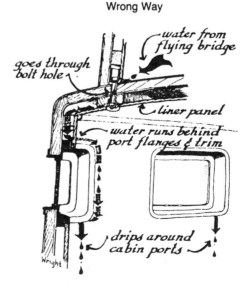

Wrong Way

Concave joint in sealant tends to crack as it dries.

Right Way

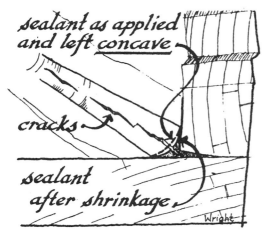

sealant as applied and left <u>concave</u>

cracks

sealant after shrinkage.

Wright

A leak's origin may be much higher than first indicated.

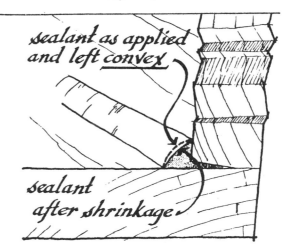

sealant as applied and left <u>convex</u>

sealant after shrinkage.

The correct caulking method (above) leaves convex bead that should not crack.

openings visible, water has a tremendous affinity for such joints—it seems to find its way in through crevices or tiny gaps that are invisible to the human eye. One way to determine if this is the source of trouble is to inspect this area carefully immediately after a heavy rain. If the joint is covered with molding, pry part of this molding off to see if the surfaces underneath are damp. If so, you'll know that water is finding its way in behind the molding and the only way to cure the problem is to completely remove the molding and rebed it.

If it is held in place by screws that are covered with wood plugs then you'll have to first remove the plugs by digging each one out with the point of a knife blade. After the molding is off, scrape away any old compound that remains. Dry the surfaces thoroughly, then apply a liberal bead of caulking along the entire length of the joint where the vertical and horizontal surfaces meet. Press the molding firmly in place to squeeze out all the excess compound and then replace the screws to secure it permanently.

When the joint where a hatch or cabin side meets the deck has no such molding, all you have to do is scrape out all of the old caulking material, wipe down with acetone, and then apply a fresh bead of new sealant. Use masking tape on each surface to create a neat-looking bead, but avoid the common mistake of wiping off all excess with your fingertip to create a neat-looking concave bead. For maximum durability the bead should be *convex* rather than *concave* because when a concave bead shrinks as it dries it tends to crack down the middle. A convex bead includes enough material to prevent this.

Another frequent source of leaks is window frames and portlight frames. All too often careless workmen leave voids or gaps where bedding compound is missing, or they use poor quality compound that dries out and loses resiliency. Either way, sealing around the outside with a bead of silicone rubber or Thiokol-type caulking often helps, but this is at best only a temporary cure. The only sure cure lies in removing the window frame completely and then rebedding it properly with an elas-

tomeric sealant before replacing it.

Bear in mind, however, that just because a leak shows up around the bottom of a window frame on the inside, this does not necessarily mean that the leak is originating around the outside of that particular frame. Very often water will seep down from above (between the inner and outer lining of the cabin sides) until it meets the window frame; then it runs down around the frame and seeps out under it on the inside.

How do you actually find out where the water is coming from so that you don't have to take everything apart and, in the process, make many needless repairs? More often than not you can locate the source of trouble with a hose.

Let the water run slowly (not full force) without a nozzle. Use a piece of line or tape to position it so that the flow runs over the affected area, starting at the lowest possible point and then working your way up in stages. Direct the stream in such a way that the water runs over the suspected joint, frame, or deck fastening, and let it run in each position for at least thirty minutes while you check on

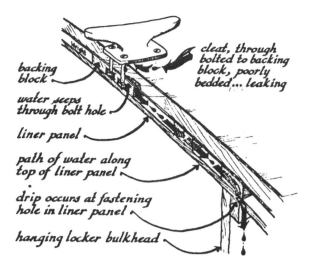

Water can and will flow horizontally along a stringer or other structural member.

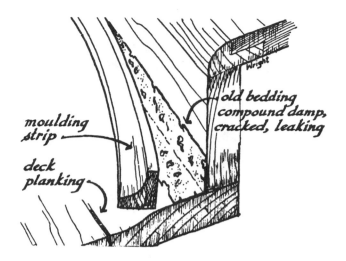

Leaks often occur due to poor or missing bedding.

the inside for signs of moisture. If none occur, move the hose up to the next highest point where there is a possibility of water entering.

On my own trawler, the leak showed up under a section of deck covered with teak planking, so the first step was to let water run over the teak planking in this area. But after half an hour nothing showed up below.

Since the deck slopes aft, the next step was to move the hose farther forward by several feet so that the water still flowed back over the suspected decking. Not until the third move, when the hose was approximately eight feet forward of the place where the leak showed up below, did we find the source—a loose wood plug that covered a broken screw that had never been properly bedded. Water was apparently running down through this loose plug and seeping under the teak planks, then running aft until it finally found its way down into the cabin below.

To repair this I removed the plug, drilled out the old screw and inserted a new, slightly larger one in its place. Before driving the new screw home, a blob of rubber sea-lant was squirted into the hole. The seams on each side of this deck plank were also caulked.

If this progressive testing with the hose had failed to locate a leak in any of the deck planking, then the next step would have been to let the water run down the sides of the cabin in stages, starting at the joint where the deck and the cabin sides meet, then gradually working up in stages until water was allowed to run down over the top of the cabin alongside the window frames and down onto the deck. It takes time and patience, but eventually the leak can be located and the necessary corrective measures taken.

Using the Newest Two-Part Polyurethane Paints

Probably the greatest improvement ever made in marine paints was the development of two-part polyurethane finishes. These paints dry to an exceptionally high gloss, which they retain for years without fading, dulling, or discoloring.

However, when first introduced, two-part polyurethane was the province of skilled professionals trained in spray techniques—since none of the early products could be brushed on. The spraying had to be done under carefully controlled conditions because temperature and humidity were critically important factors in achieving good results. Also, the solvents were highly toxic, so careful handling, proper ventilation, and face masks—to protect against inhalation of the vaporized solvents—were required.

Then a few years ago, in answer to increasing demand from boatowners who wanted to use these paints themselves, several national manufacturers introduced two-part polyurethane paints that were specifically designed for do-it-yourself application: They could be brushed on by the average boatyard painter or semi-handy boatowner, and were not as tricky to handle. Equally important, they could be applied over most existing paints and finishes without having to strip all of the old paint off—a preparatory step that was essential to the success of professionally applied, sprayed-on polyurethane finishes.

For best results, apply the two-part polyurethane paint with a solvent-resistant foam-type roller, then brush lightly across the strokes with a pure Chinese-bristle brush.

I tried several of these new two-part polyurethane paints on my own boat about two years ago. I found that these paints were really a great improvement over most conventional finishes—they have a much higher gloss and they dry to a harder, brighter finish that stands up well under repeated scrubbing and constant exposure to the elements (I live on my boat up North, so the boat is never covered or sheltered, and is in the water all year).

However, as I reported at the time, these two-part polyurethanes not only cost considerably more than regular marine paints, they are also more difficult to work with. They require careful mixing and preparation of the old surface beforehand, and are very sensitive to the need for proper thinning. In addition, more care is required in applying the two-part paints. But in spite of all these limitations, in my opinion the extra work—and extra cost—were worthwhile based on the quality of the finish.

Now, after twenty-four to thirty months of exposure, I can report that these paints *do* seem to stand up better than conventional one-part marine finishes—they certainly hold their gloss and color better. However, after about a year, a careful examination showed that, good as they are, they still did not match the gloss and color retention, or the resistance to staining and discoloration, of the "professional grade" two-part polyurethanes that were being sold to professional applicators at that time (and were not available to regular consumers through regular paint outlets).

On discussing this with the companies who make two of the most widely sold brands of "professional grade" two-part polyurethanes (Grow Group, Inc., makers of Awlgrip; and International Paint Co., makers of Interthane), I learned that many experienced boatyard painters agreed that there was a difference—the products designed primarily for professional use *did* give a tougher and longer-lasting finish when properly mixed and applied.

But these had to be sprayed on, didn't they? No longer, I was told. In answer to demands from professionals, as well as from the general public, the Interthane line was expanded to include a special brushable catalyst, and the people who make Awlgrip soon followed suit with the same thing.

In both cases the basic paint is the same—it's just that mixing it with the brushing catalyst (instead of the spraying catalyst) makes it possible to put the paint on with a brush instead of a sprayer (a roller can also be used—but more about this later). Using the paints in their brushable form not only eliminates the need for expensive spray equipment and trained operators to use it, it also eliminates much of the hazard involved in working with the paints' solvents—they are only strongly toxic when atomized and used in a relatively enclosed area. When the paint is applied by brush or roller it is not nearly as toxic—as long as there is *good* ventilation.

But since these paints are primarily designed for professional use, can the do-it-yourselfer boat-owner who is willing to pay the price (a hefty $30 to $35 a quart) and go to the extra trouble of following the instructions recommended by each manufacturer, actually buy these paints? Until recently, the answer would have

After the surface is sanded perfectly smooth, wipe with solvent or thinner to remove dust.

been either a "no" or a qualified "maybe." The products were sold only to professionals through wholesale distributors.

Now the picture has changed. Awlgrip, which does not officially condone sales to do-it-yourselfers, is still sold only through wholesale distributors; but many of these distributors will sell to nonprofessionals who come in and ask for the product. And the Interlux people have just started to market Interthane nationally through their regular dealers and distributors (many dealers will not actually stock it since they already carry Polythane, but they can order the Interthane products for you).

The biggest single drawback to these professional-quality polyurethane finishes is that they normally cannot be applied over existing paint. The powerful solvents will soften and/or lift many old paints. (The various "over-the-counter" versions are formulated with different solvents so they can be safely applied over most old finishes that are still sound.)

There are two ways around this drawback: (1) You can take all of the old paint off by sanding or scraping, or by using a remover; or (2) you can apply an intermediate or "transition" coat that will provide a good base for the new paint. For this transition coat the Interlux people recommend their two-part Polythane (which is their "over-the-counter" consumer product). The people who make Awlgrip recommend taking the old paint off, or using their epoxy primer as an intermediate coat.

If you are in doubt as to whether such a transition coat is needed before you start, there is a simple test you can make. Saturate a piece of cotton with some of the special thinner that is sold for use with each of these paints, then tape this on top of the old paint for about thirty minutes. When you pull it off, see if the thinner has softened, blistered, or otherwise attacked the old finish. If it has, *don't* put the new paint on directly over it. If it hasn't, chances are you are safe in going ahead.

In an effort to learn more about these professional-grade, brushable, two-part polyurethanes, I went to several yards that use them.

What I heard prompted me to obtain some brushable Awlgrip and brushable Interthane and try them out myself.

After discussing application techniques with several pros, I decided to follow the method they have found most successful in getting a smooth finish with both the brushable Awlgrip and the brushable Interthane—I put the paint on with a foam paint roller, then immediately smoothed it out with a fine bristle brush. The results, to say the least, were amazing.

When you first roll the paint on, it has a slightly dimpled or "pebbly" surface with very thin bubbles showing all over, but then when you cross-stroke lightly with the brush, you smooth all this out and the paint flows out like glass. It dries to a smooth, brilliant gloss that has the bright "wet look" of freshly applied paint or varnish, and it retains that "wet look" long after it has cured hard (both of these products come in clear, as well as in regular colors).

This is not to say that these paints are foolproof, or that they will give you a beautiful finish even if you are careless or sloppy. Quite the opposite—they require a lot of *extra* care in mixing, thinning, and application, and they require more-than-average attention to preparation if you really want to get a professional-looking job.

For example, you must use the right kind of brush and roller to put on the paint if you want to get the kind of finish these paints are capable of providing when properly applied. The roller must be a foam-type paint roller that is solvent-resistant—a cheap foam roller will be eaten up by the solvents and will fall apart in short order (each company sells solvent-resistant foam-roller covers through their distributors).

The brush used must be a top quality, pure Chinese bristle brush, preferably the kind that is a mixture of badger hair and bristle. These are not easy to find, and when you do find them, they are not cheap (expect to pay $20 to $25 for a 3″ brush). If your dealer doesn't stock them, he can order one for you through his distributor. Don't think you can get by with an inexpensive brush or with a synthetic bristle brush—you'll only be wasting a lot of very expensive paint and a lot of time.

In addition to making certain you have either taken all of the old paint off or applied one of the recommended primers or transition coats mentioned above, here are some pointers to keep in mind when working with these two-part polyurethane finishes:

- Take extra care in smoothing the old surface and filling in even the smallest blemishes. The mirrorlike gloss achieved with Awlgrip or Interthane means that slight imperfections will be much more noticeable after the finish dries. Sand carefully with progressively finer grades of paper, and use nothing coarser than #150 or #180 for the final sanding.
- After sanding and smoothing, wipe the surface down with the recommended thinner or solvent to make sure you remove every bit of sanding dust, as well as all dirt or other foreign matter. A clean surface is important before applying any paint, but with a two-part polyurethane paint you have to be almost hospital clean.
- Be sure to follow mixing directions exactly. The proportion of catalyst to be used with the paint is critical, so don't try to guess if you are mixing less than a full can. Use a small measuring cup or glass to measure out amounts precisely, and be careful not to contaminate the contents of the paint can with some of the catalyst until you are ready to mix both together. Mix the paint about thirty minutes ahead of time and allow it to stand. Then stir again before using.

- Some thinning is almost always required, especially in warm weather, and additional thinner will have to be added periodically as you work. When you feel the paint is starting to thicken a bit and is getting harder to smooth out, add a little more thinner. This is probably one of the trickiest parts of the application process for those who are inexperienced since it takes a little while to get the "feel" for just how much thinner to add.

  Too much thinner and the paint will run or sag; too little and it will "pull" and tend to dry "ropey" with brush marks showing. (This was also a problem with the "do-it-yourself" two-part polyurethane paints that I tried a couple of years ago—in fact, if anything, I found it easier to hit a "happy medium" when thinning these "professional" grade finishes than I did with the "do-it-yourself" versions).

- Avoid working when temperatures are below 55° F. or above 85° F., and try to avoid working in direct sunlight if possible—especially if temperatures are above 70° F. These paints need some moisture in the air to cure properly, so the relative humidity should ideally be above 50 percent. However, really humid days (above 85 percent RH) will make the paint set up too fast.
- Use the roller-and-brush technique everywhere you can. On surfaces that are too small for this, use the brush alone. Spread the paint on evenly across the shortest dimension if practical,

In addition to sanding, all cracks, nicks, and gouges should be filled with epoxy before painting.

then cross-stroke lightly along the length with an almost dry brush to smooth out the finish.

- With all polyurethanes you have to be careful to avoid trying to put on too thick a coat—two thin coats are always preferable for best results. Allow the first coat to dry overnight, then wet sand with #320 or #340 grit paper and wipe off all sanding dust with a rag saturated with solvent before applying a second coat.

How to Get a Mirror-Smooth Varnish Finish

There is probably nothing that contributes more to the appearance of any boat than the condition of its brightwork. Regardless of whether the boat is a sleek fiberglass cruiser with just a few varnished handrails and hatch covers, or a well-kept

Lift brush up and away from the work at the end of each stroke.

classic wood boat that has miles of brightly varnished toe rails and cabin sides, a mirror-smooth varnish finish adds immeasurably to the "Bristol" look of any boat, and it is always a beautiful sight to behold.

Unfortunately, building up and maintaining this kind of finish is not quick and easy; it takes time and patience and requires careful attention to some important details. But it doesn't necessarily require more time, or even a great deal more skill, than is required to do a job that will dry full of streaks, dust specks, and runs. It's just that you have to learn the proper working techniques and then follow them carefully. Furthermore, you have to use a top-quality varnish that is applied only when working conditions are right.

One of the most important "secrets" for achieving a smooth varnish finish is using the right brush. The best ones are those made of badger hair, or a mixture of badger hair and pure Chinese bristle. Unfortunately, good ones made of these natural bristles are hard to find, and they are quite expensive when you do find them.

Many experienced boat painters have found that they can also do a good job with a brush that is made of synthetic bristles, but it must be one of the best models; one that has a very high percentage of "flagged" bristle (bristles that have "split ends" similar to the kind found in natural bristle) and one in which most of the bristles are tapered.

Brushes made of polyester filament bristles seem to work better than those made of nylon bristle, and they are not affected by some of the strong solvents used in some of the newest finishes (such as the two-part urethanes). Nylon bristles tend to get soft and floppy when used in strong solvents.

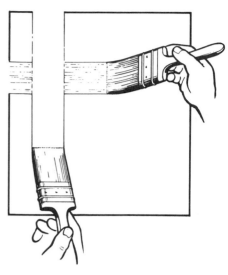

Apply varnish across the grain, then cross-stroke lightly with the grain.

There should be a mixture of different-length bristles in the brush so it will flow the varnish on uniformly when flexed and as it starts to wear. Also, the brush should feel comfortably balanced when you hold it in working position. The shape of the brush should be such that it tapers on both flat sides as the bristles approach the tip; when the bristles press lightly against a flat surface the tips should "fan out" to form a neat, straight edge. When you flex the brush against the back of your hand, the bristles should have a nice springy feel to them.

Just as important as using the proper kind of brush is the need for taking the time to do a proper job of preparing the old surface before the varnish is applied. No finish can be any smoother than the surface under it, and no finish can stand up any better than the coating over which it is applied (if you are applying new varnish over old).

When sanding raw wood, start with a medium grit paper such as #80 or #100, then switch to #150 or #180. Do your finish sanding parallel to the grain with #220 paper. You should try to do all your sanding parallel to the grain when possible and avoid rubbing in circles. If you use an electric sander, use an orbital sander (also called a finishing sander). Never use a disk sander—it will leave swirl marks and gouge marks that will be almost impossible to remove.

If you want a really smooth job on open-grain wood such as mahogany, teak, or oak, you will have to use a paste wood filler to fill in the open pores. This is not the same as the filler you would use for filling screw holes or cracks; it is a filler specifically designed to fill in open pores in the grain. Use it on previously unfinished wood only or on wood that has been stripped clean with a chemical remover. On previously finished surfaces, when you sand down to the bare wood the filler in the pores usually remains, so a new coat of filler is normally not required.

Although these fillers all come in paste form, you don't use them that way. Thin the paste with turpentine or paint thinner until it is about the consistency of heavy cream, than apply it to the wood with a brush. Fillers are usually available either in a no-color natural, light tan, or in colors such as mahogany and brown mahogany, although not all stores stock it in colors. The colored fillers serve as a stain as well as a filler for the open pores of the wood.

Natural filler can be used on some light woods such as oak and some teak, but on darker woods such as mahogany, you will probably want a colored filler. If you cannot find a filler in the shade you want, tint it with oil colors or universal paint colors. This will act as a stain as well as a filler, so add color a little at a time and keep testing on scrap wood. You can always add more if the filler is too light, but it is hard to lighten the

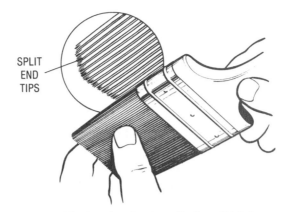
The best brushes have "split end" bristles.

SPLIT END TIPS

color after you have added too much.

The thinned-down paste wood filler is applied to the surface by brushing it back and forth over a section at a time (no more than three or four square feet). Wait until the filler just starts to dry, as evidenced by the fact that it starts to lose its wet look and starts to turn dull, then start rubbing off the excess immediately by using a folded piece of burlap or similar coarse cloth. Rub across the grain first, then rub in a circular motion. The idea is to pack the filler into the pores while rubbing hard enough to remove any excess that remains on the surface. If the surface gets very sticky or gummy, dip the cloth into some paint thinner and wring out the excess, then continue rubbing immediately.

Timing is important here. If you wipe too soon, you will rub the filler out of the pores. If you wait too long, it will start to dry and will be almost impossible to wipe off, although you can sometimes save the day by using a rag dipped into thinner. Otherwise, you may be faced with a sizable sanding job and may even have to start all over again.

When you finish wiping, allow the filler to dry overnight, then sand lightly with the grain, using

#180 sandpaper. Give the surface a final sanding with #220 paper. Then dust thoroughly.

If you are applying new varnish over wood that already has relatively sound varnish on it, you won't use stain or paste wood filler. Sanding is definitely required, however, to smooth down any rough areas and to ensure a better bond for the new coats. Sand until the old finish is absolutely smooth; judge this by stroking the surface lightly with your fingertips, not just by how it looks. Start with #120 paper, then finish with #220.

When recoating old varnish you will almost always find some places where the old varnish has cracked or lifted or started to turn white. Cracked areas can sometimes be sanded smooth without going all the way down to the raw wood, but areas where the varnish has lifted or where it seems to have turned white (indicating that water has gotten underneath), should be scraped off and sanded down to the bare wood. On mahogany you may also find places where the wood underneath has started to darken, also indicating that water has worked its way under the varnish and into the wood.

To make these spots blend in smoothly with the rest of the finish, scrape off all the old varnish and then sand the bare wood. If sanding doesn't get rid of the dark spot, you may have to use a bleach (such as oxalic acid). In some cases you can hide the discoloration with a little stain or paste wood filler. Stain is also needed if the wood is too light after sanding. You want to darken the wood so that it matches the rest of the finish around it, but don't depend on the varnish alone to do this.

Wherever possible, remove handles, catches, and other hardware before varnishing. This will not only make sanding and smoothing easier, it will also make it easier to flow the varnish on more smoothly with straight strokes and avoid stopping and starting strokes repeatedly (all of which causes more brush marks to show).

After sanding, on raw wood or on old varnish, it is essential that every bit of dust be removed before you apply the first brushful of varnish. The best way to do this is in three steps:

(1) Use a cloth, brush, or vacuum to remove most of the dust, but remember to shake out the cloth or brush so that the wind carries the dust away from the rest of the boat.

(2) Wipe the surfaces down with a tack rag (also called a tacky cloth). You can buy these in any paint store and in most marine supply outlets. It is a folded piece of cheesecloth that is permanently tacky so that it picks up and holds dust when wiped over the surface. As each side gets loaded with dust, turn the cloth or refold it to expose a fresh surface.

(3) Just before you start varnishing each section, wipe that area down again with a clean cloth dipped into paint thinner and partially wrung out. If you are using a varnish that requires a special thinner (other than ordinary turpentine or mineral spirits), use that thinner or solvent instead.

Most clear varnishes should not be stirred before use, but some may need thinning for the first coat or two, so obviously some stirring will be required. Do not shake the can, and do not stir violently. Pour some of the varnish out of the original can into a clean container, then do your mixing and working in this container. It should not be filled more than half way while working, and you should pour off (and thin) only as much varnish as you will use that day. The idea is to avoid pouring any partly used varnish back into the original can. This will only contaminate the original contents and will make it harder to get a smooth finish the next time you use it. If you do mix the old with the new, strain it through several layers of old nylon stocking before using it again.

When applying the varnish, never dip your brush in by more than about one third the length of the bristles, then tap off the excess by patting the tips lightly against the inside of the container above the varnish level. Don't wipe the bristles across the rim of the can; this will create tiny air bubbles in the varnish as it runs back into the can and these bubbles will be very hard to remove from the varnish and the finish.

Hold your brush down near the ferrule and turn it over while carrying it from the can to the surface to keep it from dripping, then flow the varnish on with smooth strokes. Don't scrub it on by bearing down hard. As a rule, except on narrow moldings where it may be impractical, the best method is to brush the varnish on with smooth strokes across the grain, then cross-stroke lightly with an almost dry brush going parallel to the grain.

When painting individual panels or sections, start at one end and go all the way across to the other end if you can do so comfortably. Otherwise, start at one end and go past the center before lifting the brush up and away from the surface with a gently arcing stroke, as shown in the drawing. Then start at the

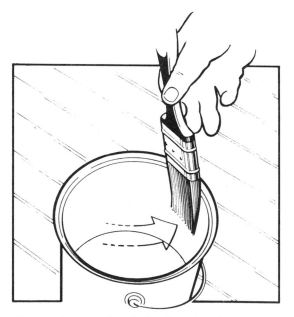

Always pat, never wipe, the brush against the can to avoid bothersome varnish bubbles.

other end and come back toward the center again from the opposite direction. Make sure you go past and overlap the spot where the first stroke ended, and again lift the brush up and away with an arcing motion. In all of this, the brush should be well loaded with varnish, and you should pick up more as soon as it feels as though the brush is running dry.

As each section or panel is coated, start cross-stroking immediately, but don't dip the brush; the bristles should be almost dry. Use only the tips of the bristle for this final smoothing, dragging them lightly over the surface to smooth out brush strokes and pick up runs before they can actually develop.

The size of the section you complete each time will depend to some extent on how fast the varnish dries; cross-stroking should be done before the varnish begins to get the least bit tacky or sticky. The time it takes for the varnish to get tacky will vary with the brand you use, the amount it is thinned, the porosity of the surface, and the temperature and humidity on that particular day.

When varnishing close to the edge of a board or panel, never drag the brush across the corner or edge; instead, brush from the center of the panel out to edge or corner and lift the brush gradually as you go past the edge. Dragging the brush across the edge or allowing the bristles to wipe across the edge is certain to result in runs and drips. The same thing holds true when brushing around permanently installed hardware that cannot be removed. Be careful to avoid having the bristles rub against the edges as you go past; this can also cause runs and drips.

On inside corners, the opposite is true. You obviously cannot go beyond the end, so start in the corner and brush out toward the cen-

ter of the panel, then lift up and away as you pass the halfway mark in the center. Next, start at the other end, again in the corner, and come back past the center until you overlap where the first stroke ended, then curve up again.

Varnish should not be applied when temperatures drop below 50°F., though you can sometimes varnish on a sunny day in the middle 40s if you stand the varnish in a container of hot water to keep it warm while you are working. If doors or hatches are removable, it may pay to take them off and do the varnishing indoors where you won't have to worry about temperature extremes, and where you can better control the amount of dust that will settle on the wet surface. When this is not practical, avoid varnishing in direct sunlight, especially on days when temperatures are expected to climb above 80°F., and never varnish on very windy days because dust and other air-borne debris will settle on the wet varnish and ruin even the most carefully applied finish.

In early spring and fall be careful about varnishing too early in the morning when there is still dew on the surface, or too late in the day when dew or condensation can form on the varnish before it dries. This will result in a loss of gloss and may cause the varnish to turn white or cloudy looking.

With varnish, as with most other marine finishes, several thin coats are always better than one heavy coat. As a rule, this means a minimum of four to six coats when varnishing over bare wood (up to eight coats if you want that really deep gleaming finish you may have admired on some professionally maintained yachts). When revarnishing over an existing finish that is still in relatively good condition, two coats are generally advisable, though if you do it before the old

coat starts to show signs of wear, one coat will often do the trick. When applying multiple coats, the first one or two coats should be thinned anywhere from 10 to 15 percent so the varnish will soak in properly. For specific recommendations, consult the manufacturer's directions on the can.

Most varnishes require a light sanding between coats to ensure a good bond, but some of the newer formulations recommend no sanding as long as you apply the second coat within a specified number of hours. After that period, or if you are varnishing over an old finish, sanding is definitely required. Removing every bit of sanding dust is imperative if you want to ensure a smooth finish when the next coat is applied.

Brightwork: The Clear Urethane Solution

There is probably no problem of more universal interest to the boatowner, power or sail, than the maintenance of exterior brightwork. Whether the wood is teak, mahogany, or some other species, all boatowners seem to be faced with the same problem: What preserves and protects brightwork with a durable finish that will retain its gloss without endless hours of preparatory sanding and without almost monthly recoating during the boating season?

Even if a top-quality varnish is carefully applied at the beginning of the season (four to six coats are recommended for initial buildup by most experts), most boatowners discover that if they want to maintain the original bright luster, and if they want to avoid having to wood down the entire area within a year or two, at least one more coat

Two-part urethanes represent a dramatic improvement in marine paint.

also help to ward off the damaging effects of every marine coating's greatest enemy—the ultraviolet rays of the sun. In addition, when wood darkens under paint, no one sees it; when the wood darkens under a clear film it is immediately noticeable and detracts from the overall appearance.

Probably the most dramatic improvement in marine paint durability during recent years has been the development and widespread use of two-part urethanes, paint finishes that have exceptional gloss retention and often stand up as long as five to eight years.

Hence, great interest was shown in the two-part clear urethane coating introduced a few years ago by the U.S. Paint Division, Grow Group, Inc., the people who make Awlgrip, a two-part urethane that

already had a well-deserved reputation for durability and gloss retention.

What made this product especially interesting is that the clear urethane could be applied by brush when used with a special brushing catalyst developed for Awlgrip.

Unfortunately, when first introduced some years ago, the clear urethane evidenced some problems—problems with application mostly, but also some disappointment with the hoped-for durability of the finish. Apparently, while U.S. Paints opaque urethane finishes were designed for use on relatively stable surfaces such as fiberglass or metal, the clear urethane was being used on wood—a natural product that varies in surface texture, moisture content, oiliness, and tended to

Traditionally, teak needed bimonthly coating for best appearance.

will have to be applied before the season is over.

Leading manufacturers of paints and varnishes have long been aware of this problem, so many have done (and are doing) considerable research in this area. But the "ideal solution" or "perfect coating" has yet to be discovered. However, there are some developments that do seem to show promise of lasting longer than the usual two to three months between coats.

Actually, more progress has been made in this area with paints—"opaque" coatings—than with clear coatings because clear coatings obviously do not have the same amount of solid, in the film. The solids and pigments not only add strength and durability, they flex or move more than fiberglass or metal.

As Chris von der Heyde, sales manager of U.S. Paint, explains it, "We originally introduced clear Awlgrip for use over our regular opaque paints, especially our metallic finishes. It was the dealers and applicators who decided to use it on wood."

Since that time, clear Awlgrip has been modified to a great degree principally to improve its brushing and working qualities and its resistance to attack by ultraviolet. But according to Mr. von der Heyde, the company still does not have a complete system for coating wood with a clear finish—in other words, they do not yet have a base coat they can recommend for sealing and priming the wood before the urethane is applied.

The big problem seems to be that the clear urethane does not stand up well when used directly over most woods because all urethanes are exceptionally sensitive to moisture content in the material over which they are applied. Since wood varies greatly in this respect, and since one can never be sure how dry or well-seasoned the wood is, there is always a danger of premature failure when the clear urethane is applied directly to the wood.

Nevertheless, Hi-Solids Clear Awlgrip is being used by many boatyards and boatowners who have worked out systems that involve using products made by other manufacturers for the first several coats and then applying the Hi-Solids Clear Awlgrip as a finish coat. Although the Awlgrip producers do not "officially" recommend any of these systems, they recognize that some of these have worked quite well in providing a good foundation for an overcoating of clear Awlgrip.

According to Mr. von der Heyde, the company is working on several products that will answer the need for a base coat which will bond well with most woods, while still providing the protection required against darkening and other damaging effects of ultraviolet. These products are currently being tested on boats and test panels in various locations, but as of yet none have been tested long enough to thoroughly satisfy the manufacturer.

In spite of this, and in spite of the fact that systems vary among different applicators, boatyards that have been using clear Awlgrip on brightwork are reporting some remarkable results—beautiful high-gloss finishes that retain their gloss for up to two years of continuous exposure without recoating, and have better-than-average resistance to attack by salt water, frequent scrubbing, and mild abrasion.

As these stories have spread, and as owners of boats that have been finished with this product tell others how pleased they are with the results, more and more people have been asking about the feasibility of using a clear two-part urethane finish on their own brightwork. (To my knowledge, Awlgrip is the only two-part brushable urethane in a clear finish at present. It is a *polyester* resin, while other leading brands are *acrylic* resins and can only be sprayed on by professional applicators.)

In an attempt to gain some answers, I have spoken to the people who make Awlgrip, to several distributors and professional applicators, and to owners of boats that have had their brightwork finished in this manner. Based on a consensus of what I have thus far heard and seen (and until I finish some tests of my own), here are the techniques that seem to be working well when using Hi-Solids

Clear Awlgrip as a finish for marine brightwork—techniques that also seem to be giving long-lasting results.

Applicators have been relying on one of two bases—either several coats of top-quality marine spar or clear two-part epoxy.

In each case, several coats are applied, after which a suitable aging period must elapse before the clear Awlgrip is put on over it. When questioned about the two methods and which, if any, they would recommend, Awlgrip's technical people are understandably reluctant to make any "official" recommendations about the use of products made by other companies.

However, they are honest enough to admit that their dealers are using these products under clear Awlgrip and getting excellent results, so they don't hesitate to describe the techniques involved in sealing the wood.

But which is better to use as a base coat—a marine spar varnish, or a clear epoxy?

A lot depends on who you ask and on how much darkening you are willing to accept as the finish ages.

If you use varnish underneath, you will have to wait months before the final coats of Awlgrip can be applied; if you use an epoxy, you can apply the clear Awlgrip in a matter of days after the last coat of epoxy has cured. On the other hand, most applicators seem to agree that epoxy tends to darken more as it ages and is exposed to the sun, while a good varnish that contains a UV shield will tend to hold the color better and will keep the finish from darkening as much.

John Jacques, of Dutch Wharf Boatyard Marina in Branford, Connecticut, a yard that has had a considerable amount of experience in finishing brightwork with Awlgrip's Hi-Solids Clear, says

Properly applied, clear Awlgrip on wood should last for years.

that he uses Pettit's Polypoxy Clear on the brightwork after stripping it down to bare wood.

He advises thinning the first coat of Polypoxy about 50 percent so that it will soak in deeply, then sanding lightly after it dries hard. The second coat is thinned only slightly—about 10 percent in most cases. When dry it is again sanded lightly and dusted off, after which a third coat of the same material is applied, thinning only as necessary to achieve easy brushing.

The third coat of clear epoxy is allowed to cure for a few days, then four coats of the Awlgrip Hi-Solids Clear are applied about one day apart (you don't have to sand between coats if you recoat within thirty-six hours). All coats are applied by brush, using top-quality badger-hair brushes, and on large areas at least two or three men work together to avoid any chance of lap marks.

A sailboat with an all-wood hull was refinished in this manner some time ago, and after having been exposed to the weather continuously for more than two years it still has most of its original gloss, although there are some places where nicks and scrapes obviously had to be touched up.

In another example, a large fiberglass motor yacht with teak wing doors, handrails, and mis-cellaneous other bright-work was done with this method in the spring of 1980. Although the yacht was uncovered and in the water continuously for two years after that, the finish was still as glossy and lustrous looking as the day after it was applied—and the only maintenance it has had during this period was the normal washing down after each cruise.

According to Mr. von der Heyde, some yards in Florida, where there is obviously more year-round demand for this kind of work and where any finish gets its severest test, there is another technique some applicators are using to achieve a long-lasting Awlgrip finish, particularly on teak. They prefer to use several coats of a good marine varnish as a base (as least four or five coats). They allow this to age for at least six months to a year, then the customer is asked to bring the boat back for a light resanding, touching up, and final coating with four to six coats of the Awlgrip Clear.

One of the reasons they prefer varnish, particularly on teak, is to keep the wood from darkening as much. Teak tends to show up light where it is scratched or nicked, and even when these spots are promptly touched up they are lighter than the rest of the finish, creating an uneven or blotchy appearance in time.

For the maximum in durability and appearance, there are even some applicators who apply the finish in a three-step sequence: Pettit's Polypoxy first (usually three coats as previously described), then three or four coats of marine varnish with a UV shield. They allow this to age for several months, then finish with three or four coats of the Awlgrip Clear.

Is the labor (and cost) worth it?

According to those who have

tried it, the answer is a definite yes—if you really want a clear finish that will not need recoating every couple of months, and if you want a gloss that will keep its shine for two to three years without recoating.

All this does not mean that you can completely neglect the finish during this time. Just as you would with any other type of marine coating, if you really want to get maximum life out of the coating, you still should wash off salt spray at the end of each day, and then wipe down the brightwork with a soft cloth or chamois.

The question that most often pops up in the boatowner's mind is: Can I apply it over my existing varnish without having to wood it all down?

This depends on the condition of your old varnish, the type of varnish, and the number of coats that were originally applied. The people at Awlgrip, as well as the pros I spoke to, generally advise wooding down before you start as being the safest procedure.

However, if you have a solid base of good varnish that has aged for about six months, and if the varnish is still in good condition, then chances are that with a moderate amount of sanding and touching up you may be able to go over the varnish with the Clear Awlgrip. To test for compatability, tape a wad of cotton that has been saturated with Awlgrip's reducer to the surface of your existing varnish finish and wait about fifteen to twenty minutes. Then see if there has been any lifting or softening of the old varnish. If not, it is probably safe to go ahead. However, if the reducer reacts with the old varnish in any way, then you plan on wooding before you get started.

(In addition to Awlgrip Clear, there are a number of one-part clear marine finishes on the market that also seem to promise exceptional durability and gloss retention. A number of these, as well as the Hi Solids Awlgrip Clear, are currently being tested by this writer on his own boat, and an in-use report, as well as the results obtained, will be published as soon as possible in a future issue of "Boatkeeper.")

For a Smooth Finish, Don't Stir

Although the instructions on most cans of paint will tell you to stir thoroughly before using, this is definitely *not* the case when working with varnish. If possible, varnish should never be stirred. If stirring becomes necessary (as when you add thinners) do so with care. Don't stir vigourously or whip the varnish into a froth. Stir gently, with a wide paddle, and try to let the varnish stand for an hour or so before you actually use it.

The reason for all this is that vigorous stirring of varnish introduces small air bubbles—and these bubbles are almost impossible to brush out on the final finish. Careful stirring, or no stirring at all, prevents this.

Copolymers: The Bottom Paints of the Future?

One very unpleasant—and very time consuming—job that the average boatowner has to face each year is cleaning, sanding, and repainting the bottom of his boat. Aside from the mess and hard work, the job can also be dangerous because sanding bottom paint releases toxic dust that makes it advisable to wear a good face mask when you work in order to avoid possible damage to your lungs.

Regardless of whether the boat is stored in the water or on dry land, every year the boat must be hauled so the bottom can be scrubbed, then sanded smooth and recoated with an antifouling paint shortly before it is launched again. Without this annual maintenance routine it doesn't take long for the bottom of the boat to become coated with a fuel-robbing growth of weeds, barnacles, and grassy slime.

Although some bottom paints do last longer than others, until recently none of the bottom paints on the market could be honestly classified as being multi-season coatings—that is, you could not count on getting much more than one year out of each bottom painting job. On my own boat, which stays in the water all year long, I have been able to go as long as eighteen months between paint jobs, but this is mainly because little or no growth occurs during the cold winter months.

Now, however, a new family of multi-season antifouling bottom paints, originally developed for use on naval vessels, tankers, and other commercial vessels, gives every indication of being capable of lasting for several years, even if the boat is hauled and left out of the water for up to six months at a time.

These new antifouling paints have a *copolymer* base that contains special tin-based, organo-metallic, antifouling toxicants that are chemically combined with the paint so they are actually part of it—instead of just being mixed in with (or suspended in) the paint as is the case with conventional antifouling paints. The result is a com-

A short-nap roller with an extension handle eliminates the need to lie on your back when applying the new copolymers.

pletely different type of bottom paint that will not only last longer when properly applied, but will also largely eliminate the need for heavy sanding and scraping when the time comes for repainting.

First marketed and tested in Europe, copolymer bottom paints have actually been widely used in England and other countries for some years. It was only a few years ago that this type of paint received EPA approval here, permitting it to be sold and used in this country. The first one accepted was Interlux's Micron 22, but it is not sold "over the counter" to consumers (do-it-yourself boatowners) because it must be sprayed on by a trained professional who has the proper equipment. It is not intended for sale to—or application by—the boatowner who does his own work.

However, new versions of these paints have been put on the market and *are* being sold to any boatowner who wants to apply them himself, as well as to boatyards that are not equipped to do spraying. These newer versions have the same chemical base, but they use different solvents so they can be easily applied with a brush or roller. But you must be willing to carefully follow the manufacturer's directions as to mixing and application if you want to get the promised results (proper preparation of the old surfaces and correct rate of coverage or spread are especially important).

There are at least two manufacturers who are marketing do-it-yourself copolymer bottom paints: International Paint Co. (Micron 33) and Pettit Paint Co. (Offshore). Each comes in a choice of conventional colors (four for Micron 33 and five for Offshore).

Several other companies are working on similar types of bottom paint, so chances are most of the major paint companies will soon have a copolymer bottom paint.

To understand how these new paints work, you have to understand how they differ from conventional bottom paints:

All antifouling paints have a biocide (poisonous chemical) mixed in with the paint to help kill off barnacles and other marine growth that comes in contact with it. In conventional bottom paints this biocide is mixed in with the paint during formulation, but chemically

Hosing down the hull with high pressure will help remove the accumulation of slime.

it is not actually part of the paint—the paint merely acts as a binder or vehicle to hold it in place.

The biocide works by leaching out of the paint film while the boat is in the water, until eventually all, or at least most, of the biocide is gone. Then the paint no longer has any antifouling properties—even though it still retains much of its original color and still looks as though it is covering the bottom well.

Unfortunately, the biocide does not leach out at a uniform rate. It leaches out much more rapidly when the boat is first launched than it does after the boat has been in the water for a few months. Very often the paint will have lost much of its original effectiveness after only three or four months have gone by—sometimes the loss is as much as 70 to 80 percent.

This aging process and loss of the biocide's effectiveness continues when the boat is out of the water, and is hastened by exposure to sunlight. Any boat that has been out of the water over the winter has to have its bottom repainted in the spring before it is launched.

A further problem with conventional bottom paints is that as the biocide leaches out of the paint film it leaves tiny pockmarks or pockets in the surface, and this in turn means that the surface of the paint gets rougher and rougher as it wears. This roughness causes greater drag when the boat is under way, which translates into a loss of speed and greater fuel consumption (these factors will depend on the normal cruising speed of the boat, its size, and other variables).

A rough finish means that lots of scraping and sanding is usually required before the next coat of bottom paint is applied (if you want a reasonably smooth finish), and periodically the old bottom paint has to be scraped off completely.

Copolymer bottom paints generally use a completely different type of biocide, which is chemically bonded to the paint and is actually part of the paint film. Thus, there is no separate biocide to leach out; instead, microscopic layers of the paint itself wash off at the surface to kill any underwater organisms that come in contact with the film.

Unlike the leaching action of traditional antifouling paints, this "washing" action is not only gradual and continuous, it also takes place at a rate that remains constant from the day the boat is launched until the day that all of the paint is gone. As long as there is any of the actual paint left on the bottom, that paint is just as effective in killing marine organisms as it was immediately after it was applied—even after months (or possibly years) of underwater exposure. Another way to express this is to say that as long as you can see the paint on the surface you can be sure it is still working. That is why the paint can last for several seasons—the actual life of the paint

will vary with the number of coats applied (the thicker the film, the longer it will last).

The gradual erosion or washing away of the paint has another important benefit—the surface actually gets smoother and slicker as it wears. Since there is no leaching biocide, the paint wears off in smooth layers—much the same way that a bar of soap washes off and gets slicker as it is used. This not only adds up to less friction and underwater drag during the life of the film, it also means that when the time finally arrives for repainting there is very little sanding to do.

Speed-conscious sailors can buff this bottom paint to a smooth, slick surface without in any way affecting its antifouling qualities, so they can have the best of both worlds: a highly effective antifouling finish and a minimum of drag to interfere with speed.

How long will these copolymer paints actually last under normal conditions? None of the companies now marketing will make precise predictions, and rightly so. It really

Slime washes off easily with a sponge or soft brush.

depends on several variables: how many coats are applied; how much the boat sits still in the water; how fast it normally travels; the temperature of the water, etc.

Trial tests made on pleasure boats in various areas have shown that if two to three coats are properly applied, the boat can go a minimum of at least two years, and in several cases up to as many as four years, before a new coat of paint will be required.

Of course, there are also some drawbacks. For one thing, these paints are expensive—they list for about $150 a gallon as of this writing—and in many cases, when applied at the recommended coverage they don't go as far as traditional bottom paints. In other words, you will need more paint to cover the same area, and in all cases you will need at least two, and preferably three, coats to achieve a truly lasting job. Within obvious limitations, the more coats you apply and the thicker the final film is, the longer the job will last before a new coat is required.

Brushable copolymer bottom paints are best applied with a short-nap (⅜") roller, although a brush can also be used. To avoid the need for lying on your back or working on your knees, an extension handle can be used with the roller to permit reaching down to the bottom of the keel without crawling under (see drawing).

Though not essential, Interlux recommends using a different color for each coat—not only so that you can see where the paint is being applied without skipping spots, but also so that you can tell when it is starting to wear later on. If, for example, you use green for the first coat and blue for the second and subsequent coats, then you will know that you are getting down to the base coat when you start to see

the green showing through, and you can plan your next haul-out and repainting accordingly.

Before applying the new paint, you must first do a thorough job of cleaning off and preparing the old surface. Copolymers cannot be applied over the soft copper bottom paints, but they will stick well to an old coat of hard-drying vinyl or epoxy antifouling paint that is still in sound condition. The old paint must be well sanded to provide a smooth surface, and any flaking or poorly adhering spots should be removed before the first coat of new paint is applied.

Each coat needs sixteen to twenty-four hours' drying time before the next coat is applied, and at least the same amount of time before launching after the last coat is applied.

Although these paints keep barnacles and similar growth from adhering as long as there is paint present, they will accumulate some buildup of slime in time, especially if the boat sits idle in the water for lengthy periods. This slime can eventually accumulate to the point where it covers the paint surface and thus interferes with its antifouling qualities, so it should be removed periodically.

This is not hard to do; the slime washes off easily with a high-pressure hose when the boat is hauled, as shown. If the boat is not hauled, the slime can be removed by simply wiping the bottom with a sponge or soft brush while the boat is anchored in shallow water, or even while it is tied next to a dock. Or you can hire a local diver to do the job underwater every few months. Most power boats capable of moving through the water at better than 12 or 14 knots can usually get rid of the slime by simply running the boat at high speed for thirty or forty minutes.

Keeping the Metal Hardware Bright and Shiny

One sure sign of a boat that is really kept in "Bristol fashion" is when all the deck hardware—bow rails, chocks, stanchions, control handles, and other visible metal fittings—is bright and shiny with no signs of pitting or oxidation. Of course, you expect this on a new boat, especially when it is on display at a boat show, but what happens after you have bought that same boat and lived with it through several seasons?

With regular care, and with reasonable attention to maintenance, the metal fittings on your boat can be kept looking just as good as new; and you can prolong almost indefinitely the need for replacing or replating many pieces of deck hardware just because they are dull and tarnished.

On most boats there are four types of metal you are likely to encounter around the exterior: stainless steel, chrome plate, bronze, and aluminum. There are variations in how much care each type of metal needs and in the techniques that should be used when cleaning and polishing different metals, but there is one rule that should be followed in maintaining the appearance of all these metals: Keep the metal clean by washing it frequently.

In order for oxidation to occur, both air and moisture must be present—two things you cannot do much about on a boat. But metals are much more susceptible to this kind of chemical attack when there is also pollution present. Salt, airborne dirt, and even the chemicals contained in many bodies of fresh water, are pollutants that help this oxidation process along, so clean-

Frequent washing and drying keep metal hardware shiny.

ing often is a great help in slowing down this process.

This doesn't mean you have to scrub the metal daily; but it does mean that hosing it off after every cruise and washing if off with soap and water at least once a week is definitely a good idea. When hosing, wipe the metal down with a wet sponge or cloth at the same time because simple hosing doesn't always get the salt off.

When you wash the metal with soap, pay particular attention to the joints and crevices. Dirt that lodges there tends to stay caked in place and is often the cause of crevice corrosion. This can severely weaken structural strength and welded joints (even in stainless).

Washing is most important for aluminum—particularly on boats that are used in salt water. Salt water is a vicious enemy of aluminum, especially if the metal has not been painted or properly anodized, or if it is a poor-quality alloy that was not formulated specifically for marine use.

Of course, merely washing your metal brightwork will not keep the metal from oxidizing or pitting. You will still need to use a polish occasionally, and in most cases it will be advisable to apply some kind of coating to protect the metal even longer.

Although even the "experts" don't always agree on what is the best way to take care of each type of metal, there are a number of techniques that I have found work well. These recommendations are based on more than two decades of boating experience during which I have owned a dozen different boats—power and sail—and on discussions I have had with a number of professionals who spend their time taking care of boats.

Stainless Steel

Stainless steel alloys used on boats are supposedly corrosion-resistant, but as most boatowners discover, quality varies greatly. Even the best-quality stainless will get dull looking and take on a tarnished look if neglected. And the poorer-quality alloys will pit and develop surface corrosion in a short time if the metal is not regularly cleaned and polished.

For routine polishing of stainless steel I have found that a fleece-type polishing material works well. Consisting of a specially impregnated cotton or fleecelike wadding, these are fast and easy to use, and they get surface corrosion off easily. To use, you simply pull out a piece of the impregnated cotton and rub the metal with it. As you rub, the cotton will turn dark and leave a dull, grayish film on the surface. Keep turning the cotton as it gets dirty, and throw it away when it is all black. Let the hazy film on the metal dry for a few minutes, then polish with a clean, soft cloth.

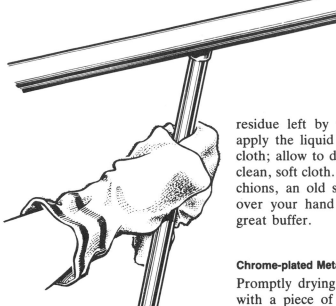

For buffing tubular metal hardware, such as rail systems, an old sweat sock is a handy helper.

If the stainless is too far gone for this to work, I use a regular metal polish—the kind that is sold in all marine supply and auto supply stores. These usually contain a small amount of very mild abrasive and are more work to use; but they work better on surfaces that are severely oxidized or that have a fair amount of rust on them.

Most metal polishes claim to leave a slight film on the surface that helps protect against further oxidation and corrosion, but I have found that you can't count on this to keep stainless steel bright for very long. Instead, after polishing, I apply a separate coat of liquid wax—either a marine wax or one of the liquid auto waxes that are formulated to combat rust.

After washing, dry the metal thoroughly and rub with a clean cloth. If you use a metal polish, wipe down afterward with a rag dampened with paint thinner or similar solvent (to get rid of any residue left by the polish). Then apply the liquid wax with a damp cloth; allow to dry and buff with a clean, soft cloth. For rails and stanchions, an old sweat sock slipped over your hand like a glove is a great buffer.

Chrome-plated Metals

Promptly drying chromed surfaces with a piece of clean toweling or chamois helps to maintain the shine and remove any streaks or spots left by the water. If washing doesn't restore the shine, then I use the impregnated cotton or fleece as with stainless steel. However, this is seldom required if the metal has been cleaned regularly. Polishes that contain abrasive should be used only when necessary. After cleaning and polishing (if necessary) I have found that the best way to protect chrome is to wipe the metal down with a rag that has been sprayed with a moisture-displacing penetrating lubricant (WD-40, LPS-1, CRC, and WGL are some of the most widely sold brands). These moisture-displacing lubricants actually penetrate the pores of the metal to keep moisture out, thus protecting the metal against oxidation and pitting.

Wipe on only a light film, not a heavy coating that will feel sticky or tend to attract and hold dirt. On hardware that is fully exposed to the elements this film will have to be renewed every few weeks, but metal that is protected from salt spray and weather will only need coating once or twice a year. If the chrome is fully exposed and frequently doused with salt water, then I prefer to use a liquid wax after cleaning and polishing.

On small items of decorative hardware that are hard to reach— such as horns and searchlights, for example—I have found it easier to spray the metal with a clear lacquer or clear metal coating.

Bronze

This metal, still widely used on trawlers and other "traditional" style cruising vessels, tarnishes or oxidizes faster than most other metals. It usually develops a greenish or dark gray-green film on the surface. This film doesn't actually hurt the metal, but it detracts from a boat's overall appearance. Also, it sometimes runs down and stains painted or gel-coated fiberglass surfaces.

To clean and brighten tarnished bronze, start by scrubbing with a strong detergent, using a pad of very fine bronze wool. When clean, polish with a good metal polish that is made for use on brass and bronze, or make your own by using a solution of salt and vinegar. This is an old remedy that cleans off the tarnish, but it may not leave the metal as shiny as a metal polish will.

When the metal is clean and bright, there are several things you can apply to keep it that way:

(1) You can apply a clear lacquer or clear protective spray made for metal—the kind sold in most marine stores. The trouble with this is that when it starts to wear away in spots, you will have to get the rest off with lacquer thinner or similar solvent before you can repolish.

(2) You can apply a coat of moisture-displacing penetrating lubricant as described above under "Chrome." The drawback to this is that the coating will have to be re-

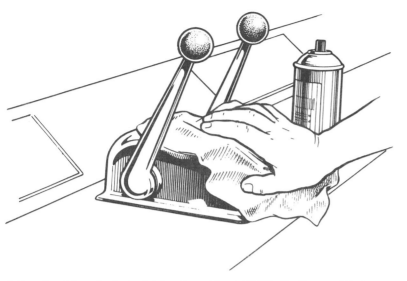

A film of moisture-displacing lubricant provides protection for chrome-plated hardware.

newed fairly often if you want to keep the metal from tarnishing again.

(3) You can apply a clear teak oil, which I discovered quite by accident works great on bronze! Several years ago I was applying Deks Olje to the teak on my trawler and I accidentally dripped some onto a bronze porthole frame that was coated with green tarnish. I immediately took a rag and wiped it off, but I noticed that the oil had wiped the tarnish completely off and the metal had the dull brown, clean appearance of new bronze.

I left the metal that way as a test and a year later found that there was still no tarnish on that bronze porthole.

Aluminum Alloys

On boats, aluminum is used mainly for spars, and for some of the fittings attached to these spars, as well as for moldings and window frames or door frames on production boats.

When aluminum oxidizes it turns dull and often develops a whitish film. In many cases it will also pit, and around salt water some alloys will actually disintegrate in time if not protected. Good anodizing prevents this and will last for many years.

Poor anodizing, however, will allow metal to oxidize and develop severe pitting in a comparatively short time. Also, some alloys are just poorly suited for marine use and will start to pit and oxidize even if they have been anodized.

The only way to clean up and brighten oxidized or pitted aluminum is to scrub with fine steel wool or bronze wool. Rub until fairly smooth (till most of the pit marks are gone), then scrub with a strong detergent. A time-saving trick is to scrub with a soap-impregnated steel wool pad—the kind sold for use on pots and pans.

When the metal is as clean and smooth as you can get it, dry thoroughly, then apply a good coat of marine paste wax. Renew this wax

coating at least twice a year under normal use; more often if the metal is frequently scrubbed.

Cleaning Inflatable Bottoms

Those who leave an inflatable tender in the water for weeks at a time invariably find that the rubberlike bottom fabric is almost irresistible to marine growth—yet there is no antifouling paint one can apply that will last for any length of time due to the continual flexing of the inflatable bottom. This means that regular cleaning is a definite requirement.

I have found that the easiest way to do this is to flip the dinghy over on a beach or dock and soak the bottom with lots of fresh water. Then scrub with a strong solution of liquid bleach and water. The bleach not only kills the marine growth, it also helps to loosen its grip on the fabric so you can scrub it off easier. When finished, hose the bottom off thoroughly.

To inhibit future growth, a heavy coat of marine wax keeps the bottom clean for weeks.

Scrubbing Off Grass Skirts

Over the course of the season in Long Island Sound, my boat develops a "grass skirt" of marine growth. In the past I have tackled *fin de saison* cleaning by leaning over the rail and scrubbing from the relative comfort of the deck. This approach is not satisfactory because one cannot exert much leverage at this angle. A secondary disadvantage is that soon one develops purple spots before the eyes and tends to fall overboard.

Recently I have discovered a means that is so effective I feel stupid not to have thought of it before. One simply gets in the dinghy and uses a rowlock as a fulcrum to push the scrubber against the hull. My dinghy is an inflatable, and the air-cushion effect enables me to maintain pressure easily up against the hull. One would expect a solid dinghy to have the same effect by tipping slightly. A to-and-fro rowing action cleans off the boot topping very effectively, one hand holding the dinghy in toward the big boat. An up-and-down pumping action, still with the brush handle in the oarlock, reaches under the turn of the bilge equally as well.

It may be my imagination, but my boat sure goes faster without her grass skirt.

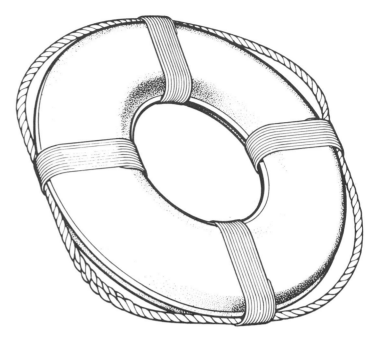

Braided rope is used to replace worn webbing straps.

Ladder Footwear

Worn sneakers have a new lease on usefulness attached to your boat's ladder during lay-ups. Top sides are protected from harmful scratches and wear.

Refurbishing an Old Life Ring

Even if it hangs unused all season, a flotation life ring will start to show its age after a few years because the bindings or straps of webbing tend to rot and crack. Instead of discarding the ring, an easy way to make it look new again is to strip off the old bindings completely, then replace them with multiple wraps of nylon solid-braid rope.

You can make the new bindings as wide as you want just by adding more wraps of rope. I used ⅛" solid braid and found that ten wraps in each section gave me the equivalent of a 1¼" band or wrapping (using ⁵⁄₃₂" braid, only eight wraps would be required for the same width). Measure how much rope it takes to go around once, multiply this by fifteen, then add a foot or two, for knotting and tuck-ing in the ends, to give you the length needed for each wrapping. Cut four pieces to the same length (so all will be the same width on the ring).

Now splice the ends of a length of ⅜" or ⁷⁄₁₆" nylon rope together to make a circle big enough to go around the outside with a fair amount of slack when it is in place (an 80" circle is about right for a 19" ring). Hold this ring of rope in place against the outside as you start the first wrapping and tuck the end of the ⅛" braid under the first few wraps to lock the end in place. Keep wraps tightly together until all the braid is in place. The end is secured by knotting and tucking under the last few wraps.

Finish by doing the wrap on the opposite side of the ring, then do the two wraps in the 90° positions in between. When finished with all four, apply two coats of marine enamel to the braid.

Keeping Acrylic Plastic Scratch-Free

Acrylic-sheet plastic is more in evidence on the water than ever before. Windshields, hatch covers, and instrument panel covers are, more often than not, being made of this strong, safe, crystal-clear material. Like everything else on a boat, however, it is subject to deterioration and damage. CY/RO Industries, an acrylic-sheet manufacturer, offers the following suggestions for maintaining and restoring sheet plastic.

When acrylic sheet becomes dirty, wash it with mild soap or detergent and plenty of water. Use a soft clean cloth or a soft mop for larger areas. Do *not* use any pressure; let the soap do the work. Then dry with a clean, damp chamois. Rubbing a dirty sheet of acrylic with a dry cloth will scratch its surface. Grease and oil can be removed with hexane or naphtha. Do not use other cleaning agents, solvents, or sharp tools to remove spots.

Fine scratches can be removed by hand polishing. Several companies manufacture special cleaners and polishes for plastics. If you cannot obtain these locally, good-quality auto cleaner will suffice. Apply it to a soft flannel pad and rub back and forth or with a circular motion. When the scratches have disappeared, remove all residue and apply a quality auto wax.

Power Buffing

To remove scratches that are too deep for hand polishing use a polishing wheel in a bench grinder or electric drill. On a grinder, use a 6″ to 12″ diameter by 1½″ to 2″ thick wheel, or whatever size your grinder will accept. Smaller wheels,

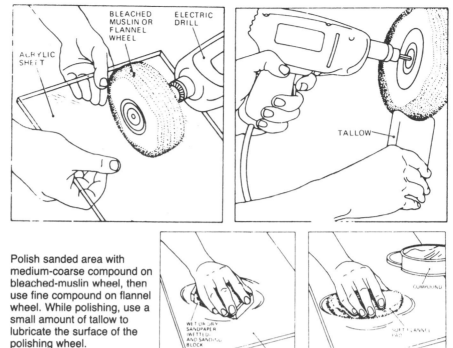

Polish sanded area with medium-coarse compound on bleached-muslin wheel, then use fine compound on flannel wheel. While polishing, use a small amount of tallow to lubricate the surface of the polishing wheel.

chucked into a drill, are best for large workpieces that are too difficult to handle on a stationary buffing wheel.

The first step in buffing is to use a bleached muslin wheel with a medium-coarse or fine compound, depending on the depth of the scratches. Keep the piece in motion at all times. Too much pressure can soften and burn any spot on which you linger.

Do not start near the top of the piece as the wheel may catch the edge and tear the piece from your hands. Start approximately one-third of the way down, and keep moving back and forth until you have reached the bottom edge. Then turn the piece upside down and repeat the operation. For final finishing, use a Domet flannel wheel with a little tallow to lubricate the surface of the wheel.

Removing Deep Scratches

A scratched acrylic surface should not be sanded unless the imperfections are too deep to be removed by polishing alone. If the scratches are deep or cover a large area, a portable pad sander should be used. Use wet-or-dry sandpaper for best results and apply water to its surface with a sponge. Don't apply pressure; let the sander do the work.

If the scratched area is small, sanding can be done by hand. Wrap a piece of wet-dry sandpaper around a block and sand an area that is slightly larger than the scratched area. This is to avoid the formation of a sharply defined "low spot," which would cause optical distortion.

Whether you sand by hand or use a machine, start with the finest grit sandpaper that will remove the imperfections. If you start with too coarse a paper, it may cause additional scratches that are deeper than the original ones. Unless the scratches are very deep, 240-grit or 320-grit paper is coarse enough to start with.

As you change from coarse to medium to fine paper keep in mind that you are continuously replacing a small number of deep scratches with a larger number of shallow scratches. It is essential that you remove all deep scratches before you change to the next-finer grit.

After rinsing, use a 400-grit, then a 500-grit paper; use plenty of water to sponge off the sandpaper frequently. Once a satin-smooth finish is obtained, you can polish.

How to Beat Those Waterline Oil Stains

A few years ago, a tongue-in-cheek article appeared describing the pesky fiberglass mite—a distant cousin of the feared wood borer of Southern climates.

Well there *is* such a destroyer of fiberglass. It's not really an animal, but its damage to gel coat is just as injurious. The gel-coat-eating monster is the petrochemical waste found in practically any busy harbor, and the brownish coating that gathers along a boat's waterline.

If the line is removed within a few weeks, gel coat can be saved. The longer the stain remains, however, the more difficult it is to remove. After a season, for example, the ring may have to be literally sanded out using a powdered fiberglass abrasive—a process that destroys the gel coat. The residue from diesel smoke may have the same damaging effect if left on for long periods. From a distance, the effect is a gray shadow. But on closer examination, it is apparent that tiny black dots of soot have penetrated the gel coat.

While the oil or soot coating is fresh, practically any fiberglass cleaner will remove it. However, one of the most effective cleaners is an item probably already in use in the galley—the household dishwashing detergent Joy. Some of this liquid on a long-handled brush does an excellent cleaning job. Just dip the brush in the surrounding salt water (or a bucket of salt water containing Joy), rub some on the coated areas and let the solution stand for a few seconds. Dip the brush in salt water and rinse. Harder stains will require a more abrasive cleaner.

Be sure *not* to use steel wool cleaning pads on or near fiberglass. Bits of the steel can become embedded in the gel coat and ugly rust stains will result.

By the way, Joy is also an excellent bilge cleaner and emulsifier and works well for washing clothes in salt water.

Care of Your Boat's Canvas and Plastic Drop Curtains

When the canvas covers or curtains around the outside of a boat look worn and shabby, the whole boat looks shabby. Although no one expects these items to last forever, that doesn't mean you should have to buy new ones every year or two—or that you have to live with cockpit enclosures, bridge covers, and drop curtains that are dirty, torn, and generally weatherbeaten in appearance.

To keep your canvas from deteriorating before it should, all it takes is some time and effort— time to regularly clean all your canvas covers and curtains, time to attend to all minor repairs promptly as soon as the slightest damage is visible, and time to periodically clean and polish the clear plastic "windows" in your drop curtains, dodgers, or other enclosures.

Here are some pointers on how you can keep all your canvas looking good, while at the same time also helping to lengthen the life of these expendable—and expensive—exterior covers and curtains.

Cleaning and Caring for Canvas

Regardless of whether the material is dacron, nylon, vinyl, or any other blend of synthetic fibers (to simplify matters I will call all of them canvas in this article), the greatest enemy of all exterior boat fabrics is dirt. Not only from the point of view of appearance, but also because dirt helps mildew to get started, and as it works its way into the fibers of the fabric the material will tend to rot—especially if there is also dampness present. This is why regular cleaning and washing is so important.

At the end of each weekend (or at the end of each day) hose off all the canvas when you wash down the rest of your boat, especially if you cruise in salt water. Dried salt attracts moisture and keeps the surface damp. This catches airborne dirt and allows it to work its way deeper and deeper into the pores of the fabric—so that eventually it becomes almost impossible to get out.

Every few weeks give the covers and curtains a more thorough cleaning by washing them with mild detergent and water. I have found that a regular boat soap works well, but it is best not to dilute it as much as is specified on the label. I use about double the amount recommended for normal washing.

Lubrication and proper cleaning are essential for long life of canvas and plastic.

Lay the covers out on a fairly flat surface such as a dock or deck, then get down on your hands and knees and use a sponge or soft brush to scrub over the entire surface. Don't use a very stiff, hard-bristle brush, and don't bear down hard; just rub lightly. Scrub over one section at a time, then rinse off promptly.

Stubborn Stains

If you find the dirt isn't coming off, make the solution a little stronger, and for really stubborn stains keep some concentrated detergent handy (mixed half-and-half with water). Scrub the bad spots with this concentrated solution, but don't allow it to remain on the fabric for more than a couple of minutes. Then rinse off *thoroughly*.

Some vinyl materials—especially the ones that have a stiff, plasticlike feeling when cold—can be cleaned more effectively with a vinyl shampoo or upholstery cleaner. Sold in auto supply and marine supply stores for use on vinyl cushions and upholstery, such cleaners are stronger than regular detergents. But here again I have found that you should ignore the dilution instructions—in fact, with some brands the shampoo must be used straight out of the jar if you want it to work effectively on very dirty covers.

While cleaning the canvas, keep a sharp lookout for tears, badly abraded areas, and other signs of severe wear. Patch these sections promptly to keep them from getting worse. It doesn't take long for a small tear to develop into a long rip when the wind gets at it. If you can, sew the rip or tear together or sew on a patch. You can also use sail-mending tape as a temporary repair, then as soon as practical take the item to a canvas shop where it can be sewed.

One of the most common causes of tearing is when snaps become stiff and stubborn. This makes you yank hard on the fabric every time you want to undo one of the snaps, and soon small tears develop around the snaps—or they rip out completely. When one snap lets go it's not too bad, but all too often

after the first one goes the wind gets at the fabric and all the others soon tear out.

The best way to prevent this is to keep the snaps lubricated so they will pop open (and snap shut) with a minimum of strain. About once a month spray each of the snaps with a little moisture-displacing penetrating lubricant such as WD-40, LPS-1, CRC, or WGL.

Lubricate Zippers

This also holds true for the zippers—stubborn zippers are probably the second most common cause of torn canvas and plastic. Tugging and yanking cause the fabric to pull apart along the seams or cause the zipper to rip out. To keep the zippers working smoothly you can spray them with either a silicone lubricant or one of the penetrating lubricants mentioned above. You will find it easier and more effective to do the job while the zipper is closed. Spray lightly along the full length of the zipper, then work the zipper open and closed a few times to spread the lubricant evenly.

The clear vinyl used in most dodgers, drop curtains, aft deck enclosures, and cockpit enclosures is uaually the first part of the canvas to go—the plastic turns cloudy and gets brittle, then splits. Fortunately, in most cases the clear plastic can be replaced by a marine canvas man without having to replace the entire curtain or enclosure. Still, since this is expensive, it pays to do everything possible to lengthen the life of the plastic.

Many boatowners do not realize that all clear vinyl materials are *not* alike; quality varies depending on the brand or manufacturer. Unfortunately, when you order canvas curtains or a dodger you have no way of knowing what quality you are getting—and you often have no choice. Canvas men usually stock and use only one brand.

However, if you notice that a neighbor's curtains have lasted much longer than yours, or if you find that vinyl curtains ordered from one dealer stand up better than those ordered from another dealer, then you have something to go on. Also, you should let your dealer know whenever clear plastic deteriorates more rapidly than it should—your complaints may lead him to switch brands.

Cleaning and Caring for Transparent Vinyl Curtains

In addition to trying to make sure your clear vinyl is the best quality available, you can prolong its life by following these simple procedures:

- As with canvas and other fabrics, dirt and airborne pollutants (smoke, exhaust, etc.) are constant enemies of clear vinyl, so get in the habit of hosing off the plastic each time you come back to the dock.
- Never wipe the plastic with a dry cloth or paper towel, no matter how soft. When wiping or cleaning is necessary, use a wet cloth or sponge.
- Washing with mild soap and water is advisable every two or three weeks, but not necessarily every time you hose the curtains off. The soap helps take out some of the plasticizers that keep the plastic supple, so don't wash with soap any more often than necessary.
- If the curtains are rolled up while the boat is underway, unroll them before hosing off or washing the boat. Do not let water accumulate inside a rolled-up curtain or folded dodger because water also tends to extract the

plasticizer when it stays in contact with the vinyl—and this is what often causes the plastic to get stiff and turn cloudy looking.
- After washing or hosing, dry the plastic with a soft towel or clean chamois. This minimizes the effect the water will have on the plasticizer in the vinyl, and it keeps the sun from doing too much damage to the plastic (another cause of premature aging).
- Two or three times during the boating season, apply a light coat of spray wax to the plastic to keep it supple and to replace some of the plasticizing agents that have been lost. One brand of spray wax favored by many professional captains is Pledge (*not* Lemon Pledge). Apply this right after washing and drying. Spray on a light coat and wipe it around with a clean, soft cloth without rubbing hard. Wait a couple of minutes, then buff with another clean cloth.

Fiberglass Maintenance and Repair Guide

Although no one can argue with the fact that a fiberglass boat is a lot easier to maintain than a painted wood boat, fiberglass is still a long way from being the completely maintenance-free product that some newcomers to the boating field think it is—at least until they have owned and taken care of their first fiberglass boat.

The gel coat that gives fiberglass its bright, glassy-smooth appearance is only a skin-deep surface coating that, like all coatings, will eventually start to dull and lose its luster—especially if it is not regularly maintained by frequent washing and periodic waxing. The

gel coat is also easily scratched, scuffed, chipped, and otherwise marred during the course of a typical boating season; and when this happens repair work is often trickier than repairing similar damage on a painted wood boat—if you want it done in a professional manner so that the patch will blend in neatly after the job is done.

Many people do not realize that most gel coats are actually quite porous. Dirt stains can penetrate and become extremely difficult to remove if left on the surface too long, and even water will penetrate porous sections or crazed areas if the surface is worn and not protected by wax. In extreme cases prolonged water penetration can result in partial delamination of the fiberglass.

The best way to prevent problems of this kind is to seal and protect the surface of the gel coat with applications of a good grade of marine wax at least twice a year.

This is a good place to point out that while you can save money by using an automobile wax instead of a marine wax, this is foolish economy in most cases because, contrary to popular opinion, there *is* a difference. A good-quality marine wax is formulated to resist marine growths and to better withstand staining from the chemical pollution that is present in most large bodies of water. This is particularly important if your boat is used in salt water.

For washing a fiberglass boat, use a mild detergent solution—avoid using abrasive scouring powders or detergents that are so strong they also remove all of the wax. Use a sponge or soft-bristle brush for general scrubbing, never an abrasive pad; and on stubborn streaks that won't come out easily use a stronger detergent solution if necessary. Let it soak on the stained area for a couple of min-

After masking and filling crack, cover with plastic to insure curing.

utes, then scrub again. Rust stains or streaks left by deck hardware or by metal left in contact with the fiberglass can often be removed by rubbing with lemon juice, but if this fails, use a commercial rust-removing gel like Naval Jelly.

Scuff marks that won't come off with normal scrubbing or washing can be removed with a fiberglass polishing compound (follow the directions on the can). Just remember to go easy with the rubbing—the gel coat is quite thin and if you are not careful, you can go right through it, especially if you are using a power buffer and you hold it in one place too long. Rub only enough to take out the scuff mark, then apply a new coat of wax over the area immediately (the polishing will have removed all of the old wax).

Polishing compound is also used to restore gel coats that are badly dulled or faded due to a lack of proper care over the years—the mild abrasive in the polishing compound will remove a microscopically thin layer of the worn gel and expose a clean layer that can then be brightened by proper cleaning and waxing.

Repairing Small Nicks and Gouges

All marine supply outlets sell gel-coat repair materials, as well as complete kits that include a can of gel coat resin (with or without pigment added), a small tube of catalyst (hardener) and possibly the pigments or color needed to tint the gel coat so you can try to match the existing color of your boat as closely as possible.

Incidentally, in all gel-coat repairs, mixing to match the existing color is probably the trickiest part of the whole job (even whites are different!). Like paints, gel coats fade and oxidize in time, so the freshly applied material will seldom match the old material exactly.

If the crack or gouge is very small (less than about ⅛″ width), then the first step is to cut out the crack slightly in order to insure a good bond for the filler. The best tool to use for this is a small pointed burr and a small portable hand grinder, or you can use a small abrasive bit chucked in an electric drill. Make sure you hold the drill with both hands to keep it from slipping.

You can also cut the crack out by hand, using the corner of a small chisel or the point of a regular beverage can opener (a "church key"), but grind or file the point down to bring it to a sharper point.

Next, use a small piece of fine sandpaper (#150) to sand on each side of the crack so the gel coat will bond, then wipe the area clean. Place a strip of masking tape along each side of the crack, about ¼″

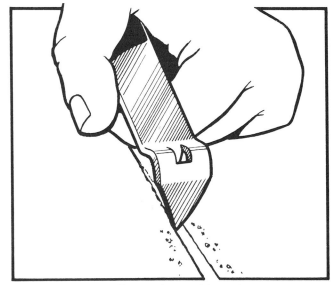

For gouging out thin cracks to provide a good trough for filler, a sharply pointed can opener is handy.

away from it, and extending past the crack by about ½″ at each end. The tape will keep the patching material from being spread too far, and build up the slight extra thickness required to simplify sanding and working out to a "feather edge" on each side.

Mix a little of the gel-coat resin with the amount of catalyst recommended, working on a smooth sheet of cardboard or plywood and blending the materials evenly with a small putty knife or spatula. If color must be added, do this first and keep checking the color to get it as close as possible before you add the catalyst. Colors will change a bit after they dry, but you can come pretty close by smearing a little on a stick and holding this next to your boat until it matches. Then add the catalyst and mix again.

The catalyzed mixture dries quickly, so mix only as much as you can use up in about ten minutes (less if the temperature is high). Spread it on over the scarred area between the strips of masking tape, using a flexible putty knife or a plastic spreader. Press the compound in firmly, so no air pockets are left and scrape off any excess so the surface is flush with the top of the masking tape.

Now take a piece of cellophane or lightweight plastic kitchen wrap and place this over the entire patch, smoothing it down firmly so there are no air bubbles trapped underneath. The best way to do this is to attach one end of the plastic to the surface with a strip of masking tape while holding the rest of the piece away from the surface. Then use the edge of a plastic spreader to smooth it down neatly before taping the other end down. Another way to smooth the plastic down is to roll over it lightly with a piece of dowel after taping one end down as just described.

The purpose of this procedure is to insure complete curing of the gel-coat resin. Unlike epoxy and polyester resins, gel coat will never harden completely if exposed to the air while curing. That's why you must smooth the plastic down against the surface of the freshly applied resin without trapping any air underneath (it won't stick to the resin when it dries). Apply additional strips of tape around the edges to hold the plastic in place while the patch cures.

After it is hard (you can feel it is hard by pressing on top of the plastic) peel off the plastic and start sanding. Use sandpaper that is #150 or finer, and sand parallel to the scar to the length of the scratch if possible to avoid sanding the surfaces on each side.

When you have sanded the patch down flush, switch to #400 wet-or-dry paper, but use it wet. Stop every few minutes and wipe the surface clean so you can see when the scratches left by the first sanding are gone. Then finish with wet-or-dry #600 paper (again, using it wet) to give it the final smoothing.

Polish with a fiberglass polishing compound, using a lamb's wool pad and an electric drill, or by hand rubbing with a cloth pad. Wipe the surface clean, then apply paste wax and buff to restore the luster.

Repairing Larger Scratches and Chips

Because ordinary gel-coat repair materials are more like a heavy paint than a putty, they usually cannot be used for larger scars such as cracks or gouges that are more than ⅛″ wide. The material would simply sag and run, especially on vertical surfaces. For these larger damages there are two methods you can use to make the needed repairs.

One method is to fill the depression almost flush—but not all the way—with an epoxy putty or polyester resin putty. When this dries you smooth it over by filling it flush with gel coat as described above. This is the method that will work best where the damage is fairly deep or goes through the gel coat and into the fiberglass itself.

The other method is to make a putty out of the gel coat by adding some chopped fiberglass or similar filler to the catalyzed resin to stiffen it before you spread it over the scar. (Most dealers sell such fillers, mainly for use with polyester or gel-coat resins.) Some experimentation may be required to hit the right amount of filler to add—just use enough to make a workable mix that will stay in place, yet will also be easy to smooth on.

Spread this over the scratch or gouge with a wide plastic spatula or

Fill large cracks and gouges with epoxy putty or polyester putty applied with a wide spreader.

spreader. *Do not* put down strips of masking tape first. Just spread the gel putty on and smooth it off so that the depression is filled and there is no material left on the surfaces around it. Then cover with a sheet of plastic as described above, smoothing it out and taping it down to hold it in place while the patching material cures.

When the material has cured, remove the plastic and sand with #150 paper to remove any irregularities and to sand the surface of the patch slightly lower than the surrounding surfaces. Dust thoroughly and wipe clean, then put strips of masking tape down on each side and fill with regular gel coat as previously described—again covering with plastic to insure a proper cure, and again sanding the surface smooth and level with wet-or-dry paper.

There is one shortcut you may want to try that will save some sanding time on these larger repairs: When applying the thickened gel coat (or an epoxy or polyester putty) don't fill the depression all the way to the top—leave it slightly hollow at the top. Then apply the strips of masking tape and smooth on the gel coat in the manner described above—but this time wait until the gel coat just stiffens enough to feel rubbery (you can poke through the plastic with a finger to check for this).

Carefully peel off one end of the plastic and pull it up away from the surface, then use a razor blade to carefully shave the excess compound off flush with the surface. Then press the plastic back down and smooth it over the surface to eliminate air bubbles. Leave it in place till the gel coat is completely cured, then peel it off and sand as usual. That way you eliminate the need for the first sanding and can go right to the wet-or-dry sanding with the #400 paper.

Repairing Craze Marks

This is in many ways the most difficult of all cosmetic repairs to make. If not too large an area is involved, it may be possible to treat the craze marks as a series of fine cracks which you can then cut and fill individually.

However, if there are too many craze marks to treat individually, or if the cracks are so fine that it makes no sense to start cutting them open, then your best bet is to cover the area with gel coat that you apply just as you would a paint. The big problem here—as in most other gel-coat repair jobs—is in matching the color. A slight mismatch on a small crack or chip might not be too noticeable, but on an area of a couple of square feet it will show up prominently if the color is not perfect.

The ideal way to apply the gel coat is to spray it on, using a small artist's airbrush or a regular paint sprayer. You can also buy small aerosol units that use disposable aerosol cans and have empty glass jars that you can load with your own paint. These will work fine on small jobs.

Either way, the gel coat will have to be thinned considerably, using the solvent recommended by the manufacturer (often as much as 50 percent). Some experimentation will be required to get the right percentage, so try the spray on some scrap surfaces first before you tackle the actual job.

If the area is small, you can also paint the gel coat on with a brush, but make sure you use a top-quality soft-bristle brush—most synthetic bristle brushes will not withstand the solvents used. And a poor-quality bristle will make it impossible to get a smooth job.

For extensive cases of crazing, or for gel-coat finishes that are really hopeless, the best way to rejuvenate the surface is to paint it. Any of the top-quality two-part polyurethane paints now on the market will do an excellent job on fiberglass if application instructions are carefully followed.

Easy Name Removal

If you are buying a used fiberglass boat, chances are you'll be changing the boat's name and home port. You may not want to tackle the name painting. However, you can save a few dollars by removing the old name yourself. The method here was given me by the experts at Wayfarer Marine, Camden, Maine.

The name can be removed without damaging the gel coat by using lacquer thinner or acetone. Both chemicals are highly toxic if inhaled, so a suitable mask should be worn.

Apply the acetone with a brush on one or two letters at a time. Allow a minute or two for the paint to soften, then scrape off the letters with a putty knife. With sufficient soaking, the paint will scrape off easily. If the lettering has been on the boat for any length of time, the gel coat under the letters will be a slightly different shade than the surrounding area. The new name, however, will generally cover these unwanted outlines.

If the boat is to be documented, the U.S. Coast Guard has specific requirements for placement, lettering style, and size. These are detailed on the back of the form, "Affidavit of Marking." In practice, some deviation from requirements is tolerated, the major concern being legibility.

Repairing Dockside Water Hoses

One important piece of marine equipment that always takes a beating is the hose.

In recent years the flat hose—the kind that collapses and drains itself after the water has been turned off—has become exceedingly popular, but when one of these hoses develops a split, or when one of the ends becomes damaged and needs replacing, repairs are nearly impossible to make. The reason is that conventional hose mending kits that have metal replacement couplings or ends just don't seem to work well with flat hose. You can sometimes get by with an old-fashioned brass crimp fitting if you then use a steel hose clamp around the outside, but more often than not even this unsightly lash-up will usually let go when pressure builds. In addition, the steel edge or bolt on the hose clamp is always catching on things when you drag it around.

However, I recently found there is one type of replacement hose coupling and hose mending kit that

will work with flat hose, as well as with any other type of conventional plastic or rubber garden hose. They are manufactured by Gilmour Manufacturing Co. (P.O. Box 486, Somerset, PA 15501).

Widely available in regular hardware stores and home centers, as well as in some marine supply outlets, these hose couplings and repair kits are made of plastic and are designed so that a tapered stem slides inside the end of the hose after you cut off the damaged fitting. Then, a two-part clamp locks on around the outside when you tighten the two halves together with the rustproof bolts and nuts that go through the flanges. This clamp holds the fitting securely and prevents it from slipping out, even under full water pressure.

One size fits all rubber or plastic hoses with inside diameters of $7/16''$, $1/2''$, or $9/16''$. The only tool needed to install one of these Hose Menders is a screwdriver. Gilmour makes both male and female end couplings, as well as a hose mender or splicer for joining two lengths together (after you have cut out a damaged section).

Better Finishing for Wood Spreaders

The varnished wood spreaders on my mast took quite a beating on their upper surfaces (but not the lower) from the action of the sun, wind, and rain, requiring extensive refinishing at the end of each season.

I found the solution was to paint the upper surface with a good white paint or an aluminum paint. Paint protects the spreader for several seasons, yet when viewed from the boat deck, only the traditional varnished wood surface is seen.

I used masking tape to insure a neat, well-defined line of demarcation between paint and varnish.

Sail Repairs You Can Do Yourself

If you are one of the many sailboat owners who have taken your sails home over the winter (rather than having them professionally cleaned

Two-part clamp works with any type of hose to lock new end-fitting in place.

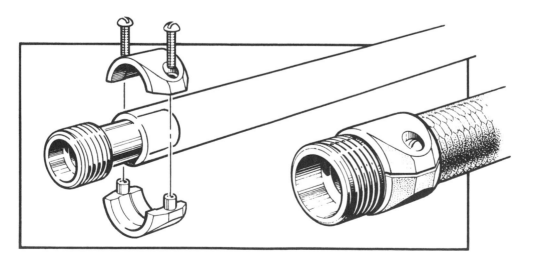

and stored), then now is a good time to get each sail out so you can inspect it carefully for signs of wear and for places that need repair. Even if the sails are free of obvious tears, there will probably be some parts where the sail is particularly susceptible to wear or chafing that are in need of repair. A thorough inspection of these potential trouble spots will enable you to make the necessary repairs before the boating season really gets under way. Here are some points that should be checked:

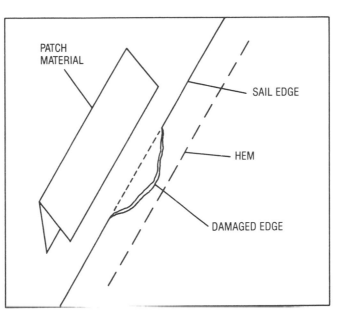

Seams: Stitches are a weak point in any Dacron sail because they rest on top of the fabric and are thus exposed to serious chafe. If you see a partially chafed seam, reinforce it with new stitches by sewing machine or by hand. It is much easier to restitch a seam before it actually lets go than it is to sew the panels back together smoothly after they have come completely apart.

Sail sewing is really quite straightforward and the type of stitch that you use is not critical. If you are doing the sewing by hand, an in-and-out progression along the seam at ¼″ intervals will do fine. Staggering the penetrations is slightly stronger and better-looking, but care is required to keep the spacing uniform. If you are sewing with a machine, the zigzag stitch is best because it distributes the stress inside the edge of the seam. Straight stitches are also acceptable, especially if you put down two rows about ³⁄₁₆″ apart. If your stitch length is also ³⁄₁₆″, this will approximate the normal sailmaking zigzag stitch of the same dimensions.

There are special polyester threads available that have far greater strength than anything to be found in the notions department of a local store, and there are special twines and needles designed

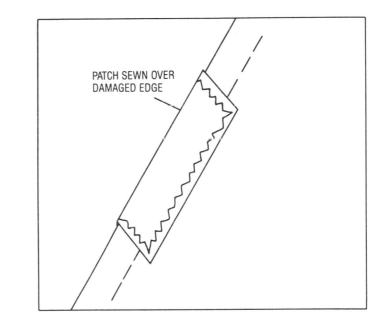

Use matching sailcloth to make patch for sail edge. Fold patch in half and stitch it in place.

specifically for sewing sails by hand. But if you can't find these locally, don't hesitate to use materials that you have close at hand. They may not be as strong or as durable as the materials in the original sail, but they don't have to be—after all, the sail doesn't have its original strength and durability, or repairs would not be necessary.

Edges: Look for chafe on the mainsail's leech where it may be hitting the backstay, or along the genoa's leech where it hits the spreaders. Anywhere damage to an edge is noticed, use a narrow strip of fabric, folded in half, to cover the damaged surface. Cut the patch out with a soldering gun or a wood-burning tool to keep the edges from raveling, then sew it carefully in place after first basting it with transfer tape or silicone glue. Once again, it is best to use matching sailcloth for this purpose, but any handy piece of fabric will serve.

Corners: Look at all corners for signs of stress breakage and wear or tear. The two usually go together. Very seldom will a sail fail in a place where there has been no chafe damage first. Fortunately, reinforcing a corner area is really quite simple. With rings and grommets, all one need do is loop a length of webbing through the hardware, fold it back on the sail, and then sew it in place.

The head area of a mainsail that runs up a tunnel or groove in the mast is often a problem spot because the bolt rope very quickly begins to pull away from the head of the sail. The best way to fix this is to take the headboards off and cover the bolt rope with a rectangular piece of sailcloth folded down its center. (Best results are obtained with a special bolt rope sleeve cloth that has Teflon beads in its center area.) After the headboard is put back on, this repair will hold until the patch material wears through in its turn.

Another approach to this problem is to accept the inevitable and simply trim away the bolt rope along the front of the headboard as shown. The head area will not be as well supported as it was when the rope was there, but the chafe problem will no longer exist. A plastic sail slug can be attached to the headboard near the top if support in the head area is needed to maintain sail shape.

Batten Pockets: Any hard object constantly rubbing against a sail will cause trouble, and battens are no exception. If the cloth in a batten pocket wears through, it is a fairly simple task to take off the old pocket, cut a new one and then

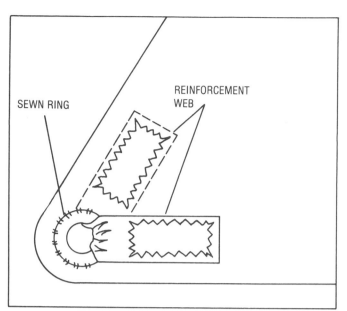

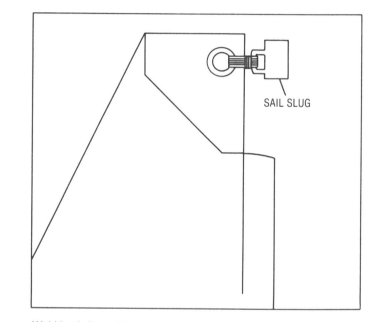

Webbing is looped through grommet, above, to reinforce corner. Worn bolt rope is trimmed from headboard and replaced with plastic sail slug.

sew it in place. (Be very careful to baste it well with silicone glue or double-sided tape—if the pocket slips while it is being sewn in place, there will be an obvious hard spot in the sail.) If the sail itself wears, remove the pocket patch, place a patch of sailcloth over the worn spot, sew it down carefully all around, and then replace the patch.

There are several types of pocket patches employed by sailmakers, but many of them include a small piece of elastic at the inner end to keep the batten in place against the leech. If this material has lost its elasticity, you may find that your battens tend to slide away from the leech, allowing it to flutter. Or you may find that the battens actually tend to fall out. To replace this

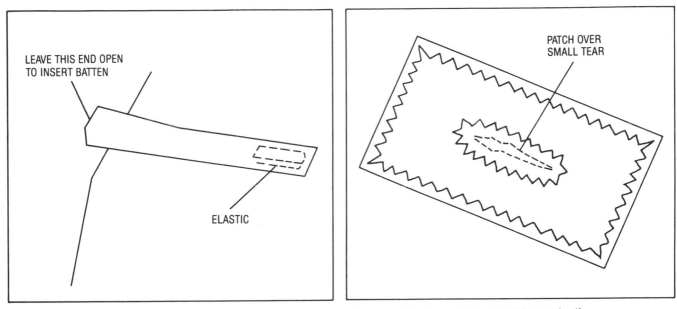

Elastic band keeps batten in place against the leech.

After patch is in place, stitch around the tear itself.

elastic, lift the forward six inches of the pocket away from the sail to expose the elastic. Then replace the worn-out elastic with a new strip. This elastic is available in any fabric shop—it's essentially the same stuff that is used in clothing waistbands.

Tears: Fabric tears in an otherwise sound sail are always the result of either chafing or snagging, so be sure you correct the causes as well as the symptoms. A tear in any sail should be patched with a piece of cloth of similar weight and feel. It should overlap the tear or opening in the sail by two or three inches. Carefully sew the edges of this patch to the sail after gluing or taping it in place, then sew all around the opening or tear so that there is no loose fabric left to snag on anything. Use your "hot knife" to dress the edges of a ragged tear.

Cleaning and Storing: Most sailmakers recommend nothing more than rinsing the sail with freshwater to remove salt and surface dirt. A more thorough cleaning will have the same effect as several weeks or more of hard use. If you are willing to pay that price, spread the sail on a smooth, clean surface and brush it lightly with a mild detergent solution. More thorough cleaning is simply not worth the cost in terms of shortened sail life.

After cleaning a sail, dry it completely before storing. Mildew will not grow on modern synthetic cloths, but it can grow on the dirt that they accumulate if moisture is present. Although mildew will not harm the fabric itself, it will certainly discolor or spot it.

Finally, fold the sail and store it in a cool, dry place. The method of folding is really not very important—just try to keep folds to a minimum. There are several schools of thought regarding how this can best be done—choose whichever seems most convincing to you.

Emergency Sail Repair

While cruising a long way from home last year, the genoa on our 32′ sailboat developed a 15′ rip along the leech. We applied some of the sail-mending tape we always carry on board, but after about three hours of 15-knot breezes, this too let go.

Scrounging around for something else to help us sail home, we found two other types of tape that seemed worth a try. One was a film-type Mylar package tape, and the other was the translucent reinforced packing or strapping tape, both about 2″ wide. We used both of these along the leech to seal the tear, then applied additional strips across the tear, at right angles to the leech and extending about 6″ into the body of the sail.

Both held up beautifully till we got home without causing the sail to wrinkle, and they permitted us to sail close hauled most of the way.

Some Tips on Sail Care

It isn't crucial to have wrinkle-free cruising sails, so it's okay to leave them stuffed in their bags for a week or so. It's also okay to leave them wet for short periods of time, although if you're planning on storing your sails for long periods, it's important they be dried thoroughly to prevent mildew. Mildew won't grow on synthetic fibers and will not affect their strength, but it can grow on the dirt that gets on sails, and it can develop into an unsightly mess.

Unlike racing sails, washing cruising sails will not damage them. In fact, while removing salt and dirt, washing your sails will make them softer and easier to handle. Use warm water and a mild detergent. Probably the easiest technique is to lay the sail flat on an asphalt driveway or lawn and scrub it with a long-handled brush. Be sure to rinse the sail thoroughly and dry it in the shade if possible.

A good cover is essential for the cruising sail. Ultraviolet radiation over a prolonged period can seriously weaken your sail fabric, and a sail that is left in the sun, especially in the tropics, can lose a serious amount of strength after less than a year. Acrylic fabrics, although expensive, make the best covers because they are absolutely insensitive to ultraviolet rays and because they won't fade.

Make sure your sails are furled securely before leaving your boat for any length of time. Sails can become completely destroyed in a squall or a storm because a portion of the sail was left loose and started flapping. That goes for roller-furling headsails as well. Make sure that your mainsail and headsails are furled smoothly and furling lines are secure.

It's extremely worthwhile to have your sails checked periodically by your sailmaker. He'll be able to repair small rips or weak seams before they become a problem, and he'll wash and fold them properly.

Basically, a small amount of time spent caring for your sails can, in the end, make you race fast or cruise efficiently. Fortunately, there are no mysteries in sail care—only a little common sense.

Tuning Your Rig

Some cruising people tend to think that a well-tuned rig is strictly for racing boats. This can be a dangerous misconception. A poorly tuned rig, besides making your boat sluggish, may also put unnecessary strains on the mast, shrouds, stays, and hull, and perhaps shorten the life of your sails.

Masts, whether wood or extruded aluminum, are very strong in compression when they are held straight, but when they are allowed to bend, the compression exerts forces the mast was not designed to sustain. In general, then, a well-tuned mast is perfectly vertical and held firmly in place by standing rigging of an adequate size.

Initial tuning begins with the bare rig at the dock. First, position the mast vertically fore and aft (unless, of course, rake is desired for proper balance; your spar and rigging plan should show the amount of rake). Determine whether the boat is in trim or not. Eye the boat broadside from shore or another boat. Then sight up the mast from deck level as if you were aiming a gun: Press your check against the mast and close your outward eye. Sight up all four faces of the mast—starboard, port, forward, aft—at first, just to see what you're dealing with. Then restrict your sightings to whichever two faces you are tuning.

Also, the main and genoa halyards can be effectively used as plumb lines. Free the business ends of both halyards and drop the genoa halyard to a few inches above the deck and the main halyard to a few inches above the gooseneck. (Be sure to cleat the bitter end of the halyard!) They will both hang close to the mast amidships when the mast is straight. Tighten one stay and loosen the other to achieve this position.

If your mast steps on the keel, remove the partner wedges and center the mast in the deck opening, giving the mast a nudge now and then during adjustments to settle it in position. (Be sure the mast hole itself is centered—builders' tolerances may allow some leeway here. Check by measuring from the side of the hole to each rail.) The mast must be in column from butt through the partner all the way to the truck.

When the mast is vertical fore and aft to your satisfaction (sight up the mast again), tighten the headstay and backstay equally using hand tension on the turnbuckles. For leverage, employ an average-sized screwdriver inserted through the center of the turnbuckle. The stays should be taut but by no means straining. Pull with your weight against the stays—the average yachtsman should find them deflecting about 2″.

(There is, of course, a more exact measurement for proper initial tensioning. If you have a tension gauge—Loos sells an inexpensive one—tighten all standing rigging to 20 percent of its breaking strength. The builder should be able to tell you the rigging's breaking strength; if not, any rigger or wire rope manufacturer can.)

Next, center the mast amidships. Run a check by dropping a masthead halyard to just above deck level and swinging an arc with it to the same port and starboard shrouds. If the mast is off center, the halyard will appear shorter on one side. (Under sail in a breeze

Drop main halyard to deck at dock to determine if mast is vertical. If rake is not desired, ease after shrouds and stay, tighten forward rigging.

Lowers are fine here. Ease backstay and take up on headstay. Uppers may need easing. These adjustments are critical if you have fixed spreaders.

Ease forward lowers, take up on after lowers. When lower mast is vertical, check for bend in upper mast. Fixed spreaders make this critical.

Everything is too tight here, causing dangerous compression. Ease backstay and headstay first, then ease lower shrouds. Uppers may need easing.

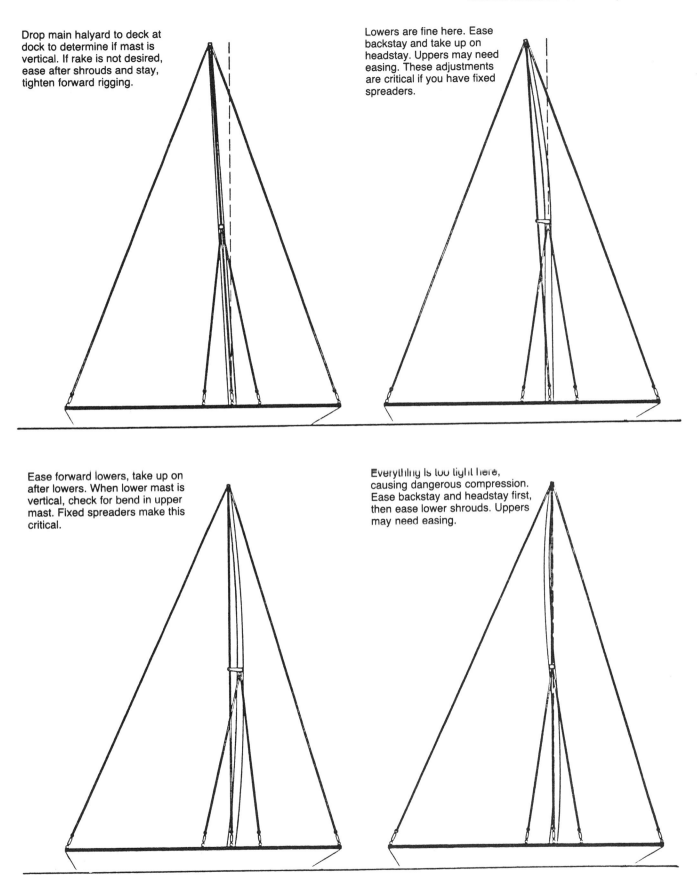

something has to give, and the mast will inevitably fall off a bit to leeward.)

Then start with the lower shrouds. When tuning, always begin with the lowers and don't move on until that section of mast is vertical. Think of single-spreader rigs as two distinct masts, and double-spreader rigs as three distinct masts. With the lower shrouds it's best to begin with the forward lowers, if any, then move to the after lowers. When the bottom section of the mast is vertical amidships and all lower shrouds are equally tensioned—the 2″ rule (or 20 percent rule) applies here as well—move to the upper shrouds and proceed in similar fashion. Again, the upper shrouds should have equal tension. At this stage, they should also have the same tension as all the lower shrouds.

Finally, be sure the spreaders are holding the upper shrouds securely. A spreader must bisect the angle of the shroud—in other words, the angles formed by the spreader and shroud above and below the spreader must be equal. If not, the load on the spreader will be uneven, putting strain on the spreader. Like the mast, the spreader is very strong under compression when the force is directed down its length. Now tape or otherwise secure the spreader to the shroud.

Fine-tuning must take place under sail. Fifteen knots of apparent wind is ideal. (Too little wind and the rig may not show a tendency to bend; too much and you may have difficulty making fine adjustments.) Hoist the largest headsail the boat can carry under the conditions, and put her hard on the wind. Trim the sails hard, let the boat settle in the groove, then sight up the mast. One of the mast configurations shown here may be evident. Simply follow the instructions under the configuration that most matches what you see, easing the sheets off completely to remove the tension from the rig before making adjustments.

There is one important thing to remember about fine-tuning: If you make a mistake, go back to the beginning.

Again, start with the lower shrouds, and then, when the lower section of the mast is aligned, move to the uppers. After each series of adjustments, trim the sails hard and bring the boat back up close-hauled. If the mast looks straight, come about and sail close-hauled on the opposite tack until you can determine whether the

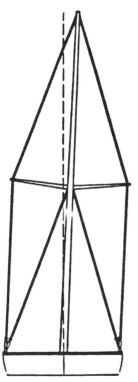

At dock, when mast is straight is it vertical? Swing an arc with a halyard, then adjust shrouds. (Under sail, mast will naturally fall to leeward a bit.)

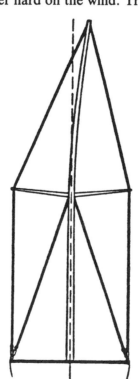

Lower shrouds seem fine—the problem lies with the uppers. Ease the starboard upper. If necessary, tighten port upper. Then tack to check results.

Lower mast has too much compression. East port lower. Check starboard lower. If upper mast is still bent, see above, right. Then tack and check.

Both upper and lower mast have too much compression. Ease port lower and port upper; also check starboard lower—it may need easing.

mast is straight or not. If not, make the necessary adjustments.

Ordinarily, unless the mast has a considerable bend in it, your adjustments will be no more than a few turns of the turnbuckle. Remember the initial tensioning rule: Though cruising rigs can be tensioned to 25 percent of their breaking strength, don't go over that figure, and it's best to stay under 25 percent. Tuning is as much a process of loosening turnbuckles as it is of tightening them.

Note that the leeward shrouds will have reduced tension, particularly when the boat is close-hauled in a strong breeze. This is as it should be. But the leeward shrouds should not be slack. There is some difference of opinion about this

point. Some authorities recommend that the leeward shrouds of their own rigs have appreciable tension at all times. Chuck Poindexter of Sound Rigging Services in Essex, Connecticut, suggests that leeward shrouds can be slack. Certainly there should not be enough slack to allow the rig to slop around in light air and a confused sea.

Rigs, like pianos, have a way of coming untuned after a time. The wire rope will stretch to a small degree, and the chainplates may settle, particularly with new rigging. You will want to retune a *new* boat after about fifty hours. Examine the mast regularly on both tacks during the season, and retune accordingly.

When you are convinced the rig is properly tuned, insert cotter pins in the turnbuckles and spread them about 10°. Install chafing sleeves over them or tape the pins. Be sure the spreader still bisects the upper shroud angle and is securely fastened to the shroud.

On Going Aloft

Going aloft used to be easier. Much of my early experience was on boats with ultra-conservative aspect ratios and gaff rigs with sturdy mast hoops to hold the luff of the mainsail to the mast. The hoops provided a convenient and safe stepladder arrangement right up to the gaff. Quite often, by standing on the gaff or on the spreaders that were just a little higher, you could reach whatever had to be dealt with. Even when there was some motion, the low aspect ratio minimized the effort of the boat to shake you off.

With the swing to the Bermuda rig, aspect ratios increased, but rather gradually. Many of the boats were quite narrow and sailed well up to 35° or 40° heel angle. If you could match a good breeze and smooth water with a helmsman you could trust, it wasn't hard to "walk" up the mast, especially when there was a good handful of external halyards as an assist—and as long as the really wide heel angle was maintained and the spar was dry enough to provide good footing. Still, if there was more to do than impress the passengers, it was better to use the bosun's chair.

The swing to wider boats that have the sail more upright and the general cleaning up of the rig, which includes leading most halyards inside the spar, has forced us to rely more on the bosun's chair. At the same time, the job of those on deck has changed from just taking up slack to straightforward hoisting. Given these facts, what is the best kind of chair?

The best type—particularly if you want to get something out of your pocket (difficult with a canvas sling type)—has a plywood bottom crisscrossed underneath by synthetic lifting ropes that form a backup.

The hoisting apex of this bosun's chair should have a $5/16'' \times 2''$ outside diameter ring or $5/16''$ bow shackle, with the lines seized tightly around. The length of the line should be kept to a minimum so that the hoisting point is as close as possible to the chair bottom. This is important for two reasons: First, it enables you to hoist the chair higher up, simplifying the difficult-to-reach jobs at the top of the mast. Second, the person in the chair is more secure because it is difficult to slide out in either direction.

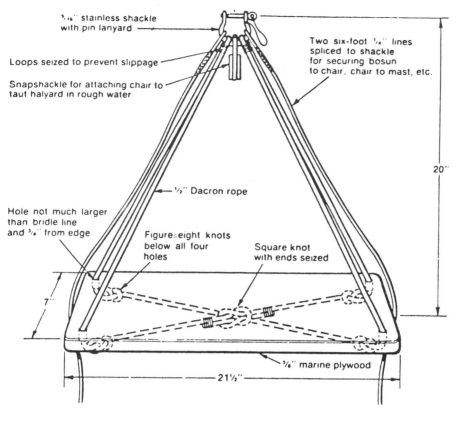

¼" stainless shackle with pin lanyard

Loops seized to prevent slippage

Snapshackle for attaching chair to taut halyard in rough water

Two six-foot ¼" lines spliced to shackle for securing bosun to chair, chair to mast, etc.

½" Dacron rope

Hole not much larger than bridle line and ¾" from edge

Figure-eight knots below all four holes

Square knot with ends seized

20"

7"

¾" marine plywood

21½"

Rod Stephens prefers this type of bosun's chair. He points out that the board can be painted or varnished except for the center area that is the actual seat—leave this bare wood. Distance between the corner holes is 5½" on the short side and 20" on the long side.

The chair lifting lines go through reasonably tight holes on each corner of the chair bottom, and there should be figure-eight knots in the bridle, immediately below each of the corner holes. These knots prevent the chair bottom from sliding or tipping, which makes going aloft safer and permits the masthead man to devote more of his energy to the job in hand and less to self-preservation.

The lines should be about ½" diameter and—most important—should be synthetic. I remember one spring day in City Island, New York, when I was swinging around aloft on what looked to be a pretty good chair with manila bridle lines. After one rather extreme swing out around the forestay to get to the other side, I happened to notice that one strand of the three-strand rope had carried away. I immediately put an extra line under my shoulders and hitched around the halyard, and asked to be lowered as smoothly as possible. When I reached the deck, it was quite easy to break the line—or what was left of it. Moral: Shoulder the extra cost and use synthetic.

You should fit your chair with two ¼" diameter lines, each about 6' long and spliced under the shackle or ring. Their primary function is to secure you in the chair when necessary, and to secure the chair in the position desired when working aloft. It is also a good idea to hitch on a couple of similar lines that can be disconnected when needed. These can secure something you may be working on which has to be temporarily unfastened during the operation.

In rough weather, an extra halyard—if available—should be set very tight against the mast. A snatch block snapped around this halyard and hooked into the hoisting part of the chair should provide added security against the possibility of swinging away from the mast and colliding with it. A rough landing can result in injury to the occupant of the chair.

In addition to these short lines, there should be in really rough weather two strong tag lines, one leading from each side of the chair bottom. They can be secured to the crisscrossed lines under the chair with bowlines and should lead to strategic deck positions and be carefully tended throughout the hoisting operation to maintain tension so that the gyrations of the chair are minimized. When lowering, these tag lines should be taken in steadily for the same purpose.

No one should go aloft when it is rough without being strongly secured to the chair. If there is a bad collision, at least the injured person can be lowered without falling into the water.

In addition, it is a good fundamental rule to wear long pants and long-sleeved shirts, and to double up everything to provide padding when conditions are rough. It's also essential to eliminate sharp objects aloft while fitting out. Either pad them or round them.

There are chairs with various pockets for tools and gear. This is well and good, but in case you don't have such a fine arrangement, be sure to have a deep canvas bucket with rings at top and bottom. A bag-type of bucket is no use as you cannot see what's in it, and it's hard to come up with what you want when you reach in and the bag closes around your hand.

Any tool of real weight should

be securely tied with a light line to the lifting ring in the chair. The lines should be long enough to permit using the tool without disconnecting it. It's all too easy to lose your grip on a wrench or large screwdriver when you are putting a load on it. It may get to the deck before anyone has time to dodge it. Even if it doesn't hit someone, it may damage the deck. Beyond that, I've yet to see a good wrench or screwdriver that knows how to swim.

Generally, it's better to avoid any kind of snapshackle. If you must use one, tape it for good luck and, as a precaution, take one of the small lines and hitch it securely around the halyard just above the snapshackle.

When there's a choice, it's good to go up the weather side abaft the mast, presuming the mainsail is set so the luff of the mainsail will minimize the amount of swinging, at least in one direction. Also, depending on the importance of the job and the state of the sea, remember that bringing all the sea abeam while keeping enough sail to minimize rolling gives you the best chance to go aloft and do the job safely.

Before going up, it's a basic rule to test the chair by securing it to the halyard and jumping up and down as hard as you can. It's better to spot a potential weakness (looseness, a crooked line-up) at 18″ above the deck than when you're at the top of the mast.

An all-rope halyard lets the person going aloft help a lot by going hand-over-hand on the hauling part. If the halyards are all internal and if there is a shortage of power on deck, you can use an internal halyard to hoist up a single block with an all-rope external halyard temporarily rigged.

Those hoisting on deck should avoid excessive winch turns that are all too frequently used in a misdirected quest for additional security. Four turns is the absolute maximum. Remember that excessive turns waste considerable power and increase the chance of fouling.

Self-tailing should be used only when there is no alternative, and only if the line easily matches the self-tailing gear and arrangements are such that the line coming off leads down in such a manner that its weight puts some tension on the line feeding off to help the effectiveness of the self-tailing gear.

Never use reel winches when going aloft.

Remember to go slowly both up and down when passing spreaders or any other obstructions such as a radar antenna and any fore and aft stays. Hand motions are very effective to signal those below. Some simple ones are clenching a fist for "stop" or "hold," moving the hand in a circular motion for "go ahead," and pointing up and down to indicate direction.

When it is rough, the person aloft should be particularly careful to avoid putting unreasonable fore and aft loading on spreader ends. This is especially important for a large person on a relatively small boat.

When the foretriangle is less than masthead, there should be an arrangement that makes it possible from the deck to rig a gantline (temporary halyard) that can be pulled through at the masthead, presumably using a messenger that might also serve as a flag halyard. This can be important in case there is a problem with a main halyard.

In case of heavy work to be done, two chairs can be useful. I can remember three or four aloft on one Twelve Meter on the way to the starting line when a lot of last-minute work was needed the day after a dismasting.

As for coming down, again avoid extra turns. Two full turns generally suffice, but this depends a little on the relative weights of the person being lowered and the person tending the halyard. The target is to pay out line smoothly all the way and to avoid the usual stop and go that is uncomfortable and creates unnecessary peak loads.

Just one more tip: When the option exists, always come down directly over the person tending the halyard. This invariably improves his concentration!

Attaching Fittings to Aluminum Spars

Perhaps the best way to attach fittings such as strap eyes, cheek blocks, cleats, and the like to an aluminum spar is by drilling and tapping holes and then using stainless steel machine screws. They are more easily removed than blind ("pop") rivets and stronger than sheet-metal screws.

When choosing screw sizes, try to use fine threads wherever possible. For example, there is a 10-24 (coarse) thread and a 10-32 (fine) thread. The fine thread will put more threads in a given wall thickness. An engineer's rule of thumb says that for maximum strength when threading thin sections, at least three threads should be engaged. It is sometimes difficult to find the fine thread fasteners, but the search is worth the effort.

Be sure you use the right size drill for a given tap. This will usually be a "number" drill; for example, a 10-32 tap takes a #21 drill. Drilling and tapping into aluminum goes much faster and more easily with the use of a proprietary cutting oil formulated for working with aluminum. One brand I've used is called Tap Magic Aluminum Cutting Fluid.

Attaching a flat-bottom fitting, such as a cleat, to a curved mast or boom presents a special problem because the two contact only at the line where the flat surface of the cleat is tangent to the curve of the spar. This creates a tremendous stress on the fastenings. One way to solve this problem is to file a curved depression in the base of the cleat in order to increase the contact area between the cleat and the spar. A much easier way is to mix up some 2-part epoxy putty and apply a thick bead of it to the perimeter of the cleat base. Then screw down the cleat onto the spar. This will squeeze out the excess putty, which can then be scraped away before it hardens. If you ever want to remove the fitting, be sure to rub some candle wax onto the surface of the spar before you screw down the epoxy-loaded fitting.

Use of an anaerobic thread adhesive, such as Loctite, will prevent all threaded fittings from loosening.

To avoid electrolysis between stainless steel fittings and an aluminum spar, cut a thin sheet of plastic, then use this as a shim between the fitting and the spar.

EXTERIOR PROJECTS AND IMPROVEMENTS

Surprising Facts About Cleats

Most of us when looking for a cleat to put on our boat, think in terms of matching style with what hardware is already there and in terms of size for the job at hand. After all, a cleat is a cleat is a cleat, right? We thought so once, at least to the extent that a cleat with a 5,000-pound rated working strength ought to be capable of holding a line with a 5,000-pound load. We were disabused of our casual thinking quite by accident when testing some marine hardware coatings for resistance to abrasion by rope.

We designed a test in which the standing part of a piece of line given a half turn around the base and half a figure eight over the horns of a sample cleat was to be alternately slacked and tensioned to the rated working strength of the cleat. The action of the line riding back and forth and the tremendous pressure on the cleat surface would surely be a good test of the coating's ability to take punishing. We made up a test fixture with an air cylinder to cycle the line,

picked 1½" manila for its rated working strength and abrasive quality, and started the test.

Surprise! The rope broke well before the load reached it, and the cleat's rated working strength. That is, at less than 25 percent of their ratings. The sample cleat seemed a little small for the manila rope, so we decided to try again, this time using a smaller diameter dacron line. Again the rope broke prematurely. Why?

We found the lines had both parted where they had made the first turn around the cleat base. The sample we were using was a fairly stylized cleat, rectangular looking, but with slightly convex surfaces and with visibly rounded edges. We could not say that the line had been cut, at least not in the usual sense. Recalling a discussion we once had about the proper diameter of a sheave for a given diameter rope, the problem became clear.

A line when viewed closely is simply a collection of fibers patterned in some fashion for strength and handling characteristics. These fibers can move to some extent relative to one another so that the load borne by the line as a whole is

more or less equally shared by the individual fibers. Under straight-line tension the system works well. But when going around a bend the load-sharing system is limited.

This effect can be well illustrated with a Slinky toy. Pulled in a straight line, the coils are more or less equally separated. As more tension is applied to the spring, the coils become more separated. In fact, the separation of adjacent coils is a good measure of the tension on the spring at any point. By stretching the Slinky halfway around progressively smaller wheels, we would quickly find the following:

(1) When the wheel diameter is large compared to the spring diameter, the distance between coils along the wheel surface isn't much different than that along the outside of the turn.

(2) When the wheel diameter is approximately twice the spring diameter, the difference in distance between coils along the inside and the outside of the turn is significant, but the coil is everywhere in tension.

(3) When the wheel diameter is small compared to the spring diameter, the inner coil surfaces touch

and the outer coil surfaces are significantly farther spread than the coils in the straight portions of the Slinky which apply the tension.

The same findings hold for cordage. Passed around a small enough post, the inner portion of a piece of line can actually be subject to compression. The compressive force must to some extent be added to the tensile load borne by the outer part of the line. Cumulatively, the effect of passing a line around too

tight a turn is that more than the applied load is being borne by less than the total number of filaments in the line. Worse, especially for a hard-laid line, the greater part of this amplified load is taken by the lesser number of outer fibers.

What does this mean for a cleat? Its useful working load should be estimated as the lesser of its rated working strengths, or better, the working strength of the strongest line you can use on it—that is, the *diameter* of the line should be no

greater than *radius of the smallest curve* on the cleat's working surface.

Some points to look for:

- Are base posts and horns round, ideally with diameter about twice that of the line you intend to lead to the cleat? (See Figure 1.)
- Better, are junctures of the base posts and horns filled out to hold the surface curvature? (See Figure 2.)
- Better still, are the base posts flared so that the surface of the line is continuously supported as it passes over the cleat? (See Figure 3.)

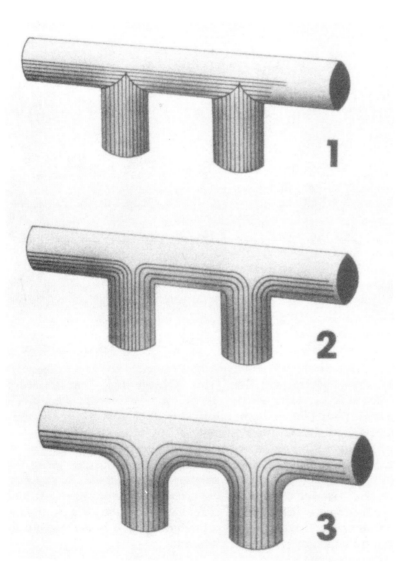

Installing a New Cleat

Cleats are often much too small or one is used where two are desirable. When a cleat is too small, it soon becomes overloaded with line, creating a confusing and potentially dangerous situation.

Installing a new cleat is not a very difficult job, especially if you know a few tricks—and the same basic principles can be used in mounting other items of deck hardware as well.

Assembling the parts and tools needed is the first step—finding the right cleats, stainless steel bolts, sealant, and preparing a backing plate. If the deck is cored, two backing plates may be necessary—one under the deck and one directly under the cleat—to distribute stress and avoid crushing the liner. And with cored decks, bolt holes must be thoroughly sealed—not only to prevent water from leaking into the cabin, but also to keep it from starting rot within the deck itself.

Backing plates can be fabricated of hardwood, stainless steel, or aluminum. If aluminum is used (it is

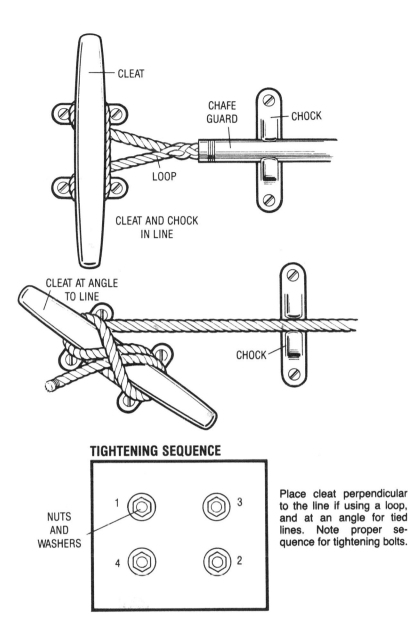

CLEAT

CHAFE GUARD

CHOCK

LOOP

CLEAT AND CHOCK IN LINE

CLEAT AT ANGLE TO LINE

CHOCK

TIGHTENING SEQUENCE

NUTS AND WASHERS

1 3

4 2

Place cleat perpendicular to the line if using a loop, and at an angle for tied lines. Note proper sequence for tightening bolts.

cleat and interfere with the cleating process. In determining position, also check to see that the cleat will not block walkways or other hardware, or catch running lines, etc. After determining the proper position, you are ready to drill the holes. To be sure of the proper drill size, drill a test hole in a scrap of wood first. The bolt should fit snugly but not have to be forced in.

Drilling requires two persons— one to drill from above, and the other to hold the backing plate in position and then attach the hardware. For convenience, one hole may be predrilled in the backing plate. The corresponding hole is then drilled through the deck so the cleat and backing plate can be attached with washer, lock washer, and nut (or locknut).

Using the cleat as a drill guide, the remaining holes are drilled through both the deck and the backing plate separately. Predrilling four holes in the backing plate is very risky, since drilling, particularly through a thick deck, is rarely precise, and the two sets of holes will be almost impossible to align. During the drilling operation, the helper should hold the backing plate in place using a large block of wood.

For bedding the cleat, a silicone-type sealant—or any of the marine sealants—will do. The material should be "buttered" into the holes with a knife, as well as onto the bottom of the cleat; then the bolts may be pushed into place. Sealant is usually not required on the backing plate, since enough squeezes through the holes onto the plate.

When tightening the hardware, tighten diametrically opposed bolts first. Tighten them almost all the way, then let the sealant set for about thirty minutes before tightening the rest of the way. This period allows the sealing material to adhere to critical surfaces and

the easiest material to work with and the cheapest), choose ⅛" to 3/16" plates that are at least 2" wider and 2" longer than the cleat. After cutting to size, rough edges should be filed smooth to remove burrs.

Be sure that the bolts you buy will properly fit the cleat. Recently, when installing two 10" cleats, we found that 5/16" bolts fit the holes, but the oval heads protruded and would constantly cause chafe. With ¼" bolts, the heads were properly recessed, but the shafts had too

much clearance, so we decided to use the 5/16" bolts, but ground the heads to fit.

A cleat may be placed in any position, depending on how it will be used. For example, if the line is normally secured with a loop, the cleat should be approximately perpendicular to the direction of the line, as shown. If the line is to be cleated, then the cleat should be placed at an angle to the lay of the line. Without the angle, the line would rest against the side of the

keeps it from all being squeezed out. Clean excess sealant off the deck before it cures.

Epoxy Mounts for Fittings

When you need a small, but odd-shaped mounting pad or block to fit an odd-size fitting, or to fit against a curved or irregular-shaped surface, trying to fashion a wood mounting block that will fit both surfaces can be very time consuming and difficult to accomplish.

A much easier way to make such a mounting pad is by using a two-part epoxy putty. It is easily molded to match any contour, and it serves to insulate against contact from dissimilar metals. It will also fill any voids between the two, and thus can prevent corrosion from developing.

After drilling the holes, clean both surfaces and mix the putty according to the directions on the package. Shape it to match the outside dimensions roughly, then press the fitting into place and insert the bolts or screws (don't use rivets) that will hold it in place (don't clear the putty out of the holes). Tighten the fasteners only enough to hold the fitting in place and slightly compress the putty so it squeezes around the edges, then trim off the excess on the outside and around the heads of the bolts or screws. Let set till almost fully hardened, then give the fasteners their final tightening and trim off any additional excess that squeezes out. Allow the epoxy to cure completely before applying tension.

Modernizing Rode Markers

One day when we were anchored in Annapolis the skipper of an ad-jacent boat objected to our position. I asked her how much rode she had out, and her reply stuck with me. "How would I know! Marking the rode is a chore, and besides the markers don't last." It bothered me she didn't know her own rode's length, but I had to sympathize—the plastic markers on our rode always broke off, and the spacing between markers was eccentric. Previously, I had tried marking our rode in the class sequence, but found remembering the sequence a problem.

After several months of trying different methods of attaching easily read markers to our anchor line, I can recommend the following solution. I cut some 1" nylon webbing we had aboard into 6" to 8" lengths, sealing the ends of each piece in an open flame. I then marked each piece on both sides with a waterproof black laundry marker in intervals of 25' Finally, I unlaid our nylon rode at each appropriate spot and tucked the webbing between the strands.

I've found the webbing stays in place so reliably I don't have to worry about the untimely disappearance of a crucial marker. Also, the markers are so big relative to the ½" rode I can easily count them by feel when anchoring at night. Best of all, cost and labor were minimal.

Extend Line Life with Snubbers

A small but vitally important item on any boatowner's checklist is the condition of the dock lines.

Even top-quality mooring and docking lines with good chafing gear require constant monitoring. Stress and strain take their toll and expensive lines have to be replaced quite often.

With the current cost of lines, any method of extending line life is welcome. We have developed such a "line saver" by using trunk tiedown devices available in most automotive or discount department stores. These 12" to 18" rubber snubbers sell for about $1.00 a pair. We used #4 (slightly larger

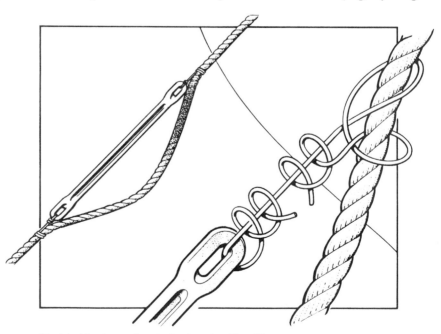

Stretchable straps absorb shock, extend line life.

than ⅛″ diameter) nylon multi-strand cord to attach them to the lines. However, any cord that has adequate strength and will fit through the eye of the snubber will do.

Tied across a bight of docking line, the snubber acts as a shock absorber, stretching to its limit as tension is exerted before the stress is taken by the line itself.

To fasten the snubber to the line, attach the cord to the hole in each end of the snubber with two half hitches. Attach the other end of each cord to the line with a clove hitch that is pulled very tight. For insurance, fasten the free end to the standing portion of the cord using two half hitches.

The homemade snubbers have survived two Maine winters and have extended line life several times at very low cost.

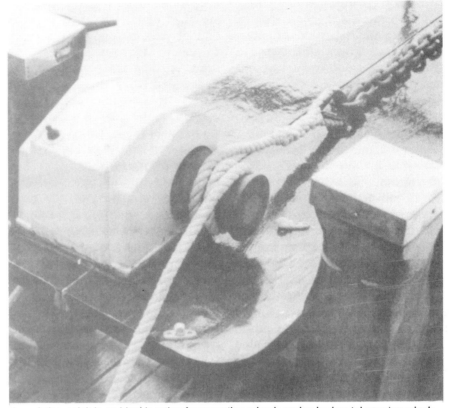

An existing pulpit is an ideal location for mounting a back-saving horizontal capstan winch on deck.

Installing a Deck-Mounted Anchor Windlass

A motor-driven anchor windlass can make anchor retrieval a lot easier and quicker on any size boat, especially if you frequently anchor in an area where a muddy bottom means that you have to lift half a ton of mud along with the anchor each time you pull it up. At least that's what it feels like after a long, hard day of swimming, lying in the sun, and probably drinking and eating too much.

Installing a pulpit and a heavy-duty anchor windlass with a vertical capstan that has the motor recessed below decks can be a sizable project involving cutting through the deck and requiring more-than-average skill in carpentry, fiberglassing, and wiring. However, there are a number of moderately priced, deck-mounted power wind-lasses that have horizontal capstans, which can be easily installed by any boatowner who is reasonably handy with tools and able to do a fairly simple 12-volt wiring job. In most cases, the whole job can be finished in less than one day.

When I took delivery of my 49′ Marine Trader trawler over four years ago, it had no anchor windlass on it, though it did have a pulpit and an anchor davit with a roller in the bow. I had ordered a large name-brand anchor windlass, but due to various problems it was not installed by the time I had to take delivery of the boat in the late fall. The plan was for me to bring the boat back to the dealer the following spring to have the windlass I had ordered installed.

As so often happens, other plans interfered the following spring and I did not bring the boat back. After anchoring out once or twice and almost breaking my back while hauling up the 35-pound Danforth by hand, I decided that a motor-driven windlass was a must. Noting that the owner of a comparably sized yacht near me had installed a moderately priced deck-mounted model with a horizontal capstan, I asked how it worked and was assured that it handled his 35-pound anchor with ease, even when it was buried deep in the mud after two or three days at anchor.

Convinced, I bought one and installed it myself in less than one day, and I can honestly say that it really does the job. Bear in mind that like most boatowners I don't use the windlass to actually break the anchor out of the mud—my boat's main engines are used for this. After starting the engines we move forward slowly while pulling line in until the anchor rode is straight up and down, then I take a turn or two around the sampson post or bow cleat while we continue to move forward slowly until a lack of tension in the line indicates that the anchor has broken free.

Then we put the engines in neutral while I wrap the line around the capstan and switch it on to finish the job of bringing the anchor on board. After taking three or four turns around the capstan all I have to do is maintain tension on the free end of the line while the motorized capstan does all the work. Up comes the anchor and its entrapped cake of mud, shells, and other back-breaking bottom cargo.

If the anchor is really loaded with mud and I don't want to bring all that mud up onto the bow, I release the line after it is about three-quarters of the way up so that the anchor falls free back into the water. This dunking usually cleans the worst of the mud off, after which I rewind the line on the capstan and lift it back up again.

Suitable for use on most small to medium-size cruising boats, deck-mounted windlasses with a horizontal capstan come in all price ranges, some selling for about $250 to $300, and others well over $1,000. You can choose from models that will handle either rope or chain, or both, and there are even some "automatic" models that feed the line directly down into the rope locker when operated by a remote switch located on or near the helm (these are generally a bit trickier to install, and require more wiring than a simple capstan model which is activated by a switch located on or near the windlass).

When comparing specifications you will be surprised to find (as I was) that many of these moderately priced deck-mounted units

have a maximum working-load rating that equals or even exceeds that of units costing several times as much. However, they won't bring the line up as rapidly when under load (they are geared down more to provide the torque needed, so the capstan turns slower when under load), and they cannot run for as long a period of time without overheating.

In addition, the less expensive units may contain less expensive components, and they generally do not have the same rugged, handsome look that is characteristic of the more deluxe models. On the other hand, these models draw less power than most of the larger and more expensive units, so this means you can use a smaller gauge wire to make electrical connections for the windlass to the battery, and this can sometimes add up to sizable savings.

The first step in the installation is deciding exactly where you want to mount the windlass—a job that would seem to be quite simple, but

one that calls for taking several factors into consideration before proceeding:

(1) The unit must be through-bolted, so you should select a location where you can get at the bolts underneath. If the unit is to be mounted on an existing pulpit as shown in the opening photograph, then this should not be a problem, but if you are mounting it on the deck you may find it advisable to move it aft a bit in order to locate it over a more accessible area than the extreme forepeak.

(2) In most installations you will also need a backing plate of wood or metal on the underside of the deck, so if the plate will be visible from below, take this into consideration when choosing a location. The backing plate can consist of a ½"-thick sheet of marine plywood, or a heavy sheet of stainless steel or aluminum plate (it must be thick enough so it won't bend easily when the bolts are tightened).

A backing plate under the deck

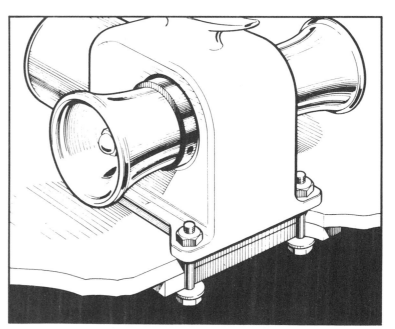

Access to through-bolts and space for a backing plate determine the position of the windlass.

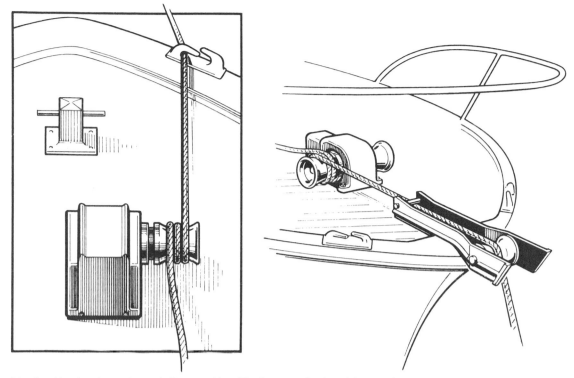

Line feed-in also determines windlass position. The line must feed straight onto the capstan.

will be needed if the deck is made of a single layer of fiberglass, or if it is of a sandwich-type fiberglass construction with a foam or balsa core (the backing plate will spread the pressure and keep the bolts from crushing or tearing through the "sandwich"). However, if the boat has thick, solid wood decks with a sturdy king plank down the center, or if the deck consists of solid teak laid on top of heavy fiberglass, then you may not need a backing plate on the bottom (though it is almost always a good idea).

(3) If your line and anchor will be coming up through an anchor davit or pulpit of any kind, then you will want to locate the windlass slightly off-center so that the capstan will be in line with the roller or opening in the center of the anchor davit, or at least as close to the center line as it is possible to get it.

If your anchor line normally comes up through one of the bow chocks on either side of the bow, then try to position the capstan so that its center is approximately in line with the chock. The idea in every case is to try to position the windlass so the line will feed onto the capstan from straight ahead whenever possible, not in from a sharp angle. In extreme cases when this is impossible, you will have to install a fairlead or turning block of some kind to insure a comparatively straight feed before the line runs onto the windlass's capstan drum.

(4) Since the winch will need a cable to supply the needed electrical power from the battery, and since this will have to be a fairly heavy size cable—usually at least No. 6, but even larger in some cases—some thought must be given to the problems you may encounter when running this wire from the windlass to the battery (you have to go directly to the bat-

tery for adequate power for a windlass).

After these factors have been considered and you have selected the location for the windlass, use a punch or awl to mark the holes required for the mounting bolts. In some cases the manufacturer will supply a template or pattern that you can use as a guide; in others you simply place the windlass in position, then use an awl or similar instrument to mark the locations of the mounting holes in the base.

The bolts used should be about 1″ longer than the total thickness of the windlass base, plus the deck and the mounting plate under it (if a mounting plate will be necessary). You will also need at least one hole for the wiring to go through, so drill this at the same time, preferably where it will be covered up by the base of the winch when it is mounted in position, making it waterproof. If the wires must come through elsewhere in an exposed location, then be sure you use a water-tight deck connection so you don't create a potential deck leak.

Feed the lead wires for the power supply through the hole under the base, then apply bedding compound or caulking around each of the mounting holes and around the perimeter of the base. After tightening all the bolts from below, apply a bead of caulking around the base as further protection against water seeping under.

If the deck or mounting surface has a curve on it, then you will have to fashion a wood mounting block (preferably of teak) to compensate for the curve. The top should be flat to accept the base of the windlass, and the bottom should be contoured to match the curve of the deck. Drill holes to match the mounting holes in the base, then apply a good bedding compound under the block surface before mounting the windlass on top.

To wire up the windlass, cable of the size recommended by the manufacturer should be run directly from the battery to the lead wires coming through the deck. The hot wire going to the positive post on the battery should have an in-line circuit breaker (often furnished with the windlass) connected to its end, just before it connects to the battery post. DON'T install the circuit breaker at the other end of the wire; it should be right next to, or as close to the battery as possible. The other wire goes to the negative post on the battery.

Windlass Cover

Windlasses are very expensive items that should be rinsed of salt water often and protected by a canvas cover. Since most windlasses are a rather ambiguous combination of curves and points and cylinders, two choices are left to the yachtsman. The first is to fabricate a simple drawstring bag that can be pulled over the windlass and tightened.

But, for the typical windlass with a wildcat for chain and a drum for line, two cylinders, with one end of each closed (much like a winch cover), can be made.

If the windlass has no other eccentricities, each side can then be covered with the addition of two more pieces of canvas. These will have to be fitted with a goodly number of darts to allow for the curve of windlass housing, and a hole in each to allow for the wildcat and the drum. First, cut the holes as tight as possible, then continue darting around until you have a proper fit. Cut a slit below the wildcat to allow the cover to be put in place over the chain that goes through the deck fitting. Hem the slit as well as the rest of the cover, then sew the two cylinders in place.

Lastly, sew a piece of dacron tape to the bottom of each side of the slit. These will be ties to keep the cover from sailing off into the sunset.

Anchor Davit and Roller

I recently built the anchor davit and roller unit pictured here for my boat—at far less cost than any of the commercially made models I could find. In addition, my homemade anchor davit has features that few of the ready-made units had, and all the materials were purchased at local hardware stores and lumberyards.

Bolted to the deck of my 26′ cruiser, this unit has made anchor handling much easier than ever before. It holds the anchor firmly in place and ready to go at all times with the line cleated to the regular bow cleat. The dimensions shown are designed to fit my 13-pound Danforth-type anchor, but could be easily modified to fit other anchors.

As indicated in the drawing the basic frame for the davit is made from two heavy gauge (¼″ thick) aluminum "L" sections which are cut to length and then clamped back-to-back for drilling the ⅞″ holes for the roller axles, and for sawing the ends off on the same diagonal. Drilling and sawing both pieces at the same time will insure that they will match exactly.

A piece of aluminum plate, ³⁄₁₆″ thick, fits inside of and on top of the two aluminum "L" sections to serve as a top plate and to join the two pieces of aluminum angle together. After placing it in position as shown, drill four holes for the bolts that will go through and bolt the whole thing together. The four ¼″ bolts, which should be 1½″ in length, should be flat-head bolts so the heads can be countersunk on the underside of the ¾″-thick mahogany base on which the whole unit is mounted (see drawing).

Cut the wood base to size and sand the edges smooth. Then position the metal parts of the anchor davit on top and drill the four holes for the bolts. Insert the bolts from below, then install the nuts on top and tighten securely.

The two rollers are standard trailer rollers, available from most marine supply outlets. The axles for each are cut from pieces of aluminum-bar stock, then holes are drilled through each end so cotter pins can be inserted to hold the rollers in place.

To finish the project, rub all the aluminum down with #200 abrasive paper, then polish with #400 wet-or-dry paper, using it very wet.

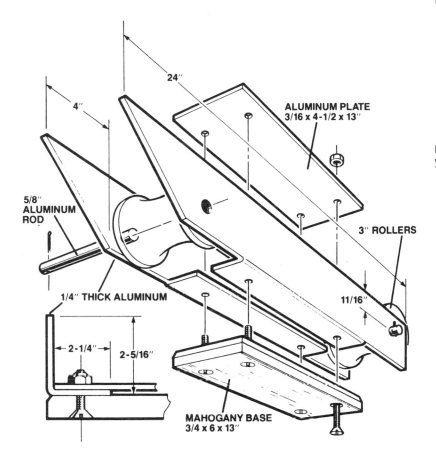

ALUMINUM PLATE
3/16 x 4-1/2 x 13"

24"

4"

5/8"
ALUMINUM
ROD

3" ROLLERS

1/4" THICK ALUMINUM

11/16"

2-1/4"

2-5/16"

MAHOGANY BASE
3/4 x 6 x 13"

Building this anchoring aid yourself allows you to custom-fit the unit to your boat.

Apply a couple of coats of wax to the metal and a couple of coats of spar varnish to the wood. Mount the finished unit on the bow so it projects out far enough to clear the anchor as it comes up. Then through-bolt it to the deck, using heavy stainless bolts. Make sure you use plenty of caulking or bedding compound under the base before you set it in place. A compression pad of wood on the inside, under the deck, is a good idea where the bolts go through. This will prevent crushing or otherwise damaging the fiberglass when the bolts are fully tightened.

An Inboard-Outboard Table

Temporary work counters are scarce, but here's one that's easy to build.

Table mounts inboard or outboard of gunwale, and can be stowed flat against the bulkhead.

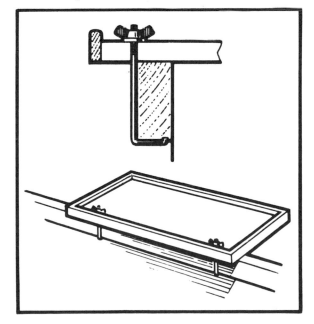

A rather narrow taffrail was backed up with a strip of 2" × 4" mahogany. A pair of holes were drilled horizontally through the taffrail and the back-up strip, and vertically through the strip. A panel of Formica-covered plywood, about 3' × 4' had a matching pair of holes drilled on one edge. With brass bolts and wing nuts, the plywood panel could be hung out of the way, flat against the weather cloth or secured horizontally and inboard as a handy table. In this particular installation, a freshwater supply was available and a kitchen-sink spray hose was attached. This made a fish-cleaning counter when the table was mounted outboard.

It would be easy to adapt a similar three-way table to fit the gunwale of most small boats.

A mahogany lip about ½" thick, extending approximately ½" above the working surface, would keep tools or other materials from sliding overboard when the table is inboard. When outboard for cleaning fish, it would keep the entrails from sliding aboard.

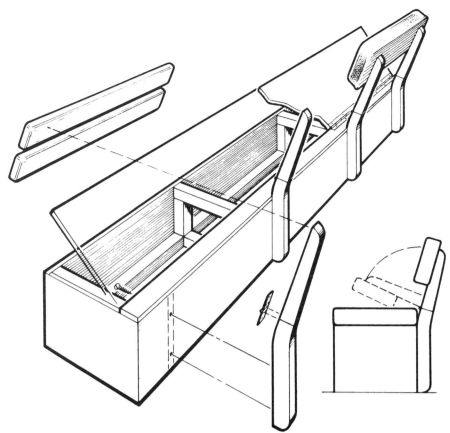

The folding-back design of this seat/locker unit permits use of the backless cover of the original seat.

Combination Flying Bridge Seat/Bench Locker

As on many other boats, the flying bridge on our boat came with only a single, permanently installed bench-type seat of open construction, so it performed only one function—it provided seating for those on the bridge.

I decided to replace this with a combination seat/locker that would also include some much needed storage space for such things as the canvas bridge cover, life preservers, extra lines, and similar items. At the same time, I decided to make it easily removable by attaching it to the bridge deck with thumbscrews so the seat/locker could be easily moved out of the way when I had to work under or behind the steering station (this was always a problem with the original fixed seat).

My original seat had no back, so my existing bridge cover did not allow for one.

I built the new seat with a hinged back that can be folded down before the cover is snapped into place over the top. This meant cutting the seat supports as shown in the drawing, then hinging each so the assembled back could fold down.

The seat/locker box was made of ½" exterior grade plywood (mahogany plywood should be used if you want to varnish it, but ordinary exterior plywood can be used if you plan to paint it). A framework of 2 × 2s on the inside provides rigidity and forms a solid surface for fastening the plywood in each corner (use screws or ringed nails to form the joints). After assembling, the inside joints were fiberglassed and the inside of the box was given a coat of fiberglass resin.

The hinged top of the bench was also made of ½" plywood, so one or two cross braces (short lengths of 2 × 2) will be needed across the opening under this to support the top and prevent sagging when people sit on it. A piano hinge should be used to fasten this to a lengthwise strip that goes across the top along the back of the box.

The vertical frames that support the back of the seat are cut out of 1¼" thick stock, and they should be securely through-bolted to the upholstered cushions with a plywood backing on the inside; or they can be made entirely of wood—usually by fastening wood slats spaced a couple of inches apart horizontally across the vertical supports.

Poor Man's Radar Reflector

We have "borrowed" this item from Pete Smyth's old "TLC" column in the February 1969 issue of *Motor Boating*. He gives credit to P/C Anson G. Hoyt, who in turn acknowledges borrowing it from the Coral Ridge Power Squadron Newsletter, who in turn borrowed it from something called "Twin Lights." It has been around.

Buy a 36″ square sheet of aluminum at your hardware store or building supply store. Cut the sheet into four 18″ squares. You need just three of these pieces to make the reflector, cutting them as indicated in the sketch. Drill the four holes as indicated on each of the two oddly-shaped pieces. Assemble, when needed, as shown in the sketch and suspend from any high location on your boat. It is said to make a little wooden boat show up like the U.S.S. *Missouri* on a radar screen.

When not needed, disassemble the screen and store it under a mattress, or in any other convenient flat spot.

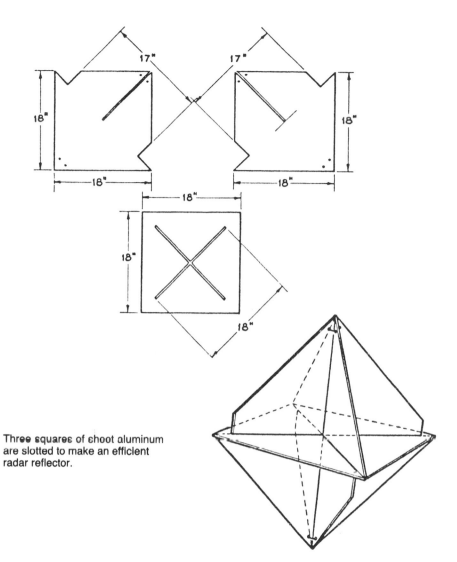

Three squares of sheet aluminum are slotted to make an efficient radar reflector.

Freshwater Windshield Washer

Electric windshield wipers are now standard on a good many small boats. They work fine in rain or when quantities of water frequently strike the windshield, but on a clear day salt spray can coat the windshield and quickly evaporate, leaving the salt. It's glareproof, but impossible to see through.

I took matters into my own hands. In a junkyard I found an automobile windshield washer tank with a 12-volt pump attached to its base from an old Chrysler.

Mount the one-quart tank on any convenient bulkhead near the helm, then wire the pump by running the "hot" lead through a pull-type momentary switch (pull for on, let go for off). Mount the switch conveniently on the dash.

To carry the water to the windshield, buy a length of flexible hose sized to fit snugly over the outlet tube on the tank. (I got my hose at a fish tank supply store.) Run the hose to the top of the windshield, then drill a hole in the frame to pass the hose through. Then con-nect the hose to a length of copper tubing that will run along the top of the windshield. Drill one or two tiny holes in the tubing aimed down at the windshield, then crimp the far end of the tube so the water exits only through the holes.

For a two-piece windshield, use two copper tubes, bridged with a length of plastic tubing.

To hold the copper spray tube, I cut a piece of sheet metal (use copper or aluminum) about 4″ × 6″. I drilled holes along one side (see drawing) large enough to fit under

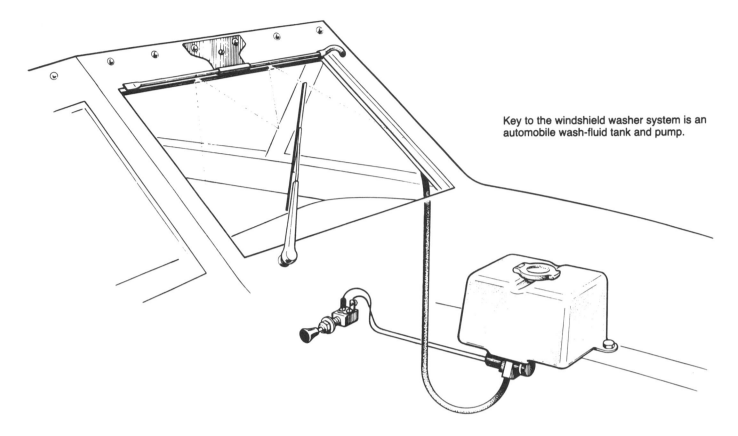

Key to the windshield washer system is an automobile wash-fluid tank and pump.

the removable snap buttons on the frame, then curled the other long side to wrap around the copper tube. Slide the tube in and crimp gently, making sure the curl does not cover the spray holes nor impede the easy flow of fluid.

In conjunction with your wipers you'll have—*Voila!*—clear vision.

Cooler Seat for Inflatables

Replacing the forward seat of an inflatable boat with a sturdy cooler will give you a place to stow food and beverage, a place to sit, and it can be used for dry stowage.

Choose a well-built cooler, preferably metal, and, depending on the size of your inflatable, one that will allow you room to maneuver around it. In a 12′ sportboat a 13″ × 18″ cooler fits well.

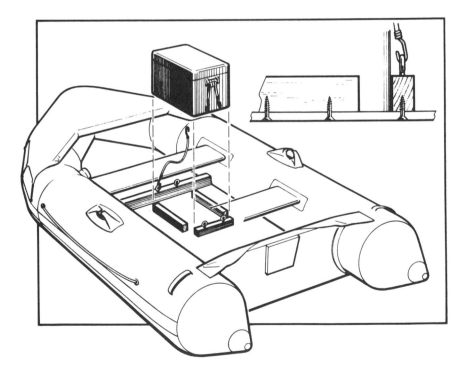

Cooler chest replaces forward seat in this inflatable.

Center the cooler on the floor and draw its outline. Cut three 8″ strips of wood approximately ¾″ × 1″ and place two along the sides and one at the aft end. The front of the cooler should rest against the thwartship floor brace. These strips are screwed into the flooring system from underneath using recessed stainless steel flathead screws, recessed so they don't rub against the fabric floor. Secure two ½″ × ½″ × 1½″ stainless steel eye straps to each of the strips below the cooler handles. Then use thin line or shock cord run through the cooler handles from the eye straps to secure it in place.

Dinghy Seat Tab

Knee-knocking becomes a problem in a small dinghy when a second person sits facing you in the stern

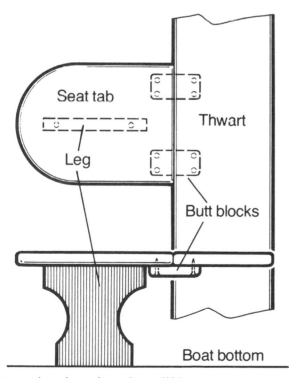

Rower, when alone, sits on thwart. With passenger on aft seat, rower can slide forward onto tab to keep the dinghy in proper trim.

sheets. Also, your knuckles can come unpleasantly close to his face when you're leaning on the oars.

One yachtsman solved his dilemma, and improved the trim of his dinghy, by adding a small seat tab, or extension to the forward edge of the thwart.

Consisting of a single piece of ¾″ mahogany, cut to approximately 9″ × 12″ and rounded at the forward end, it attaches to the thwart with a couple of screwed-on blocks beneath.

For support, the new seat tab has a vertical leg attached to its underside with a couple of long screws, as shown. When finished to match existing woodwork, you have a double purpose seat for whatever rowing conditions come along.

Homemade Rod Rack

A vertical rack for fishing rods, similar to the one illustrated here, is a handy addition to any open boat or runabout, not only for rods but also for spear guns and boathooks, an extra hand bilge pump, etc. Easily built of materials that can be found in local hardware stores or building supply houses, you can make one up for comparatively little cost—and in the exact size and configuration you may need to fit your particular boat.

When selecting a location for the rack, make sure you allow at least 19″ from the boat deck to the top of the rack, and space individual holders so they are at least 6″ apart, center to center.

The tubes that serve as the rod holders are 14″ lengths of 2″-diameter PVC plastic pipe, available from most plumbing supply outlets if you cannot get it from your local hardware store. Buy enough to permit cutting as many lengths as you will need, then use any fine-tooth saw to cut the pieces. The cut edges can be sanded smooth with fine sandpaper. If some of the manufacturer's lettering shows on the outside of the pipe, it can be wiped off with acetone, or you can sand it off with fine steel wool. Drill two ⁵⁄₁₆″ holes through one side of each tube, locating the two holes in line with each other, and positioning each 2″ in from the end.

Two horizontal strips of 1″ × 2″ wood are used to mount the row of tubes (rod holders) as shown in the illustration, making each one at least 2″ longer than the overall width of the rack so that the holes at each end will be at least 1″ in from the ends. Drill ⁵⁄₁₆″ holes at 6″ intervals to match the holes pre-

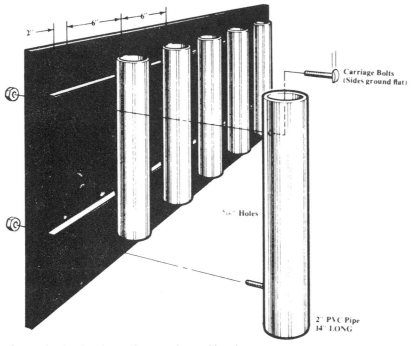

Customized rod racks are inexpensive and handy.

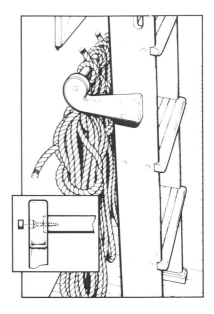

Bracket holds line behind bridge ladder.

brackets can be screwed to the underside of the wood steps instead of to the side rails, as shown.

Either way, the completed rail provides enough room on our boat to hang a total of about 300 feet of ½" and ⅝" lines.

viously drilled in the tubes, then use these wood strips to mark and then drill matching holes in the surface against which the strips will be mounted.

Since the rod holders should be through-bolted, you can mount them against the side of an engine access cover in most open boats, or you can mount the assembled tubes and strips to a suitably sized sheet of exterior plywood, then mount the whole sheet of plywood to a bulkhead or other surface.

Carriage bolts to hold the tubes in place are inserted from inside the tube so they go through the holes drilled in the tube, then through the holes drilled in wood strips behind the tube, and then through the mounting surface or board. Rubber washers can be used under each bolt head to keep them from digging into the plastic too much, or you can grind a straight edge on two sides of each

bolt head then align these vertically to avoid scratching rod handles when they are dropped into place.

Neat Line Storage

In order to store all our various lines we built a rail behind the ladder that leads up to the flying bridge on our boat, as shown in the illustration. Two teak brackets were cut out of 1"-thick lumber (¾"-thick stock would probably work as well) and screwed to the sides of the ladder, as shown. Then a teak bar was mounted between them to act as a rail from which the lines could be hung (when properly coiled). We used teak, but mahogany or other less expensive wood could be used if desired.

If the bridge ladder has steel tubes for the side rails, then the

Scupper Drains to Prevent Stains

On most boats as the water runs off the decks in various places—often through gaps in the cap rail—this runoff creates dark streaks on the sides of the hull that are very hard to remove, especially if the decks are oiled teak.

A neat solution is to install drains of soft plastic tubing that will carry the water overboard without having it run down the sides of the hull. As shown in the drawings, the tubing extends past the sides of the hull by an inch or

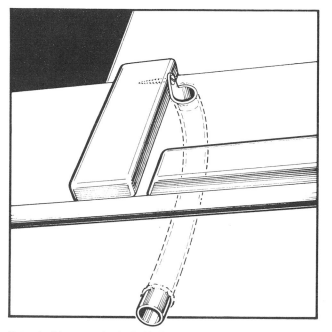

Extend tubing past the hull side by an inch or two to keep stains from forming as water runs off.

At the deck level trim off the tubing so most of it is flush, but with a good size tab still protruding. Fold this tab down and fasten in place with a stainless screw and washer. At the other end leave about 2″ protruding, then trim off the excess later if experience shows this is too much.

Hidden Lock for Hatches

Many boats have large hatches or lazarettes in the cockpit sole—sometimes these are merely engine hatches, but sometimes they are storage compartments for fishing gear, fenders, extra lines, boarding ladders, scuba diving gear, etc. Yet in a surprisingly large number of boats there is no easy way to lock these hatches for security when you are not aboard. Some people install hasps and padlocks, but these leave a lot to be desired in appearance, and they are easy to trip over.

An ideal solution is to install a hidden sliding bolt that locks the

two so the water will fall free without running down the hull. And, since the tubing is flexible, no harm is done if the boat brushes up against a piling or dock.

For most boats, tubing that is either ¾″ or 1″ in diameter will be about right. Use an electric drill and a bit the same diameter as the tubing to bore a hole through the deck, then bore another hole through the side of the hull a few inches below the cap rail. To seal the opening when the tubing is inserted, epoxy cement is applied to the outside of the tubing. The tubing should be several inches longer than necessary so you can let it protrude at each end. The excess will be trimmed off afterward.

Spread epoxy over the outside of the tubing, then have someone feed it slowly down through the deck opening. Insert a long thin dowel from the outside (through the hole in the hull), aiming it up the hole in the deck. Get the end of the dowel into the end of the tubing coming down through the deck, then use the dowel to guide the tubing to the hole in the hull as the other end is pushed and twisted to feed it downward. Poke a long thin screwdriver in from the outside to help snag the end of the tubing by partially depressing it as you pull the end through.

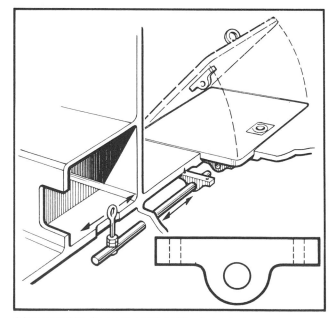

A broomstick is the basis of this hidden hatch lock.

hatch from underneath, as shown in the accompanying illustration. Inexpensive to make and install, this sliding-bolt "lock" is invisible from the outside and virtually trouble-free. It consists of a broomstick or similar pole that slides through two guides that are permanently fastened under the deck as shown. One is secured to the bottom of the hatch cover, and the other is fastened to the deck so that it is exactly in line with the first one. When the pole projects through the two, it keeps the hatch from being opened.

To slide the broomstick back and forth to lock or unlock the hatch, attach a bolt at right angles to form a handle. This "handle" projects up through a slot cut in the cabin sole inside a space that is normally concealed. In our boat the slot is in the sole under a dinette seat, but it could be in almost any convenient location inside the boat where the projecting "handle" will be out of the way, yet easy to reach.

For accurate alignment of the two hardwood guides, install the one under the deck first, after boring the hole through the bulkhead that will serve as a guide for the broomstick. Then, while inside the hatch with the cover in place, you position the second guide to make sure the pole will slide back and forth easily.

Lid Preventer

One simple way to hold a locker cover open so that it won't come crashing down on your fingers (or head) is to use a piece of shock cord with a plastic hook at the end as shown here. One end of the shock cord is attached to the underside of the hinged cover with a wad of epoxy putty, while the

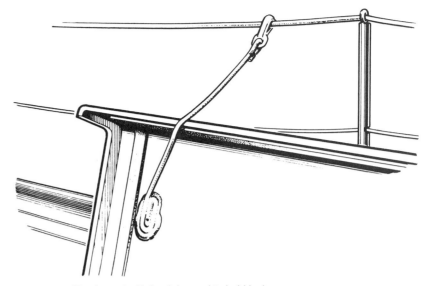

Shock cord with hook is used to hold locker cover open.

other end is equipped with a plastic snap hook of the kind that is widely sold for use with shock cord. When the lid is lifted you snap this hook onto one of the lifelines. Simply unsnap it when you want to close the cover.

Two Easy and Complete Cockpit Screens

Those of us who gunkhole know that aggressive insects can turn an otherwise pleasant anchorage into a minor nightmare for the unprepared.

Aside from chemical repellents (which must cover every square inch of exposed skin and will wear off), the best line of defense is a set of closely meshed, snug-fitting screens for all ports and hatches. Such screening can easily be extended to include the entire cockpit of a cabin cruiser or sailboat. The necessary nylon netting is readily available at most large camping supply stores and relatively inexpensive.

If you have full cockpit canvas to

use as a pattern, the job is already half done. Simply spread the cover out and lay the sections of netting over it. Ordinary straight pins can be used to hold the panels of netting together until they are sewn into the single large screen. Attach snaps to the screen (of the same type as on the canvas cover) where the snaps are on the cockpit cover. Attach the snaps about 2" closer than they are located on the cockpit cover to allow you to stretch the screen taut when it is installed.

Leave plenty of material to hang loose below the snaps to aid in sealing little gaps and openings. If you double back the netting and install the snaps through the double thickness, it will be both a neater and stronger finish. Add some stitching to tie down the loose edges of material and you are finished.

If you don't have a cockpit cover already, just install snaps at 1' intervals around the cockpit periphery and sew enough netting panels together to make a large screen to drape over the cockpit. Then install the mating snaps on the screen in place—front first, then the back, then the sides. Trim the excess net-

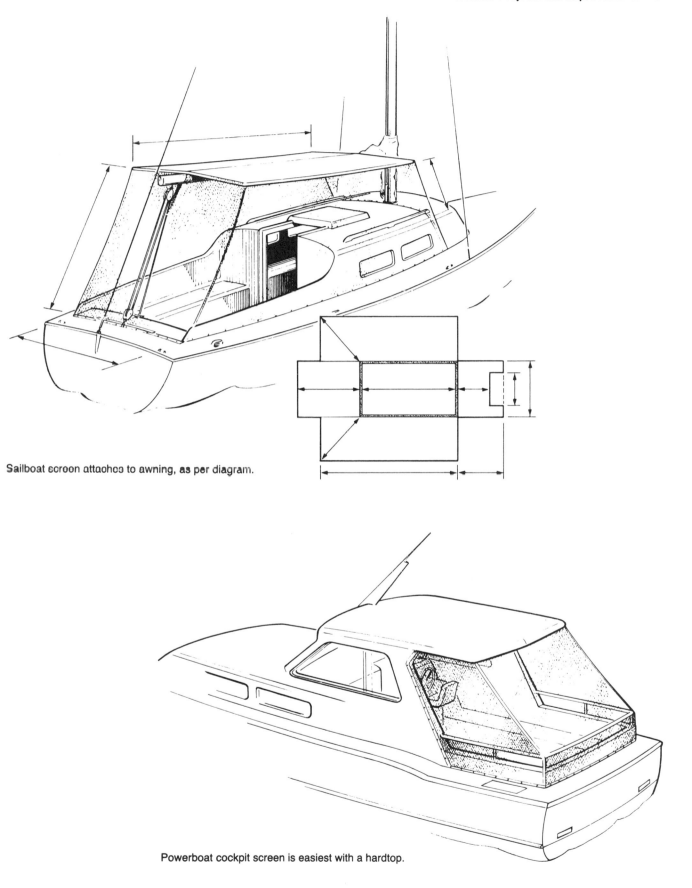

Sailboat screen attaches to awning, as per diagram.

Powerboat cockpit screen is easiest with a hardtop.

ting, stitch the loose edges as above, and you're done.

The construction of a cockpit screen for a sailboat is a little more difficult. The easiest way to screen the cockpit is probably to combine the screen with a sun awning. Snaps or Velcro strips around the top edge of the sun awning will permit ready attachment of the screen while still preserving the flexibility needed for adjustment of the awning and movement around the outside of the cockpit.

The first step is to make the proper measurements. Set up your awning and make complete measurements. Then determine the amount of screening that you will have to buy. Be sure to add at least 10 percent to this quantity to account for overlaps and the inevitable minor errors. At the same time, determine the quantity of snaps and/or Velcro.

Start by laying the sun awning on the ground. From each side of the awning, lay out panels of netting of appropriate size and orientation to conform to the measurements made earlier. Sew the panels on each side of the awning together. Add Velcro to join the center segments of the forward and aft sides together. This will be the dividing point for the finished screen. Sew the right and left sides of the forward part of the screen to the respective edges of the right and left sections of the screen. Unless you are very sure of your measurements and ability, do not sew the rear section to the side sections yet.

Set up the sun awning on the boat, attach all sections of the screen to it and fasten the bottom edges of all screen sections. Then fasten the right and left edges of the rear section of the screen to the respective rear edges of the side sections with straight pins. This will allow adjustments to the attach-

ment points to obtain a smooth finish before any cutting or sewing of this seam. Once you are satisfied with the attachment of the panels, cut off the excess and sew the final seams.

In all cases, allow enough excess material to drape around the bottom edge of the screen to insure that the bottom is sealed. Closure of the screen around the stays, lines, or the boom can be easily done with Velcro.

The screen can be removed and stowed in a remarkably small space, or the forward and rear sections can be folded back to the sides and the sides rolled up to store on the sun awning, held there by simple ties.

Deck Box Vent

This is an idea that someone should have thought up sooner. Two dorade vents are incorporated into a deck box for storage of heaving lines, sail stops, and winch handles. The unit is easy to make and can be scaled up or down to suit any sized vessel. The interior may be merely painted with a synthetic paint or can be fiberglassed. The cowl ventilators and hardware can be ordered from any marine supplier.

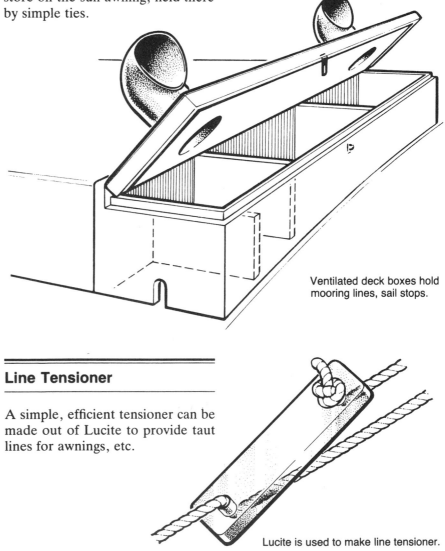

Ventilated deck boxes hold mooring lines, sail stops.

Line Tensioner

A simple, efficient tensioner can be made out of Lucite to provide taut lines for awnings, etc.

Lucite is used to make line tensioner.

A Pivoting Mast: Not Just for Bridges

It was the attraction of cruising through the French canals that gave me the idea of having pivoted masts fitted to my ketch *Aventura*. Although my cruising has led me to the South Pacific instead, it is a decision I have never regretted. As more and more cruising and racing boats are opting for a mast stepped on deck, there is no reason why the mast should not be stepped in a tabernacle allowing it to be lowered and raised without outside help. On *Aventura* the arrangement is kept as simple as possible, and in five years of cruising I have dropped the mast on average at

least once every year, never using a crane. The operation can be easily carried out by two people and takes about one hour, although in a real emergency I could do it on my own in even less time. The mizzen mast, which is also pivoted, is so light that it can be dropped in a matter of minutes. The two masts are rigged independently of each other, a precaution against losing both of them if one or the other breaks and goes overboard.

When lowering a pivoted mast, the critical moment occurs when the mast reaches an angle of about 25° to the horizontal, and it is at this stage that the head of the mast has to be supported from a point situated at a height equal to at least one third the length of the mast.

This problem can be easily overcome by improvising an A-frame out of the boom and spinnaker pole. As I have two running poles of equal length, I use these for the A-frame. The poles are 13′9″ long, while the mast has a length of 38′4″ and weighs approximately 220 pounds. including all rigging. The operation step by step is as follows:

The A-frame is laid down facing forward, with its legs shackled to the cap shroud chainplates. The poles are shackled together at the apex to form a rigid frame. After securing the mast from falling backwards by attaching the jib halyard to a strong point, the forestay is taken off and made fast with a shackle to the apex of the frame, although a second jib halyard could do the job equally well. Also from the apex, a line is led through to the bow roller or to a block fixed to the stem and from there to the windlass, where a few turns are taken on the rope gypsy. In fact, when lowering the mast, the use of a winch or windlass is not really necessary. All standing rigging forward of the mast is then taken off and the cap shrouds slackened by a few turns on the rigging screws. The backstay(s) and lower backstays do not have to be touched at all, and even the cap shrouds, whose lengths should remain constant, are only slackened to allow the mast a small amount of lateral movement.

The lowering of the mast can now begin. While one person is taking charge of the line attached to the A-frame, the other person gives the mast a slight push backward to start it going. As the mast starts going down, the A-frame is gradually lifted from the deck, the line man easily controlling the fall by paying out line gradually. Two turns on the gypsy are sufficient as with more turns it is easier to get a riding hitch. Down to an angle of

The A-frame, made from running poles, is attached to the mast head with a forestay or jib halyard, while a line is taken via the bow to the windlass.

Here the A-frame is ready to take up the mast again.

45° the operation is simple, but when this angle is reached, the weight of the mast starts being felt and, although I have successfully carried out this operation more than half a dozen times, I still feel the adrenaline rising in my blood as the mast dips its head lower and lower while the line creaks and groans under the strain. But the A-frame is doing its job and by the time the mast has reached the angle where its weight is greatest, the frame is close to the vertical. A padded place is now prepared on the aft deck and the mast is gently lowered onto it. Throughout the operation the helper keeps an eye on the rigging and other fixtures so as to warn the line man in case anything is snagged or caught. The fall can easily be halted at any stage by cleating the fall line.

The raising of the mast is, if anything, simpler as the critical stage is passed at the beginning of the operation. When raising the mast, the A-frame starts off in a vertical position and the line running from the apex of the frame to a windlass or winch is slowly winched in. On *Aventura*, my old windlass, which sometimes cannot get the anchor out of the mud, is powerful enough to raise the mast back to the vertical. Once the mast is standing again, a jib halyard is used to steady it forward while the forestay is returned from the frame to the stemhead. If any of the other rigging had been dismantled for the operation, the mast can be steadied with halyards, topping lifts, etc., while the standing rigging is fixed up again.

Obviously, there are countless variations for carrying out this operation and I found it much easier to lower and raise the mast when a higher point of attachment than the one offered by my own A-frame was available. Thus, the A-frame can be mounted on a dock, with the yacht facing it. An even easier solution is to simply take a block and attach it to a high structure facing the boat and then lower the mast by paying out a line that runs from the masthead to the block and back onto the foredeck. Or one can do the operation by using a halyard from another boat conveniently moored in front of one's own yacht.

On *Aventura*, the main tabernacle is made of ⅜" stainless steel plate with a 1" × 8" stainless pin running through the mast, the pin crossing the mast at 8" from its base. Originally the pivot sleeve inside the mast was not reinforced, something which I had to do recently when I noticed signs of corrosion between the aluminum mast and the stainless pin. At the same time, I also reinforced the mast itself on both sides of the sleeve. The distance from the mast heel to the bottom of the tabernacle is 4" and the space is now filled with wooden wedges, although for a long time I relied on the pivot alone to support the mast. The spar makers, who also fabricated the tabernacles, did not recommend the insertion of wedges under the mast, but after many thousands of miles of windward work, I decided to fully support the mast under its heel.

All these suggestions refer to a mast pivoted to be lowered backward. On a ketch or yawl though, the main mast could be pivoted to allow it to go forward, in which case the mizzen mast itself can be used to act as the high point in question. There are many boats with pivoted masts, especially in Holland, where the frame used for lowering and raising the mast is a permanent fixture on the foredeck, the two legs of the frame being also used to steady the boat when drying out. But if the mast is only supposed to be lowered on rare occasions, the improvised frame can do the job just as well.

The advantages of being able to drop a mast anywhere and without any outside help are too many to mention. I have been able to drop my main mast in the morning, rivet twenty steps onto it, replace all wiring inside the mast, and have it back up again by the same evening. If we want to explore a place that is cut off from the sea by a low bridge, we can do it. But the greatest advantage by far of being able to drop one's mast, especially in remote places, is to reduce the windage dramatically in the event of a hurricane. With the mast down at virtually deck level, the windage of a sailing boat can be reduced by more than 50 percent as the windage on the spars and rigging can exert tremendous pressures in winds over 50 knots. This is something that we haven't had to do yet, but would certainly consider in such a situation. And then, of course, there are still all those French canals beckoning!

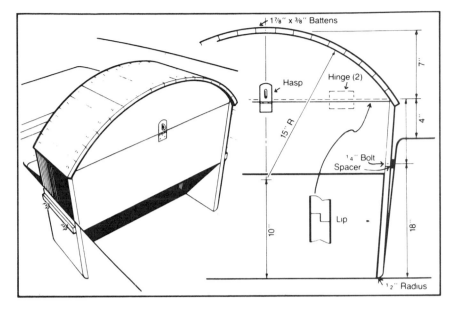

The curved top on this locker-seat storage unit serves as stable helm position when boat is heeled.

Cockpit Seat/Locker

In many sailboats visibility is quite limited when seated, especially when heeled over and in a boat that has a high cabin. To correct this problem on my 36' sailboat, as well as to provide a reasonably comfortable seat while the boat is heeled, I built the combination curved top seat-and-locker unit pictured.

Dimensions will, of course, vary according to the width of the cockpit and the amount of space available between cockpit lockers along each side. Cut the two vertical side pieces first and hold them temporarily in position so you can measure the lengths needed for the cross members that will form the front and back sides of the seat. Most cockpit sides are tapered or sloped, so be sure you allow for (and install) spacer blocks at each side, as shown in the drawing, in order to permit opening and closing the seat lockers when this seat is in place.

Made of teak or mahogany, the seat has a hinged top that provides space on the inside for storage of emergency equipment such as flares, EPIRB, etc. The seat is through-bolted to the cockpit sides to keep it from shifting, and the curved top makes it easy to sit comfortably on either tack.

Scupper Strainers

Self-bailing cockpits are a great invention—except that scuppers can become plugged with debris after several seasons of carelessness and neglect.

We have heard of two sailing auxiliaries whose cockpits no longer drain because of blocked outlets. One fiberglass sloop required hours of labor to free the delicate tubing of its burden of leaves, bugs, food, paper, hair, and other memorabilia of days on the water.

The second boat is finishing out the season afloat, its owners hoping no huge waves will swamp the cockpit. Reluctant to haul out, they are fearful that probing with a pointed instrument to remove the dirt might damage the inside passage and the connections between the scuppers and the hull fitting. Suction with a "plumber's friend" and other emergency measures failed to dislodge the clogged mass.

In the light of these two current experiences, we are passing along our solution to this problem, which in eight years of sailing has kept our Tripp 30's cockpit scuppers free, clean, and clear: In a regular hardware store, we purchased two stainless, perforated cuplike strainers, slightly smaller in diameter than the scuppers, so that they

Sink drains are used for scuppers.

nest neatly in the top of the opening. They fit flush with the cockpit sole and have a lip that enables them to be lifted out easily for weekly cleaning, which is accomplished by swishing them in clear water. They effectively collect and filter out just about everything but water and a few innocuous crumbs. This operation is quick, easy, and cheap compared to the major surgery required when scuppers refuse to drain. The strainers come in several sizes and cost under a quarter.

Sold on the need for vigilance, we have also placed a smaller model of this same kind of strainer in our cabin sink drain—after once losing a kitchen knife down that opening!

Isolate That Lazarette

As in many mass-produced fiberglass sailboats, I found that the lazarette in the cockpit of my boat opened into a vast empty area under the cockpit sole and around the coamings. Any water that leaked in past the hatch cover drained into the bilge, and often accumulated in spaces that were inaccessible because they were behind glassed-in bulkheads or similar dividers.

Water is not so bad, but any gasoline or other flammable liquids that might spill from cans in the lazarette could also end up there, posing a potential explosion hazard. In addition, if the hatch cover ever got torn off during a storm, water that came aboard would pour through the lazarette and soon swamp the boat.

My solution to all this was to isolate the lazarette from the rest of the boat by glassing in plywood bulkheads that made it a separate, watertight compartment. Now, if anything spills, or if water does come aboard, it is contained—and as a bonus I have a lazarette that is not always "swallowing up" small items that would otherwise tend to get lost in the bilge.

Since you will be dealing with tight spaces and odd shapes, the best way to start is to use sheets of corrugated cardboard to make a template for each piece of plywood. This will take some trial and error with scissors and a ruler, but cardboard is cheap and pieces can be joined together with masking tape if one piece of cardboard is not big enough (you can buy large sheets in art supply stores). After cutting the cardboard to fit, use it as a pattern for cutting the pieces of plywood to the right size and shape.

Before you can fiberglass the pieces of plywood in place you must remove all dirt, paint, or other coatings from the surface. A disk sander is the fastest tool to use, but wear a respirator to protect you from breathing in the sanding dust (it can be hazardous). After sanding, remove all dust with a vacuum cleaner.

The fumes from the resin that is used to do the fiberglassing can also be dangerous in a confined area, so use a fan to blow air into the compartment while you work. Also, wear a good respirator with dual chemical filters.

Use polyester tape and wide fiberglass tape (4″ to 6″ wide) to hold the plywood bulkheads in place. Fill the joints first (where the plywood meets the fiberglass of the hull) with a putty made by mixing the resin with glass beads or powder, then spread the glass and resin over this to create a neatly rounded joint. Finish with another layer of glass and resin over the entire surface of the plywood.

Remember that if this lazarette will be used to store gasoline cans or other inflammables, it must be ventilated. Install suitable air scoops or louvered vents—one facing forward and one facing aft.

Lubber's Louvers

One happy solution to the problem of boat ventilation is the use of adjustable louvers fitted with screening, which let in the air but keep out the rain and the bugs.

These louvers, available for little cost at lumber and hardware dealers, can be fitted to whatever opening is available, in this case a sliding door opening. True, a full screen door could be installed, but once in place it would remain and not keep the rain out. And the partial closure has the advantage of allowing passage in or out without removal. Further, the smaller panels can be stowed when not in use.

To get started, measure the opening to be used, then match it with the next larger size or combination of sizes available at the store. Then cut off and mill edges to suit. In the case shown, the vertical side to starboard was milled with a tongue, the other edge with a groove to fit the door jamb and the door edge.

The top edge of the top section was tongued to fit in the overhead track. The upper section is also cut to overlap the lower section on the outside to prevent water seepage to the wrong side.

Depending on a particular boat's frame and door construction, there may have to be fillers added and cavities cut along the edges of the panels to fit around door latches. Bugs are great at finding an un-

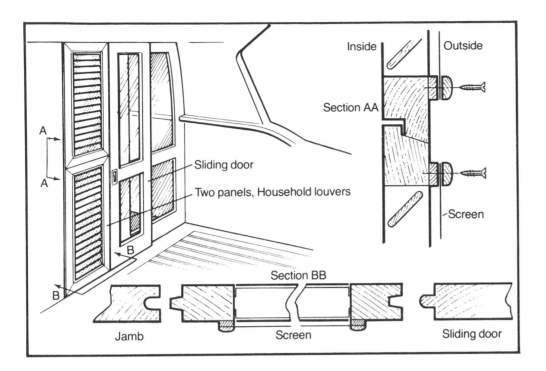

Section AA

Inside | Outside

Sliding door

Two panels, Household louvers

A

A

B

B

Screen

Section BB

Jamb | Screen | Sliding door

Two panels of ordinary household louvers, positioned in the sliding door of a deckhouse, let air in while keeping out insects and rain.

closed gap where light shines through.

Nylon screening was used, tacked to a ¾" × ½" frame which provided clearance for the louvers to operate.

Boom Preventer

When our boom comes flying across in a jibe, or even in a windy tack, the potential for damage is considerable. Our rig is stout, but I can't say as much for the upper reaches of our guests and charterers.

I solved this worrisome problem by devising a preventer which dampens the boom's violent movements but does not impair its swing from tack to tack, or materially effect trimming.

The heart of the system is a stationary turning post arrangement made of aluminum with a spiral groove machined into it large enough to accept a ¼" piece of line. The line makes four revolutions around the post from its deadend on the boom, then returns to the boom where it runs to a small winch and accompanying cleat. During trimming or an easy tack, the line passes freely around the post, but the moment the line comes under sudden strain—during a jibe, for instance—it closes around the post producing an astonishing amount of friction, and the suddenly civilized boom crosses slowly and predictably.

I manufactured the crucial post in my own onboard machine shop, but any suitably equipped shop should be able to make one.

Topping Lift-Tension Holder

On a moderately sized cruising sailboat the boom topping lift must be slack when under sail, otherwise it will tend to lift the end of the boom and cause the sail to twist. Yet if the topping lift is too slack the line will flog about and may hang up on one of the battens.

The simplest way to solve this problem is to cut a 2' or 3' length of elastic shock cord and attach a shackle to one end. Fasten the other end to the fitting at the end of the boom to which the topping lift is attached. Now stretch the shock cord to about three fourths its maximum stretch, laying it along the length of the topping lift. Mark this point on the topping lift and then seize a small brass or stainless ring onto the line at this point; use waved nylon or polyester cord.

Before raising the main, stretch the elastic and snap it onto the ring attached to the topping lift. After the main is raised you slack off the topping lift a bit in the usual manner before cleating it at the mast, but this time the elastic cord will keep it taut, while still allowing some up-and-down movement of

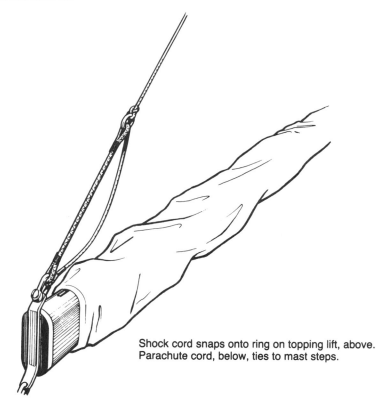

Shock cord snaps onto ring on topping lift, above.
Parachute cord, below, ties to mast steps.

the boom. When not in use the shock cord is unsnapped and stored, usually by rolling inside the mainsail.

Nonfouling Mast Steps

For a long time after I added those half-A aluminum mast steps, I wondered if the convenience of climbing to the spreaders really offset the fouling of halyards every time I set sail in even the slightest chop. The halyards tended to snag on the steps when the boat rocked. As a result, I was forced to climb the steps to unlace the halyards before I could raise or lower the sails. And since my steps go all the way to the top of the 48′ mast, it could be a slightly harrowing experience in any kind of sea. Finally, I hit on a solution so simple I'm surprised I've never seen it on other boats.

Starting at the top, I tied ¼″ parachute nylon cord around the outer

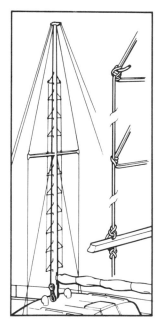

bend of the rung with a double rolling hitch; then I pulled the line tight and led it to the next rung down, where I tied another hitch, and so on down to the bottom rung. Instead of continuing the line around the spreaders, I tied the bitter end to two small stainless

hookeyes inserted in the top and bottom of the spreaders. Below the spreaders I followed the same pattern, down to the lowest rung.

Compass Mount for Small Sailboats

The previous owner of my Cal 2-24 sailboat had mounted the compass permanently on top of the sliding hatch cover, but I found this unsatisfactory for a number of reasons: When the hatch cover was slid forward the compass was too forward to be seen easily from the helm; the compass was constantly being jarred by crew members sliding the hatch open and closed; the compass, being permanently mounted on the hatch, was a tempting target for thieves when the boat was left tied at the public marina during the week.

The solution I worked out to solve this problem was to mount the compass on a removable mounting board that clamps to the lowest of the sliding hatch boards. The compass itself is supported by an aluminum (or brass) bracket that fits inside a wood support bracket, as shown (use only brass or aluminum screws to assemble this to avoid magnetic problems). On most boats this wood bracket will have to be tapered or shaped in back where it attaches to the removable mounting board so that the compass will sit vertically even though the hatch board slopes forward slightly.

Permanently installed brass or stainless steel bolts go through the hatch board and are held in place with a recessed locknut, as shown. The bolts should be long enough so that about 1″ protrudes through into the cockpit. This enables the end of each bolt to go through

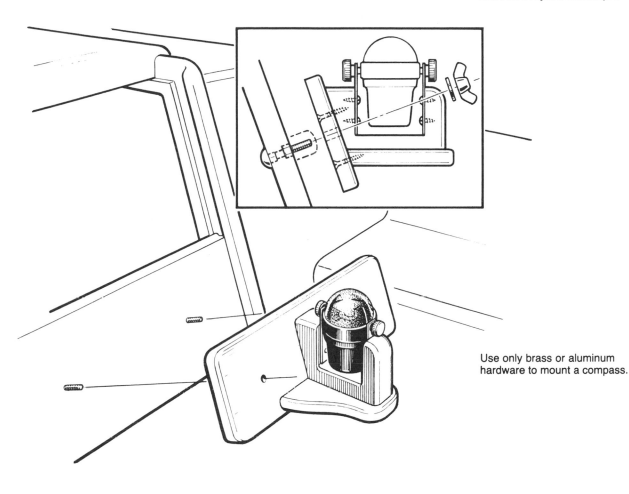

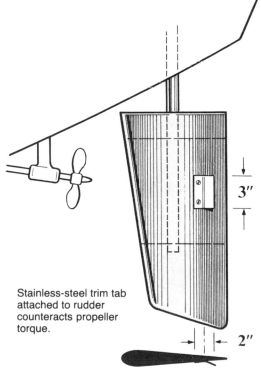

Use only brass or aluminum hardware to mount a compass.

matching holes drilled in the compass mounting board.

Wing nuts are then used to secure it when the compass mount is in its "working" position, and it's a good idea to cover these with some sort of rubber caps. Removing the two wing nuts enables the boatowner to take off the entire compass mount, with the compass, and store it safely inside when the boat is not under way. Yet when in place, the compass is in a safe and comfortable position for easy viewing, and out of the way of most crew activities.

Rudder Trim Tab

My 27′ sloop has a spade rudder that is located on the centerline of the boat, and auxiliary power is supplied by a 30-horsepower engine that is equipped with a right-hand propeller. As with many other auxiliaries that are set up in this manner, I found that when under power there was a strong tendency for the boat to pull to port because of the rudder's reaction to the right-hand propeller. On a long trip this would prove quite tiring— I was continually fighting the pull of the rudder. The more power I applied, the harder I had to work on the tiller.

After spending an entire season struggling with this problem, I finally came up with a simple solution that has worked well ever since. Having been an airplane pilot during my days in the service, I knew the value of a trim tab on the aileron of an airplane's wing or

Stainless-steel trim tab attached to rudder counteracts propeller torque.

3″

2″

rudder. Figuring that this should work just as well on a boat's rudder, I made a trim tab out of a piece of stainless steel that was 3″ high and 2″ wide. I then gave it a slight bend of about 10° along the center, as shown here.

Next I drilled two holes in the flange and fastened this to the port-side of my rudder along the aft edge, using stainless screws and bedding compound. I made certain it was located in the slipstream of the propeller.

Although my choice of size and angle (degree of bend down the center) was pure guesswork, it works great—my rudder stays easily amidships when I am running under power, even when wide open, and I no longer get arm-weary from fighting the tiller. The tab is so small that I have noticed no appreciable loss of speed, or any other problems when steering, either under sail or under power.

Spreader Thumb Cleats

Here's a simple arrangement that will end the rap of halyards against a mast. A pair of thumb cleats are positioned on the spreaders, about 18″ out from the mast. The halyards are pulled out along the spreaders until they slip into the thumb cleats, and then they are tensioned. Peter Mere noted this rig in Eric Hiscock's book, *Voyaging Under Sail*. An alternative, with wooden spreaders of sufficient strength, is to provide notches in the after edges.

Leach Cringle for Roller Reefing

By installing a reefing cringle on the leach of the mainsail, and a cheek block on the boom below the cringle, it is possible to eliminate the boom-droop that's a common problem when roller reefing is used.

When it's time to reef, the boom is topped, and the reefing cringle is pulled down as near to the boom as necessary, and the reefing line is cleated. The sail then will reef very neatly, and the boom will not sag when the topping lift is slacked off. If the line from the reefing cringle is led forward to a tube cleat near the gooseneck, reefing can be a single-handed operation.

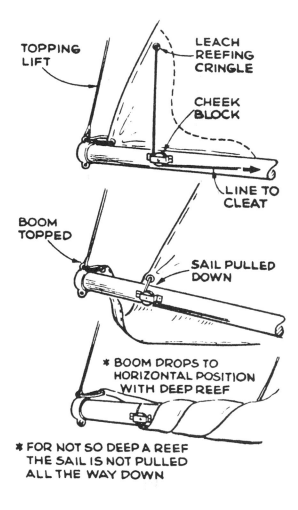

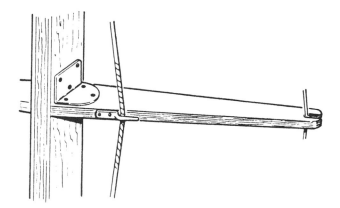

Cleat on after edge of spreaders keeps halyard from slapping against mast, left. Above: Leach cringle eliminates boom drop when the sail is reefed.

Jib-Sheet Tweaker

At least that's what Roger Tuck calls this arrangement he devised to provide a downward pull to headsail sheets. He notes that it is to be used where a smaller boat has only one fixed sheeting point for a variety of headsails.

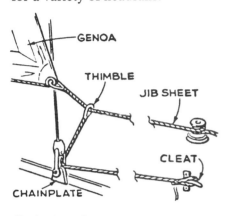

Jib-sheet tweaker

A nylon thimble has a length of line eye-spliced to it. The sheet is run through the thimble and back to its winch. The line with the thimble is led down through a chainplate shackle, or other suitable fitting forward, and back to a cleat. By adjusting the downward pull, a sail such as a genoa will set better and reduce or eliminate leach flutter. Mr. Tuck notes that a thimble arrangement should be provided for each side of the boat.

Bow Nets

On most cruising boats, especially ones with bowsprits, bow nets are an almost indispensable item. They are a great help in keeping lowered headsails and headsail handlers out of the water.

Some beautiful handcrafted nets have appeared over the years but the most useful, least expensive, and least time-consuming nets are those cast away by fishboats. The very fine herring nets are, of course, of little or no use, but the old woven hemp and the newer acrylic nets with substantial strands, make perfect boat netting.

The cleanest method of installation utilizes a single line reeved, or really stitched, over the bow pulpit for the top, while a similar line can be reeved through small pad eyes attached every 8″ or so to the sides of the bowsprit platform. This single-line method enables one to remove the net with ease for washing, varnishing, etc.

Acrylic nets should be cut with a hot knife to seal the strands and prevent them from excessive unravelling.

Normally bow nets terminate at the first set of stanchions, but I've seen numerous cruisers with small children or dogs run netting completely around their boats. If this procedure is to be followed, one must cut lead holes in the netting for genoa sheets. To avoid the tearing or chafing of the net, a frame of dacron tape should be sewn around the holes.

I have found bow nets most useful when used in combination with shock cords to hold down folded sails. The shock cord can be hooked into any loop of the net, hastening all foredeck activities by eliminating the need to search out and snare miniature pad eyes hidden somewhere beneath five hundred square feet of genoa.

Cockpit Chart Stowage

Charts in the cockpit can be disastrous. When most needed, they fly overboard or end up under hurrying crew's feet, triggering graceless somersaults. But charts abovedecks are often compulsory, and at all times great fun to use, and even the tiniest of cockpits will have space for this clever pouch.

It is a large canvas pocket that can be snapped or attached with Velcro to the aft wall of the cockpit. The size of the chart pocket should be 11″ high by 18″ wide. You have to fold a chart in half again to get it in, but this can easily be done without permanent creasing. An additional pocket of 2¾″ × 11″ should be added to the outside for stowage of parallel rules, and another 2½″ × 7″ pocket should be sewn for one-handed dividers. If desired, the back portion can be extended to create a flap. Sew three small bits of Velcro onto it (one in each corner and one in the middle) to help keep the pocket flap shut. A piece of Velcro in each top corner, or a snap in the same, should be enough to provide adequate fastening to the cockpit wall.

Deadlights

Lucite placed into openings cut into your companion slide provides extra light below on rainy days. The job can be done with fiberglass tape and resin, which will adhere to Lucite plastic.

Boom-Supported Cockpit Cover

Here's a simple cockpit cover of a type that's easy to make and to rig. This can't be used while the boat is under sail, as the boom provides the central support. You'll need a sturdy boom crutch, or topping lift, to support the after end of the boom.

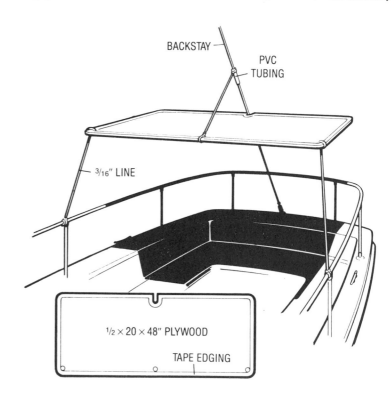

If your boat's cockpit is of Type (A) (see sketch), some curvature will have to be worked into the bottom side of the cover. For the ends, the sailcloth should be cut to fit snug with any camber in the deck.

For a cockpit of Type (B), a straight bottom will do. Install grommets along the bottom edges and sew jib snaps to the grommets. The snaps then can be hooked to screw eyes mounted on the outboard side of the coaming. Note that brass rings are sewn to squares of sailcloth, which, in turn, are securely stitched to the front flap. Jib snaps on a flap at the forward edge of the matching side panel can be hooked to these rings to seal off the forward end of the shelter.

Helmsman's Sunshade

Here's an easy way to provide some welcome shade for your sun-drenched helmsman.

On our sloop we cut a 20″ × 48″ piece of ⅛″ plywood notched in the middle of one edge to fit around the backstay, as shown. Three ¾″ holes were then drilled along the opposite edge for tying ³⁄₁₆″ lines—one line in the center going up to the backstay, and the two lines from each corner going down to the stanchions of lifelines. We covered the edges of the plywood with duct tape and rigged the piece as shown in the sketch.

A piece of PVC tubing over the stay provided a slipproof point for attaching the single "halyard." As the sun swings, the shade can be adjusted to keep the helmsman happily cool.

Pattern for boom-supported cockpit cover is shown at lower left. Below: A simple sunshade is suspended from the backstay.

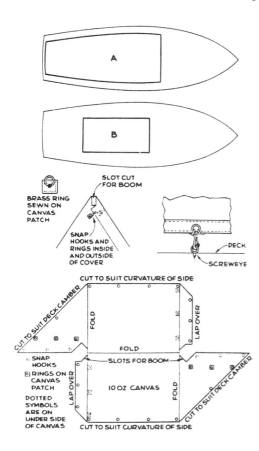

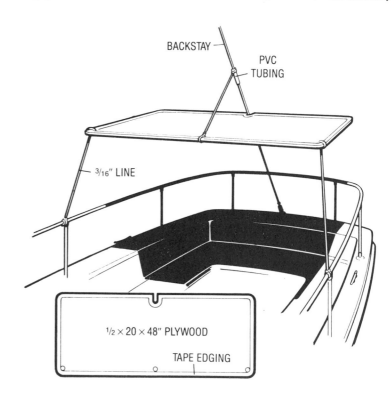

3 INTERIOR PROJECTS AND IMPROVEMENTS

Pointers on Choosing, Installing, and Caring for Boat Carpets

At one time, the only kind of carpet anyone would think of using inside a boat was one of the various "outdoor" or "indoor/outdoor" carpets most often seen around swimming pools and patios, but these days that has changed considerably. We now see all kinds of regular carpet, the same kind you use in your home, used on the inside of many cruising boats. In most cases there is nothing wrong with this; the inside of a modern boat is more like the inside of a land-based home or apartment than it is like the spartan interior of the boats our grandfathers used.

However, as many have discovered to their sorrow, a boat *is* different than a house. Carpets that will last for years at home may develop mold or mildew, or may start to show other signs of deterioration after only one or two seasons on a typical boat. Even if the carpet is in a fully enclosed cabin, moisture is always a potential problem inside a boat—the carpet can get wet from unexpected leaks such as those caused by a broken water line or a poorly fitting hatch that lets rain blow in during a storm. And in chilly weather condensation can create damp spots under the carpet that will go unnoticed for weeks at a time.

In addition to problems associated with dampness and mildew, there is also the fact that boat carpet gets tougher wear than most home carpets. People walk in directly from outside and their feet or shoes are often wet and dirty

Synthetic carpets can withstand a good dockside scrubbing with ordinary detergent; thorough rinsing is important.

from the docks or from unpaved parking lots. Fishermen drop wet rods, bait, and other objects on the carpet when things are happening in a hurry, and every time the captain (or yard mechanic) works on engines or other below-decks equipment in the boat, the carpet on the inside stands a good chance of being stained by grease, dirt, oil, dirty tools, hoses, or machine parts. And, of course, the carpet is also much more subject to fading due to long hours of exposure to sunlight—at least in some parts of the boat.

Pointers on Choosing Carpet

Almost all of the brands labeled as being suitable for outdoor use will stand up well inside a boat, but you may find the selection quite limited in many areas, and some stores in smaller communities may not carry outdoor carpet at all. Fortunately, you are not limited to just those—you can use almost any carpet that is made entirely of man-made (synthetic) fibers such as polypropylene, acrylic, or nylon. Of the three, polypropylene carpet seems to be the most resistant to staining and exposure to frequent dampness and sunlight. Acrylic is almost as tough. Nylon also wears well, but it is not quite as stain-resistant as polypropylene and is not as resistant to fading as the others.

It's best not to take the salesman's word for what the carpet is made of or what he claims it will withstand—read the manufacturer's label to see what the primary fibers and the backing are actually made of. The backing, by the way, is even more important than the carpet fibers insofar as resistance to moisture and mildew is concerned. If the backing is not made of a man-made material that is resistant to moisture, then you are sure to run into problems later

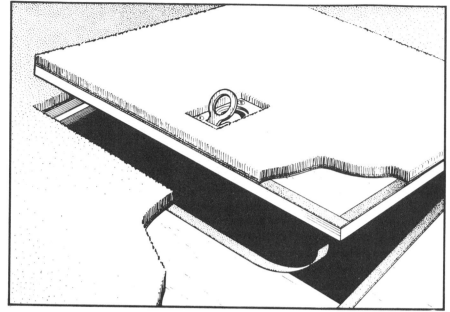

Double-stick tape holds carpet in place but loosens if carpet is lifted frequently. Velcro is better.

on (a jute backing, for example, is very durable when used in a home, but it will soon show signs of mildew if installed in most boats).

Many indoor/outdoor carpets and some regular carpets designed primarily for indoor use come with a foam or cushion-type backing, a material that closely resembles sponge rubber in feeling and consistency. Although this material is not harmed by water or being constantly damp, its principal advantage is that it gives the carpet a more "cushiony" feel and eliminates the need for a padding or liner underneath (padding not only makes the carpet feel better underfoot, it also helps it to last longer). The cushion backing also offers a little additional sound insulation, though this is relatively minor in most cases.

There is one drawback to a foam-back carpet, however. If and when it does get wet, the foam backing absorbs and holds the water and seems to stay wet almost forever—at least this has been my experience with this type of carpet

when I used it inside a boat on several different occasions.

In smaller boats owners sometimes decide to buy inexpensive bathroom carpeting and use this in the cabin. While it is true that these carpets are usually fully washable (many are designed so they can be thrown into a washing machine), they are not really intended to take much heavy wear. They will mat up and tend to lose their original appearance in a fairly short length of time, so be prepared to replace them every year or two. Also, they don't come in wide sizes, so seams will often be required and some varieties are hard to join neatly.

Pointers on Installation

Where practical, or possible, carpet in a boat is best loose-laid; that is, not fastened down at all. That way you can lift it quickly in an emergency (for example, when you have to get at a hatch underneath) and you can pick it up to take it outside when you want to clean it, or when it needs drying out.

Of course, you don't want to create a hazard that people can trip over when edges lift up or curl back, and you want to be sure that the carpet won't slip, slide or bunch up underfoot. It is for all these reasons that it is generally advisable to fasten the carpet down, at least around the edges. However, don't use nails, tacks or staples if you can avoid it. Beside the fact that unless you use copper or stainless fasteners they will rust and create stains, they will also make it that much harder when you have to lift up the carpet when emergency repairs are required or because cleaning is required.

I have found that there are two techniques that work well: (1) Use double-stick carpet tape around the edges and along all seams by applying this to the plywood or fiberglass cabin sole, then press the carpet down onto this. (2) Use Velcro strips around the edges instead. These are placed at intervals along the edges and in the corners by fastening one half to the deck with copper tacks or adhesive, and the other half to the back of the carpet with adhesive. Double-stick tape is cheaper and quicker, but after you pull the carpet up and down a few times, you will find that much of the adhesive quality is lost and the tape will probably have to be replaced.

Using Velcro strips solves this problem, but you may find it difficult to make the Velcro stick to the underside of the carpet with some types of backing. I found a clear two-part epoxy the most effective adhesive, but hand stitching may be necessary to keep the strip from pulling away on some synthetic backing materials.

You will obviously have to pick up the carpet repeatedly when there are engine or bilge hatches under them. Many boatowners elect to lay the carpet over the area

Carpet cleaning machines are easily rented and are ideal for scouring out stains in onboard carpet.

in one large piece, then flick it back out of the way when they have to get at one of the hatches. A better method is cut the carpet along the outline of the hatch, then fasten the carpet to the hatch by one of the methods mentioned. Cut a small opening over the lift ring so you can get at it easily. That way when you open the hatch the carpet will come up with it and the rest of the carpet in that area will not be disturbed. Just make sure you secure the edges of the carpet around the hatch so it will stay put and not come up with the hatch when you lift it.

Pointers on Care and Cleaning

Because boats are used for fishing, swimming, and other activities, the carpet on the inside is often soiled or stained when someone drops things on it—things such as wet fishing or snorkeling gear, oily pieces of bait, etc. One way to protect the carpet against this type of abuse is to cover it while activities of this kind are going on. Some use plastic sheets or runners, but these are also slippery when wet, and spills tend to run off them around the edges.

A better way to cover the carpet is with a sheet of canvas kept handy for just this purpose, or keep several large beach towels on hand. These can be neatly folded and kept out of the way when not needed, but when out fishing, or when working on the engines under the hatches, the beach towels make easily cleaned and highly absorbent protective covers for the carpet.

All carpet will live longer and look better if it is regularly cleaned with a vacuum cleaner or carpet cleaning machine, and if all spills or dropped foods and other materials are wiped up as soon as possible. If the carpet is made of synthetic fibers, you can wash stains off just as you would from any other washable surface.

Start by first blotting up as much excess liquid as possible, using clean paper towels or absorbent cloths. Then use a clean wet sponge or folded piece of wet cloth to wipe up as much of the residue as possible. If the spilled material is greasy or oily, use a small amount of soap suds or one of the liquid carpet cleaners to scrub the spot out. Then sponge with clean water. You can also use a solvent-type carpet cleaner, but test it first on a scrap piece to make sure it won't hurt the fibers or the dyes in the carpet.

When a thorough cleaning of the entire carpet is required, one of the best ways to do the job is by renting one of the carpet cleaning machines that are now so widely available in supermarkets, hardware stores, and home centers. These spray hot water mixed with special cleaning detergents into the carpet, then use a powerful vacuum to draw out the detergent and liquid, along with the loosened dirt.

If the carpet is in pieces and can be easily taken out of the boat, another method that works well is to lay the pieces out on the dock and then use a hose and scrub brush, with ordinary detergent, to scrub the carpet clean. Though this may sound severe, with most man-made fibers the scrubbing and the water won't hurt the carpet at all. You just have to be sure you do a thorough job of rinsing all the detergent suds out, then give the carpet time to dry completely before replacing it inside the boat. It will dry faster if you can drape it over a railing or hang the carpet vertically, rather than if you leave it lying flat on the dock.

Inexpensive Boat Carpet

Carpet does have a place on boats, particularly if you spend a lot of time aboard and have small children. After a thorough search we found that bathroom carpet, widely available in such stores as Penney's and Sears, is ideal.

The carpets are entirely nylon or polyester, so mildew is not a problem. The bottom is textured latex, which means the carpet is slip-resistant, and can be trimmed with ordinary scissors to fit the irregular patterns found on most cabin soles. To clean, either shake the carpet or machine wash and tumble dry.

The carpet is available in a wide variety of colors, several sizes from 4' × 6' to 6' × 10', and has pile depths from ½" to 1".

We spent $35 to partially carpet our 32' sailboat, dividing up a 5' × 9' section to cover the major traffic area, companionway stairs, and both the galley and the head. We can enjoy the beauty of our laid fir sole and still have the warmth and comfort that soft carpeting brings to our sailboat home.

Applying Laminated Plastics

Formica, or one of the similar decorative laminated plastics, makes an excellent surface on tabletops, and it can be used on countertops, even on bulkheads, to good advantage. Its application certainly is within the scope of anyone reasonably handy with tools.

The instructions provided here come from Leo J. Carling, Jr.:

"First of all, power tools are unnecessary. To be sure, their use could make parts of the work go faster, but the end result will be exactly the same. All you need is a crosscut saw, 6' straight edge, hip and rafter square, ruler, scriber (an awl will do), pair of dividers or draftsman's compass, coarse file (not a rasp), soft-faced mallet (substitute a block of soft wood and a hammer), scissors, pencil, sandpaper, and a cheap paint brush.

"In addition to the DLP (decorative laminated plastic), you will need the type of contact cement that's supplied by U.S. Plywood Corp., and some brown wrapping paper. Get enough paper to completely cover the area involved, and try to keep it in a roll rather than folded, as creases could cause trouble.

"Basically, there are two kinds of projects, the simpler being an application to a free-standing area such as a tabletop. A slightly more difficult job involves a piece that must be fitted to one or more fixed boundaries.

"First we will show how to make a free-standing unit—a tabletop with what is known as a 'self edge.' In the choice of plastic, give some thought to the satin-finish surfaces, as the absence of glare may be most welcome. Make a sketch approximately to scale of a 4' × 8' sheet of the material, and lay out the pieces you will require. The sketch should include principal dimensions, and the direction of the grain or pattern if this is a factor. See the figure on p. 73. You will note the order in which major saw cuts are to be made. The first and second cuts will quickly reduce the large sheet to manageable pieces. If you are using a hand saw, the work must be well-supported as close as possible to the line of the cut.

"The dimensions shown in the sketch are about ¼" oversize. This is a little generous; an eighth will do if you are sure all the edges of

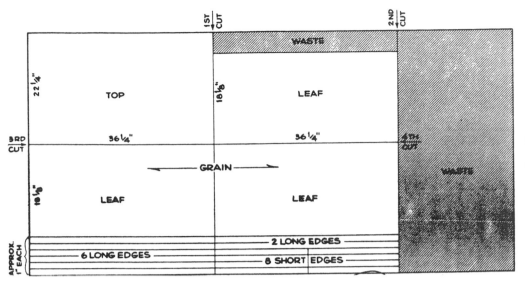

Lay out pieces and order of cut on sheet of plastic, left. Below: Filing ends of edge pieces flush with panel

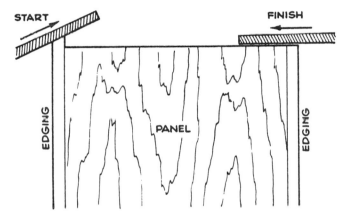

the tabletop are perfectly straight, and all corners are exactly 90°. If in doubt, make the pieces a little larger; it will necessitate a bit of extra filing and sanding later, but it's better than having a piece a bit too short.

"In laying out the edge pieces for the long sides of the table, be sure to increase their length by twice the thickness of the pieces for the short sides—about 1/8".

"A crayon pencil, ballpoint, or felt-tip pen can be used to lay out the cutting lines, but try first in a scrap area to be sure the marker does not leave a permanent stain. On high-gloss surfaces, you may have to use a scriber or scratch awl for accuracy, but take care to avoid scratches where they're unwanted.

"The edges of the plastic panel should be straight, and the corners square. Check them anyway. If they're true, your layout work is simplified. If not, strike a couple of lines, such as cuts 1 and 3, far enough in from the edge to allow the waste to fall outside the required pieces.

"Use of a hip and rafter square is suggested because its 16" and 24" legs make for considerable accuracy. With care, the 24" leg also can be used in place of the 6' straight edge by making a series of marks about 20" apart and connecting them with a line drawn along the long side of the square.

"When you have finished the layout and checked to be sure all pieces are accounted for, you are ready to saw. A cross-cut hand saw, preferably #10 point or finer, will do nicely. If you are using a portable circular saw or a saber saw, choose a very fine-tooth blade as these machines cut on the 'up' stroke, and coarse teeth plus fast feed will shatter the plastic's surface, perhaps beyond the 1/16" per cut you must allow for final finishing. Such blemishes cannot be removed. I have used a standard 10" cross-cut blade on my table saw successfully.

"After making the major saw cuts, cut the strips for edging, as it is easier to manage them from a fairly wide piece of material than one only a couple of inches wide.

"Before applying the laminate, make sure all surfaces of the table or countertop are smooth. Small nail holes and similar indentations are no problem, but a missing knot or a large void in the edge of a piece of plywood could result in the plastic being fractured should that spot be struck sharply when the table is in use.

"Questionable areas can be filled with wood dough or some similar material, or you can whip up a mixture of epoxy resin and sawdust. Whatever is used, sand the patch smooth after it has hardened, and use a sanding block to insure a level surface.

"Now you are ready to apply the cement. Follow the instructions on the can. Usually two coats are required on all surfaces to be bonded, both the plastic and the wood. If the project is large enough, by the time the last piece has been coated, the first is dry and ready for its second coat. The final test for dryness is made with brown wrapping paper, a piece of which should not stick to the cement coating. On your first project, it might be prudent to coat only the edging surfaces first, and apply the cement to the main surfaces only after the edging is in place.

"In any case, apply the edging first. Start with a short side. It is best to put the work in a vice, or have someone hold it firmly on end for you. Hold the edging material between thumb and forefinger of each hand, by its edges, and bring one end down in light contact with the edge of the panel. Allow about ⅛″ of the strip to overhang at that end; it should also overhang the top and bottom surfaces by ⅛″. 'Aim' the strip with care down the length of the panel edge, and ease it into place with a sort of 'rolling' motion from one end to the other. Do not let it buckle and skip a section, only to make contact up

ahead with an air gap in between. Should this happen, you will have to cut the buckle to bring it down to the panel, as the laminate cannot be slid once contact is made.

"This is not a disaster, but it will give you an unwanted joint. Now apply the edging to the side opposite the one just done.

"With the panel standing on edge on a smooth, firm surface, with one laminated edge down and the other up, tap the upper edge with a rubber mallet, or a hammer using a soft pine block for a cushion. Take extra care to avoid striking so hard that the overhanging edges and ends of the strip are fractured. It takes just enough pounding to insure a solid bond. Flip the panel edge for edge, and repeat.

"Trim the excess from both ends of each edge piece, using a coarse file. Lift the file clear of the work after each cutting stroke. At the start, cut the plastic at an angle of 30° to 45° and then gradually decrease the angle. Make the last cut or two almost, but not quite, parallel to the adjacent panel edge.

"Now apply laminate to the two remaining edges, using the same procedure. After the ends have been trimmed, you are ready to dress the upper and lower edges. Maintain the bevel cut down to ¹⁄₁₆″ of the panel surfaces, then drop the front end of the file into contact with the surface for the final couple of passes. The file can be worked along the edge as each cut is made, using the edge-milling of the file somewhat in the manner of a saw.

"The top is the last piece to be applied. Before actually putting it in place, experiment with the handling of it. Is it so large it sags badly in the middle when held by its edges? If it does, or if you have any doubt about your ability to control it well, don't risk a serious blunder. Make a wrapping paper 'sandwich.' Cut a sheet of the paper several inches larger than the surface to be covered, and lay it over the wood surface after the contact cement has been allowed to dry. Now you can set the plastic laminate panel down on top—after its contact cement has dried—and slide it about to get a uniform over-

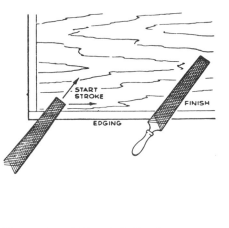
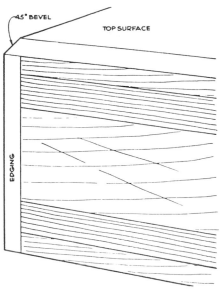

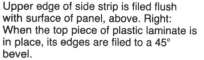
Upper edge of side strip is filed flush with surface of panel, above. Right: When the top piece of plastic laminate is in place, its edges are filed to a 45° bevel.

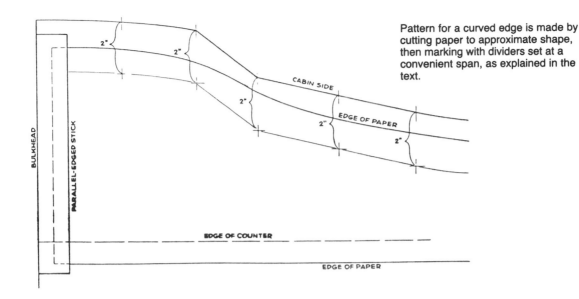

Pattern for a curved edge is made by cutting paper to approximate shape, then marking with dividers set at a convenient span, as explained in the text.

hang on all sides. Then, while you hold it in position carefully, someone else can slide out the wrapping paper. Rap the top down firmly with a rubber mallet or hammer and soft pine block, working from the center outward toward all edges.

"The excess is trimmed from the top in the same way as from the edges, but in this case the final cut is made at a 45° bevel. Be sure to stop short of cutting into the upper surface of the edging: See the drawing. Finish up with #120 sandpaper on a sanding block. Work the length of the edge, not across it as you did with the file.

"Now for a countertop job where curves or irregular shapes are involved: Preparation of the wood, planning the project, tools, quantity of material, and order of applying the pieces are all the same as for the tabletop job. The big difference comes in cutting the laminate for the top. It must fit against the bulkhead or other parts of the boat accurately. This fitting must be done *before* any cement is applied.

"Again, wrapping paper is used. This time cut out a piece that, when spread flat, will leave an inch or so of bare wood showing adjacent to be fixed boundaries of the counter area. Use a few thumb tacks to hold the paper in place.

"Set the legs of a drafting compass for any convenient span, such as 2". With the pointed end set snugly at the junction of the fixed bulkhead or cabin side and the countertop, strike a very short arc with the pencil end, at approximately a right angle to the fixed member: See the sketch. If the member is curved, strike as many arcs as needed to produce a smooth, representative curve on the paper. If the adjacent member is straight, such as a bulkhead would be, the compass method is not needed. A stick with a parallel edge laid against the bulkhead will allow you to transfer the line to the paper with a single pencil stroke. Another method calls for a short block of wood to be slid along the bulkhead with the pencil point held in contact with the block and the paper.

"In the case of intricate details, a small square may help in projecting points to the paper. Don't hesitate to write reminders of special features in the appropriate places on the paper you are developing.

"When the pattern is complete, lay it on top of the laminate. Hold it in place with masking tape. With the same compass setting, or the same parallel-edge stick, transfer the marks back to the laminate.

"There are several ways the laminate can be cut to the lines now drawn on its surface. The choice will depend on the fineness of detail to be carried out, and your skill with the tools available. Naturally, straight cuts will be handled in the usual way. 'Slow' curves may also be cut to ⅛" with a hand saw; a compass saw will be needed on 'tighter' curves, again leaving ⅛" for final trimming. Fine detail may have to be done with a jigsaw, either hand or power. Experiment on some scrap laminate first, to see how your saw leaves the edge. Very fine-toothed jig blades should require no final finishing with file or sandpaper. The finished edge should be a snug fit against the bulkhead or other fixed member. A gap of more than $\frac{1}{32}''$ or a shattered surface will be unsightly, so take your time and check the fit frequently.

"When you are satisfied with the fit against all fixed members, it is time to treat the 'open' side or sides. If you have not already done so, apply the laminate to these edges, finishing them flush with the top and bottom surfaces of the counter. Place the plastic-top panel in position, and on its underside mark the location of the 'open' edges. Allow $\frac{1}{8}''$ for trim, and make your cuts.

"Now use the laminate as a template, place it on a sheet of wrapping paper, and draw its outline on the paper. Cut the paper to the outline, leaving a generous overhang at the 'open' side. Apply contact cement, in two coats, to both the countertop and the underside of the laminate. When the second coat is dry, set the paper on the countertop, exactly in position. It should completely cover the top and overhang only at the open edge. Place the plastic laminate in position over the paper. When you are satisfied that it is exactly in place, lift the open edge slightly, and have your helper carefully pull out the wrapping paper. Then follow the same steps as for the tabletop.

"With either the countertop or tabletop installations, you may find the glue lines show up in an objectionable manner. They will show up rather prominently, particularly if the plastic is dark. You can hide this glue line with wood stain, such as a medium mahogany. Don't leave it on too long, and avoid letting it slop over onto the plastic surface. A rag moistened with turpentine will remove any excess stain from the laminate, yet leave the glue line materially darker."

Extend the Season with Central Heating

Most boatowners agree that anything that extends their boating season—or at least anything that makes boating more comfortable in nasty weather—is well worth investigating.

That is why more and more cruising boats are being equipped with heating systems these days, especially in the northern half of the country where late fall and early spring can provide some gorgeous sailing and boating weather—even though it can be awfully bone-chilling at times.

However, with some type of heating system on board you can be assured that at the end of the day's sailing there is a warm stateroom in which you can change clothes and then sit down comfortably for a pleasant drink followed by an equally pleasant hot meal.

A heated boat not only helps in extending your actual boating season, it also makes it possible for you to come down and work on the inside of your boat during the off-season. Many a pleasant weekend can be spent in the fall or winter, or early spring, doing some much needed cleaning or maintenance or making modifications and improvements that you just don't have time for in the boating season—as long as you can be reasonably comfortable and warm while working. You can even continue to spend some pleasant weekends aboard after outside temperatures drop down to near freezing or below. And as a bonus, keeping the inside of the boat warm is a great help in preventing the development of mildew and fungus growths, along with the damp musty smells that this often leads to.

Of course, you don't necessarily need an automatic central heating system to accomplish all this. There are many excellent space heaters you can buy, and built-in bulkhead heaters you can install, which will also keep small-to-medium-size cabins warm and toasty. However, as a rule, these cannot be left unattended for very long because they generally have limited fuel supplies that must be replenished at fairly frequent intervals. Also, while some are per-

Espa's hot-air unit is a typical heating system for a boat.

Neptune heater circulates hot water through boat radiators.

Typical installation of a hot-air unit.

fectly safe, others can be hazardous if not vented properly to the outside.

Another drawback to many space heaters (including many bulkhead-mounted units) is that they don't really spread the heat uniformly throughout the boat if there is more than one cabin. Heads, galleys, or other compartments that are partially or fully closed off from the area where the heater is located may remain chilly—unlike a boat that is warmed by a good central heating system that spreads its warmth throughout the boat by means of ducts (in the case of a hot-air system) or hoses (in the case of hot-water heating systems).

All this is important to those who really want to use their boat or spend time aboard during cold weather, and it is essential to those who want to live aboard. These boatowners need a completely automatic, thermostatically controlled heating system that will operate dependably even when no one is on board, or while occupants are gone for days at a time. This means a central heating system that is not unlike those in private homes.

Before you can choose a heating system for your boat, one of the first things you will have to consider is how much heat you will actually need to keep comfortable. This will, of course, depend on the

outside temperatures you expect to encounter, on the size of the boat's interior spaces, on the construction and design of the boat, and on what insulation, if any, it has.

A boat is not insulated the way a house is, so there will be greater loss of heat to the outside. But a boat also has much smaller spaces that have to be heated. If it has double-walled cabin sides or an inside liner and sandwich-type construction, then it will be less of a problem to heat than one that has only a single thickness of wood or fiberglass between you and the outside.

Although all those variables make it almost impossible to give specific figures as to how many

BTU's would be needed for a particular size boat, there have been enough installations made in recent years to permit fairly accurate estimates. You start by first figuring the volume of space to be heated—this means multiplying the average width (in feet) of each cabin by its average height and then its length. The total number of cubic feet of air to be heated is then multiplied by a given factor to tell you the amount of BTU's recommended for winter heating.

As a rule, for cabins above deck level that have lots of windows, use a factor of 15. If the cabin is below-decks and has only average size portholes, then you can probably use a factor of 10 or 12 to determine your BTU requirements. And if you boat in the frozen north in the winter, you may want to use a factor of 20 for above-deck cabins and saloons that have lots of uninsulated windows.

Like home heating systems, marine heating systems come in three basic types, depending on how the heat is distributed to the different areas: an all-electric system that uses individual resistance heaters in each area, forced hot-air systems, and circulating hot-water systems that use radiators or convectors to distribute the heat.

There is also a fourth category, the heat pump, which circulates cooled or heated water (depending on whether you want heating or cooling), but in marine installations this is almost always part of a water-cooled marine air-conditioning system (it heats when on reverse cycle). This heating, however, is only practical when the water temperature is definitely higher than the air temperature—and this makes it impractical for winter heating in most parts of the country.

Electric heat is the simplest to install, and in many cases it is also the least expensive system to put in. You can easily locate baseboard units in each stateroom area, and then have each controlled by its own thermostat so that only as much heat as is needed is supplied to each area when it is actually needed.

However, there are some drawbacks. Electric heaters take lots of current—high amperage at either 110 or 220 volts—and this means you can only use them dockside when you are at a marina or shipyard that has adequate power you can draw on (unfortunately, not many do). Of course, an onboard generator will give you heat underway if the generator is large enough, but you wouldn't want to depend on this for long when dockside. And with electric rates being what they are in most parts of the country these days, heating with electricity is probably higher in cost than heating with most other fuels.

If you do decide to go for electric heating, make sure you buy heaters that are UL and USCG approved, and make sure that the marina will be able to supply you with the amount of power you need. To estimate the total wattage you will need, divide the number of BTU's required by 3.4 (for 6,800 BTU's you will need about 2,000 watts). Select radiant, baseboard-type units that do not have fans but heat by convection or radiation only (they are safer and they use less power).

Forced hot-air systems, which have long been used in RV's and large buses, have become increasingly popular since special models designed for marine use have been put on the market. These will heat up a boat quickly and keep the inside very dry—so there is never a problem with condensation. However, in cold weather they often make the indoor air so dry that occupants will actually feel mild discomfort, especially when living aboard.

Most forced hot-air units are designed to burn either diesel oil, kerosene, or regular home heating oil. A built-in blower circulates the heated air throughout the boat by means of flexible 4″ or 3″ ducts (usually made of fiberglass or a similar non-combustible material). In boats that have diesel engines, the same fuel tanks can be used to provide fuel for the heater. In boats with gasoline engines, a separate tank can be installed, or a collapsible fuel tank can be used during the heating season.

One of the more widely sold hot-air heating systems is the one made by Espar Inc. (P.O. Box 2346, Naperville, Ill. 60566). It is a diesel-fired heater that has a 12-volt blower built in and comes in various sizes, from a small model that will put out about 6,000 BTU's to a very large unit capable of delivering up to 48,000 BTU's.

Each is controlled by a thermostat that will turn the heater on and off automatically to maintain a preset temperature, and all units have built-in safety features that will shut them off automatically if the unit overheats, runs out of fuel, or malfunctions.

The inside cabin air is drawn in and heated through a heat exchanger, then recirculated, so there is no chance of combustion air entering the living areas. The combustion air is vented directly to the outside through a flexible stainless steel vent pipe that can be removed or capped in the summer. Prices for these Espar units range from about $800 for the smallest units, to about $1,900 for the largest ones.

A hot-water heating system is generally more expensive to buy and install, but it may actually be easier to install because it means you only have to run small-diame-

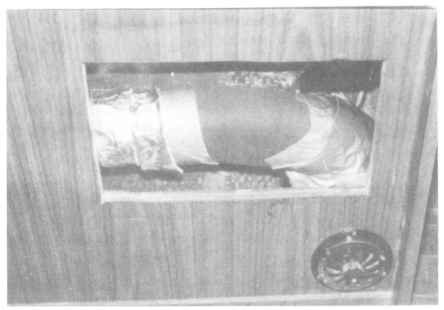

Hot-air system requires room for ducts behind bulkheads.

ter flexible hoses around the boat, instead of large-diameter, bulky ducts. In addition, hot-water heat is more uniform and thus more comfortable for long-term living aboard (not so many alternating cycles of hot and cold blasts of air), and it does not lead to the overly dry atmosphere that is created inside when a hot-air furnace runs for many hours.

For larger boats that have more than one cabin, and for motor yachts where cabins are on several levels, a hot-water heating system offers one other advantage: You can set up the system so that there is more than one heating zone, with each controlled by its own thermostat. Thus, the main saloon can be turned way down at night while the staterooms are kept warm, and the reverse can be done during the day. This eliminates the common problem of one area being overheated while another part of the boat is near freezing.

Until recently, hot-water heating systems for private boats were not very popular. One company (Way-Wolff Associates of Long Island City, NY) has been marketing them for years, but these were primarily used in large yachts and were never widely used in small-to-medium-size cruising boats. However, now there are more moderately priced hot-water heating systems available that are also simpler to install and much more compact—making them ideal for use on boats as small as 32'.

Made and distributed by Neptune Marine Heaters (412 City Island Avenue, City Island, NY 10464), these heaters burn diesel fuel or home-heating oil. They are made with standard components that are used in all home boilers, so parts are widely available in regular plumbing supply outlets anywhere in the country. In addition, if and when repairs are needed any home heating or plumbing contractor can service one of these units—eliminating a problem that often develops with some of the more specialized units when there is no regular dealer nearby.

Measuring about 33" in length and about 20" in height by less than 12" in width, the unit is compact enough to fit in almost any cruising boat—sail or power. There is also an optional waterproof dock enclosure which permits setting the heater up on the dock so you don't take any space at all inside the boat. Connections are made to the hot-water system inside the boat (using rubber heater hose) so that in the summer the entire unit can be left on the dock or carted away and stored until the cold weather returns.

Neptune heaters come in two styles, horizontal or vertical, both capable of delivering up to 60,000 BTU's per hour—enough to heat any boat up to about 60' in length. They sell for $1,695, complete with circulator motor, high-speed flame-retention burner, hot-water safety relief valve, temperature and pressure gauge, low-water pressure switch—and all the other safety controls normally found on home boilers and furnaces.

The boiler is a wet back, welded steel, tube type unit that has urethane insulation around it, and the burner is a forced-draft type that requires only a small diameter vent stack, which can be located anywhere you can install a suitable through-hull fitting.

To radiate heat in each stateroom or cabin area, the Neptune system uses either regular baseboard radiators, or special compact convectors that include a small silent squirrel-cage blower. The convectors come in two sizes—a smaller unit that will put out up to 4,200 BTU's (equal to 9' of baseboard radiators). Both sizes can be installed horizontally in "kick-spaces" under counters or bunks, or they can be installed vertically like a regular radiator.

Hot water is carried to each radiator or convector through rubber heater hose. The system is controlled by a regular household thermostat, and regular 110-volt current is required for the boiler. Current will also have to be supplied to each of the convectors (for the built-in blower), though each draws only about one-third of an amp.

Mahogany Drop-Leaf Table

Because there was no place on our sailboat where I could store my sewing machine, we designed a drop-leaf table that would incorporate a large locker under the center leaf for the sewing machine. This design works well for anyone who has a large item to stow, or who needs an extra locker for galley gear.

We used mahogany for the table because it matched our interior, but you can use a less expensive wood if you wish. You want lumber that is surfaced on both sides to a finished thickness of approximately ¾". It helps if you have a table saw and a router, but if you don't, the lumberyard can cut the pieces for you.

You will also need a saber saw, a drill, countersink, counterbore, a flush mounting ring or latch lock, several hinges, 1″ stainless steel wood screws, four 4″ angle brackets, and a hook-and-eye strap.

The table is basically a box with the ends of the box continuing down to form the legs and the top of the box a little larger than the sides all around. There are two drop leaves, with one narrower than the other since the table is offset to one side of the saloon. Dimensions are shown in the drawing.

To adapt this design to your own boat, assuming you have a fore and aft settee on each side of the cabin, first measure the width between

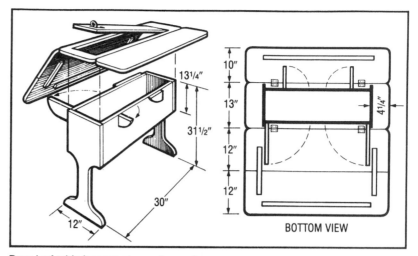

Drop-leaf table incorporates a storage box.

the settees. Each leaf should overlap its respective settee by about 1″ when raised. The height of the settees, plus approximately 11″, will be the total height of the table, but sit on the settee and try to determine what would be the most comfortable height for you. The length of the table is a matter of personal preference, but to seat two persons on a side comfortably, the table should be at least 40″ long.

The items you wish to store in the table will determine the size of the locker in the center. The tabletop will be about 2½″ wider and 8½″ longer than the locker underneath it, as shown in the illustration below. Since the locker is fairly deep, it must be away from the settee by at least 10″ or 11″ as shown, to provide knee room when sitting.

Draw out the shapes of the separate pieces on the planks of lumber, as shown. There will be two main legs, two sides for the locker, a top and a bottom for the locker, three leaf pieces, two folding legs for the leaves, two braces for the large leaf, and four support arms that are optional. Use differing plank widths and lay out your pattern in such a way as to minimize waste. Don't forget to take into ac-

count the fact that the saw blade reduces your cut ⅛″ to ³⁄₁₆″, depending on the blade.

The main legs will be as wide and deep as the locker section and shaped as shown. The bottom of the locker is the same width as the inside dimension of the box, and the side pieces will overlap the ¾″ thickness of the bottom piece on the outside. Thus, the inside of the locker, plus ¾″, is the height of the side pieces. Cut out the pieces and sand the edges, but be careful to round only *exposed* edges and not any edges that will butt up against another piece.

Assemble the box, taking care to keep everything square. Simple butt joints work well and won't be noticeable under the tabletop. If you wish to conceal the screw holes, they must be counterbored so you can plug the holes afterward. Screws should be spaced 6″ apart along all overlapping edges, and the edges should be coated with glue before fastening them together.

The top and the two drop leaves will be of equal length but varying widths. Since the lumber isn't wide enough to make the wide drop leaf in one piece, you'll have to cut two pieces and join them together, edge to edge. Though doweling is strongest, we felt edge-gluing with the additional support of two braces under the leaf was adequate. It has held up well in 6,000 miles of cruising. The two braces for the large leaf are roughly 15" × 1" × ¾". They are screwed to the leaf in four places and glued. Place them about 5" in from the edge of the leaf, across the seam, as shown.

Before putting the top on, you must cut out the door for the locker underneath. The distance between the inner sides of the box, plus ½", will determine the width of your opening. That way the edge of each side of the box will form support lips on which the door can rest. Use a saber saw so you can start the cut in mid-plank, and be careful not to splinter the wood. Put two small brass butterfly hinges on one end of the door, and on the other end install a flush lifting ring or a latch-lock mechanism that is recessed into the tabletop.

Center the top of the box and fasten it down with wood glue and screws. Then turn the table upside down on a flat floor to attach the drop leaves. Butt each leaf against the edge of the top and install two hinges 2½" wide on each side.

We added two small support arms on hinges under each leaf which fold up against the sides of the locker when the leaves are down. You may not feel they are necessary, since the main support for the leaves comes from two hinged folding legs that are 1" × ¾" and the same height as the main legs. To secure them when up, use Velcro hook-and-loop tape, or clips.

We bolted 4" angle brackets to the main legs with ¼" machine screws and acorn nuts, then secured them to the sole with #14 self-tapping sheet-metal screws the same length as the thickness of the

sole. We painted the brackets to match the table.

Finally, install a hook and eye on each leaf to secure it when down. Make sure all exposed corners and edges are well rounded. Fiddles may be added if you wish. Finish by oiling or varnishing.

Removable Shelf Fiddle Holds Better

The fiddles built across the front of most shelves on stock boats are usually neat looking and hold books and other tall items in place when the boat is relatively steady or at anchor. But they are often too low to hold these items in place when the boat is under way and heeling.

I have devised a good way to solve this problem with shelves that are recessed or built in between ribs or bulkheads so that fiddles can be placed across the front to hold things in place. I fashioned strips of flexible ash wood about ¼" thick, like the kind used for sail battens, to make new fiddles that are higher up, and that can be removed when you want to take something out from behind them.

As shown in the accompanying drawing, near the end of each wood strip I drilled a hole and then cut this out to form a keyhole-shaped slot. The widest part of this "keyhole" is large enough to fit easily over the head of a typical wood screw that is partially driven into the vertical members at each end of the shelf. The screw head should stick out from the wood by about ½".

The narrow part of the slot is just about wide enough for the body of the screw, but not wide enough to allow the head to slip through. This enables me to install

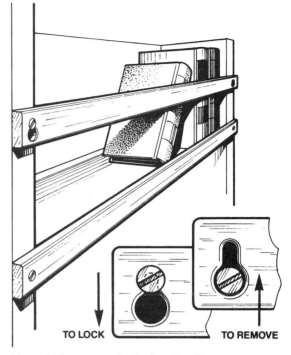

TO LOCK   TO REMOVE

Upper fiddles prevent books from toppling off shelf when boat is heeled.

each fiddle by simply sliding the wide part of the keyhole over the screwhead, then allowing it to drop down into the slotted part of the hole. The strip then holds everything firmly in place.

When I want to remove something, I simply raise the strip of wood high enough so the wide part of the keyhole will slip over the screwhead, then lift the fiddle off.

Expand Your Hanging Space

Like most boatmen, I often wished I had more hanging locker space for all the clothes that get brought aboard each weekend. Finally, I came up with an idea that doubled our hanging space for a very small price and very little work.

Our 33' cruiser has a settee that converts into top and bottom bunks—a common installation. But this area is rarely used for guests. So I decided to use this ex-

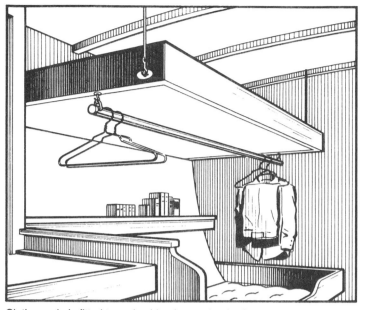

Clothes pole is fitted to underside of upper berth of unused convertible settee area.

prevent the table from sliding off either seat and we had a simple cockpit table. Application of some wood stain and several coats of varnish finished the job.

The end result is a perfectly usable table that will not slip or slide with motion of the boat or even bumping it. Stowage could not be more simple; put it in a locker or shove it under a seat cushion or even a berth and it is securely stowed. A side benefit is that there are no extra pieces to lose or break. If you wish to get more elaborate you can add fiddles to the edges, and strips of rubber under the overhangs for extra nonskid.

tra space for hanging clothes. I attached two brass hooks to the underside of the raised bunk near its outer edge. Then I took the clothes bar we keep across the rear seat of our car—any bar or pole will do—and presto, instant extra hanging space.

It so happens that on our boat this area has its own privacy door, but a small fabric curtain will work just as well. And when company comes, the top berth is still available.

Most sailboats have a cockpit configured with two benches on opposite sides. A glance at this configuration immediately suggests a modification. Why not have a slightly larger table that will overlap both seats and do away with the separate legs?

That is exactly what we did. I used a piece of ½″ plywood, cut it long enough to overlap both seats by about 2″ and made it wide enough to serve as a table. Two blocks of wood on the bottom to

Easy-to-Stow Table

This simple fold-up table serves well where floor space is at a premium. It will accommodate two persons nicely—and a third by using a stool. Aboard one boat this type was used to replace the original folding table, which had one end attached to the toilet-room bulkhead, the new type held by a single leg. This permitted installing

Simple Cockpit Table

On frequent occasions while we were at anchor and often when under way in light air we found it a great convenience to have a table in the cockpit where we could have a meal rather than going below. Although there are a variety of tables on the market with folding legs, the legs have an unfortunate tendency to fold at the wrong time or else the table is simply unstable.

Table fits snugly between cockpit seats.

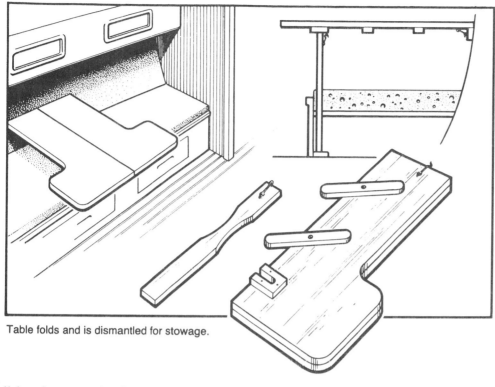

Table folds and is dismantled for stowage.

a small heating stove in the corner where it was convenient, but out of the way.

Adding Pressure Water and Dockside Water to Your Boat

Cruisers who are intent on adding all the comforts of shoreside living to their boats inevitably run into the nuisance of having to use a hand pump for all their fresh water. Fortunately, there are two simple answers to this problem; first, install a dockside water system that will handle all your needs while in port, and second, add a freshwater pressure pump for convenience while cruising and at anchor.

Many people do not realize how easy it is to add a pressurized water system that will provide running water at the turn of a faucet handle. All you have to do is replace the existing hand-pump-and-spigot

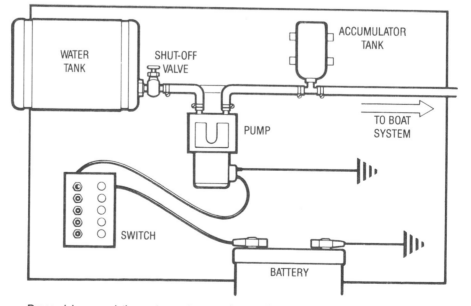

Pressurizing an existing water system requires cutting the supply pipe.

unit with a regular faucet, and then near the water tank install an electric pump is activated automatically every time you open the faucet.

This assumes your boat is equipped with a 12-volt DC electrical system, which includes the usual 12-volt battery for starting the engine. Ideally, the boat should also have a second battery for operating the electronics, lights, and other electrical accessories, but this is not essential if you want to add a pressurized water system (although it certainly would be a good idea). In that case, the second battery would be used to provide power for the new water pump.

There are many different kinds of freshwater pumps available in most marine supply stores. Though similar to an electric bilge pump, a freshwater pump differs in one important respect: it should have a built-in pressure switch that kicks the pump on automatically when it senses a drop in water-line pressure on the discharge side of the pump.

In a pressurized water system, all the water lines inside the boat are under constant pressure, just as they are in a house. (In a house the pressure comes from the domestic water supply; in a boat the, pressure is built up by the pump.) When this pressure has built up to a preset level, usually between 25 and 30 pounds, the pump stops running. However, when a faucet is opened and some pressure is released, the pressure switch on the pump senses this and after a drop of more than a few pounds, it kicks the pump on. The pump keeps running until the faucet is closed and the pressure has returned to the shut-off level.

One drawback to this system is that if a leak develops anywhere in the system the pump will just keep running until the tank runs dry. That is why it is essential that if you are going to pressurize your

system, you should first make certain all loose connections are tightened and all defective hoses or pipes are replaced. It is generally a good idea to turn off power to the pressure water pump when the boat is left unattended for any length of time.

After checking all hoses, pipes, and fittings in the system to make sure there are no leaks, the next step is to select a suitable location for the new pump. Try to select a spot that is reasonably close to the existing water line leading from the tank and as close to the tank as practical. Mount the pump on a flat surface where it will be reasonably easy to get at for servicing.

In most cases you can find a place near the tank, or near the water line leading from the tank, where you can mount a sheet of exterior-grade plywood that can act as a base. Screw the plywood down solidly, then mount the pump on this, but use shock-absorbing rubber or plastic pads under the pump to minimize noise and vibration when the pump is in operation.

To connect the pump into the boat's water system, shut off the valve at the base of the water tank, then cut the water line where it passes the pump. Using the appropriate elbows or other fittings, connect the pipe leading from the tank to the inlet side of the pump. Make sure you use a piece of flexible tubing that is approved for use with potable water and secure this to the pump fitting with double hose clamps. The flexible tubing is not only easier to work with, it will also help to eliminate the banging noise that sometimes results when metal tubing is connected directly to the water pump.

The next step is to connect the other side of the cut water line, the piece that goes on to the rest of the boat, to the outlet (discharge) side of the pump. On this connection

try to include an extra loop of hose before it connects to the rest of the system. This loop helps eliminate "water hammer" (banging noises) in the system when the pump is in operation.

An even better help in eliminating noises in the system, while at the same time insuring a smooth flow of water that will not pulsate as much, is to install an accumulator tank similar to the one made by Jabsco. The tank will help to absorb surges and will minimize the number of short on/off cycles the pump must go through to maintain pressure in the system, thus lengthening pump life.

As shown in the drawing, this tank is connected to the water line by cutting a T fitting into the discharge line leading from the pump. The two cut ends of the line are connected to opposite sides of the T, and a pipe nipple is inserted in the third leg so that the accumulator tank can be connected. The tank must be solidly mounted, preferably in a vertical position, to a convenient bulkhead, engine compartment divider, or to a bracket that will hold it firmly.

After the pump has been connected, the next step is to remove the hand pump on the galley sink (and the head sink, if you have one) and to replace it with a con-

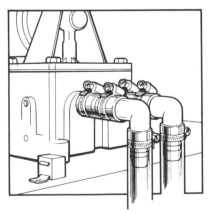

Hose clamps and elbows are used to connect tubing to the water pump.

ventional faucet. Any style will do, from an inexpensive bronze spigot to a fancy chrome-plated model. Since you will probably have to visit your local plumbing supply dealer to buy adapter fittings or connecters needed to connect your boat's water line to the inlet fitting on the faucet, bring the faucet and a piece of the boat's water tubing with you and the dealer should be able to fix you up with the parts you need.

On many boats a small check valve in the water line leads directly to the sink. The valve helps keep the hand pump primed between uses, but you won't need it when you convert to a pressurized system, so it is best to remove it when you replace the hand pump with the new faucet.

After all plumbing work is done, the final step is hooking the pump up to a source of electric power, as shown in the drawing. Good practice calls for running a line for the "hot" wire from the boat's main circuit-breaker panel (or fuse block) to the pump—that way the circuit breaker serves as a convenient shut-off switch for the pump. You could run a line directly to the battery or to an engine room busbar, but then you will have to install an in-line fuse, and you will have no easy way to shut the pump off when you leave the boat.

The ground wire for the pump can go directly to a common ground in or near the engine room, or to part of the engine block if that is more convenient. Just make sure that the gauge of wire used, for both the "hot" wire and the ground wire, is at least as large as that recommended by the manufacturer of the pump (the specification sheet will tell what gauge to use for various lengths).

When everything is hooked up, open the faucet and open the water-line valve leading from the tank. Turn on the pump by throwing the switch or circuit breaker. As water starts to flow it will spit and run erratically at first, but once all the air is out of the lines it should run fairly smooth. Shut off the faucets and wait to see if the pump stops after a few seconds, then have everyone sit quietly and listen. If the pump comes on by itself again after a few minutes, or at any time when no one is running the water, you have a leak in one of your water lines, fittings, or one of the faucets is not fully closed.

A pleasant added luxury that can be easily installed on almost any boat that already has a pressurized water system is a dockside water connection to supply a constant stream of pressurized water to the system.

Already "standard" on many of the larger cruising boats, a dockside water connection provides you with an unlimited supply of water as long as you are tied to the dock. A hose links the boat's internal water system directly to the municipal water supply so that you can run the water as long as you like without depending on the boat's freshwater supply. No more warning guests against taking long showers or using too much water when shaving or washing up.

Aside from the obvious benefit of drawing on an unlimited supply of fresh water, you also greatly extend the life of your water pump by not using it as much—advantages that are of particular interest to live-aboards and to those who often spend weekends aboard while dockside.

Of course, along with the luxury of having an unlimited water supply, there is a possible danger: if a pipe should burst or a connection loosen inside the boat while the water is hooked up and no one is around, then the boat could be flooded with water and sink. Luck- ily, there are a couple of common-sense precautions that will prevent this from happening.

The first and most obvious precaution is to get in the habit of always shutting the dockside water off when you leave the boat. Though this can be done at the dockside connection where the water hose is hooked up, it is much easier to do, and you are much less likely to forget to do it, if the inlet connection *on the boat* is a regular faucet or spigot that can be turned off at the boat end of the hose. It helps if this spigot or faucet is located near the hatch or gate where you normally step off the boat because you are more likely to see it each time you leave.

Because the city water pressure as it comes off the dock can be much higher than the boat's plumbing system is designed to take, it is imperative that a pressure reducer (also called a pressure regulator) be installed in the line before it enters the boat's plumbing system.

One way to do this is to buy one of the special plastic dockside water inlet connections that are sold in marine supply stores. These have a threaded fitting that accepts a regular water hose on the outside, and they have a built-in pressure regulator that reduces the water pressure to about 35 pounds, equal to that which most boat plumbing systems can safely take.

Although this is very convenient, I prefer to use a regular metal garden spigot as an inlet valve (you can get chrome-plated ones if appearance is a factor). These enable you to shut the water off when you wish without getting off the boat, and since they are metal, they are less prone to damage when someone bangs against the boat or steps on the hose while it is connected to the fitting.

This spigot should be conve-

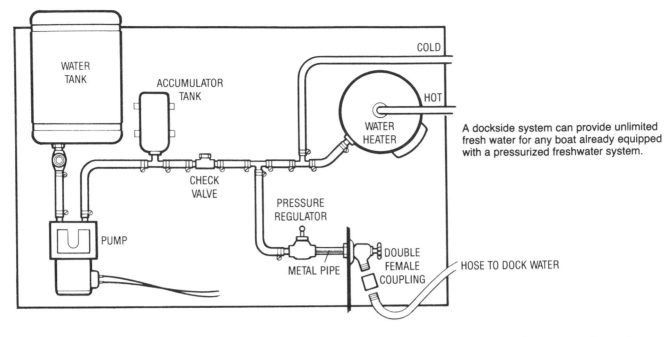

A dockside system can provide unlimited fresh water for any boat already equipped with a pressurized freshwater system.

niently mounted in a cabin side or cockpit coaming where you can get at the back side to make the necessary plumbing connections, and where there will be space behind it for a ½″ metal pressure regulator or reducer. One popular location is on the cabin side where there is a locker or set of drawers on the inside that can provide access. Another good location is in the side of a seat locker or permanently mounted deck box. On power boats that have a cockpit, installing this inlet valve under the coaming, or next to the dockside electric connections are other convenient locations.

When selecting the location for this inlet valve, you will want to take into account how difficult it will be to run the connecting water line from the proposed location to the main supply water line. As shown in the accompanying drawing, the dockside water connection has to be tied into the water line after the pressure water pump, but before the water branches off to the hot-water heater and all other fixtures inside the boat. Generally, this means cutting into the cold-water line fairly close to the pressure water pump. The dockside water inlet connection can be almost anywhere—it's just that the farther from the pump it is, the more additional piping you have to install.

The spigot and the pressure reducer are connected together—back to back, or alongside each other—with metal pipe nipples and fittings. Using metal pipe and fittings to connect the spigot directly to the pressure regulator inside the boat is important because this part of the system must still withstand the high pressure that comes off the dock; plastic pipe or tubing could burst if there were a sudden surge of pressure.

Another way to get around this problem is to buy the kind of pressure regulator that screws onto the outside end of the spigot. It screws onto the end of the spigot in place of the water hose, then has a fitting on the other end so that you can screw the water hose directly to it. That way pressure is reduced before it ever gets inside the boat. The only trouble with this setup is that it is not very neat looking, and there are instances where the projecting regulator can be a nuisance when handling lines or when moving around on the boat while under way.

After drilling the hole required for the water-line connection and installing the inlet valve or spigot in the desired location, hook up the pressure reducer on the inside, using metal nipples and/or elbows to make the connections. Then run the water line inside the boat from this connection to the place where you will tap into the existing water line. This can be at any point after the freshwater pump, but it should be before the water line leading from the pump branches off to the hot-water heater. If you have an accumulator tank next to the water pump, then cut into the water line after the tee leading to the accumulator tank.

To make the actual connection you will have to first cut the water line in the spot selected, then install a tee fitting so you can connect the new dockside water line to one leg of the tee. The line going to the rest of the boat is connected to another leg of the tee, and the line coming from the water pump will be connected back to the third leg of the tee. Needless to say, you have to select the type of tee that matches your boat's plumbing system (soldered copper or compression-type fittings if you have copper water lines, and plastic fittings if your boat has plastic water lines).

Before reconnecting the line coming from the pump to the third leg of the tee, you should install a check valve as indicated in the drawing. The check valve protects the pump (and the accumulator tank, if you have one) from being damaged by excessive dockside water pressure coming to it in reverse. It lets water flow from the pump out to the boat system when the pump is drawing water from the tank, but when dockside water is pressurizing the system none of the water can flow in reverse back to the pump.

also work) was cut to cover the slot, and fastened to the top of the opening with screw and washer, allowing it to swing freely. This cover was then slotted to capture the arm when the window was wide open. When the window is fully open, the cover swings down, slips around the slot, and the bugs are locked outside.

Detail, right, shows the slot in the screen frame that allows the operating arm to move up and down as the windshield is opened or closed.

With the windshield open, the teak cover (shown raised, below) will be swung down to block the opening under the operating arm.

Custom Windshield Screen

Aboard our Grand Banks 32 we wanted to improve summertime ventilation in the deckhouse and keep the bugs out, so we decided to screen the only opening window in the three-section windshield. However, the top arm of the window opener complicated matters—an opening in the screen was necessary to permit the arm to move vertically as the window opened or shut. Our criterion was a good-looking, permanent screen. A marina neighbor, Benny Dupuy, solved the problem simply.

An opening was left in the wood-framed screen during construction to allow the arm to ascend to its highest point (window open). A small piece of teak (aluminum will

A Home-Grown Chronometer

In need of a diverting winter boat project, I searched through some old "Boatkeeper" sections for an idea.

One bit of data jumped out at me—companies that sell low-cost, but very accurate, quartz-crystal clock movements made in Germany. I decided to purchase one of these units and see if I could make a home-grown chronometer for small craft.

I ordered one quartz movement, a set of hands including a sweep second hand, and a marine clock face (it has an anchor painted on it). All of this, including shipping charges, totaled under $20.

The only assembly required is to mount the clock face to the unit using a small brass slotted nut provided. The hands are but pressed onto the shaft including the sweep

The $12 quartz crystal chronometer is shown in its custom-made box.

second hand which is held in place with a small threaded fitting. Everything fit the first time.

In order to make the chronometer look authentic I patched together a small pine box from scraps. The little brass hinges were salvaged from an old jewelry box. Sanded and colored with an antique stain it looks rather well.

One "C" cell battery powers the unit for three years. The current drain is so low that the cell will last for its shelf life. On the back of the unit there is a tiny knob for setting time and a start/stop button.

The unit's accuracy appears to be phenomenal for the price. It is warranted to be plus or minus fifteen seconds per month by the manufacturer. My unit is doing better than that judging by weekly time ticks based on radio signals. It would appear to be well within the Swiss standard for chronometers of plus or minus five seconds per month, and makes a comfortable and old-fashioned ticking sound as it is running.

These units can be ordered from: Selva Borel, 347 13th St., Box 796xw, Oakland, CA 94604; Klockit, Dept. WN8, Box 629, Lake Geneva, WI 53147; Fort Products, Drawer 544, Hwy 31 North, Spanish Fort, AL 36527.

Fitting an Air-conditioner into a Small Cruiser

Any boatowner who is handy with tools can convert a home-type window air-conditioner for marine use. I'm not talking about those all-too-common and unseamanlike installations through the aft bulkhead, but one in which the entire unit is out of sight, out of the weather, and completely built in.

My boat, a 28' Bayliner, has a generous amount of unused space below and forward of the bridge control station—space ordinarily used only for access to the bridge controls. Into this space I installed a common 4,000 BTU General Electric CarryCool. It weighs less than 40 pounds and has a plastic case. However, any portable 110-volt unit in the 4,000 to 6,000 BTU category will work just as well. The main points to consider are its weight—it must be light if installed well above the waterline—and it should have a corrosion-proof (preferably plastic) case.

Start by measuring the available space. Make sure access to instruments, steering cables and the like won't be compromised. Next plug in the unit to determine four things: (1) location of cool-air outlet duct (normally top front of the unit); (2) location of the cool-air return or discharge opening (normally in front of the cabinet covered with a filter pad); (3) location of the condenser ambient air intake (normally in back); and (4) location of the condenser hot-air outlet (normally on the perimeter of the rear casing). A piece of paper held in the air flow is a good indicator.

Next, buy a sheet of .020″ aluminum and a selection of aluminum pop rivets from any large hardware store or home center. Remove the front air-intake grill and filter from your unit, then cut a piece of aluminum large enough to cover the cool-air intake and rivet it in place. To insure a leakproof seal, apply a strip of sticky-back foam weatherstripping around the perimeter of the duct before riveting. Now cut two 3″ holes (using snips or a hole saw) in the aluminum cover directly in front of the duct, and use rivets or screws to fasten two 3″ plastic duct flanges over these holes (available at marine stores for bilge vent holes).

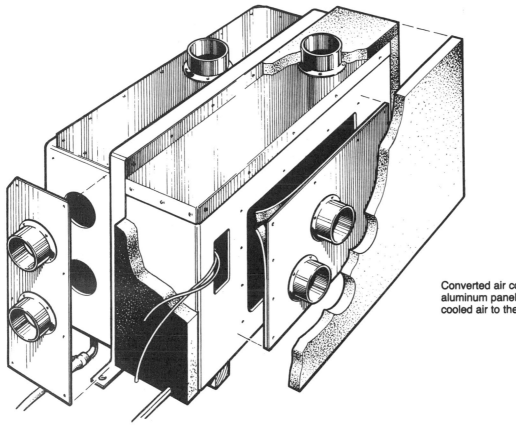

Converted air conditioner: Note the sheet-aluminum panels and insulation. Ducts feed cooled air to the boat's interior.

Next remove any louvers from the cool-air outlet duct, then fabricate an aluminum cover, seal with foam tape, and rivet in place. Cut a 3″ hole and install a duct flange. Be meticulous with your metalwork—gaps will waste precious cool air. Since aluminum is an excellent conductor, glue insulation over both the panels installed—either foil-backed fiberglass or ½″ to ¾″ elastomer rubber. The latter is preferred and available in sheets through insulation suppliers under the trade name Armaflex.

At the rear of the cabinet, fabricate a panel (or panels) for the condenser (hot) air exhaust after cutting away all louvers. Allow for a plenum or air space of at least 1″ between your panel(s) and the condenser for sufficient air circulation. Cut two 4″ or three 3″ holes into the panel(s) and fit with duct flanges. Insulation here is not desirable. Leave the condenser air intake grill on the back of the unit untouched, since it will receive no flanges.

NOTE: When drilling the cabinet for the rivets, be careful not to puncture the coils or interfere with other functional parts.

Locate the condensate sump in the bottom of the unit, then drill and tap a hole at its lowest point so you can thread in a ¼″ right-angle hose adapter, available through any R.V. supply house.

Now plug in the unit and turn the controls to maxcool/high speed. Diligently caulk any cold-air leaks. If the unit has inside-air/outside-air controls, lock these at the inside-air mode.

Installation will vary from boat to boat, but first start by gluing a piece of Armaflex large enough to cover the base dimensions of the unit to the bridge sole. This will act as a vibration and sound barrier. Position the unit with its rear facing aft. If the condensate drain hangs below the base, mount the unit on strips of lumber. Fasten with brackets, or better, lash with copper straps through-bolted to the cabin top. Remember that the unit may be subjected to fairly violent motion at its elevation—good seamanship dictates secure fastenings. Connect a rubber or plastic hose to the condensate drain and lead it overboard via a bridge scupper.

Depending on the number of hot-air discharge flanges you've installed, locate an equal number of cowl or neck vents on the exterior of the flying bridge bulkheads, facing aft. Connect plastic bilge vent hose from the vents to the flanges. Keep the hose as short and straight as possible, and use tie wraps to immobilize the hose. Make sure the condenser intake grill has ready access to air—you may have to install louvered vents in the forward bridge bulkhead.

Next, determine the best cabin locations for cool-air return and supply ducts. The cabin top directly below the bridge will probably be the simplest and most direct. You'll need to cut two well-spaced 3″ holes in the cabin top for the cool-air return and one 3″ hole for supply air. Separate the supply and return holes enough so the air circulates in the cabin, not simply in and out of the machine. Louvered vents allow you to direct the air for maximum effectiveness. Connect ducts to the unit's flanges with duct hose, again keeping the hose runs as direct as possible. Insulate the thin cool-air hoses with large-diameter Armaflex tubing or fiberglass to prevent them from absorbing heat. Then caulk around the hoses where they pass through the cabin top.

Wiring involves running a 15-amp 12-gauge circuit of wire from your distribution panel through a S.P.S.T. wall switch to an all-weather receptacle box near the unit. Use only marine-rated wiring, not the common NM-T household Romex.

For simplicity, I use the wall switch to turn on and off the unit, leaving the controls of the unit always on. I also removed the thermostat from the cabinet and placed it in the saloon overhead so it cycles in response to cabin temperature.

Teak Knife Rack

The teak knife rack illustrated here keeps all galley knives instantly ac-

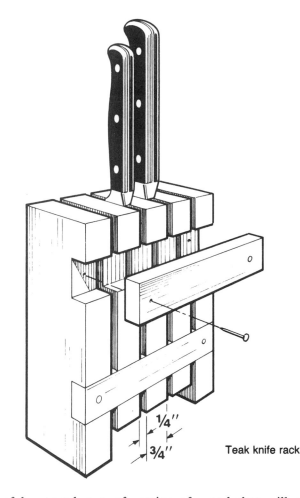

Teak knife rack

cessible yet safely stored out of harm's way. After deciding how many knives you wish the rack to hold, cut enough pieces of ¾″-thick teak to the length needed so there is one more piece of wood than the number of knives. The length of each piece should be at least ½″ longer than the longest knife the rack will hold, and the width should be at least ¼″ wider than the widest part of the widest blade.

Now clamp all the pieces together and cut the two sets of notches in all pieces at once—preferably with a radial arm saw or table saw. If you don't have access to one of these power tools, use a hand saw and sharp chisel to cut out the notches.

Each notch should be ½″ deep and 1¼″ wide to accept the two strips of wood that will go across and fit inside the notches. These wood strips are fastened in the notches with glue, after spacing the pieces apart by ¼″, as shown. They are fastened to the end pieces with bronze brads or small nails. To avoid splitting the wood, drill clearance holes through the wood strips first, then drill smaller pilot holes in the two end pieces. The completed rack is then fastened to a convenient bulkhead in the galley with screws.

Glass Rack

Here is a simple way to store plastic glasses free from dust, where they are easy to reach, and without using valuable storage space. All you need is a vertical bulkhead conveniently located, such as over the sink or ice box or beside the cockpit entry.

Materials needed are six or seven stackable plastic glasses (the hard reusable kind), a 2″ shelf bracket, a wood dowel 6″ long by 1½″ diameter—a damage-control plug works fine—and five wood screws.

Place the dowel in one of the glasses, mark it even with the rim, remove the dowel and saw it off where marked. Make a screw-sized hole in the center of the bottom of the glass (off center if the glass is very wide) with the tip of a soldering iron, and bevel to form a countersink. Screw the dowel inside of and to the bottom of the glass. Mount the shelf bracket to the bulkhead with the perpendicular arm on the bottom. Position the dowel on the perpendicular arm of the bracket so that the glass almost touches the bulkhead. Screw the dowel just firmly on the bracket.

Stack the remaining glasses upside down on the mold.

The bracket can be bent to any desired angle so that the glasses are vertical and touching the bulkhead or so that they angle out from the wall. If you want to disguise the dowel, use dark colored or opaque glasses.

Neat Galley Storage

Short pieces of white PVC plastic pipe, about 4″ in diameter, and 10″ to 12″ in length, can be used to quickly create neat holders for storing all kinds of galley items—cups, bottles, silverware, etc.—as illustrated here. Buy pieces of the white shiny plastic pipe so it will be easy to keep clean, and fit each piece with a wood base for holding bottles, silverware, and knives.

To form a base for the bottle holder or cup holder, use wood about ½″ or ¾″ thick and then cement the plastic pipe to the wood with epoxy cement. An alternate method of mounting to a base is to cut a shallow hole of the right size to make it a press fit for the pipe. Force the end of the pipe into the recess. Sand the wood smooth and round off all sharp edges and corners, then paint with several coats of white paint.

For the cup holder, you form a groove through which the handles will project by making two lengthwise cuts about ½″ apart, but leave the last inch or so at the bottom

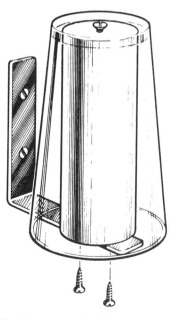

Plastic glass screwed to dowel can hold a stack of similar glasses.

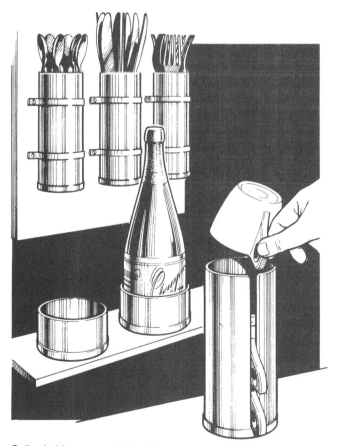

Galley holders are easily fashioned from plastic pipe.

end intact as shown. Now break this strip out carefully and use a file to smooth the cut edges.

Bottle racks are created by cutting the top ends at a slight angle to make it easier to slide the bottle in. Several can be attached to a single board as shown.

Holders for silverware can be made from smaller diameter pipe—2″ pipe is about right. These can be attached to the back side of a cabinet door or bulkhead with metal or plastic straps, and the bottoms can be sealed with end caps that are sold for use with PVC pipe.

Prevent Propane Leaks with a Plenum

The danger of propane stoves in marine applications is well known. Since propane is heavier than air, any leakage tends to settle in the bilge where it can accumulate and perhaps explode from a stray spark. Various safety precautions, such as locating the storage bottle on deck, shutting off the gas at the bottle when not in use, and checking regularly for leaks, have made these stoves acceptable. Propane is worthy of enough effort to make it as safe as the stove in your home. A leakproof sub-box or plenum with an overboard vent will do just that.

Cut the countertop to accept the stove with ¼″ clearance on all sides. Glue and screw 1″ × 1″ cleats on the underside of the countertop ¼″ outside the cut opening. Now the box. Using ¼″ plywood, make the sides of the box deep enough so the top of the stove will be 1″ below the countertop plus an additional 3″ depth for shaping. For example, assuming the stove is 4″ deep, figure 1″ below the countertop plus 4″ for the stove plus 3″ for shaping, or 8″ overall depth. The corners of the box can be glued and nailed with small brads to hold it together while shaping the sloping bottom. Cut the bottom of the inboard side so that the forward lower corner is at least ¼″ below the bottom of the stove and the aft lower corner is 1″ lower than the forward corner. Cut the aft side of the box from this point on the inboard corner to the full depth (8″) on the outboard corner. With these two sides cut, a bottom of ¼″ plywood can temporarily be laid in place and the slope of the other two sides can be marked and then cut. Now glue and nail in place. The outer edges of the bottom can be trimmed even after completion. At the outboard rear corner, the lowest point, drill a ½″ hole and epoxy in a short piece of ½″ PVC. Attach the box to the countertop, glueing and screwing to the cleats previously installed. Fiberglass the inside of the box completely including the edges of the countertop. Two layers of glass should be used; however, the glassing should be done with a high percentage of resin to assure that the box is leakproof and as smooth as possible. Install a through-hull near but below the end of the PVC and connect it with high-quality fuel hose and stainless clamps. Install cleats on the inside of the box to support the stove. Now install the gas-feed line. A one-piece copper tube from the bottle shutoff valve to the inside of the box, sealed where it passes through the box, assures you that any leakage, even from a missed light, will be

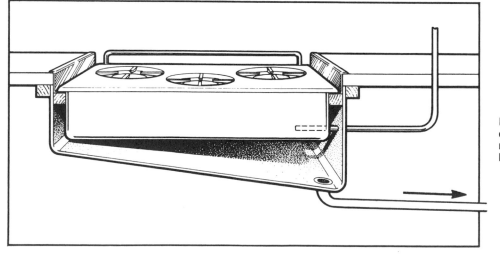

Fumes descend toward the drain, and then overboard by means of a hose and through-hull fitting.

containcd within the box and flow harmlessly out the through-hull to be blown away or absorbed. The countertop edge should be covered with an aluminum shield to prevent scorching when there is a large pot on the fire.

Galley Food Locker

Do-it-yourself aluminum materials available at hardware stores and lumberyards can be used in a variety of ways aboard boats, as Gordon Manning demonstrates. Here's another of his projects; this one uses both decorative ventilation grill stock and aluminum piano hinges.

Of course dimensions will have to be adjusted to suit your boat. The cabinet illustrated is 5″ deep, so all the shelves were cut 5″ wide from a ⅜″-thick panel of marine plywood. Note that one end is higher than the other, in order to fit snugly under the cabin overhead.

Start by assembling the two ends to the bottom shelf and the top panel. Note that the top panel must be cut about 1″ longer than the bottom piece, because it runs on an angle. Be sure to trim each

end to the proper angle to insure a tight fit against the sides. See the drawing.

Next cut out the three shelves (or however many you need) and the shelf supports. With the supports in place, total side width is ¾″. The supports are glued in place and fastened with ¾″ brass wood screws, driven from the inside. The shelves themselves and the top and bottom panels are glued and fastened with small galvanized brads.

A piece of ⅜″ plywood is cut to fit between the top of the doors and the headliner. This may need a

slight curve in many installations. It is glued and nailed with brads to the top and end panels.

The two doors are also ⅜″ marine plywood. After the center sections are cut out and sanded smooth, they are backed with the decorative aluminum grill. Gordon Manning used grill that was anodized gold in color, which was very effective with the mahogany-faced plywood. The doors are attached with two lengths of aluminum piano hinge, and the necessary catches are installed. He used magnetic catches, which are good if they hold well, and they are well away from your boat's compass.

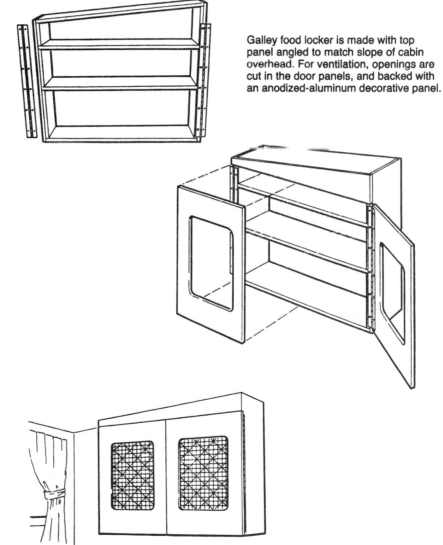

Galley food locker is made with top panel angled to match slope of cabin overhead. For ventilation, openings are cut in the door panels, and backed with an anodized-aluminum decorative panel.

Pot Holes

Why would anyone in his right mind want pot holes in his boat? you ask. The answer is simple: To keep pots in, of course. They are very close to being the perfect solution to pot stowage—enabling removal of any single pot without disturbing others, eliminating the possibility of any rattling and clanging at sea, and being extremely simple to construct and adapt to any vessel's cabinetry. Beyond all that, they have one great advantage over any other pot stowage method I can think of, in that the lid to each pot can be stowed *on* the pot, again eliminating endless digging and searching through some bottomless pit. When at sea, the lids can be stowed upside down in the pots to lower their center of gravity.

Into most above-counter cabinets, at least two shelves of holes can be installed. The pots having the largest surfaces should be on the top shelf where the curvature of the hull usually allows more room.

Rough cut ½″ sheets of plywood to fit, then lay out all your pots and pans and arrange them in the most economical order. Don't forget to leave space for the handles in such a fashion that they will be readily accessible.

Draw in the shape of each pot and very accurately cut out the hole with a jigsaw, remembering that any overcutting will result in irritating rattles under way. Very shallow pots, like frying pans, whose handles prevent them from slipping into a hole to sufficient depth, will require the fabrication of chocks (see illustration), the height of which will be determined

by the lip. Three short ones will do. Install these to make a very snug fit as shown.

Round the edges of the holes with sandpaper to prevent splintering. Next, lay out the position of the shelves inside the cabinet and install ¾″ quarter-round as shelf supports. Glue and screw them into place. Sand all edges of the shelves, then screw the shelves onto the cleats. Do not use glue here, for you may one day get sick of your current pots or you may one day lose some of them overboard and logic tells me that it would be infinitely easier to make new holes for the new pots than to hammer a pot to fit properly into the old ones.

Holes cut in shelves are used to hold pots securely.

Safe Mount for Oil Lamp

I needed an extra oil lamp inside the cabin of my boat, and I wanted it centrally located where it would also be firmly secured even when under way or in a bumpy anchorage. The most appropriate support was a vertical tie rod (metal post) that serves as a support for the cabin top—a feature found in many sailboats.

As shown in the accompanying illustration, I mounted the lamp by cutting out a banjo-shaped piece of teak which was long enough so that when the lamp was fastened to the round part of the "banjo," the top of the teak would be about even with the top of the glass chimney on the lamp. A shallow V-shaped groove was cut in the back of this teak piece, running lengthwise from top to bottom so the wood would fit snugly against the tie rod when fastened against it.

Next, a slot was cut through the side of the banjo-shaped piece of teak just above the round section

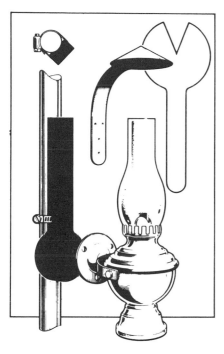

Pole-mount for an oil lamp includes hood cut from copper flashing.

Engine-Room Stowage

Possibly nowhere in a vessel will one find as great a need for stowing obnoxiously shaped objects as in the engine compartment. For the many odd pieces like spare alternator belts, oil sump pumps, and spare injectors, one will require nooks and crannies that are both secure and readily accessible.

For general stowage, the slat-faced bins seem to be most practical. Through the slats, adequate vision can be gained of the bin's contents, and because of the slats construction can be rapid. The bins should be narrow, about 8″, and moderately deep, about 12″, to allow most things to be wedged into place to prevent unscheduled flights. On fiberglass boats you can fasten the two end pieces to the hull with fiberglass tape and resin. On wood hulls you can screw, or clamp and glue, directly to a rib. This newly created vertical space can now be converted into bins with their plywood bottoms attached to each bulkhead and enclosed with ¼″-thick slats cut to 1½″ width. The topmost slat should have a butt hinge at one end and a barrel bolt at the other to effect a gate.

One small point: Spare engine parts are best left and stowed in their cardboard boxes. Not only will the boxes afford vital protection to delicate things like gaskets, but they'll provide a quick record of part names and numbers for the reordering and restocking which should be done as soon as possible after the part is used.

to permit slipping a stainless steel hose clamp through as shown (you will have to open the clamp all the way so the end of the band comes out of the worm gear housing in order to do this). To cut the slot, drill several holes close together, then use a rasp or saber saw to cut out the wood between the holes.

A piece of copper flashing (sold in hardware stores or lumberyards) is then cut out as indicated to fashion the hood. The cone for the hood is formed by cutting a small pie-shaped wedge out of the circle, then soldering the seam together as the piece is bent to shape. The hood is nailed to the teak with copper nails or brads.

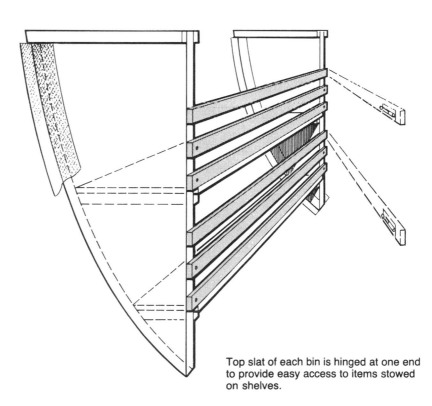

Top slat of each bin is hinged at one end to provide easy access to items stowed on shelves.

4 MISCELLANEOUS INTERIOR MAINTENANCE AND REPAIRS

How to Lick On-Board Condensation

You climb aboard after the boat has been closed up for a week or more and the cabin smells musty. Also, there are signs of mildew in some of the hard-to-reach corners . . .

You reach inside a cabinet and discover it is dripping wet—yet there is no leak in sight . . .

You pull a pair of sneakers out of a hanging locker and learn they are not only damp, they are covered with ugly mildew spots . . .

You wake up on a cold morning inside the boat and see that the windows are all "steamed up," and the moisture on the glass is dripping down onto the lovely teak trim and cabin sides . . .

You take a box of crackers out of the galley and get ready to bite into one with relish—but the crackers are all soggy and tasteless. . . .

All these unhappy incidents are caused by one of the more annoying problems that plague boatowners in all parts of the country during chilly weather—condensation that forms inside the boat when the outside air is colder than inside air. This not only creates interior dampness and mildew, it also results in the development of annoying musty odors and unpleasant persistent smells.

Although this is a problem that is probably of most concern to those who live aboard—either when cruising, or full time—it also affects most others who own boats large enough to have a closed-off cabin.

As one who has lived aboard for about ten years now, I have faced more than my share of con-

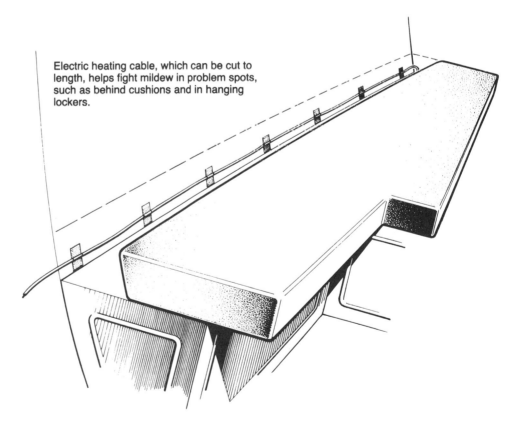

Electric heating cable, which can be cut to length, helps fight mildew in problem spots, such as behind cushions and in hanging lockers.

densation problems—one wood and one fiberglass—and while I don't claim to have the answer to every condensation problem, I have come up with a number of solutions that have eliminated practically all condensation problems inside my own boat, even during the winter when temperatures outside drop below freezing for days at a time.

In order to sensibly attack the problem, you first have to clearly understand exactly what causes condensation to form.

All air contains moisture, but the amount of moisture it contains (its humidity) varies considerably from place to place and from time to time. At any given temperature, the air can hold only a certain amount of water vapor before it becomes saturated. The higher the temperature the more moisture it can hold.

Therefore, when warm moisture-laden air is suddenly chilled, the excess moisture condenses out. That is how dew forms. Air that is warm and moist becomes chilled during the night, so small drops of water form on the ground and other exposed surfaces.

The same thing happens inside your boat. The air inside starts out warmer than the outside—either because it is heated or because you have closed up the boat at a time when temperatures inside were relatively high. Later the air and the water on the outside combine to cool off the hull and outer structure of the boat (remember, boats are usually not very well insulated against the cold—even against a mild drop in temperature).

When the warm air inside the boat comes in contact with these "chilled" surfaces—especially in closed-off or poorly ventilated spaces where air does not circulate easily—the result is condensation on the colder surfaces of the hull,

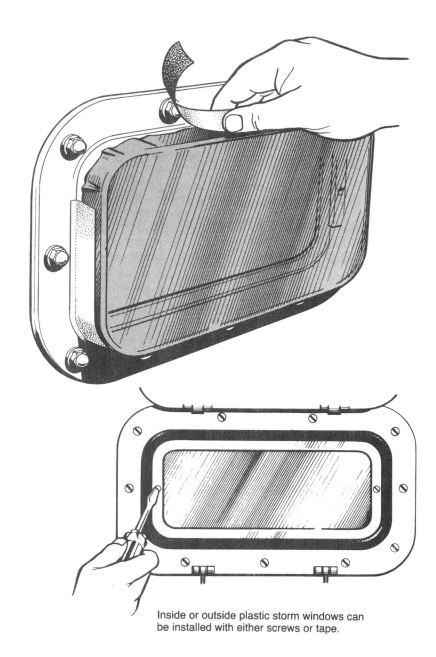

Inside or outside plastic storm windows can be installed with either screws or tape.

cabin, or locker sides (this is much the same as what happens when a pitcher of ice water "sweats" when it sits outside on a hot summer day).

So what can you do about all this?

You can do what I did—that is, attack the job piecemeal; one section or one place at a time. All you have to do is remember the basic

principles I have outlined above: Regardless of where it occurs, condensation or "sweating" will only take place when moisture-laden air comes in contact with a surface that is colder, and it will be intensified by a lack of ventilation when it occurs in a closed-off place (like a cabinet or locker) where there is little or no circulation of air.

Therefore, the way to eliminate

the problem is to take one or more of the following precautions:

(1) Insulate the cold surfaces on the inside so they won't lose so much heat to the outside. That way their temperature will not drop much lower than that of the air inside the boat.

(2) Keep the warm, moisture-laden inside air from coming in contact with the cold surfaces on the inside of the hull or cabin by installing some kind of barrier (a vapor barrier).

(3) Add heat at the point of contact so that the normally colder surface is kept warmer, and so that air in the vicinity won't be chilled enough to cause moisture to condense out.

(4) Provide plenty of ventilation in all areas where condensation could be a problem, because a flow of air will help moisture to evaporate quickly if and when it does form. In addition, ventilation helps to actually prevent it from forming because it spreads the moisture around and helps to even out the sudden temperature drops, which cause condensation.

If you could do all of these things, you would actually eliminate any possibility of condensation or "sweating" even taking place—but, of course, all this is easier said than done.

However, the task is by no means hopeless. You can whip it as I did, though it may take some time and extra effort. Just see when and where you can apply each of the four preventive rules I have outlined above.

Here are some of the things I have done in my own boat to stop condensation problems—things that illustrate the points outlined above, and things you can also do on your own boat where the same problem is present:

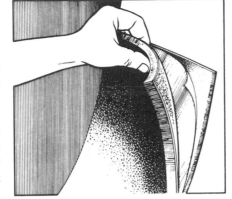

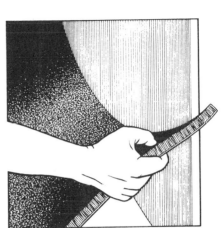

Carpeting is a good insulating material; a sheet of plastic between layers (top) helps prevent condensation.

Condensation that occurs under or behind mattresses or cushions, even though the boat is heated.

This is a common problem in fiberglass boats, especially where there is no hull liner. Where the cushion rests against an outside surface that is normally chilled, mildew and condensation form on those parts of the cushion that come in contact with the cold fiberglass. Where possible, the simplest solution is to keep the cushion pulled away from the hull or backrest in order to allow air to circulate behind it. That way there is less chance of condensation forming. Even if any does form, it will dry up quickly as heated air from inside the boat carries it away. As a live-aboard, however, I had a more serious problem with mattresses whose edges came up against the sides of the hull. Condensation kept them continuously damp along the edges at night, and

mildew soon started forming. All this even though the hull was lined with plywood and vinyl—it wasn't enough to keep the chill out. The first thing I did was line the hull at these points with another layer of carpet. This helped quite a bit, but in cold winter weather we still had a problem.

I finally used a new type of electric heating cable—similar to the kind used to keep pipes from freezing. This new version, called Frostex II, is sold by the foot, and you can cut it to any length you want (ordinary electric heating cables come in set lengths and cannot be cut without ruining them). It contains a dielectric conductor on the inside that eliminates the need for a thermostat—the colder the ambient temperature, the warmer the heating cable gets. The higher the ambient temperature, the cooler the cable remains and the less current it draws.

All you do is stretch it out along the area where a small amount of extra heat is needed (in this case I stretched a length along the hull sides next to the mattress) and then fasten it in place with ordinary duct tape. Then use a lightweight extension cord to connect it up to the nearest 110-volt outlets and forget about it. The cable draws very little current even when on, and it will heat up only when needed. It gets only mildly warm to the touch even when fully heated, and is UL-approved.

Condensation that occurs inside hanging lockers and cabinets.

Where these lockers or cabinets are against the hull I have found that lining with carpet or layers of plastic foam helps a lot. This insulates those sides and keeps them warmer. However, carpet does not stop air from getting through, even if rubber-backed, because it is not a vapor barrier. As a result, moist air goes through the carpet and then condenses, saturating the back side. This water then seeps down and creates a soggy mess at the bottom, even if the rest of the carpet-lined surface seems dry.

To get around this, I put a vapor barrier—a sheet of polyethylene—on top of the carpet (on the warm side) so that moisture could not get through to the back. This seemed to solve the problem, but I found that putting a second layer on top of the plastic helped even more and made a neater job. Also, leaving the doors to the locker open or, better yet, cutting vents in the doors so that warm air can circulate also helps a great deal. Remember, you're always trying to create a buffer.

In places where this double layering of carpet and plastic is not practical, the simplest solution is installing one or two of those electric heating rods that are sold by many marine stores for this purpose. Place these along the bottom, near the back, and the heat will rise along the back side, warming surfaces enough to eliminate condensation problems.

In really cold cabinets, like in an unfinished space I had under one of the head sinks, I used both methods. I lined the fiberglass with carpet and sheet plastic, then buried a length of the Frostex heating cable mentioned behind the bottom edges of the carpet. The heating cable draws less current than one of those "damp chaser" rods, and it works fine behind the carpet.

Condensation that forms inside windows and portholes.

The best cure I have found for this is installing some type of storm window—an extra layer of glass or plastic over the existing one with an air space between the two. You can install this "storm sash" on the inside or on the outside. If you put it on the inside, it will keep warm inside air from coming in contact with the cold outer glass, so no condensation will form. If you install it on the outside, it will keep the glass from getting so cold, so again, no condensation will form.

For your "storm windows" your best bet is to visit a regular hardware store or home center. You can use rigid sheets of clear Plexiglas or Lucite over large windows, fastening them in place around the outside with duct tape, or on the inside by drilling holes near the edges and then using a few screws to hold them in place.

You can also use sheets of clear, flexible plastic that come with special self-adhesive plastic moldings. The moldings are put up first, then the sheet plastic is stretched across and fastened in place with a plastic spline that fits into a groove in the molding. You can even secure the sheets of plastic across the window or porthole opening with strips of tape—though this will not look as neat.

Condensation that forms on bulkheads or ceilings of heads.

As a rule, ventilation is the best solution to this problem. If nothing else, leave doors open in cold weather when the boat is heated, or during fall and spring days when the boat is closed up during the week. Add Dorade vents if possible to insure a flow of fresh air, and leave doors open when the boat is unoccupied for more than a day. If the boat is in a slip with dockside electricity, leave a very small heater going inside the head—even a 60-watt bulb burning all the time will usually be enough. When people are on board use a small fan to circulate air into that area.

Stain-Killing Primer

Although most of the belowdeck surfaces in the average boat—inside the engine room, in the bilge, under the various hatches, inside lazarettes, etc.—are seldom if ever seen by anyone but the skipper, the boatowner who really likes to keep things shipshape will still try to keep these areas clean and neatly painted, especially during spring fitting out.

However, applying paint over surfaces that have been saturated with oil and grease, even after a thorough scrubbing, will more often than not result in extensive peeling before the season is half over. To avoid this there are special primers you can use that will stick over mildly greasy or oily surfaces—primers that will also cover such stains as creosote, rust, and soot without having them "burn through" after the new paint dries.

These primer-sealers, which are sold in most paint and hardware stores, are pigmented, shellac-base primers that dry to a flat white finish. The two most widely sold brands are Enamelac and BIN. Both dry fast and can be painted over in less than an hour, and both can be used for priming wood, metal, or fiberglass. This makes them ideal for many jobs where you want to get a primer and a finish coat on in the same afternoon, as well as for painting many surfaces over which ordinary paint won't stick.

Solving Head Problems

Understanding the six major differences between a head and a toilet can help you avoid headaches in the future.

Before Englishman Thomas Crapper invented the modern toilet early in this century, a well-worn oaken bucket was a boatowner's only choice for on-board sanitation. Although not aesthetically pleasing, the bucket was inexpensive, simple to operate, foolproof, and virtually indestructible. In addition, it required little maintenance and there weren't any moving parts to replace, wear out, or break down.

Today, thanks to technology—and some stringent water-pollution standards—the oak bucket is a bit of nostalgia, and the choices for marine sanitation devices (MSD) run the gamut from simple to complex. There are porta-potties that store waste; manual and electric flush toilets with direct discharge or holding tanks; and on-board treatment plants with macerators, chlorinators, incinerators, and more. The options are staggering, with

each unit offering its own distinct advantages—either in cost or convenience. But despite the best scientific advancements in sanitary engineering, all of the marine heads currently on the market have one glaring similarity: Unless properly maintained and used with care, they will all break down or fail.

In truth, a marine head (so named because a ship's toilet is squeezed in near the bulkhead) is a simple, reliable device. Water enters through the inlet sea cock, advances through an intake hose, flushes waste material out of the bowl, and exits through a discharge hose. Eventually, water and waste material are pumped overboard or disposed of on land. Simple as this sequence seems, a head often breaks down because yachtsmen, used to the convenience of modern sanitation at home, forget that a head on a boat is *not* the same carefree device as the American Standard flush toilet that graces the bathroom at home. And, of course, the basic operating differences between these two types of units are at the root of most head problems.

The most important difference between a marine head and a land-based toilet is that the use of a head requires forethought: Before it can be flushed some preliminary steps must be taken. As one twelve-man racing crew found out, one of the most important preliminary steps is opening the outlet sea cock. A few years ago, about two days from home in the middle of the Newport to Bermuda race, the crew on board a custom Frers 47 began to notice an obnoxious odor emanating from the bilge and hanging lockers. In their haste to make speed, the crew had neglected to open the outlet sea cock to allow waste water to escape

from the head. With every flush, water and waste built up inside the discharge hose until finally the pressure became too great and the hose blew off the sea cock. Every successive flush after that pumped raw sewage and waste water into the hanging lockers and the bilge.

Unlike the toilet at home, which delivers six to eight gallons of water per flush at the touch of a fingertip, the marine head has a pump—either hand or electric—which must be primed. The pump, as is the case with both piston and diaphragm models, is called upon to do double duty. It draws the water in, and forces the effluent out of the bowl, with the direction of flow being controlled by a weighted rubber flapper or valve. Too often, especially in the case of manual pumps, head users only continue pumping until the waste disappears from view. Unfortunately, habitual underflushing can become a serious problem if waste solidifies in the outlet tube or sediment restricts the size of the discharge hose. It can lead to problems such as slow flushing and backwashing. To avoid potential problems, live-aboards, such as Bernard Gladstone, *MB&S*'s "Boatkeeper" Editor, insist that "everyone get in the habit of giving the toilet a good long flush after any solid waste or toilet paper has been in the bowl. This is important, because even after the bowl is clean and empty, solid waste can remain in the hose." If this waste hardens it can cause a buildup that partially clogs the hose. To avoid clogs many yachtsmen make it a rule to pump fifteen times after the waste disappears from view.

While the toilet at home uses fresh, purified tap water, a marine head utilizes ambient water. Be it fresh water or salt water, it is water that is full of marine life. Algae, eel grass, microorganisms, and floating debris are some of the items you'll want to filter out, hence an inlet strainer is recommended to keep flotsam and jetsam out of the head.

The Enemy: Weeds

When the strainer becomes clogged, water flow is impeded: This can lead to slow flushing action and clogs in the discharge hose. If the strainer cracks, breaks, or falls off, the intake hose and the head run the risk of becoming clogged with weeds or constricted by a buildup of algal growth. As the diameter of most intake hoses is only ¾", you can appreciate the need for constant vigilance and inspection of the strainer.

Probably the most significant difference between your sanitation unit at home and your MSD is the diameter of the discharge pipe or tube. A home toilet can easily swallow tissues, napkins, wads of paper, and other objects because the sewer pipe is 3½" to 4" in diameter. A marine head is much more sensitive because the diameter of the discharge pipe is a mere 1½", *less than half* the diameter of the waste pipe that leads to your home's sewer or septic system. That physically limits the size of an item that can be safely passed through, and even toilet paper can be a problem. A tightly wadded ball of toilet paper measures almost two inches across; and if the discharge hose interior has been narrowed by sediment or solids, a clogged pipe can easily result, especially if you underflush.

Because two-ply tissue is harder to break down than single-ply tissue, many yachtsmen use only single-ply tissue on board or buy special marine toilet tissue, which is designed to decompose faster than ordinary toilet paper. According to Terry Yuncker, national sales and marketing manager for

Mansfield Sanitary, "Biodegradable tissue is not a hype, it is very necessary. Especially for boatowners who have a holding tank. You don't have any agitation in a tank, only the sloshing from side to side underway, and it is difficult to dissolve ordinary tissue under those conditions." Mansfield's Sani-Soft "is as soft as Charmin," according to Yuncker, "but designed to break down quickly. It is not made from wood fibers or newspapers, as many toilet tissues are; it is a chemical composition specially formulated to fall apart rapidly in a holding tank."

Paper is no problem in pulverizing toilets such as Raritan's Jet, which utilizes a powerful jet of water, ejected at the bottom of the bowl, to break up paper and solid waste. But the jet toilet is not compatible with most treatment systems and it is primarily intended for large seagoing boats that operate outside the three-mile limit.

If you do use ordinary toilet tissue on board, single-ply is preferable to two-ply papers. "In general," says William Ruffin, spokesman for the Scott Paper Company, "one-ply tissue is recommended for holding or septic tanks."

To avoid headaches some yachtsmen don't allow *any* toilet tissue into their MSD. They encourage guests to use a wastebasket for paper disposal and carefully tack up a list of do's and don'ts for visitors. Bernie Gladstone poo-poos the use of cute signs that say, "Don't throw anything down the head unless you've eaten it first," or even the ones that manufacturers supply. "I've found the best solution," Gladstone claims, "is to print directions on a sheet of plain white cardboard with a red Magic Marker. You don't have to leave it up all the time, but every time you have guests aboard tape it right by the switch or anywhere in clear view."

Backflow Blues

At home, when the waste water flows out of your toilet, it oftens goes *straight down* from your tenth floor apartment or street-level house to the sewer or septic connection in the basement. On board a boat, where space is at a premium, it is not always possible to have the holding tank installed directly below the discharge fitting of the head. Often, elbows will be used or the discharge hose will have a number of bends and curves—all of which are prime targets for the buildup of waste and sediment accumulations.

Whenever possible, multiple elbows, which dramatically slow the flow of waste, should be avoided. While they can be space savers, one manufacturer estimates that each 90° elbow is equivalent to adding almost 18' of discharge hose to the line. If you have an elbow installation, you can appreciate the need for a good, long flush.

To prevent backflow many boats have a vented loop installed on the head. This is especially important on sailboats, where heeling can cause the bowl to be much lower than normal, and thus place it well below the waterline. A vented loop in the discharge line prevents siphoning of water back into the bowl. According to Donald Beck, customer service manager at Raritan Engineering Co., Inc., "Boatbuilders will normally include a vented loop if the head is going to be below the waterline. A vented loop is almost like a trap in a sink, except it's the other way around. There is a small vent in the top of the loop, and once the water gets over that loop it cannot get back into the head because the siphon effect is broken by air coming in. The loop is taken from the head discharge," says Beck, "up above the waterline and then back down to the discharge valve. So even when a boat is heeled, the boat will not be able to siphon the water back in, should a valve fail."

Fighting Neglect

To prevent problems from developing and causing headaches later on, proper care and maintenance of marine toilets is recommended *before* any signs of trouble begin.

Live-aboards, such as Bernie Gladstone, agree that constant attention is necessary to forestall headaches, and he suggests replacing all of the parts of a head that are susceptible to wear, on a regular basis. At the beginning of every boating season, Gladstone recommends replacing all the rubber parts that are included in your manufacturer's spare-parts kit. Year of experience have taught him that his type of preventive maintenance, which includes replacing the rubber joker valve or flapper valve, gaskets, seals, belts, and impellers, is your best insurance against unexpected breakdowns.

Second to the deterioration of rubber parts, the greatest enemy of the marine head is calcium carbonate scale which builds up in the bowl, on the valves, and inside pipes. "Every six months," says Gladstone, who lives aboard in brackish waters, "I have to take the hose off one of the heads and replace it entirely due to the buildup of salt and calcium that looks like mother-of-pearl." If you don't replace the hose or use vinegar or muriatic acid to dissolve the scale, Gladstone warns, "Little by little this scale reduces the diameter of the hose to the point where a 1½" hose is down to ¾". I've seen that on my own boat." Restricted diameters will lead to flushing difficulties and clogs.

Even if you surmount all odds and get your waste into the discharge pipe without any hassles, don't think you're home free. You still have to contend with the Marine Sanitation Device which the Coast Guard has mandated for all vessels operating in U.S. waters within the three-mile limit.

Methane Buildup

There are three classes of devices on the market that meet Coast Guard standards for acceptable performance: no-discharge systems (Type III), macerator-chlorinator units (Type I), and Type II models, which are roughly equivalent to an on-board secondary sewage treatment plant.

The least expensive units are the Type III: A porta-pottie or a holding tank that stores waste until it can be disposed of properly. "The most important step with holding tanks," according to Gladstone, "is to make sure the vent doesn't get clogged." If the holding tank overflows and clogs the vent, a dangerous situation could result if there is a buildup of methane gas, a by-product of bacterial action. Gladstone says, "You can build up sewer gas (methane) that will actually explode. It sounds farfetched, but I know of one case where it happened." Even if the methane doesn't cause a fire or explosion, it does have another drawback. The characteristic odor that one associates with sewerage treatment plants is actually methane. Besides being dangerous, methane is extremely offensive to the olfactory senses.

Interestingly, the Coast Guard does not have stringent standards concerning the construction and durability of holding tanks. Apparently they assume, since the holding tank will be aboard *with you*, you will choose a unit that is both sturdy and durable and not subject to failure.

If you do have a holding tank, an important piece of equipment to consider is a holding-tank level monitor; a device that a handy yachtsman can install in about one hour. This monitor will save you needless trips to a pump-out station to empty a tank that is only one-quarter full, and it can save you from the inconvenience of having a full tank in the middle of an afternoon's cruise.

No matter what type of head or MSD you have installed on your boat, it pays to read the owner's manual. Donald Beck of Raritan has found that many boatowners experience trouble because they don't always take the time to read the instructions. "Often I'll get a call from a fellow with a problem," says Beck, "and the first thing I'll do is go over the procedure that's in the owner's manual. That usually takes care of the problem.

Preventive Maintenance

Donald Gross echoes Beck's sentiments: "Always read the instructions that apply to all sanitation devices, both heads and MSD's" to forestall any problems from developing. "Basic maintenance of the equipment is paramount," says Gross. "Remember, you're dealing with mechanical and electrical devices, often in a salt-water environment where there are extreme hardships on the equipment. Preventive maintenance and not corrective maintenance is the key. Treat it right before it fails, is the best advice I have to offer any yachtsman."

Another reason to consult your manual is the handy trouble-shooting guide that handles most common questions and complaints, such as what to do about odors emanating from a properly working head.

"In many instances," says Beck, "the smell usually isn't coming directly from the head." The problem is the type of hose that is being used. "Some people use a thin-walled polyvinylchloride (PVC) hose with ribs, similar to a swimming pool vacuum hose. And while it is convenient, it really creates an odor problem because the odor permeates right through the plastic." If odor is your problem, Beck suggests you switch to a thicker-walled rubber hose with a smooth interior.

The owner's manual also contains complete instructions on proper winterization of your head and MSD. Always follow the manufacturer's instructions because advice varies: Some manufacturers suggest draining the system completely and leaving it dry over the winter, while others recommend the use of antifreeze.

Careful operation, forethought, and preventive maintenance should forestall many problems with a marine head. Then even if the worst does happen, and an unexpected failure does occur, by familiarizing yourself with the working parts of the head and gaining an understanding of how the MSD works, you will be better able to deal with many emergencies. You might even save yourself some costly plumbing repairs, too.

Cleaner and Polish for Varnished Wood

There are many products on the market for cleaning and polishing interior varnished wood surfaces: some excellent and some not-so-excellent. Unfortunately, even the good ones have some disadvantages.

Wax-based products tend to build up on the surface, and often will ultimately cause the surface to yellow, then get dull and smeary. And before you can refinish any wood that has wax on it, you have to get every bit of the wax off or the new varnish will never dry.

Oil-based polishes give the woodwork a luster that looks as though it has been freshly varnished, but the oil cannot penetrate into the surface, so it leaves a surface residue that wears off easily and starts to show finger marks.

I have found that an excellent alternative to any of these is using a solution of vinegar and water—20 percent plain white vinegar and 80 percent water. Mixed together and applied with a spray bottle, it will polish varnished wood as well as any commercial preparation and leave no residue that can build up. It will remove greasy smudges and leave the original shine intact.

The same vinegar solution, incidentally, is also a good cleaning agent for many materials including plastic laminates or veneers, stainless steel, mirrors, glass, and other nonporous surfaces.

Balsa-Core Attachments

The standard method of bolting through a balsa-cored deck—drill-ing for a tight fit then coating the bolt or screw with silicone or some other sealant—risks admitting water over time, raising the possibility of rot.

I advise first drilling a larger hole, say two or three drill sizes larger than the bolt, then taping the bottom of the hole and filling with epoxy resin. When the resin has thoroughly hardened, drill again with a smaller bit the same size as the bolt. The resin, which will have penetrated the balsa, will act as a permanent seal. Then use a sealant to stop leaks.

Easier Filling of Alcohol Stoves

Filling the tank on an alcohol stove by pouring from a gallon can or jug almost always results in spilling some, so my son and I decided to

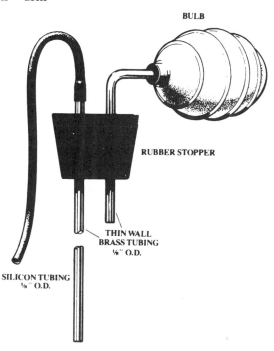

BULB

RUBBER STOPPER

THIN WALL BRASS TUBING ⅛" O.D.

SILICON TUBING ⅛" O.D.

A simple arrangement for spill-free filling of an alcohol stove

build a simple pump to eliminate this problem.

The materials required are a rubber stopper the right size to fit your alcohol jug or can, a couple of feet of ⅛" outside diameter thin-wall brass tubing, some ⅛" inside diameter plastic tubing, and a rubber squeeze bulb. All this can be purchased in a hobby shop, but if you have trouble getting a rubber stopper try a drug store or a scientific supply house (a cork will sometimes work okay, but it is more likely to leak air).

As shown in the drawing, two holes are drilled through the stopper to accept the brass tubing—they should be a snug fit for the tubing. One piece of tubing should go down almost to the bottom of the container on the inside, and should stick up an inch or two above the stopper. The other piece of brass tubing should be about 12" long and should have a 90° bend in it as shown. One end goes through the cork and sticks down for a couple of inches, while the other end is connected to the fuel bulb or squeeze bulb.

Slip the end of the plastic tubing over the top end of the longer piece of brass tubing (the piece that is not bent) and you are ready to pump alcohol from container to stove.

After taking the cap off, push the stopper into the can opening and give the bulb a few squeezes to start the alcohol flowing. When the stove tank is almost full, loosen the stopper to relieve the pressure and stop the flow instantly.

Emergency Plugs for Through-Hull Valves

All seagoing boats should have plugs aboard, for none is immune

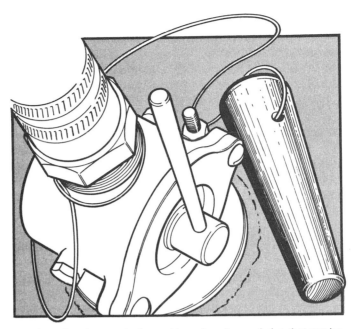

A softwood such as cedar is used to make a tapered plug that can be driven into the sea-cock outlet in an emergency.

to failed sea cocks or other through-hull valves. Indeed, many offshore racers are required to carry them as standard safety equipment. It would not seem overly cautious to have at least three plugs for each size of sea cock just in case trouble really does come in threes.

Only softwood should be used for plugs. I have heard the tragic tale of a hard-as-steel oak plug which, when driven into the sea cock by an overly anxious crew, split the housing like a blooming rose; so use softwood (cedar is perfect) and use your head. If you have no access to a lathe, fret not, an hour's whittling will supply you with fifty years' worth of plugs.

For the large ones cut 5"-long plugs from 1½" stock, tapering them from 1½" to ¾". After your first two cuts, it would be nice to place the plug into a vise (fat end only) so that two more tapering cuts can be made with a jigsaw. Next, get out the shoe rasp and rasp away.

If your wood is well chosen, rounding the plug with a rasp should not be too demanding. Round the ends to avoid splintering. Drill a ¼" hole through the fat end and run a generous lanyard through it. With this the plug can be tied to the sea cock it is to serve, for storage and as a safety line to hold it in place. When needed just tap the plug into place and wrap the lanyard around the base of the sea cock to keep the water motion from spitting the plug back out.

For smaller sea cocks (¾") cut your plug from 1" cedar (the 1" is minimum), make it 4" long and taper it to ⅜". Inspect each year for checking or cracking and rub in a little oil.

Prevent Pump Clogs with a Strum Box

In many horror stories about a boat that takes on water, the in-

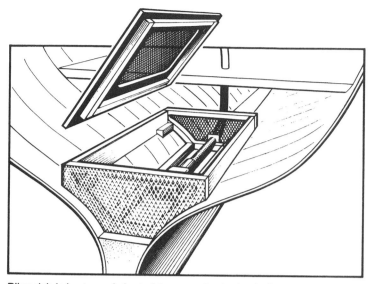

Bilge debris is stopped short of the pump intake by the box's wire mesh.

take of the bilge pump clogs with the debris found in most bilges. This occurs whether the pump is manual or electric, automatic or manually activated.

A screen over the intake hose should solve the problem, but this is not always the case. The screen itself often becomes clogged, at which point you discover it's inaccessible. Even if you can reach the screened intake and remove the clog, it soon clogs up again.

As a result the boatowner simply rips off the intake screen. This works for a while—until the pump itself gets clogged or jammed. Then the trouble really begins.

For starters, every cruising boat should be equipped with more than one pump, and preferably with at least one manual pump in addition to any electrically powered ones.

However, there is an answer to this problem that will prevent all but the worst of clogging problems with most bilge-pump installations—set up your bilge pump so that its intake terminates in a strum box located in the lowest point of the bilge.

A strum box is nothing more than a screened enclosure or cage that allows bilge water to flow into it freely, yet debris that could clog the pump is kept out. The box opens at the top to permit removing debris that gets accidentally dropped in.

The larger the strum box, and the easier it is for the water to enter, the more effective it will be in preventing clogging of the bilge pump—assuming there are sizable

screened openings. There are no set rules to follow, but as a rough guide you should make certain that the total area of all openings into the box, or the total area of the screen-covered opening, is at least 80 to 100 times as large as the area of the intake opening on the pump. In other words, if you have a pump with a 1″-diameter intake, make sure the strum box has at least 60 to 80 square inches of screened openings.

You could build such a box of wood or plastic, then drill dozens of holes (no larger than about ⅜″ in diameter) through the outside, but a much simpler and more efficient method is to cut sizable openings and then cover these with perforated metal or coarse mesh. If you elect to use wire mesh or screening, remember that it should not be too fine (otherwise it will be continuously clogging up) and it should be rust resistant.

On the other hand, it must have holes or openings that are small enough to hold back or stop the smallest particles large enough to clog the pump. Instead of regular wire mesh, which is often difficult to find in local stores nowadays, you can use perforated aluminum sheets (widely sold in local hard-

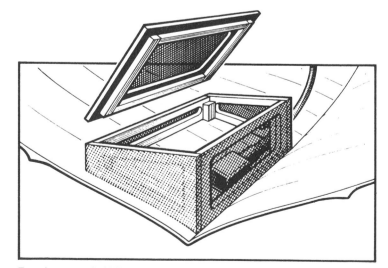

Even in a crowded bilge, place the strum box at the lowest possible point.

ware stores and home centers), brass or aluminum grillwork sold for use on cabinet doors and similar built-ins, or nylon screen. For maximum effectiveness it is essential that the strum box be located accessibly at the lowest point of the bilge. Needless to say, this location will only help if the bilge areas in your boat drain properly—in other words, if they have strategically located limber holes that permit water to run freely into the lowest areas (a problem with some of the newer fiberglass boats).

You can locate an electric bilge pump inside the strum box, or locate it elsewhere and run its intake pipe inside of the box.

The design will depend to a great extent on the type of boat—or more specifically, on the shape of the bilges. For example, in a typical sailboat or deep-keeled trawler the bilges normally taper down to a narrow V-shape so that all you really have to fabricate are two ends for the box. The inner sides of the hull will serve as the sides.

On the other hand, with a planing hull that has a relatively flat bottom, you will have to actually build a four-sided box or enclosure with two ends and two sides.

In the first case, where the bilge area tapers sharply, most of the water will have to flow in through mesh-covered openings in each end—it is only when water rises higher than the end pieces that it will flow in over the top and sides. Since there is a limitation in most boats as to how high and wide these end pieces can be, it is especially important in this type of bilge that the strum box be covered with mesh (in the form of a removable cover), and that most of the area of the ends be left open, for water to enter.

The two end pieces can be cut out of ½″ or ¾″ plywood, or out of ¼″-thick sheet plastic (such as Plexiglas). These pieces are cut so that their bottom edges are contoured for a snug fit against the bottom of the bilge and the side of the hull.

Where the strum box fits into the bottom of a deep, tapered bilge, the two end pieces are joined across the top with two strips of wood that also serve to brace the end pieces to keep them from collapsing inward.

Over this is fitted a frame covered with the same screen material. It can be held in place with small plastic wire ties (or pieces of wire) which are easily cut free when you want to reach inside for cleaning. This is simpler than securing the cover with screws which are hard to get at if you have to loosen them when they are partially under water.

In a fiberglass hull the wood pieces that form the box frame are best fastened to the hull with a liberal layer of epoxy cement applied to the edges before pressing them down into place. However, make sure you clean the fiberglass thoroughly, and wipe up any water so the surface will be as dry as possible. Use one of the epoxies that are designed to bond to wet surfaces.

On a wood hull chances are the wood is so water-soaked, and possibly oil-soaked, that no epoxy will be able to bond very well. Therefore, your best bet is to attach small brass angle braces or L-braces to the outside of the wood with screws and then screw these into the wood planking.

In most boats it will be easier to assemble the whole box first, then mount it in the bilge. But in some cases you may find it easier to assemble the box in place. In this case, if you cannot use screws to fasten the sides against the end pieces (due to the curve of the bilge), then cement them on with epoxy, or with a silicone rubber adhesive.

To insure long life for the finished box, the pieces of plywood should be soaked in a liquid wood preservative after being cut to the required size and shape. If the mesh is metal, it should be rust-resistant and further protected by spraying with a rust-inhibitive metal primer.

5 TOOLS, MATERIALS, AND EQUIPMENT

How to Pick and Use the Right Marine Adhesive

If you've tried to buy an adhesive lately, you know how difficult it is to sort through the enormous variety of products on the market. According to many of the labels and the advertisements, each sounds as if it could stick anything to anything under any conditions. While it is true that some can be used for several purposes, there is no such thing as a universal adhesive. For a permanent and satisfactory job, you have to match the adhesive to the task at hand—and that means knowing something about the kinds of adhesives suitable for the marine environment.

Woodworking Glues

The three most useful wood glues are: (1) white polyvinyl acetate glues, (2) plastic resin glues, and (3) Resorcinol glue.

White glues, the most popular of all for general woodworking, have moderate strength but comparatively poor resistance to moisture and exposure to dampness. For this reason these glues gener-ally have no place around the inside or outside of a boat: Even if the joint is located where it will never be exposed to water, damp-ness can still be a problem.

Plastic resin glues are powders you mix with water. They form a very strong joint—one that is often stronger than the wood itself—and they are very water-resistant. They are not completely waterproof, however, so they should not be used in places where the joint will be constantly under water. They work best in joints that are reason-ably snug-fitting and without voids,

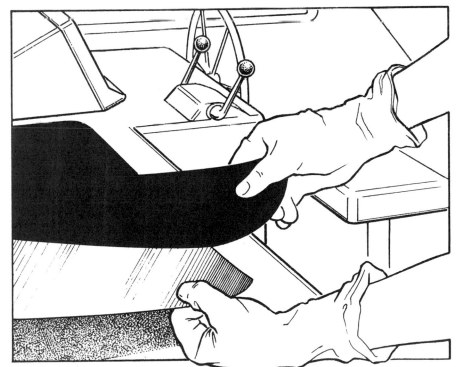

Contact cement being used to attach non-glare plastic—the middle sheet separates the surfaces until adhesion.

MARINE-ADHESIVE BUYER'S GUIDE

Adhesive	Mixing Required	Clamping Required	Drying Times	Water Resistance	Bond Flexibility	Materials Bonded	Special Characteristics
Resorcinol Glue	Yes	Yes	12–18 hours	Excellent	Not Flexible	Wood, Leather Cork, Textiles	Will fill gaps in poor fitting joints
Plastic Resin Glue	Yes	Yes	8–12 hours	Good	Not Flexible	Wood	Won't fill gaps and requires snug-fitting joints; requires temperature of at least 70 degrees.
Epoxy Adhesives	Yes	No	1–8 hours	Excellent	Not Flexible	Metal, Fiberglass, Wood, Glass, Ceramics, some Plastics	Low temperature slows drying and curing; has excellent gap-filling ability; will harden underwater.
Silicone Rubber Adhesives	No	No	1–2 hours	Excellent	Very Flexible	Metal, Painted Wood, Glass, Fiberglass, Rubber and Plastic	Resists extremes of high and low temperature and stays flexible.
Contact Cement	No	No	Instant (after contact)	Fair to Good	Moderately Flexible	Wood, Plastic, Leather, Rubber Fabric, Vinyl	Both surfaces must be coated and allowed to dry beforehand.
"Instant" or "One-Drop" Adhesives	No	No	30–90 seconds	Very Good	Not Flexible	Metal, Hard Plastic, Glass (some on Wood)	Works best on nonporous surfaces. Must be used in thin film; won't fill gaps.
Vinyl Repair Cement	No	Yes	30–60 minutes	Excellent	Very Flexible	Vinyl and Leather	Clamping consists merely of using masking tape.
Two-part Acrylic "Instant" Adhesive	No	Yes	2–4 minutes	Excellent	Moderately Flexible	Metal, Wood, Fiberglass, Ceramics, Glass, some Plastics	One part is applied to one surface, the other part to the second. Curing starts when they come together. Can be used over oily and greasy surfaces.

and they should only be used when working temperatures are above 65°F. The glue dries dark so it leaves a visible glue line in the joint, and it must be clamped for at least eight to twelve hours to insure a good bond.

Resorcinol glue is a two-part adhesive that consists of a powder and a liquid catalyst that you mix together. It forms an exceptionally strong bond on wood and is completely waterproof, so it can withstand constant immersion. It is, therefore, the preferred glue for assembling or repairing wood joints below the waterline, as well as those that will be constantly exposed to the weather or submerged in bilge water. Resorcinol is fairly good at filling gaps and voids in poor-fitting joints, and like the plastic resin glues, it requires overnight clamping to insure a permanent bond.

Epoxy Adhesives

These are probably the most versatile of all adhesives for use around the boat. They are two-part compounds that consist of a resin and a catalyst, and once mixed will bond to wood, metal, fiberglass, and most plastics. For a good bond the surfaces to be joined must be absolutely clean before the adhesive is applied, but once cured the material is impervious to attack by water, oil, gasoline, and most of the cleaning compounds and solvents likely to be found around the boat.

Epoxy adhesives come in all kinds of packages—tubes, aerosol cans, and jars—and in different types of formulations. Some are designed for mixing in equal quantities (resin and catalyst), while others are designed to be mixed in different proportions. Also, they vary as to curing time—some hardening in as little as five minutes while others take as long as eight to twelve hours. As a rule, curing time is affected by temperature: The colder it is, the longer it takes to cure.

Epoxies harden by chemical action. They don't need air to dry, so most will harden even when under water once they have been mixed. They are excellent for filling voids and gaps. No clamping is needed as long as you bring parts in firm contact with each other in proper alignment.

Silicone Rubber Adhesives

Although most boatowners think of silicone rubber as a caulking and sealing material rather than an adhesive, this compound is also useful as a bonding material where considerable flexibility is required in the joint, along with moderate resistance to stress. It bonds well to glass, metal, wood, and fiberglass, and remains rubbery over a wide range of temperature extremes— from 60°F. below zero to 450°F. above. Thus, you could use this inside an ice chest or on the outside of an engine block, where it will be exposed to considerable heat while the engine is running.

"Instant" or "One-Drop" Adhesives

These are the "miracle" cyanoacrylate glues that come in very small tubes (one to three ounces) because on most jobs only one drop is needed to make the bond. They stick within seconds and will bond to almost anything, including human skin, so they must be handled with caution. They work best, however, on nonporous materials such as glass, metal, and many hard plastics, and they must be applied in a thin film to cure properly.

Because these adhesives dry so rapidly no clamping is required— just press the coated parts together and hold them for a few seconds. But the thin film means that the parts must fit together snugly without gaps or voids, and the quick-setting characteristic of this adhesive also means that you have to align parts accurately the first time you bring them together—shifting or moving pieces around will often ruin the bond that is starting to form.

The adhesive forms a joint that is almost as strong as one formed with an epoxy when the parts fit properly, so these quick-drying adhesives can be a handy addition to any boatowner's emergency repair kit. Although claims differ, it is generally agreed that the joint formed by a cyanoacrylate will not be quite as waterproof as one formed by an epoxy.

Two-Part "Instant" Adhesives

This is the newest of the "miracle" adhesives. It forms a very quick bond that is also very strong and highly water-resistant. Falling somewhere between cyanoacrylates and epoxies in strength, it sets almost as fast as the "instants" described above, but gives a bit more time to align parts and bring them together. You apply one part to one surface and the second part to the other surface, but the actual cure doesn't start until you bring the two together. Hold for a minute or two, and the bond is made. One widely sold brand in this category is Duro Depend, made by Woodhill Permatex (18731 Cranwood Parkway, Cleveland, OH 44128).

Unlike the cyanoacrylates, it will bond well to flexible materials and many porous surfaces, so it does not require a perfect fit between mating parts. Also, it has one very unusual quality that can be of great value to boatowners—the surfaces to be joined do not have to be absolutely clean. As long as loose dirt is removed it will work on surfaces that are oily, greasy, and grimy. Just brush the liquid activator on the surface, squeeze the acrylic adhesive onto the other surface, then bring the two together. You have to hold the parts together for only a minute or two.

Contact Cement

Made with a synthetic rubber base, these cements are designed to do just what their name implies— bond on contact. They are used for such things as putting plastic laminates on countertops, furniture, cabinets, bulkheads, and similar surfaces because they eliminate the need for clamping or applying weights while the adhesive sets. The bond formed has a moderate amount of strength that is adequate for laminating and similar applications where very little actual stress will be encountered, and they can be used to join metal, rubber, leather, and many plastics to wood or to each other.

Unlike most other adhesives, contact cement must be a⁻plied to both surfaces, and it musϲ be allowed to dry before the parts are assembled. A surface coated with contact cement will adhere only to another surface coated with the same cement. But once the two parts are brought together (after both sides are dry) they bond instantly with a tenacious grip that allows for no shifting or realigning of pieces. You have to get them right the first time.

When large sheets of plastic are being laminated to a surface use a "slip sheet" of brown wrapping paper. Place the wrapping paper between the sheet of plastic and the surface to which it will be cemented, then line the two pieces up carefully (the cement won't stick to the paper because it has no cement on it). When the pieces are in position, you lift one corner of the plastic, then grab the paper and slide it out carefully. As the coated surfaces come together they will bond instantly.

Vinyl Repair Cement

Designed specifically for repairing tears, rips, and punctures in vinyl upholstery and vinyl-covered cushions, these adhesives are quick-drying cements that set up in a few minutes and cure completely in a few hours or less. They contain solvents that virtually "weld" the torn vinyl together, and are handy to have on board for repairing weather curtains, cockpit covers, and vinyl-covered furniture. The cement dries clear so in most cases repairs are inconspicuous, but one company (Duro) also packages this cement with a small touch-up kit to color the patch so that it becomes completely invisible.

Multipurpose Sealants

Few boatowners have to be introduced to sealants and caulking compounds, and many are familiar with the long-popular polysulfide types. Used as bedding compounds, as well as for caulking, they serve almost as well for both purposes.

However, there are two other compounds in the marine market that also serve as excellent adhesives, in addition to being extremely versatile caulking compounds. Both have several features that every boatowner should know about.

The first is a caulking compound with a polyurethane base; it has been on the market for years—used widely for commercial and industrial building purposes, and in the building of commercial ships. Only now is it being introduced to the retail market.

The second product is silicone rubber—a sealant and adhesive already familiar to most boatowners who have found it to be an excellent bonding, bedding, and caulking compound. Yet, many boatowners still do not really know how to use these compounds properly for maximum effectiveness. In addition, many do not realize that this material can actually be used to make emergency gaskets of all types when the usual replacement model is not available (more about this later).

Polyurethane

The polyurethane, one-part sealants or caulking compounds come in cartridges that can be used in a conventional caulking gun. They can be used either above or below the waterline, and form a tack-free film or bead in much less time than it takes the polysulfides to dry or become tack-free.

I experimented with two different brands of polyurethane caulking on my own boat—one called Sikaflex 241 (made by the Sika Corporation, of Lyndhurst, NJ), and another called Marine 5200 (made by the 3M Corporation). I found that the 241 formed a tack-free bead in just a couple of hours when the temperature was in

Polyurethane sealants dry tack-free faster than polysulfides, form a strong adhesive bond, do not shrink, and can be used above or below the waterline.

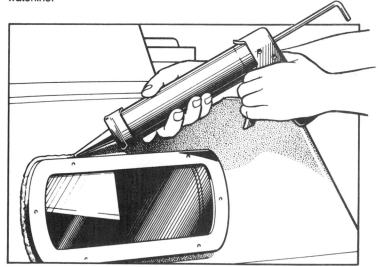

the mid-70s, while the 5200 took about eight to twelve hours to dry tack-free. This compares with the usual drying time of anywhere from thirty-six to forty-eight hours for polysulfide caulking materials to dry to the same tack-free condition. Both the polyurethanes were completely cured in about three or four days.

These polyurethane caulking compounds are also extremely flexible when dry. They won't separate or peel away from the materials to which they are applied even when joints are flexed to as much as 90° repeatedly, and they can be painted over almost immediately, although the paint will slow the final curing. They do not shrink as they dry, and since they do not sag or run, they are ideal for overhead or vertical applications where you might otherwise have a problem with oozing.

These characteristics, coupled with the unusually strong adhesive bond these caulking materials form with most of the materials normally used in building boats—including wood, anodized aluminum, painted metals, fiberglass, teak, mahogany, plywood, and many other hard-to-bond materials—is what has made them so popular in commercial ship maintenance, as well as for many industrial applications around the world.

In most cases, this exceptional bonding strength is achieved without the need for the types of sealers that are normally required before a polysulfide sealant will bond satisfactorily. On oily or fairly new teak, a sealer is still recommended, but I tried it on some weathered teak that had been scrubbed numerous times and the bond was excellent—it was very difficult to peel off after a few days, and was almost impossible to scrape off after curing for about a week.

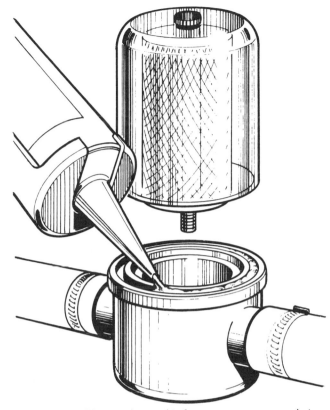

Silicone rubber can be used to form an emergency gasket.

An interesting demonstration of how this material bonds or sticks was forcibly brought home to me last fall when I used some for routine maintenance on my own trawler-yacht. I had been having trouble with a small leak around some quarter-round molding on an outside panel of one of my sliding pilot-house doors, so I carefully pried the molding off and rebedded it with a widely sold brand of polysulfide caulking.

However, halfway through the job I ran out of the brown-colored caulking I was using (it is a teak door, so I didn't want white caulking). Having a sample of the new polyurethane (from 3M) on hand in brown, I decided to finish the job of bedding the rest of the molding with that.

Both did the job—that is, they cured the leak. However, a month or two later I had to remove these same moldings again. Since both moldings had been secured with only the caulking, I anticipated no problems in getting them off.

I had no more than the usual scraping and prying problems when I started to pry off the moldings that had been bedded with polysulfide, but when I got to the ones that had been bedded with 3M's 5200 polyurethane caulking, I really did run into problems! The wood moldings would not budge, no matter how carefully I pried with a knife blade, and how forcefully I worked with two putty knives, a thin chisel—and any other tool I could lay my hands on.

I finally did get the pieces of molding off, but only after having split them in two or three places (no splitting at all on the first pieces). Things got even worse when I tried to peel or shave the compound off the narrow pieces of molding so that I could use them again. The compound stuck to the raw wood on the back side of the molding like a strong glue, so that even when I tried to shave it off with a sharp knife I did more damage to the wood than to the compound. Finally I had to discard the moldings.

Of course, there is a lesson in this that points up a potential limitation to the use of these polyurethane caulking compounds—don't use them in joints where you are likely to want to take things apart very often. Save them for those exposed joints that you really want to seal up permanently—for example, hull-to-deck joints, windshields, porthole frames, centerboard trunks, stemhead fittings, stanchions, garboard seams, all types of through-hull fittings and hardware, outdrives, and similar places where you want a tough, flexible seal that will last almost indefinitely.

The same flexibility and adhesive qualities that make this compound so good for permanent sealing also make it a superior product for many bedding applications when installing deck hardware or structural components. Used to fill bolt holes and screw holes before inserting the fasteners, it will actually stick to and coat the metal fasteners to really protect them against corrosion, as well as to literally bond them in place more permanently. But, here again, you must keep in mind the very strong bond this compound forms with the materials it comes in contact with, so *don't* use it in places where you are likely to want to take the joint apart again in the foreseeable future.

There is another limitation to the use of these polyurethane caulking compounds around boats with teak decks—both manufacturers currently do not recommend these products for sealing the joints in regular laid teak decks. The people at Sika state this is for purely cosmetic reasons because the compound tends to check or "alligator" under the frequent scrubbing and the horizontal exposure. The 3M people give a similar reason, saying that polyurethane does not stand up under scrubbing with the strong bleaches and cleaners that are repeatedly used on most teak-decked pleasure yachts.

Silicone Rubber Caulking

Silicone rubber is more often used for small jobs, such as sealing around vents, around openings where wires or pipes pass through a deck or cabin side, or where there are annoying windshield and hatch leaks that you want to seal off without taking anything apart. Unlike the polysulfides and the polyurethanes, it also comes in a clear (in addition to white, black, and metallic gray), so it is ideal for many jobs where you don't want the compound to be very noticeable.

It bonds well to metal, glass, most plastics, and sealed (painted or varnished) wood, but it doesn't stick very well to raw wood or to porous surfaces in general. Also, paint or varnish won't stick to it, so don't use it where a finish must be applied over it.

One of the best marine uses for silicone rubber is as a bedding compound. It bonds well to metal, fiberglass, and wood, but not with so strong a bond that you can't get the pieces apart when a piece of hardware must be removed for repair or replacement. It forms a thoroughly waterproof, and permanently flexible, joint that will withstand extremes of temperature, as well as constant exposure to water, sun, and salt water.

However, when using this material as a bedding compound, there is a common mistake many people make that destroys or limits its efficiency: Immediately after installation they cinch down the fasteners as hard as possible, and the result is that they squeeze so much of the compound out that there is not enough left to really seal the joint.

The right way to use silicone rubber as a bedding compound is to apply a layer of the compound under the base of the piece of hardware being installed, then insert the bolts or screws and tighten

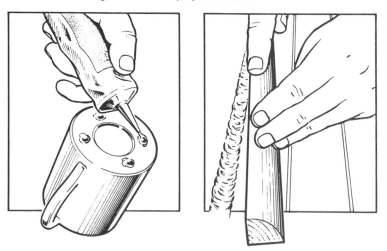

Nonskid feet are made with silicone, left. Polyurethane or silicone can be used to bed molding, but adhesion properties differ.

down *almost, but not quite* all the way. In other words, leave the last half-turn or so undone at this point. Let everything sit for about ten or fifteen minutes, *then* tighten down the rest of the way.

The ten- or fifteen- minute break will allow the silicone to partially cure to a rubbery consistency, so that when you finally do tighten the rest of the way, there will be a rubbery layer between the two surfaces that will remain permanently—no matter how hard you tighten down afterward.

This ability of the silicone to dry to a rubbery film that fits any contour, and its durability and permanence when dry, gives it another valuable use around the boat. You can use silicone rubber to make your own formed-in-place gaskets for all kinds of plumbing and sealing applications. In fact, GE, one of the two principal producers of silicone rubber compounds (Dow Chemical is the other big producer), actually packages their silicone in black under the name of "Silicone Household Gasket" (don't let the word "household" fool you—it can still be used for marine use).

To form your own gasket you clean the surfaces where the gasket must fit, then apply a layer of the silicone rubber to one part. Now press the two together, but don't draw the bolts or screws up real tight—just enough to bring them almost together. Let the assembled parts sit for about twenty minutes, then continue tightening to form a watertight seal. A sharp knife or razor blade can be used to trim off the excess that was squeezed out and hardened (while the material is soft, you wipe off as much as you can with a rag).

The technique just described can be a virtual "lifesaver" when you are stuck in a strange port or out at sea and suddenly need a gasket

that you don't have (for a head, or for an intake water strainer, for example). But remember that this method will form a gasket that will be permanently bonded to both surfaces—in other words, you cannot take the pieces apart without destroying the "gasket" you have just formed.

If you don't want the rubber to stick to both pieces, insert a sheet of waxed paper before tightening. When the compound dries take the waxed paper out and then tighten down as hard as necessary. The gasket formed will not stick to the piece that had the waxed paper layer under it, so you will still be able to take pieces apart without any trouble. Needless to say, you could put waxed paper on both sides of the layer of silicone rubber to create a completely removable gasket after drying that will not stick to either surface.

Silicone Trick

Silicone-rubber caulking makes an excellent bedding compound when fastening down deck hardware and other small fittings, particularly on fiberglass boats. In fact, it can even be used to create a rubberlike gasket that will fill in small voids and correct surface irregularities.

However, all too often the benefits are lost because most of the compound gets squeezed out of the joint when the screws or bolts that hold the hardware in place are fully tightened. Here is how you can prevent this—and yet get a better seal:

After spreading the silicone on over the base of the fitting, set it in place and start tightening the screws or bolts—but don't tighten them all the way. Tighten them about three-quarters of the way,

then let the compound cure for about fifteen minutes. Now tighten them down almost all the way, but don't do the final cinching up until the compound cures for another half hour. Then do the final tightening with full power. This sequence will leave a good film of bedding compound in place, and will result in a "custom-made," preformed "gasket" that will be really waterproof.

Another Use for Silicones

The same silicone rubber compounds that are so useful for sealing and forming gaskets can also be very useful for an entirely different purpose around most cruising boats. Apply a few drops—or a thin film—of this material to the bottom of any item that you want to stay put. The dried silicone creates an amazingly effective nonskid coating or base that will hold dishes, ashtrays, plotting instruments, glasses, small appliances, trays, etc., in place, no matter how the boat pitches, rolls, or heels (up to angles of as much as 30° or 40° in most cases).

All you do is clean off the bottom of the object that you want to make nonskid, then spread a thin layer of the silicone over the bottom—or, in the case of small objects, simply apply a few dabs or small beads to each corner of the base. Allow the silicone to set for about five to ten minutes, or until it just starts to stiffen up, then turn the object right side up and press down with moderate pressure on a flat surface that is covered with a piece of waxed paper (to keep it from sticking). Then turn it over again and allow to dry completely. The silicone will create rubbery "buttons" or "feet" that will keep items from sliding around under all normally encountered sea conditions.

Braze Welding with Portable Torches

Portable propane torches that deliver much more heat than older models did make it possible for any boatowner to do his own braze welding without having to carry around a lot of expensive, bulky welding equipment or call in a welder.

Brazing is a metal joining and fabricating technique that is almost as strong as welding. It can even be more effective than welding—the high heat of an oxyacetylene torch creates internal stresses that could cause buckling or distortion in some lightweight metals.

The technique (also called hard soldering) involves heating metal, then melting a brazing rod into the joint. Like solder, the filler metal flows in and around the joint to form a permanent bond. But solder forms a weak joint while brazing forms a joint often as strong as the metal itself. Consequently, the brazing rod and special flux melt at much higher temperatures, and the pieces being joined must be heated to a glowing red color.

Since brazing can be used to join practically all of the metals commonly found around boats—iron, steel, stainless steel, copper, brass, and aluminum—the ability to do your own brazing can be very useful, particularly in an emergency. With one of these new super-hot torches on board, and after a little practice on scrap metals, you'll be able to repair a leak in a water tank, fix a metal-framed yacht chair or a helm seat, or rebuild a broken rudder arm, stanchion, or metal table base, for a few examples.

Brazing can also be used to fabricate your own customized hardware—shelf supports, instrument mounts, or specialized brackets of unusual design.

Until recently portable propane torches using disposable one-pound metal cylinders did not deliver enough heat for reliable brazing. The theoretical flame temperature was hot enough, but the torch did not deliver a sufficient quantity of heat. Now, however, new versions have been introduced that do a more effective job of heating metal.

These torches have newly designed improved burner heads that force the gases out in a swirling, high-velocity pattern that puts two to three times more heat in the "target" area. Instead of a simple on-off valve these torches have built-in pressure regulators that automatically adjust the flame for maximum efficiency so that on most jobs you can completely braze a small to medium-size joint in about one minute.

In addition to delivering more heat for brazing, the ability of these torches to heat the metal more rapidly also makes them useful for other jobs—for example, freeing a shackle that has seized up. Directing the flame at the body of the shackle will enable you to heat it quickly without also heating up the pin, with the result that the body of the shackle will expand more than the pin and free it.

These torches also have one other big advantage for boatowners: They produce a flame that will not blow out in the wind and will even keep working when used in an upside-down position.

This torch is currently being produced by several companies, and is sold in hardware stores and similar outlets as well as in some marine supply stores. Most have burner heads that project out at right angles to the cylinder in order to make it easier to hold the torch in a more comfortable working position. Some have a burner that also swings vertically in a 360° arc so that you can swivel it to the most effective working angle.

Emergency repairs to virtually any metal fitting can be accomplished with the new portable torches, and special aluminum brazing rods are also available.

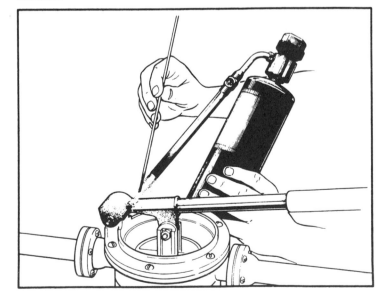

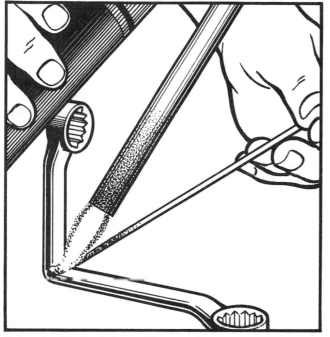

Make a handy wrench for working around corners.

Though designed primarily for use with propane gas cylinders, these torches can also be used with the new MAPP gas cylinders. This gas costs slightly more, but it also gives a slightly hotter flame and thus will enable you to complete jobs faster—or in some cases to handle a job that would be just borderline if you were working with propane. (As a rule, MAPP gas cylinders should not be used with older-style propane torches.)

Brazing Techniques

There are three rules to observe if you want to make a good brazed joint: (1) Make sure the metal parts are hot enough; (2) make certain all surfaces to be joined are absolutely clean, and that parts fit together neatly in a snug fit; (3) use the right type of brazing rod for the metals.

If getting enough heat on the joint becomes a problem because the mass of metal involved is too

great, try surrounding the work with sheets of asbestos. Or, if the piece is small enough, you can lay it on top of a stove or charcoal fire and then preheat it with this before you actually turn the torch on

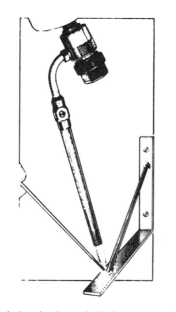

Simple bracket is made by brazing a rod to an angle iron.

(leave the metal on the stove while you work).

Cleaning and preparing the metal is a matter of filing, grinding, sanding, and doing whatever else is necessary to get the metal absolutely clean and bright before you start. Use a file or grinding wheel to make sure pieces fit snugly since brazing is a technique that works best when parts fit well and the molten metal flows into the joint by capillary action.

After cleaning and aligning the parts some method must be found to hold the pieces in position while you work—perhaps by tying them with wire, or by using clamps. To select the right kind of brazing rod consult the literature supplied with the torch. As a rule, bronze-alloy rods are used with iron and steel, although they can also be used with a wide range of other metals. They are available with or without a flux coating on the outside of each rod, but the flux-coated rods are the most popular since they eliminate the need to apply flux.

Nickel silver rods (they don't really have any silver in them) are frequently used on stainless steel and chromium because of their silvery color, but for maximum strength there are also stainless steel rods available, though these are harder to work with.

After lighting the torch, move the flame slowly around the joint until the metal becomes red hot, but keep the brazing rod out of the flame area. If flux has been applied beforehand, the flux will melt and form a clear, glazelike coating when the metal is hot enough. This serves to keep oxides from forming and helps to keep the metal clean so the brazing solder will bond.

When the metal does start to turn red, touch the tip of the brazing rod to the center of the joint, allowing the heat of the metal to melt the rod so that it flows smoothly into the joint. Direct the flame at the thickest or heaviest part of the metal—never directly at the brazing rod. If the rod doesn't melt immediately on contact with the hot metal, remove it and apply more heat before you try again. Wait till the rod melts as soon as it contacts the metal, then allow the molten metal to flow into and around the joint. As soon as it does, withdraw the flame and allow the parts to cool naturally.

Some Thoughts on Toolboxes and Bags

I have long ago stopped using metal toolboxes on board a boat—no matter how well constructed and how well painted, they will eventually rust and leave stains on the deck. Also, they are heavy, and always seem to create scratches and dents on finished surfaces.

Plastic toolboxes and plastic tool bags—the kind that stand vertically and have multiple pockets for smaller tools around the outside—are much more convenient to handle and less likely to cause damage.

However, keeping all tools in one large toolbox is seldom advisable; the box becomes too heavy to carry around easily, and there are bound to be many specialized tools that will be needed only rarely.

A system I have found that works much better is to have at least two toolboxes, or one toolbox and one tool bag. In the smaller tool bag (or box) I keep all of the most-used tools—the ones that are needed on almost every job. I call this my "90-percent tool bag" because the tools it contains will take care of 90 percent of the jobs tackled around the boat. In the larger and heavier toolbox I store the rest of the tools.

Another system that works well is to store all tools in a large chest or drawer, but then keep a small empty toolbox or bag (the bag will stow easier) nearby. That way you pull out only those tools you need—or expect to need—for each job and place them in the empty bag or box so you can carry them to where they are needed.

Strategies for Frozen Fasteners

One thing you can always count on as a boatowner is that you'll have nuts, bolts, and screws that freeze solidly, even when you've just used them. Getting them loose is a whole art, and here are some tricks to simplify your problems, reduce your costs, and soothe your temper.

Let's assume that you've found a frozen bolt. The first, and by far the most important, maxim to remember is that brute force almost always results in a great deal of damage.

If you encounter resistance when attempting to remove a fastener, stop! Don't keep forcing it, don't go for a bigger wrench, don't hit it with a hammer. Thoroughly analyze the problem. After all, you can outthink a piece of metal, can't you?

There are three key questions you need to answer before you proceed further. First, what condition is locking the fastener in place? Second, what materials are the fastener and the fitting? Last, what is the best no-slip way of applying force to the fastener?

Let's look at the first question: conditions. What can you see that might make the fastener stick? For example, a bolt that passes entirely through a threaded fitting and has protruding threads on the far side

With a rounded bolt try inserting a pin for leverage.

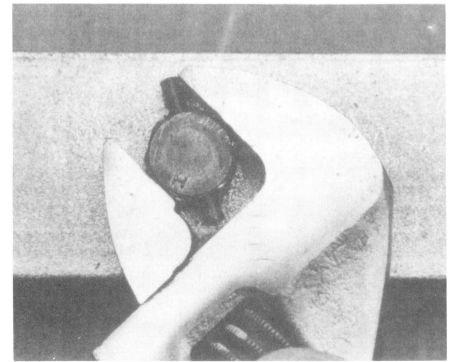

may have corrosion, rust, and gunk in the exposed threads. Clean the exposed threads with a wire brush and use a thread chaser if the threads appear damaged. A final spray with lubricant, and the bolt will probably come right out.

You may also find that there are several different conditions affecting a single fastener. For example, a bolt that has been overly tightened may also have rusted in place. You have to deal with the problems separately. You might find that you can pound out a split or lock washer under the bolthead, which releases the internal loads. The remaining slim gap between bolthead and fitting will enable a rust penetrant to attack the next problem, and you'll soon have the bolt out.

The types of metals involved will also determine the methods you can and can't use to free a frozen fastener. Engine parts are usually made of iron, steel, brass, and occasionally white-metal castings. You may also encounter bronze, stainless steel, aluminum of different grades, and, heaven forbid, pot metal.

A brass bolt threaded into a steel part will respond differently than a steel screw in a brass fitting. While you're considering the problem, make a doomsday estimate and decide which is the most expendable of the frozen parts. Check to see that it actually *can* be replaced before you take the fateful step and sacrifice it. Some bolts may be specially threaded, but generally the fitting is the most expensive part and the one you'll want to save.

The last part of the problem revolves around having (and knowing how to use) the right tools. More damage is caused by adjustable wrenches, vise grips, and worn screwdrivers than by all the rust and corrosion combined.

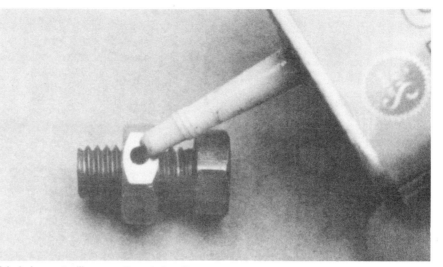
A hole in a nut will expose threads for oiling.

A hacksaw blade slotting tool; note ground notch.

A punch may redefine the points of a damaged bolt.

As a matter of course, you should have good wrenches aboard your boat, and these are invaluable for loosening bolts. The 6-point wrench or socket is far superior to the 12-point since it gives you more surface contact and is less likely to round off the bolthead. The 12-point is fine for removing bolts that are already loose or for tightening new fittings, but nothing else. You should also have box-end wrenches rather than open end, since the open ends sometimes spread slightly under load and round off the head. Don't use cheapie tool sets—they are usually poorly machined and may not be the size claimed.

You should have more than one size and type of screwdriver, in length as well as head size. The screwdriver should just fill the slot in both directions, or you'll tear out the slot under load. Last, a good set of taps and dies is invaluable for cleaning the threads.

Let's assume you've encountered a frozen bolt. The best start is to soak it daily in Liquid Wrench or a similar penetrating oil. Do it for at least a week, if you can, before you take further action. If the bolt is in a level area, build a small dam around the fitting to keep it in constant solution. Check it regularly, and wire brush away any loose rust or corrosion to further aid the oil. Brass screws or bolts may respond better to one of the liquid copper cleaners used to shine pot bottoms, but penetrating oil can't hurt. If a paint buildup seems to be the problem, apply paint remover rather than oil.

After the first soaking, tap the fastener gently with a small hammer to set up vibrations to aid the penetrant. Pick the right tool and try a "gentle test." If you still encounter total resistance, go back to oiling and tapping the fastener. If it turns slightly, add more penetrat-ing oil and work the fastener alternately tighter and looser to spread the oil inward. Don't try to force it past the point where it refreezes. You might try tapping it while you apply pressure. One word of caution about pressure: wrenches are designed at specific lengths to allow normal forces to be applied. Adding a longer handle to a socket, or slipping a pipe over a wrench, will probably break the fastener or deform the wrench.

If the above treatments are unsatisfactory, heat may be a better solution. Use a small propane torch to alternately heat and cool the fastener. The different expansion rates, even among similar metals, may break up some of the corrosion and free the bolt. Obviously, you can't use this method for a fitting on your teak deck or near bottled gas or fuel lines.

Now let's look at that common problem: You applied some pressure, there was a sickening lurch, and the bolt head sheared off.

The best retrieval method now is the screw extractor, a reverse-threaded and tapered rod somewhat like a tap, that bites into a hole you drill inside the broken fastener. As you twist the extractor into place, the reverse threading also unscrews the bolt (you hope). Every screw extractor is made for a specific-size hole. Be sure you use only that size drill bit, and pick the largest size that will still fit inside the broken bolt. Start the hole by marking the center with a punch, and use a very sharp drill bit. A dull bit may wander before biting and you'll have an off-center hole.

If possible, drill completely through the bolt so that you can pour oil into the chamber below it. To insert the extractor, you can either tap it gently into place, or you can thread it in by using a T grip from a tap set. Soft metals are usually not feasible for screw extrac-tors because they will expand and tighten the threads, but there aren't many soft metal bolts these days.

Turn the extractor gently and, with a little luck, you'll retrieve the broken bolt. Treat the extract with care and be sure that you don't bend it sideways since it is very brittle metal.

The court of last resort for a broken bolt is to drill out the fastener and then rethread the opening to accept a larger bolt. You might want to take this problem to a machine shop which can drill the hole precisely.

Dealing with a frozen nut is another ball game. The easiest method is to use a nut-splitting tool, which will neatly cut the nut away from the bolt without damaging the threads. In the absence of a nut splitter, use a good cold chisel carefully. The best method seems to be starting at the top of the nut and driving downward as close to the threads as you can get. If the nut still doesn't split, you can then chisel in from the side to break it away.

If both the bolt and the nut are disposable, you can drill holes through the flats of the nut into the bolt threads to allow penetrating oils to enter the center threads.

By the way, if you have to cut off a bolt, the easiest way to restore the threads is simply to put a stainless steel nut on above the cut. After cutting, back the nut off and it will rethread the damaged areas.

Assuming that someone (not you, of course) has already damaged the head of the fastener before you got to it, you'll have to find a way to keep your tools from slipping under pressure. If the bolthead is only slightly rounded, you can use a center punch in each angle of the hex to redefine the point enough for a 6-point wrench to grip. If the head is badly deformed, the most successful solution is to drill a hole horizontally through the bolt head, insert a steel pin, and use a wrench to remove the bolt. You can also file the sides of the head square rather than hexagonal, but you're removing strength-giving "meat" from the bolt.

If a screw slot is deformed, you can cut a new one by making a slotting tool from an old fine-toothed hacksaw blade. Tape the handle for comfort and grind out a notch so you don't damage the surrounding areas. Be sure you don't cut the new slot too deep and weaken the screw head. This will also work if the screw head has been sheared off. Simply file a slot in the shank of the remaining screw and remove it.

One tool not already mentioned is the impact driver. Resembling a thick screwdriver with interchangeable heads, this tool turns a vertical impact from a hammer blow into several hundred pounds of turning force on a screw or bolt. I'm wary of these tools, since they can shear the fastener head because of the tremendous power available.

Perhaps the best advice to remember when faced with a frozen fastener is to proceed slowly and think out the problem completely before taking action. And don't let rust and corrosion build up in the first place.

Some Thoughts on Useful "Offbeat" Tools

Although most boatowners try to carry a reasonable assortment of tools aboard, almost everyone has run across a job where he finds he is missing one or more tools that he wishes he had on hand. This is inevitable—no one can possibly anticipate every emergency. However, over the years I have found that there are some seldom-thought-of tools and related items that it does pay to include in your tool kit, along with the usual assortment of screwdrivers, wrenches, pliers, etc. Here are just a few that I would suggest:

- **A hand drill that can take up to ¼" bits.** This comes in handy for drilling small pilot holes and similar jobs, particularly when electricity is not available or when you just don't feel like dragging a long extension cord up to the flying bridge to drill one or two pilot holes. Of course, a battery-powered electric drill that comes with a rechargeable power pack would be even better—but these also cost a lot more.

- **A small hand saw of some kind.** This should preferably be the kind that comes with several interchangeable blades so it can be used for cutting wood or metal. Though you may not need this often, it can be indispensable when it is needed—for cutting an improvised wood or metal brace, for cutting tubing or fiberglass, or for fashioning a bracket out of scrap materials when you cannot get to a regular source of supply.

- **At least one or two pairs of locking pliers** (Vise Grips are the best-known brand, but they are not the only ones). These versatile tools can be used as wrenches, clamps, bolt and wire cutters, or pliers. Their powerful grip enables you to grab tiny exposed heads of broken-off screws and bolts, as well as cotter pins and nail heads. They can be used instead of a pipe wrench in many applications and are often the only tools that will grab a rounded-off nut or a slotted screwhead that can't be turned by a screwdriver. Every professional mechanic carries a couple of these in different sizes and styles, and so should every boatowner.

- **A plumber's or electrician's "snake."** Although a length of coat hanger wire will often do the trick, wire coat hangers are not always long enough—and are seldom available on a boat. A "snake" of some kind is essential every time you have to fish a wire or cable through a confined area, such as under floorboards, behind a bulkhead or built-in settee, through an overhead, etc. A "snake" can also save the day when you have to unclog a sea cock or blocked discharge lines that go overboard from the head or galley sink.

- **A small but powerful magnet.** Tied to a length of light nylon or dacron line, or taped to the end of a "snake," a magnet can be a very useful retriever for tools, bolts, and other items that drop down into the bilge where they cannot be reached. Tied to a longer length of line, I have used this same magnet to also retrieve tools dropped overboard in shallow water.

- **A small mirror, preferably the kind that comes attached to the end of a telescoping handle.** This can be indispensable for "seeing around corners" in all the tight spots that every boat seems to have. For example, I recently had to change the impeller on the water pump of my auxiliary generator, but its cover plate was so close to the sound box housing that I could not see the screwheads and had to use an offset screwdriver to remove them. The mirror enabled me to see the screw slots and thus line up the blade. After the cover was off, the mirror made it simple to line up a new impeller so that I could slide it on over the shaft.

- **A pop-rivet gun with an assortment of aluminum rivets and backup washers.** This is probably the quickest and easiest way to fasten small pieces of hardware to a comparatively thin material such as a fiberglass lazarette cover or deck box, an aluminum mast, a hollow railing, a fishing-chair leg, or anything else made of sheet metal, plastic, or plywood. Pop rivets are also great for quickly mending torn canvas or joining sheets of plastic and canvas in an emergency.

- **Some quick-drying (5–10 minutes) epoxy adhesive, preferably in both a putty and a liquid form.** This comes in handy for many emergency repairs—in the engine room, as well as around the inside and outside of the boat. Though you can often get by with a slow-drying epoxy, the fast ones can "save the day" when you don't have time to wait for a slow-drying one to cure.

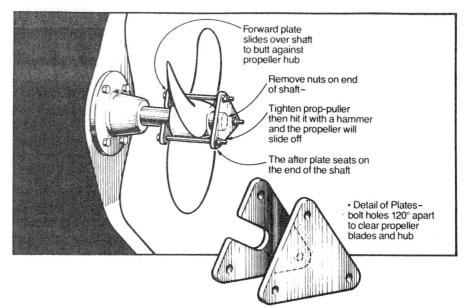

Forward plate slides over shaft to butt against propeller hub

Remove nuts on end of shaft–

Tighten prop-puller then hit it with a hammer and the propeller will slide off

The after plate seats on the end of the shaft

• Detail of Plates– bolt holes 120° apart to clear propeller blades and hub

Propeller puller is simple to make; steps for its installation and use are shown.

Inexpensive Prop Puller

There may come a time when you'll need to pull a propeller off its shaft while the boat is still afloat. This process is not only useful when in the boondocks, but it will save you the cost of a haulout at midseason should your prop become damaged. And this prop puller is simple *and* cheap.

Check out the drawing and note the materials list. Also note that the bolts must be tightened gradually and *evenly* to produce the desired effect. Be especially careful that you keep clear of the prop as the torque on the bolts reaches maximum. Sometimes a prop will be set on the taper so tightly that it will spring suddenly away as it re-leases. The force can damage anything (or anyone) in its way.

To make an inexpensive prop puller for a two- or three-bladed propeller use:

(1) Two pieces of steel plate. For my three-bladed propeller, I found a piece of scrap ⅜" steel and had it cut into two 5" × 5" squares; ¼" steel would have been strong enough. Don't use stainless steel—it's difficult to work.

(2) One ⁵⁄₁₆" threaded steel rod about 2' long. My three-bladed prop puller required three 6" No. 6 bolts and six nuts. Cutting your own bolts is easier than shopping for them.

(3) Hacksaw and blades.

(4) Electric drill and bits.

(5) A pair of wrenches to tighten the nuts.

(6) A diving mask if you plan to remove the prop and shaft underwater.

(7) Two tapered wooden plugs. As soon as you pull the shaft out, plug both holes (inside and outside). Quite a lot of water will pour in, so have the plugs close at hand.

The bolt holes in both steel plates are the only critical measurement. They must line up and they must clear the propeller hub and blades. Clamp the steel plates together, then drill all the holes.

Get the Most from Sandpaper

There are two ways to get the most mileage out of a sheet of sandpaper. The first is for sanding limited areas, and consists of (1) ripping the paper in half and (2) folding each half into thirds. This makes a small-sized pad with no two sandy sides rubbing against one another.

The second method is useful when you want a larger sanding

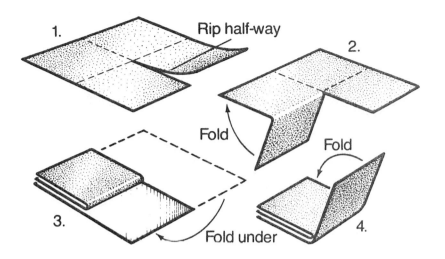

1. Rip half-way
2.
Fold
Fold
3.
Fold under
4.

When sandpaper is cut and folded as shown, there is no wear of surfaces not in actual contact with the work face.

pad. This is best explained in the diagram.

As you can see, you tear the sheet halfway across and then fold the paper into quarters so that none of the sandy sides touch. If they do touch, they'll wear out while you're sanding.

Choosing and Using Fire Extinguishers

Every boatowner hopes he will never need his fire extinguisher, but no one in his right mind would take off on even a short afternoon's cruise without one or more of them on board. In fact, the Coast Guard requires them. The number and size of the extinguishers to be carried varies with the size of the craft, and with the vessel's classification.

Although most boats come equipped with the extinguishers needed to meet Coast Guard requirements, many forget that these requirements merely specify a minimum level of protection. More often than not, most boats would be a lot better equipped to handle

a fire emergency if they had *more* than the minimum number of required fire extinguishers on board.

For example, the typical 2½-pound dry chemical extinguisher will discharge its full load in anywhere from eight to ten seconds—so, for all but the smallest blazes, it wouldn't take long to use up two, three, or even four such extinguishers (if you had that many readily at hand). And this assumes that you use the extinguisher with maximum efficiency so a lot of the

discharge is not wasted (more about this later).

There should be at least one extinguisher in each compartment or stateroom, plus others where they will be quickly and easily accessible in the cockpit, up on the flying bridge, in the engine room, and near the galley stove. These extinguishers should be mounted where they can be quickly spotted in an emergency—by comparative strangers, as well as by you. Don't try to hide them and think that you

Make sure you aim the extinguisher at the base of flames.

will remember where they are when you need them; it's amazing how confused one can become in an emergency.

Also, although the directions for use are clearly printed on the front of each approved extinguisher, make sure that you—and everyone who normally cruises with you— know those instructions by heart,

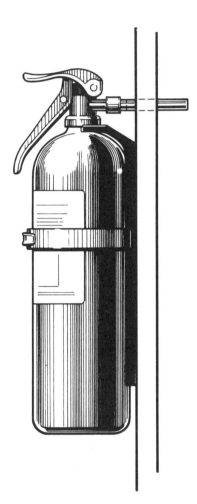

without having to read them at the last minute. That way you won't waste precious seconds studying the label when a fire suddenly breaks out.

Although they should be in the general area, don't mount your extinguishers too close to possible sources of fire if you can avoid it (stove, electrical panel, etc.). The reason is that flames may then keep you from reaching the extinguisher when you need it—another reason for having more than the minimum number required!

Locate an extinguisher reasonably close to a hatch or other exit so that you can reach it as you enter, and when you grab it you will have an escape route behind you so you can back out safely if necessary. You don't want to be way up forward reaching for an extinguisher, with the fire between you and the only safe exit.

Increasing the number of fire extinguishers you carry on your boat, and locating them strategically, are not the only changes worth making. There is another point worth considering: All UL-listed and Coast Guard-approved fire extinguishers are rated as to the size and type fire they are capable of extinguishing. This rating is clearly marked on the label of the unit with a group of numbers and letters. The letters refer to the type of fire that the extinguisher can control; the numbers to the size of the fire it can put out.

The extinguisher will be marked with one of three letters to indicate the type of fire it can control—A, B, or C. Each letter is usually enclosed in a block of a different shape—a triangle, a square, or a circle.

Class A fires are those that involve common "household" combustibles, such as wood, paper, fabric, and most plastics. Class B fires are those that involve gasoline, grease, oil, fats, paints, and most flammable solvents. Class C fires are those that involve live electrical equipment or wiring— that is, wiring that has current flowing through it (when the current is shut off, then the Class C fire becomes a Class B or Class A fire).

Most of the extinguishers sold for use on pleasure boats carry the B:C classification because this is what the Coast Guard requires. Yet many of today's boats are used for cruising and thus have comfortable living areas with carpet, upholstered settees and chairs, curtains, and wood paneling. These areas also contain many highly inflammable items made of paper, fabric, or plastic—combustibles that could fuel a Class A fire. A B:C extinguisher would be quite inefficient on this type of fire.

Actually, water is one of the best extinguishing agents for Class A fires, and there is obviously plenty of water available around a boat. But how many boats are equipped with a properly rigged bucket and line instantly accessible for throwing over the side and hauling up water? And when a Class A fire does break out, how many people are going to remember to look for a bucket and water before reaching for a more readily accessible fire extinguisher that is mounted right in the same area?

That is why it makes good sense to have at least one or two ex-

Bulkhead mounting, above, works with carbon dioxide and halon extinguishers as well as dry chemical-type. The letters printed on extinguishers, below, indicate the types of fires on which they can be used.

tinguishers in areas where Class A fires are liable to occur that are rated as being suitable for all three classifications of fire—A, B, and C. These can be used effectively on all fires.

The size of the extinguishers on board is another factor that most people pay little or no attention to—until a fire actually breaks out. As mentioned previously, approved extinguishers carry numbers in addition to letters. For example, the most popular (and most inexpensive) models sold for marine use are rated as 5-B:C. The 5 refers to the size fire it will extinguish; yet for just a few dollars more you can buy one rated at 10-B:C.

This size will put out a fire twice as big as the 5-B:C, so it is actually equal to two of the smaller units. Going still further, an extinguisher rated at 20-B:C will be capable of handling a fire that would require *four* of the 5-B:C units. There is a limit, of course, to the size you want, since the larger the unit, the heavier it will be—and you don't want one too heavy for easy handling.

Knowing how to use your extinguishers effectively is just as important as having enough of the right size and type on hand. Dry chemical extinguishers are only effective when directed at the base of the flame—in other words, aimed at the combustible materials that are feeding the fire. Stand at least a few feet away from the fire, but don't stay any farther away than you have to for safety, since the closer you are the more concentrated the stream of chemicals will be. Aim directly at the base of the flames and spray with a back-and-forth sweeping motion, but try to avoid wasting the spray. At best it won't last more than about 10 seconds.

Remember, dry chemical extinguishers are not of much use in simply flooding a compartment or space with fumes in an effort to smother a fire. They must be aimed directly at the base of the fire in order to be really effective. The CO_2 (carbon dioxide) extinguishers, which are not often seen on pleasure boats these days, and the newer Halon type extinguishers are the only ones that can be used for "flooding" an enclosed compartment to put out the flames—not the dry chemical types found on most boats. (Halon is the type used on most engine compartment extinguishing systems and on all of the automatic systems that flood an engine compartment to put out flames without someone having to actually go down into the compartment).

When using an extinguisher you should not only aim low, you should also keep yourself low if possible. Smoke and heat rise, so the air near the floor is always coolest and contains the least amount of harmful fumes. As you fight the fire, make sure you keep yourself between it and a safe escape route so you can save yourself if the fire does get out of control.

And finally, if you use water, remember: Never pour water on a grease fire or on electrical equipment that still has current flowing through it.

Fire Extinguisher Tips

Even though you regularly check the pressure indicator on each dry chemical fire extinguisher to make certain it is full, there is one other step you should take to make certain the extinguisher will work at peak efficiency when and if it is needed. Take each one off its mount and shake it vigorously at frequent intervals. This keeps the powder from caking up at the bottom so it will be dispensed more easily and more uniformly.

Another safety measure is to keep a jar full of baking soda near the galley stove at all times. The jar should be tightly capped to keep air out. It will be handy for putting out small grease fires and other flare-ups on the stove without having to use up the contents of your regular fire extinguishers. Just take off the cap and sprinkle the contents over the fire. Your regular fire extinguisher will still be available in case a larger fire breaks out.

6 ANNUAL LAYING UP AND FITTING OUT

Spring Checklist for a Trouble-Free Boating Season

Unlike fall lay-up, which is often tackled with some reluctance because it signifies the end of the boating season and the coming of cold, wet weather, most boat-owners look forward to spring commissioning with its promise of a new boating season. In their haste to get started on the new season, however, many boatowners tend to skip some routine maintenance chores that should be taken care of before leaving the dock—including those that should have been taken care of in the fall. ("We'll have plenty of time to take care of that next spring," or, "Maybe we'll come out and tackle that one weekend during the winter.")

To help you avoid such mistakes, and to keep you from overlooking all those small but important details that will make the coming season's boating a safer and more pleasant experience, here is a handy checklist for setting up a spring commissioning schedule for your boat. All outside jobs are listed first because I have found

that this is the best way to start. Do what you can when the weather cooperates, and leave the inside jobs for rainy days when you can't work outside.

Here is the first list—the "Outdoor List":

- Come down about a week before you intend to actually take the cover off and make sure there are no pockets of snow or water still trapped in the folds. If there are, arrange the canvas so it drains and will be dry when you are ready to fold it up for the summer. Look for tears and rips and repair them *now*—next fall you will have forgotten about them and the same tears will remain.
- If you have built your own winter frame, or fashioned one of bent tubing, mark each piece with tape or a crayon as you take the frame apart. That way you will save time when reassembling the frame.
- On the first dry day after the cover comes off, open all windows, ports, and hatches in the boat to air out the inside thoroughly.
- Wash the boat as soon as possible so you can see what cosmetic re-

pairs are needed. If there are bare spots on any of the painted or varnished wood, touch up those spots now—don't wait until you have time to do a complete paint or varnish job. An immediate touch-up will keep out water and help prevent rotting or further peeling and flaking.
- After washing, inspect the entire exterior for chips or scratches in the fiberglass or gel coat. If you can, repair these yourself (kits are sold for this purpose in most marine supply stores). If you don't feel confident about doing the work yourself, get the yard to do it as soon as possible. Gel-coat defects allow water to be absorbed by the fiberglass and may cause blistering or delaminating in some situations.
- Give all the fiberglass a good coat of boat wax. Contrary to popular belief, automobile wax is *not* just as good—it's not as effective in resisting salt water, and it won't seal the gel coat as thoroughly. Don't use an abrasive cleaner first unless it is really required; abrasive cleaners remove some gel coat each time, so using them too often may lead to complete erosion of the gel coat.

- Before the boat is launched, check the protective zincs on your shafts, struts, trim tabs, and rudders. If your boat has a master bonding system, check the large zincs to see if they need replacing. New ones are advisable if the old ones are more than one-third eroded.
- On sailboats that have aluminum spars, scrub each spar clean, then apply a good coat of marine wax. Naturally, this is a lot easier to do before the mast has been stepped and the boom attached.
- Aluminum window frames, door frames, hatch frames, and similar metal trim should be scrubbed clean and given a coat of wax to protect against oxidation and pitting—even if the metal was originally anodized.
- Uncoil and inspect all lines to see if any are showing signs of severe chafing, mildewing, or other indications of wear. Dock lines may need to be turned end for end, even if this means splicing another loop at the other end, in order to distribute the wear. The same holds true for anchor lines, particularly if you frequently anchor in the same spot so that you use about the same amount of anchor line each time. Inspect shackles, chains, and other parts of the ground tackle to see if anything needs replacing due to corrosion or severe wear.
- Inspect fastenings on all deck hardware, with special attention to handholds, ladder brackets, steps, stanchions, lifelines, and railings. This is mostly safety equipment that can cause serious injury if it lets go under stress, so inspect fasteners carefully and tighten those that are loose. On sailboats make sure that all turnbuckles and other parts of the rigging are still sound, and look carefully for missing or loose cotter pins that need replacing.

Spray each piece of hardware with a penetrating rust-preventive lubricant such as WD-40, LPS-1, or CRC, then wipe lightly with a rag.
- Turn on all outside lights, including the cockpit lights, running lights, and anchor light, to see if any of the bulbs need replacing. If replacing a bulb doesn't solve the problem, check the socket to see if it's badly corroded due to water on the inside. When replacing bulbs, first spray the inside of the socket with a moisture-displacing lubricant.

Here's the second list—the "Indoor (or Rainy Day) List":

- Before the boat is launched (assuming you stored it on land) scrub out the bilge and engine room areas. You can pull the drain plug and let the oily water run into an empty drum or large garbage can without worrying about pumping oily water overboard later on (illegal in U.S. waters).

- Open all cabinets and drawers to let them air out. Dust and wipe clean before you start bringing new provisions and supplies aboard, and look for signs of mildew. If you see any, spray with one of the various mildewcides that are sold for this purpose. Lining the bottom of each cabinet with a "waffle" texture or grid-pattern plastic will help ward off such problems during the summer by allowing air to circulate more freely.
- If you have used one of those nontoxic antifreeze solutions in your freshwater system, flush this out as soon as you have running water available. You may have to fill the tanks and then empty them more than once to get all the taste out, so do this as soon as possible. If a taste persists, add about half a cup of baking soda to the tank, run some out of each faucet or fixture (to make sure the solution is in the pipes), then let it stand in the system overnight. Flush out with plenty of fresh water the next day.

Replace burned-out bulbs.

Scrub out storage bins.

- Recommission the head or toilet by draining the antifreeze in it (if used); then use the manufacturer's repair kit to give it a "spring tuneup." This will include replacing such parts as the joker valve or flapper valve, as well as all the gaskets, seals, and impellers that are included in the kit.
- Disconnect the discharge hose coming from the toilet and look through the sea cock in the hull to make sure it is clear. Flush out the hoses with dockside water (under pressure) and inspect the insides to make sure the hoses are not partially clogged or heavily lined on the inside with a salt and chemical buildup (common in many saltwater areas). If in doubt, replace the hose now, rather than waiting till you have trouble in the middle of the season.
- Open and close every through-hull sea cock to make sure each one works freely—preferably before the boat is launched. Lubri-

cate those that are stiff, and replace those that seem "iffy." Replacing ordinary globe valves or gate valves with regular sea cocks is also a good idea at this time.
- Crawl through the boat and inspect all parts of the steering gear—linkage, chains, cables, etc. Tighten all setscrews and mounting-bracket hardware, and replace anything that looks doubtful. Make sure all moving parts are properly lubricated, and spray chains and cables with a moisture-displacing lubricant, preferably one that contains Teflon.
- Lubricate the throttle and clutch controls, including the control cables that are connected to them. Also lubricate the linkages at the engine where the cables are connected to the control fittings.
- Use a hydrometer to check the condition of each storage battery so you can see if any need charging—then see if it takes a full charge (otherwise it may need re-

placing). Clean off the terminals on each battery by washing with a mild solution of baking soda (don't let this get inside the cells) and make sure the terminals are on tightly. Then spray the connection with a heavy-duty corrosion preventive, or coat with waterproof grease.
- Take out your dockside electrical cord and inspect the insulation along its full length to see if it is cut or damaged. If so, wrap with several layers of tape. Check the plugs at each end to see if they are badly corroded or burnt looking. If corroded, clean with fine steel wool; if burnt looking, replace the entire plug.
- Turn on all the electrical and electronic accessories and equipment to make sure each piece is working properly. It is a lot less aggravating to find this out now, while you still have time to buy spares or send the unit out for repairs, rather than waiting till you are out on the water.
- Take a couple of hours to go over your whole stock of spare parts and emergency supplies so you can replace items that were used up (or never included) last year. This would include such items as extra water-pump impellers; gaskets for engines, generators, toilets, etc.; fan belts, hose clamps, hoses in all the sizes used in the boat, caulking compounds, spark plugs, fuses, and batteries (for flashlights, radios, etc.). Careful attention to the details on this list will pay off in the season ahead.

Protect That Seal

I own a 20′ boat powered by an OMC stern-drive that has a large rubber transom seal. This seal is susceptible to aging and attack by the elements—as well as rodents when the boat is in winter storage.

The best preventative measure I've come up with is to simply spread a liberal coat of petroleum jelly or water-pump grease over the entire seal. This not only helps to keep it from drying out and cracking, it also repels rodents during the storage period.

You will probably find it necessary to renew the coating of grease at least twice during the boating season, as well as again just before the boat is stored in the fall. Just be sure you use only a water-pump grease or petroleum jelly—other types of grease may attack the rubber and do more harm than good.

Pointers on Commissioning Marine Engines

Most of the problems that develop with marine engines—in both powerboat and auxiliaries—are due to a lack of regular preventive maintenance, especially during and right after the lay-up period.

Like most mechanical pieces of equipment, an engine often takes more of a beating when it sits idle for months than it does when it is in constant daily or weekly use. Long periods of inactivity in a cold and often damp environment tend to encourage the formation of rust on unprotected metal surfaces, as well as condensation and pitting of electrical terminals and contact points; "seizing" of water pumps, valves, and other infrequently moved parts; and loosening of bolts, nuts, hose clamps, and other fasteners due to alternate expansion and contraction of metal parts, or shrinking and drying out of hoses and flexible mounts.

That is why it is especially important that you take time out dur-

ing the commissioning period to give your power plant and its associated mechanical and electrical components some much-needed attention.

Here are some of the important points that should be checked. Use the principles they imply on all your boat's running gear.

☐ Clean coil casing and high-tension lead, as well as contact points. Inspect all cables for fraying or deterioration.
☐ To insure full starting power, disconnect starter cables and clean terminal ends and bolts. Retighten securely.
☐ Clean and adjust points on distributor, or replace if needed. Then spray with moisture-displacing penetrating lubricant.
☐ Fuel filters should be changed at the beginning of each season, just to play safe. While doing this, replace gaskets and seals.
☐ Test engine mounts with wrench to see if they are tight, and inspect rubber to see if it is badly deteriorated. If so, replace.
☐ Pay particular attention to fuel-line connections. Test for "weeping" around unions with dry paper towel after engine is run.
☐ Run engine at fast idle until warm. Open heat-exchanger cap and look for turbulence. Air bubbles could mean blown head gasket.
☐ Remove air cleaners and clean as recommended. Replace oil if yours is the oil-bath type. Make sure you tighten securely.
☐ Check stuffing boxes or packing glands to see if they need repacking. Some also hold grease that may need replenishing.
☐ Tighten every hose clamp you can find, especially those going to fuel tank. Replace clamps that are corroded or damaged.
☐ Don't forget mounting bolts

around valve covers. Look for signs of oil seepage; it could mean you need a new gasket here.
☐ Check bolts with wrench to see if any are loose. Be careful about overtightening flange-mounting bolts to avoid distortion.

Propulsion

☐ Remove battery cables to clean terminals and cable ends thoroughly. After replacing, tighten firmly, then coat with Vaseline.
☐ Don't forget to inspect all parts of steering system; linkages, cables, chain, pulleys, and mounts.
☐ To insure against water-pump failure during the season, remove end plate to check impeller.
☐ Inspect all belts to alternators, pumps, etc. Replace any that show wear and adjust tension to each.
☐ See if the terminals on all cables—for clutch, throttle, etc.—work easily. Lubricate points on each.

The A to Z Spring Checkup for Diesels

—by Ed Dennis

There are a lot of easy ways to put new life into your old puffin' chunk of iron without resorting to an expensive overhaul. A spring checkup (in capsule form) is one of them.

Most pleasure boat owners tend to shy away from diesel engines, which is downright foolish. Unless you have five thumbs, you will find that with the help of your service manual and some good common sense, there are a lot of jobs you can do just as well as any $30-an-hour diesel mechanic.

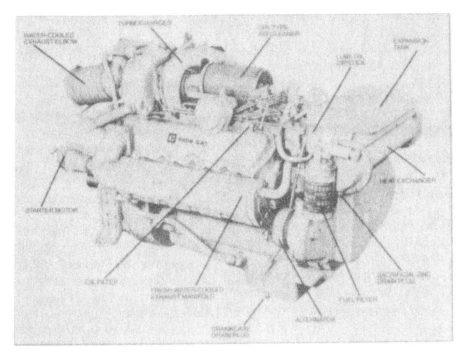

Major components of a typical diesel are indicated on the Caterpillar 3208T model.

Let's begin with your engine's service manual, a few basic tools, and some cold beer or 7-Up, as it usually gets hot below in the engine compartment.

Any maintenance should always start with ventilation. Open wide the engine and fuel compartment hatch covers for plenty of fresh air, light, and elbow room.

If you have shore current, hook up a couple of fans to keep you cool. Remember, NO SMOKING and NO OPEN FLAME.

With a flashlight or drop light, visually inspect your diesel and its components for any signs of leaks in your engine's salt- or freshwater, lube or fuel oil, or exhaust systems. Be sharp-eyed and critical. Take your time and have a good close look around. Then make a simple work plan. Pay attention to the basics first.

Quickly give all clevis pins, linkages, sea cocks, and valves a good shot of a marine lubricant like WD-40 to be sure they are working freely. Clutch and throttle controls can be inspected by sight and feel. For ease of operation, better give them a shot of lubricant too.

Air Filter

A diesel that acts like an asthmatic and runs like one should also have starting problems. So, it's best to clean or change your air-intake filter.

Fuel System

The two bugs your diesel hates most are air and water in its fuel system. So change all fuel filters and clean all strainers and water separators, then refill them with clean oil before installing them. Next, visually inspect and make sure all fuel lines and their connections are tight, not corroding or chafing. If you should have a sudden circulatory stoppage, then burp the system of air.

Any work on your injectors or pumps should be done by an authorized service dealer.

Cooling Systems

Inspect your engine overall for any signs of deterioration at connections and gaskets in both water systems.

While you are at it, check and make sure the seawater scoop and inlet strainers are clean and all intake valves are in good working order. Work them back and forth while you are spraying them with a good marine lubricant.

Then, close the inlet water valves (sea cocks) and remove the end plate on the raw-water pump and check the impeller blades. If in doubt, replace it. Then check and feel your rubber hoses and clamps to see if they are mushy or rusty; if so, replace them immediately.

Fresh Water

Today's freshwater (coolant) enclosed cooling systems usually don't give much trouble, provided they are looked at every so often. Change the antifreeze and rust inhibitor if it has been in more than a year. Old inhibitors lose their effectiveness after a year or so.

Remove all the zinc plugs in and around the heat exchanger; if they have deteriorated by 50 percent or more replace them.

Now, open up your raw-water inlet valve and inspect the system for any leaks.

Belts and Plugs

Examine all belts for cracks, wear, and lack of tension, then check the pulleys for wear and looseness.

Electrical System

Pleasure boat engines and their electrical accessories are subject to a lot of dampness and temperature variations. Look for broken, cracked, frayed, or corroded wires. If you find any, replace them one at a time. Clean and tighten all hold-down connections, then spray all with a lubricant.

Clean your alternator and starter by blowing them out with a low-pressure air gun. Fill all oil caps and wicks with a couple of drops of #10 lube oil.

Check the electrolyte level in your batteries. It should be about 3/8" above the cells; refill with *distilled* water only. Use caution since explosive gases are formed by chemical action in the cells, and an explosion could occur in a flash.

Turbos

- Turbochargers that have not been run for a long period of time require lubrication before starting. Remove the lube oil inlet line nut and pour a few ounces of oil into the open fitting

at the top of the turbo's center housing.
- Turn the rotating wheels by hand to coat the bearing surfaces with lubricant. Then reconnect the line and check the turbocharger's air tube and connections for leaks.

Safety Devices

Check and make sure your fuel electricity shutoff solenoid is working. If you have a GM, it will pay to see if the emergency flapper on the blower air intake is working properly.

Also check your engine mounts for any loose, broken, or worn rubbers or a cracked steel bolt or nut.

Lube Oil

Lubricating oil is the lifeblood of your diesel—don't cheat on it. Buy what the engine manufacturer recommends. The use of cheap lube oil or "just as good" filters might result in shorter engine life.

Never change your lube oil when your diesel is cold—bring it up to operating temperature, then drain it while it is warm and while the sludge, acids, and dirt are still suspended in the old oil.

Remember, always change the filters too. And if your engine has an oil strainer, clean it! If possible, fill both with clean lube oil before you install them.

Disconnect the lube oil inlet line at the turbocharger and pour in an ounce or two of regular lube oil. Then turn the rotating blade to prelube the bearings.

If some of your problems become too technical, it would be wise to check with your local diesel engine dealer.

Finally, run your diesel for ten to fifteen minutes at slightly above idle speed. Then with a flashlight, cautiously look for leaks and listen for any foreign noises.

Starting

- Crank your diesel over several revolutions with the governor in "no fuel" position to lubricate the engine's interior moving parts. After a half-dozen or so revolutions, turn the fuel on.
- As the engine attempts to start, it will cough, spit, and run unevenly for a few minutes until all the injectors receive fresh, clean fuel. Continue to run it at high idle for ten to fifteen minutes. While it is still running, double back and make sure there are no leaks and all pressures and temperatures are correct.
- Finish by wiping down your entire propulsion unit when it cools, and touch up any bare or rusty spots.
- Remember, fuel-injection pumps and injectors are precision built, so leave them to the pros.

Taking an Outboard out of Mothballs

—by Tim Banse

Like everything else mechanical, outboard engines live longer with a regular inspection and maintenance program. As the winter chill fades with each passing day, eager boatsmen are thinking about pulling their rigs out of mothballs and putting spring commissioning plans into action. The following checklist provides a step-by-step guide to preparing an outboard for a new season:

- Experienced marine mechanics begin their spring cleaning with an inspection of the lower unit, but only after having first opened the hood and removed the hi-tension leads from the spark plugs. These remain disconnected until just prior to the test run to prevent an unscheduled start.

Removing spark plug leads to avoid accidental startups is the first step in outboard work.

electric-shift models have special requirements because some straight hypoid gear oils destroy the shift coil wires' insulation.
• Lube the grease fittings with marine-grade grease. Old, dry grease causes wear; new grease expels moisture. If the fittings refuse to accept grease, remove them and soak them in solvent. Replace as necessary.
• Paint bare metal on the prop and lower unit housing to protect from corrosion. Broken skeg tips and bent anticavitation plates are best left alone. Heli-arc welding is a prohibitively expensive repair job, and the process often warps the gearcase. Check water intake and discharge ports for obstructions.
• The sacrificial zincs should be replaced before they have corroded away to less than half their original size. Regardless of whether or not the zinc needs replacing, remove it and make sure there is good metal-to-metal contact between the zinc and its housing surface. Before replacing, coat the bolt's threads with anticorrosion lubricant. Likewise, coat the propellor shaft with anticorrosion lubricant and reinstall the prop.
• At the powerhead, make a thorough visual inspection for loose, missing, or damaged parts. Dangling hood rubbers can be glued back in place with a tube of weatherstrip compound. Be careful when snugging up loose bolts; the aluminum threads strip easily if overtightened. Double-check the hold-down clamps that secure the motor to the transom. More than one boatsman has been horrified when he hit the throttle and the motor hopped off into the deep six.
• If the top of the battery case is dirty, clean with an ammonia-and-water or a baking-soda-and-water solution; but don't let the solution find its way into the cells. Top off

• Remove the prop nut and slide the propeller off the shaft. Examine the prop's shock absorber bushing for cracks and slippage. The bushing protects the lower unit from the smashing impact of underwater obstructions. The hub is sacrificed in lieu of the more expensive gear and shafts. If any of the blades are bent, try hammering them back into shape and filing smooth any jagged edges, or invest in a new wheel. It is imperative to keep a wheel true; otherwise the irregular blade surface sets up drivetrain vibration, causing shafts to crack and break.
• Check the edge of the prop shaft seal, where the shaft lies against the rubber lips. Fish line often gets picked up by the prop, curls onto the shaft, and cuts the seal. The resulting gear-oil leakage can ruin gears, bearings, and shafts. If there is a wad of fishline wrapped around the seal, have a repair shop pressure check the lower unit for leaks.
• Drain the old gear oil if it wasn't replaced during lay-up. Gear oil should be replaced before winter storage because water in the oil can freeze and crack the housings; in warm-weather areas the gears and bearings can rust. As the old oil drains, examine it for water, broken bits of gear teeth, and traces of the copper bushings. Refill with the manufacturer's specified lubricant;

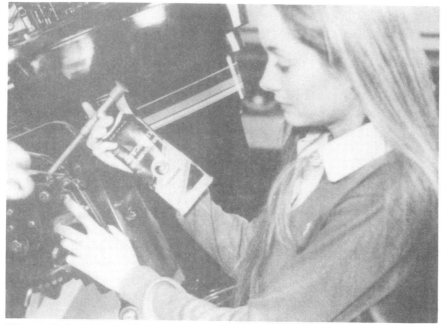

When in doubt, lubricate. Moving parts on brackets, tilt assemblies and steering systems require periodic greasing.

low cells with distilled water to avoid contaminating the plates with mineral impurities. Then bring the battery up to charge.

• Dirty electrical connections, whether on batteries or fuse blocks, resist the flow of voltage. To prevent bad connections, choose a penetrating/moisture-displacing lubricant. Read the back of the spray can to determine whether it will dry moist electrical systems and reduce corrosion. Spray terminal blocks, fuse panels, and switches, examining them for loose connections and corrosion. To prevent instrument panel lights from corroding in their sockets, give them a squirt as well.

• Examine the hydraulic lift, trim, power steering and trim tab's oil reservoirs for proper level. Check all fittings for tight connections.

• How old is the gasoline in the tank? If it was not treated with fuel stabilizer and sat in the tank for more than two or three months, drain the old gas and flush the tank with fresh fuel. Old gas will plug up carburetor jets with gum and varnish.

• Examine fuel lines and hoses for breaks and cracks. Inspect the "O-rings" on each hose connector for cuts. Does the primer bulb work freely? Replacements are readily available at most marinas. Remove the sediment bulb and clean it with fresh gasoline or acetone. Replace the filter; coat the new gasket with a light coat of engine oil to aid sealing. Lubricate throttle and spark advance linkage.

• When the engine was winterized, the cylinders should have been fogged with antirust oil. For an easier first start, pull the plugs and crank the engine to blow out the oil vapors.

• Replace spark plugs in complete sets, following the manufacturer's recommendation for heat range and combustion chamber reach.

• Outboards often used for trolling tend to carbon up, and both Mercury and Evinrude in spray cans offer a remedy. Their internal engine cleaners remove carbon deposits and restore a smooth idle. For best results, warm up the engine, and at a fast idle, poke the plastic nozzle down the throat of the carburetor to wash the throttle plate with spray. After a few seconds, the motor will begin to bog down. Keep squirting engine cleaner until the motor dies. Walk away from it for about half an hour to enable the chemicals to loosen the carbon. Restarting may require pulling the plugs and drying.

• Older, more heavily carboned engines may require removal of the exhaust port cover and scraping the area clean. When replacing covers, clean both machined surfaces and use a fresh gasket.

• Check the spark by holding one of the leads about a ¼" away from the cylinder head. Crank the engine: An orange spark signals a weak ignition, while blue is healthy. A weak spark usually indicates faulty points, either worn out or burned because of an oil mist leaking past the upper crankcase seal. Replacement of the seal requires special tools and is a task best left to a marine specialist.

• Climb inside the boat and give the remote-control box the once-over. Run the throttle up and down to make sure there is no binding. Shifting into forward and reverse should lock up the prop tight. While in neutral, it should free-wheel. Shift and throttle cables should be replaced if they bind or have cracked outer casings. To determine their proper length, measure from the control box to the stern, then across the transom to the motor connector. Add 3' to that length to form a loop in order to prevent binding when the motor is

wheeled from port to starboard.
- Check the steering. Turn the wheel hard to port, then to starboard. It should traverse freely. With a cable-and-pulley system, check for frayed cable; also make sure the pulleys and anchors are secure.
- The test run is next. To make things easy for the do-it-yourselfer, manufacturers offer flushing devices that attach to a garden hose and allow you to test run your motor far away from a body of water. Turn on the faucet and crank the engine. If you have good spark, and the engine won't start, squirt a shot of ether into the carb. If the engine starts up, then dies, something is amiss in the fuel system. If fuel is getting to the carburetor, but the engine won't start and run without the ether, stale gasoline has probably gummed up the idle passages and jets and the carburetor needs work. Consult a marine mechanic.
- If the engine starts, run it at idle to warm it up before making any adjustments. In the meantime, check the water-pump discharge, if applicable on your model. Another way to check the cooling system is to lay your hand on the cylinder head, avoiding the high tension leads. The head should be hot but not scorch your hand. You should almost be able to lay your hand on it. However, if it is as hot as a griddle, sizzling droplets of water, *immediately* shut down the engine.
- Remove the thermostat. It is usually located on the top of the cylinder head, in line with the powerheads and in the valley of V-4s and V-6s. With the thermostat out of its housing, start the engine briefly. The engine should shoot a stream of water into the air. If it doesn't, then it is likely the water pump impeller

blades are broken off or have taken an inflexible set. Also, salt water can clog up cooling passages.
- Once the engine is at operating temperature, idle can be adjusted by turning the needle-valve clockwise until the engine begins to backfire. When it backfires, turn the needle counterclockwise ½ to ¾ of a turn, depending on the manufacturer's specification. For multiple carburetor applications, do each carburetor in turn, repeating the process a couple of times to insure all carburetors are in synchronization.
- The carburetor adjustment completes this stem-to-stern checklist—now isn't it about time to launch the boat and enjoy?

Rod Stephens's Pre-Float Checklist for Sailboats

Ever since the yawl *Dorade* won a trans-Atlantic race in 1932 the name of Rod Stephens has been synonymous with "sailor," as Sparkman and Stephens has meant "naval architects." Rod Stephens's uncanny eye inspects boats under construction, boats before races, and boats just passing. He has learned what might go wrong and what should be right *before* going to sea. He has a special clarity in the way he points out the details of these matters. Following is his personal pre-float checklist for sailboats. Half a century of experience, as a professional naval architect and an amateur who loves sailing, is the basis for this working set of instructions, applicable to almost any size or type of sailing craft.

Hull

☐ Paint in good condition, even behind cradle supports.

☐ Folding or feathering prop free and lubricated. Securely attached to shaft.

☐ Speedometer transducer correctly aligned.

☐ Centerboard (if applicable) clean, smooth, operating freely. Red marks on pennant at full-up and full-down positions. Green marks: one for ¼, two for ½, three for ¾-down positions.

☐ Rudder turns freely but with no lost motion between blade and rudder stock.

Deck

☐ Nonskid surface in good condition.

☐ Winches lubricated. Spare springs, pawls, and necessary tools on board. Winch handle holders installed where needed.

☐ Compass aligned (with *no* internal correctors on sailboats).

☐ Elkhide on wheel rim. King spoke clearly marked. Quadrant with precise mark indicating when rudder is exactly straight. (To facilitate precise in-water adjustment of king spoke. If tiller, it should be precisely aligned with rudder.)

☐ Life-raft inspection certificate obtained. Raft securely stowed but easily available.

☐ Life rings and man-overboard markers in place. Water lights working.

☐ Storm covers aboard for all hatches forward of the cockpit.

☐ Genoa sheet tracks numbered on every fifth location hole. (A waterproof marking pen can be used.)

☐ All chocks (dinghy, spinnaker poles, boat hook, reaching strut, anchor), secure.

☐ Life lines set tight. Bow and stern pulpits and stanchions secure. Toggles (*not* nylon ones) on all end attachments.

☐ Emergency boarding (at stern) provided—or a swimming ladder.

☐ Fenders, fender boards, and four dock lines stowed.

Cabin

☐ Sea cocks lubricated with water-pump grease. Marked for purpose and for "open" and "closed" positions.

☐ Bilge cleaned. Limber holes clear. Internal ballast clean and secure.

☐ Bilge pumps tested. Intake screens clean. Spares for pumps on board. Floor boards not too tight (a 10° under-bevel is a good idea).

☐ All doors and drawers free. Latches working.

☐ Stove valves marked for ON and OFF positions. Flexible feed line in good condition. Stove holds pressure (if applicable) and has insulation over it on the under deck.

☐ Water tanks clean and supply pumps working. High-grade check valves installed in lowest part of supply lines leading to pumps.

Mechanical/Electrical

☐ Emergency tiller stowed with tools for installation. Spare chain and cable assembly on board.

☐ Tools clean and lubricated.

☐ Propeller shaft has double matching marks showing fixed or feathered propeller vertical, or folding propeller horizontal. Simple and effective shaft lock available (spare pins if sheer-pin type).

☐ Oil level in gear box okay.

☐ Pot drained (if water-lock exhaust).

☐ Shaft moves freely, without excess bearing clearance.

☐ Batteries clean, filled to the right level with distilled water, fully charged, and well-secured.

☐ Lightning grounding properly installed, from metal spar and from top shrouds and stays to ground plate (if ballast internal) or ballast keel bolt (if ballast external).

Rigging (Mast Unstepped)

☐ Turnbuckles lubricated with anhydrous lanolin. Right-hand thread down. Equipped with toggles; spares on board.

☐ All rigging pins lubricated. Cotter pins correct length, rounded.

☐ No longitudinal cracks in wire terminals.

☐ Mast straight. Track joints fair and aligned. Adjacent ends at each joint beveled on all sides to prevent "hang ups." Track greased with white Vaseline.

☐ All sail slides fair and rounded. (It should not be necessary to head into the wind in order to get the sail up if the corners of the slides are well-rounded to move freely in the track.)

☐ Hanks and shackles lubricated.

☐ Spreader attachment secure. Spreader tips checked for secure wire attachment under any tape and padding.

☐ Blocks and sheaves lubricated.

☐ Battens clearly marked. Spares carried for each one.

☐ Any sharp edges eliminated. (This holds true for everything on the boat.)

☐ If there are reel winches (not recommended), wire attached securely. No excess wire.

☐ On board: bosun's chair, bag of small lines, sail stops, sail covers, repair tape, waxed synthetic sail twine, good assortment of spare shackles and rigging pins.

☐ Sail bags clearly marked. (And sails should be clean and checked by launch time.)

☐ Mast wedges and (tight) mast coat at hand.

☐ Mast wiring and related electronic equipment tested.

Rigging (With Mast Stepped)

☐ Shroud rollers and turnbuckle boots installed.

☐ Windex and other masthead wind direction indicators aligned. Precise matching marks on aft centerline-fixed part of wind guide, and marks for 0°, 30° left and right, 90° left and right, 180° on rotating skirt.

☐ Clear leads on all internal lines—mast and boom. Replacement gear on board.

☐ All standing rigging clean.

☐ Bitter end eyes for external halyards. Knots in ends of all the halyards.

☐ Limit bands painted on mast and boom (optional except for racing boats).

☐ Main halyard marked at top of winch drum to show position when top of headboard is at underside of black band (at 150-pound tension, equivalent to light-air sailing conditions).

☐ Jib halyards similarly marked (tension as above) at point beyond which further hoisting would damage halyard splices and/or mast sheave boxes.

☐ Cotter pins not spread more than 20°.

Tuning Your Mast at Commissioning Time

It seems that mast tuning has acquired the same false metaphysical connotation as celestial navigation, when in fact the process is quite simple. It requires perseverance

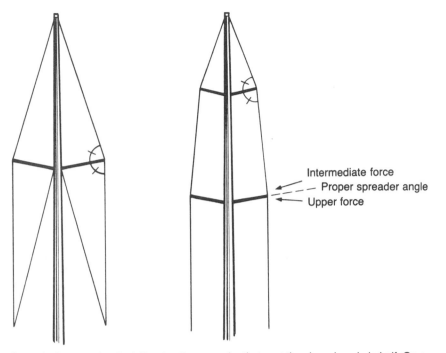

On a single-spreader rig, left, raise the spreader tip to cut the shroud angle in half. On a double rig, right, part the lowers to a lesser angle while bisecting the shroud angle on the uppers.

perhaps, but is actually simple to do.

As part of the commissioning process, the yard will install the mast and tighten the shrouds and stays with due regard to the structural aspects of rigging—but generally without regard for mast shape and performance. Any refinements will be up to you. Benefits include increased performance, knowledge of your yacht's potential under various adjustments, and a couple of interesting afternoons.

Turnbuckles are your tuning agents. Start by freeing them up with a good-quality lubricant and purchasing new cotter pins for each. Steady the threaded stud on the upper end of the turnbuckle to which the shroud end fitting is attached. If you allow the stud to turn you are also twisting the shroud and affecting the lay of the wire which reduces its strength.

On a standard single-spreader rig, supported by a headstay, backstay, upper shrouds, and fore and aft lowers, begin by slacking the uppers slightly and setting the spreaders to their proper, slightly upward angle. Set correctly, the spreaders will bisect the angle of the shroud where it turns at the spreader tip. (See drawing.) To maintain this angle, reseize the shroud to the spreader with stainless seizing wire. Apply spreader boots to the tip of the spreaders to prevent them from chafing the sails.

The next tuning process will be to plumb the mast, centering it athwartships. While the yacht sits in flat water, attach a plumb bob or similar small heavy object to the main halyard and see if it hangs at the center of the mainsail track. If it does not, slack the leeward shrouds and tighten the weather shrouds equally until the weight hangs at center.

Adjusting the fore and aft rake of the mast for maximum performance is a trial-and-error process. If you have been troubled by ex-cessive weather helm, realize that adjusting the masthead slightly forward moves the center of effort of the sail plan forward and reduces the yacht's tendency toward weather helm.

Altering mast rake on a deck-stepped rig is a simple interaction of headstay/backstay tensioning with slight changes to the lowers to set the mast bend. To adjust mast rake on a keel-stepped rig, you can either move the base aft or rechock the mast at deck level using narrower chocks on the forward side. In either case, the headstay, backstay, and possibly the lowers will need to be reset. For more than a slight rake adjustment, first check to be certain there is enough play available in the headstay and backstay turnbuckles to accommodate the change without shortening or lengthening the wire.

With the spreader angle set and the mast properly plumb, snug the shrouds and stays. You can approximate the relative tension of the rigging by feeling how easily it can be deflected.

Begin shroud tensioning by adjusting the headstay to last year's setting—easily identified by weather marks on the turnbuckle. Then set all opposing wires to equal tension, which will leave the mast relatively straight. In general, the uppers should be the tightest, followed closely by the backstay, then the forward lowers, which should be considerably tighter than the aft lowers.

Look up the mast using the mainsail track as you would the sights on a rifle. If the mast hooks one way or the other at the top, either tighten the upper shroud opposing the bend or loosen the upper shroud on the side toward which the mast hooks. If the gooseneck seems to be in line with the masthead but a bend exists at mid-mast, it is "out of column." This situation is more hazardous than an unaligned mast since the possibility of compression breaks increases.

To remedy this situation, tune the bend out using the lowers, once again tightening those opposing the bend or loosening those on the side of the bend. If the bend exists in an area above or below the spreader where it cannot be tuned out using the shrouds, the rigging may be too tight, creating the bend by compression. Loosen the backstay and the uppers, taking an equal number of turns off each, and the bend should disappear. If the bend does not disappear, then the problem is most likely a preexisting spar condition, for which compensation must be made.

After the mast is satisfactorily straight at dockside, take the boat out to examine rig tension. Sail to weather on alternate tacks in a moderate breeze while sighting up the mainsail track. If the masthead sags to leeward, the windward upper shroud is too loose. If the masthead seems to hook to weather, either the lowers need more tension or the windward upper is too tight. When the uppers are properly tuned, the masthead will not sag to leeward when close hauled, and the leeward upper will be slightly slack.

Also check for fore and aft motion. If the masthead seems to be pumping forward as you pound into the waves, the backstay could be loose. But look carefully. Midmast motion can easily be mistaken for masthead pumping. If this is the case, the windward lowers need tightening. Another cause of midsection motion is overcompression, in which case the uppers and backstay must be slackened.

Only a certain amount of headstay "sag" is permissible when adjusting backstay tension. The more the backstay is tightened, the less the headstay will sag off to lee-

ward, forming a rigid and more efficient arc along the luff of the genoa while beating to weather. As the mast is pulled aft, the mainsail is also flattened, reducing its drive in lighter air. Of course, too much backstay tension can overcompress the mast, and in extreme cases it can even change the shape of your vessel.

When you return to the dock, recheck the athwartship plumb of the mast to be certain it wasn't changed while tuning. If it has come out of plumb, then reset it using the uppers. By carefully counting the number of turns you release on one side and applying the same number of turns to the other, you should be able to move the masthead without affecting the tune. Hopefully, the adjustment will be slight enough that it can be brought back into plumb without retensioning the lowers. If adjustment seems necessary, try resetting the forward lowers using the same counting system.

Double-spreader rigs offer two additional complexities: the additional set of spreaders and an intermediate stay, running from the tip of the lower spreader to the mast at the inboard end of the upper spreader.

To adjust the spreader angle, the upper spreaders should be set like those in a single-spreader rig—bisecting the shroud angle. At the lower spreaders there is a junction of forces. The upper shroud exerts a horizontal pressure as it continues upward to the next spreader, and the intermediate shroud exerts a more acute pressure as it turns in toward the inboard end of the upper spreader. The lower spreaders should be angled upward to a lesser extent than the upper spreaders—bisecting the forces involved rather than any observable angle.

The intermediate shroud should

be tightened just enough to keep the mast from falling off to leeward when sailing close to the wind. The intermediate shroud is easy to adjust but presents a logistical problem in that it requires a man to go aloft.

Often, double-spreader rigs will have a different configuration for the lowers wherein the aft lowers are opposed by a single baby stay, which will have to be set tighter than the lowers.

This creates prebend in the mast. The mast should be supported all along the aft edge by the mainsail, which forms an extremely efficient backstay. In fact, the mast can bow quite far aft without risk of failure due to the backstay effect exerted by the mainsail.

Do not let the mast bow forward. Along the forward edge the mast is supported only by the headstay and the forward lowers or baby stay. In comparison to the continuous support along the aft side, this amount of support is minimal.

Should the mast bend forward rather than aft, chances of failure are increased. The mast can be easily overstressed in heavy weather when sailing with a fully reefed mainsail and large headsail, or worse, under headsail alone. Remember that if the mast does fail from bowing forward, the broken section will probably come aft, toward the cockpit.

When satisfied with the shape and performance of your rig, lock the turnbuckles with new cotter pins and tape them to prevent chafe.

In the fall, you can get a head start on next year's tuning by marking the threaded studs with tape where they enter the body of the turnbuckles. Then the yard will know where to set each shroud when commissioning next spring. When you come aboard for that first shakedown sail the mast should be in nearly perfect tune. But I guarantee you'll end up fiddling with the tuning anyway. It's contagious.

Fall Lay-up Checklist

Although most boatowners tackle their spring commissioning chores with gusto, very few show the same enthusiasm for winter lay-up. For one thing, most of us tend to keep stalling or putting off this chore (there's bound to be one more good weekend before cold weather really sets in, isn't there?). For another, there is a great tendency to rush through lay-up chores as the days get shorter and increasingly colder and nastier.

However, in the spring you soon regret any shortcuts that were taken, and you quickly learn how foolhardy it was to postpone tasks that should have been taken care of the previous fall. As any experienced boatyard will verify, *more harm comes to boats from neglect than from mechanical breakdowns or actual misuse*—and most of this neglect takes place during the off-season.

The best way to make sure everything will be properly taken care of is to follow the technique used by most professional yards—prepare a comprehensive winterizing checklist and follow it carefully before walking away from your boat for the season. With the exception of the engines and associated running gear, here is a comprehensive list of items that should be checked at lay-up time:

Interior Housekeeping

• Remove all foodstuffs and other perishables, as well as canned and bottled foods or drinks that you may have stowed away under seats, in the bilge, or in lazarettes and other out-of-the-way places. This includes all cans and bottles containing liquids of any kind that can freeze. When carrying all these items home, make things simpler for yourself next spring by using separate cartons (or bags) for each area and labeling each one clearly. For example, all cleaning materials that come out of the galley can be put in one carton; foodstuffs in another carton; medicines and first-aid equipment in another carton, etc.

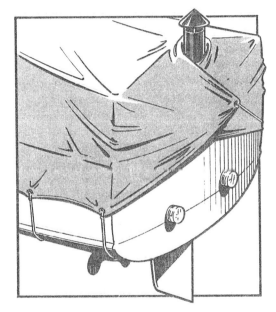

A stovepipe with cap makes an ideal opening that allows air to circulate beneath the boat cover during winter lay-up, above. Below: A checklist of this type can be used for several seasons.

• Wash all counters and similar surfaces, and vacuum carpets and furniture. Dust, dirt, and grease make it easier for mildew and mold to form, especially in enclosed spaces such as lockers, refrigerators, and ice chests. Make sure all water is drained out of the ice chest and its drain line.

• Clean all cushions and upholstered seats or bunks with a good vinyl cleaner. On fabric cushions use a vacuum and a foam-type upholstery cleaner. Remove curtains and take them to a dry cleaner for cleaning and storage till next season. Prop all bunk

DECK FITTINGS AND MACHINERY

Fittings and Fastenings:				Machinery			
Chocks	☐	☐	☐	Windlass—General	☐	☐	☐
Bitts	☐	☐	☐	Drum	☐	☐	☐
Cleats	☐	☐	☐	Wildcat	☐	☐	☐
Ring Bolts	☐	☐	☐	Wildcat Lock	☐	☐	☐
Pad Eyes	☐	☐	☐	Pawls	☐	☐	☐
Fairleads	☐	☐	☐	Pawl Ring	☐	☐	☐
Sheet Travelers	☐	☐	☐	Brake	☐	☐	☐
	☐	☐	☐	Bar	☐	☐	☐
Rail Stanchions	☐	☐	☐	Fastenings	☐	☐	☐
Rails or Man Ropes	☐	☐	☐	Winches—General	☐	☐	☐
Rail Turnbuckles	☐	☐	☐	Pawls and Rings	☐	☐	☐
Fastenings	☐	☐	☐	Fastenings	☐	☐	☐
Davits	☐	☐	☐	Handle	☐	☐	☐
Sockets	☐	☐	☐		☐	☐	☐
Brackets	☐	☐	☐		☐	☐	☐
Falls	☐	☐	☐		☐	☐	☐
Fastenings	☐	☐	☐		☐	☐	☐

cushions up so air can circulate under and around them (see drawing), and prop up bunk boards. Pull vertical cushions away from backrests and support them with tape or sticks so they lean forward and allow air to circulate behind them.

- Remove all linens and blankets, if possible, and take them home for the winter. If you have no room at home, think about taking them to a commercial cleaner for storage. Pillows (if foam) can be left on the boat, but prop them up so air can circulate around them.
- Prop open all doors on lockers in galley, head, and other spaces, and leave all drawers slightly ajar.
- Lift all hatches and either leave the covers off, or leave them partly open so air can circulate. Prop something in front of each hatch opening so no one will fall in, or place a large cardboard sign just inside the door to warn people as they enter.

Electronics

- Although some equipment cannot be easily removed (a radar unit, for example), all small items that can be unplugged and removed should be taken off the boat and stored at home—or taken to the dealer for storing, cleaning, and servicing where necessary. Taking radios, depth finders, and similar items home is not only less of a temptation to thieves, it will also keep them drier and cleaner, and thus help to prolong their life.
- As each item is unplugged wipe the plugs and contact points or connecters clean with a piece of very fine abrasive cloth or a coarse rag. Then spray with a moisture-displacing lubricant such as WD-40, LPS-1, CRC, or

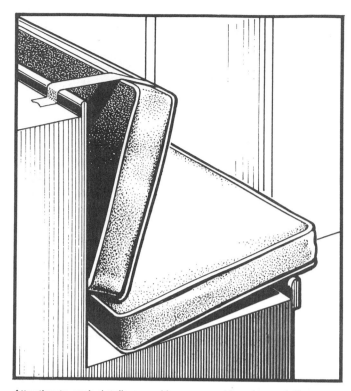

Attention to such details as making sure cushions have air flow around them to prevent mildew will make spring launching a pleasanter chore.

WGL. This will not only help dispel and keep out moisture, it will also protect against the formation of oxides and corrosion that can interfere with efficient operation next spring.

- Inspect all terminal blocks where DC circuits are connected to make certain none of the connections are loose, and that there are no signs of corrosion. Extensive corrosion means that some serious attention will have to be paid to keeping moisture out next year, and many of the terminal fittings may have to be cleaned or replaced. If only a few corroded connections or terminals are noticed, clean with fine abrasive cloth or bronze wool and then brush away all particles. The entire terminal block and all connecters should then be sprayed with a moisture-displacing lubricant.
- If your boat has a speedometer or log, take out the underwater sensing wand or paddle wheel

and leave it inside the boat. If the boat is stored in the water, this will prevent formation of barnacles and other growth during the lay-up period. If the boat is stored on land, taking this out will prevent damage when the bottom is cleaned and painted prior to launching. Either way, be sure you cap or plug the through-hull fitting to keep water out.

- Remove dry cells or rechargeable batteries from any equipment that contains one or more of these power cells, then replace them with fresh ones next spring.
- If you will be storing the equipment at home, clean off the outside of each cabinet first, then wrap with cloth or paper and seal with masking tape. Pack with a thick piece of cardboard on top and bottom to help protect against accidents and scratches.
- If possible, remove the radio antennas from the outside of the boat and store them at home—or

at least inside the boat. This will not only eliminate another temptation for thieves, it will also protect against damage from the elements or from flapping canvas and rope when something lets go during a winter storm. When you disconnect the cable from the bottom, clean the contact bolts or screws, then coat with a light film of grease or lubricant as described above. Wipe down the outside of the fiberglass antenna to clean it and coat the mounting bolts and bracket with a light film of oil to protect against corrosion.

Freshwater System

• Winterize the freshwater system. There are two ways to do this: (1) Drain it completely. (2) Fill the system with one of those special antifreeze solutions that are specially made for use in potable water systems (DON'T use regular engine antifreeze!). These are not supposed to leave any residual taste, but not all boatowners will agree with this. So before choosing this option speak to some neighbors who have used one of these chemicals to see if they have had trouble with a residual taste problem.

When using one of these antifreeze solutions, follow the manufacturer's directions as to dilution, etc. Remember that you have to flush the solution through all the pipes and fittings, so after adding the solution to the tank, you have to allow water to run out of each faucet and outlet till the color of the water indicates the chemical is present.

If you decide to drain the system, start by disconnecting the water line where it comes out of the bottom of the water tank. Let

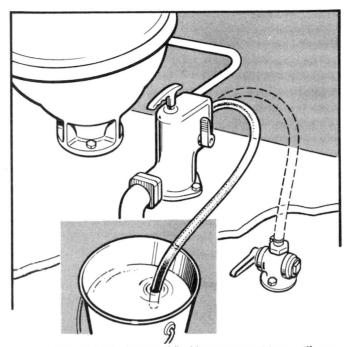

Disconnecting the intake hose and flushing permanent-type antifreeze through the system from a bucket keeps residual water in the toilet from freezing.

all water drain out. Next, disconnect the lines leading to and from the water pump. This is usually the lowest spot in the system, but you should check to make sure. If any water lines are lower, then make sure you open another connection at this low point. (If there is no connection located there, cut the line and put a drain valve or similar fitting in now.) To play safe, it is best to blow out all the lines with compressed air—if you own or can borrow a small air compressor.
• Although not essential, it may be a good idea to take the water pump home for the winter so you can overhaul it, especially if it is more than a few years old. Most companies sell repair kits for these pumps, but check your owner's manual for more specific information on the care and repair of pumps.
• If the boat has a washing machine, ice maker, or other water-using appliance, make sure the lines leading to these appliances

are also drained. Then check the manufacturer's directions as to proper winter lay-up of the machine or appliance (or call the service department of that company and ask for this information).
• Drain freshwater washdowns in the cockpit, or near the anchor pulpit—if you have them.

Heads

• Winterize toilets that discharge directly overboard by disconnecting the toilet's intake hose where it is connected to the sea cock or through-hull; then shut the intake sea cock. Fill a 2-gallon pail with permanent-type (glycol-base) antifreeze solution (do not use alcohol or kerosene, or one of the antileak antifreezes), then put the end of the hose into this pail. Flush the toilet as usual, causing the head to pump the antifreeze out of the bucket and through the toilet (see drawing). Reconnect the hose to the sea cock, then shut off the discharge sea cock if the boat will be stored in the water. If the boat is stored on land, leave both sea cocks open.

- If you have an Electra-San hooked to the toilet, use this same system, but attach a large note to the switch to remind you to empty the unit of antifreeze before you activate it again next spring. (For other brands of treatment devices, follow the owner's manual for winter lay-up procedures.)

- For boats that have holding tanks, flush the tank out several times with plain water, then pour about three or four quarts of antifreeze into the tank. Make sure the vent line is clear and fully drained, then run the pump that drains the tank briefly to make sure it is purged of water or full of antifreeze.

- If there is a sump for a shower or sink drain, make sure this is empty so the pump inside the sump won't freeze. Some pumps can be protected by putting antifreeze in the sump; others can't. Check the manufacturer's literature if in doubt.

- Be sure all medicine cabinets are empty, then clean and dry all plastic surfaces to minimize the likelihood of mildew forming. Leave locker and cabinet doors open. If the boat has a shower, take the curtain off and take it home for washing and storing.

Exterior Housekeeping

- Give the outside of the whole boat a good scrubbing before the winter cover is put on. This may sound like wasted effort, but it isn't. Dirt that remains on the surface over the winter—regardless of whether we are dealing with wood, fiberglass, or metal—

will be much harder to get off in the spring and can ruin many finishes. On metal it can hasten corrosion and oxidation; on gel coat it can cause dulling and stubborn stains to form; on paint it can result in discoloration that never will come out; and on varnish it can hasten dulling, darkening, and cracking.

- If you have the time, give all fiberglass surfaces on the outside a light coat of soft wax—*but don't buff it.* Just leave the cloudy film on over the winter. It will help shed dirt and moisture. In the spring a quick buffing will leave you with an almost clean surface that is ready for a final waxing.

- Inspect all the painted and varnished surfaces and touch up all the bare or badly worn spots now. This will not only save time next spring, it will also keep the finish from deteriorating even faster over the winter. Moisture

that is kept out cannot creep under the finish.

- Remove all exterior seat cushions and clean them with a good vinyl cleaner, then dry thoroughly before storing. If you must leave them on the boat, prop the cushions up so air can circulate, or try to store them inside.

- Take life preservers out of their storage places or containers and store them in a clean, dry location at home. If they must be left on the boat, spread them out or hang them up so air can circulate around them.

- Wipe a light film of moisture-displacing lubricant over all deck hardware, including stanchions, cleats, chocks, etc. Some prefer to wipe on a light film of petroleum jelly, but this can be messy to take off in the spring and it tends to attract and hold dirt. Using a spray lubricant, such as one of those mentioned

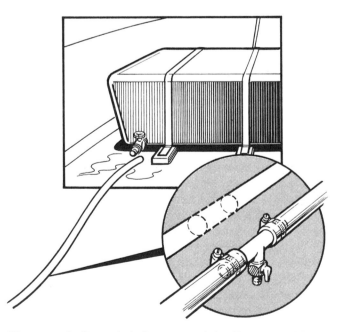

Disconnect the line to drain the water tank; but if a portion of the line is lower than the pump, drain it by adding a T-connection.

above, will not be as messy and enables you to leave a very light film on the surface. You spray a small piece of cloth till it is wet, then wipe on over the surface to deposit a light film on the metal. This will keep it bright and dry, and will not leave a greasy film that catches dirt or will be hard to remove next spring.

- Hang up all dock lines, instead of leaving them lying on the deck, and take the anchor line out so it can be cleaned (in fresh water) and then spread out to dry.
- Fold up canvas bimini tops, navy tops, or other canvas tops and enclosures. These won't last long if exposed to sustained winter storms and high winds. Where practical, take the canvas off completely and store at home in a dry location, but whether you take it off or leave it on the boat, make sure the canvas or fabric is clean before the boat is covered. Dirty canvas is a certain invitation to mold and mildew, as well as to the accumulation of impossible-to-remove discolorations.

Sailboat Rigging and Sails

- After unbending the sails, take them to your sailmaker for professional cleaning and storing and for any repairs that may be needed. If you plan to store the sails at home, wash with fresh water, then hoist them and let them flutter in the breeze till dry. Then take them home and store in a dry place.
- Grease all winches as per directions supplied by the manufacturer, and coat the outside of the winch with a light film of moisture-displacing lubricant or with a coat of wax.
- Wash all stainless hardware and fittings with fresh water, then coat all turnbuckles with a light

film of grease or auto wax. Wipe stays and shrouds with the same wax to help prevent corrosion. If spars are not painted, wipe them down with wax also.
- If the mast will be left up, try to arrange to have the masthead instruments taken off so they can be cleaned and stored indoors in a dry location.

Cover Properly

- When covering the boat with a tarp, make sure the cover is firmly tied down around all sides. Add more grommets if necessary (inexpensive kits for doing this are sold in most marine supply outlets) to eliminate loose edges or corners that can flap in a high wind. Also, make sure the cover won't sag in place to form pockets where wet snow or water can collect. Use plenty of strong synthetic line to tie the cover down, not scrap pieces of miscellaneous string or cheap twine.
- Make sure the cover is well vented to allow air to circulate underneath. One way to do this is to leave the ends open, but a better way is to include one or two vertical stovepipes with caps or hoods on top to keep out water (see drawing p. 142). Another measure that will help insure ventilation is to suspend a few small fenders around the sides before tying the cover down. These will keep the canvas away from the hull so that air can circulate more freely.
- Be sure the frame that supports the canvas is well padded with scrap pieces of carpet or foam on all corner joints and on each exposed end of wood or tubing in order to keep the canvas from tearing or chafing. Also, make sure you apply padding under the end of each vertical piece that rests on the deck or cabin top.

Miscellaneous Details

- Remove the bulbs from all outside running lights and navigation lights, then spray the sockets on the inside with a light film of moisture-displacing lubricant. This will help keep the bulbs from rusting in place—a common problem with boats that are stored outdoors.
- Lubricate all hinges, locks, hasps, catches, and other metal parts that move—around the inside as well as around the outside of the boat. Wipe on a light coat of auto wax over the steering wheel and the throttle and clutch handles, but do not buff or wipe off—let that go until next spring. Also, wipe a light coat of wax over all the exposed instrument faces and metal rings on the instrument panel.
- Lubricate all zippers on curtains and cushions—inside the boat as well as on the outside. Spray with silicone spray or with one of the new Teflon lubricants, while working the zippers open and closed a few times to spread the lubricant around. Squirt a little lightweight oil on all hinges and door latches, and squirt graphite or lock lubricant into locks on the inside to prevent freezing or seizing up.
- Give the bilge a good cleaning to get rid of spilled oil, grease, and dirt. If the boat will be stored on land, be sure the bilge pump and the hoses leading to or from it are completely drained so the pump cannot freeze. If the boat will be stored in the water, you will want the bilge pump operative, so make sure you either add salt to the bilge water to keep it from freezing or pour some antifreeze into the discharge hose and let it run back into the pump.
- Steering systems that have chains

or cables may need lubrication, but this depends on the type of system and the metal used. Check with the manufacturer if in doubt. Sheaves and pulleys may need lubrication, though some are lubricated for life.

• Be sure to go through all lazarettes and outside lockers in cockpits and on flying bridges to remove cans, bottles, and other containers that can freeze. Remove flotation cushions and preservers that are often jammed into these spaces over the summer, since condensation will form in closed-off places and this can result in mold and mildew forming on plastic or fabric materials.

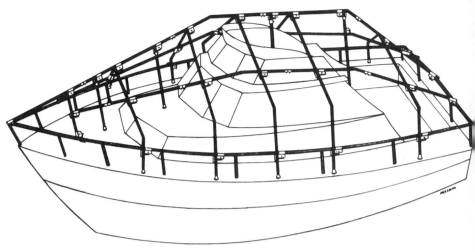

This apparently complex frame is strong, simple to erect, and reusable season after season.

Special Conduit Clamps Simplify Putting up Winter Cover

Except for those who are fortunate enough to live where boating is a year-round activity, fall is the time of year for winter lay-up—and in most cases this includes covering the boat. For boats that are stored outdoors, covering means first erecting a framework to support the waterproof canvas cover in such a way that it will shed snow and wear easily without tearing and without chafing against the boat.

A good winter cover framework will create a kind of tent over the whole boat that will not only support the canvas under the weight of heavy wet snow or pools of water, it will also permit air to circulate freely under it and will provide enough clearance on the inside so you can work on the boat when necessary.

Over the years boatowners have tried many different systems for erecting a temporary framework. Some use inexpensive furring strips (1″ × 2″ lumber) that are nailed or lashed together with string. This is knocked apart and thrown away each spring and then a whole new frame, using new lumber, is built the following fall. The trouble with this system is that you have to virtually redesign a whole new frame each fall (how many times have you tried to remember exactly how that ridgepole was put up the previous year?). And, of course, you have to haul away the pieces and buy new lumber.

Others use 2 × 3s or 2 × 4s to make semipermanent main supporting frames and ridgepoles that are carefully assembled with bolts and nuts. Each piece is then numbered or otherwise coded so that the framework can be taken apart and then reassembled in the same way.

This system also has some annoying drawbacks. First, the original construction takes a lot of time to design and to cut pieces to size, usually with specific angles for each cut end. Second, it requires accurate drilling of lots of holes while the parts are temporarily clamped or otherwise held in proper alignment. Third, the pieces of the disassembled frame are quite bulky and thus heavy to carry away and store.

In addition, building a winter cover frame out of wood usually means that pieces cannot be bent easily, so you are limited to using

Kover Klamps consist of two bolted half-round stainless-steel sections with flanges. They can be used to join two pieces of tubing in any intersection.

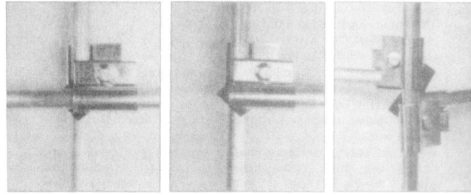

straight lengths that require many more joints than curved pieces would on most boats, and the joints form sharp corners and acute angles that require lots of padding in order to protect the cover against chafing.

But there is a third method that has become increasingly popular in recent years—building a frame out of metal tubing such as thin-wall electrical conduit. This tubing is comparatively inexpensive and it is widely available in all electrical supply outlets. The tubing is light in weight, so it is easy to carry, store, and erect—even when working alone—and it will last for many years in normal use. In addition, straight lengths can be easily bent with an inexpensive bending tool (often called a hickey) that is widely available from hardware stores and wholesale electrical supply houses.

Making wise use of curved pieces when erecting a frame often reduces the number of joints that will be required and helps to eliminate many potential chafing points. The precut and preformed pieces of metal tubing can be easily coded with numbers, letters, or colored tape, to indicate where each piece goes and how they fit together.

The one problem with this system has always been that there was no simple way to form joints where the lengths of tubing come together or cross each other at various angles. Elbows, T's, and similar fittings are available to be used with conduit, but these are not adjustable as to the angles that can be formed, nor can they be used to secure the tubing to stanchions, bow rails, or side rails.

Making joints by lashing with rope or securing with tape is not only very time consuming, it also makes it difficult to take the assembled framework apart in the spring, and this makeshift system

often allows frame members to slip or give way under stress from wind and snow loads.

To solve all of these problems one company in New York has introduced a clever new all-purpose universal clamp that enables you to easily join ⅞" or 1" outside-diameter metal tubing at any angle (this is the outside diameter of ¾" electrical conduit). The clamps can also be used to secure the tubing firmly against stanchions or bow and side rails (these are also ⅞" or 1" in outside diameter).

Called Kover Klamps, and manufactured by Klamp-It Industries, Inc., 61 Division Street, New Rochelle, NY 10802, phone—914/576-0722, the clamps consist of two pieces of metal and a thick rubber insert that goes between them. A bolt and nut that fits through a hole in each piece locks all the parts together after they have been positioned over the two pieces of tubing, and also permits pivoting the two halves so that one piece of tubing can be joined to another at any angle. The half-round segments in each half of the metal clamp lock over the tubing, while the rubber insert keeps the parts from slipping and also serves to protect polished stanchions and railings against scratching when clamping to one of these members.

Generally speaking, the best method is to erect a single ridgepole the length of the boat. On a sailboat or outboard runabout you would support this at about 4' intervals with short A-frames. On larger boats and most power cruisers, you will generally assemble suitably curved ribs instead of using short A-frames to support the pole.

Although many boats can be framed with a straight ridgepole that is high enough to clear the cabin top easily, with most powerboats, especially if they have a fly-

ing bridge, you will want to run a ridgepole from the bow to the highest point, then extend it back down to the transom.

To make a long ridgepole you can join the 10' lengths of tubing end to end with metal couplings that are sold for this purpose (they lock on with setscrews). The couplings are sold in the same outlets that sell the tubing, and they come in two types: those made of diecast metal and those made of steel. The Kover Klamp people recommend using the steel ones because they are stronger and will stand up better without bending (like the tubing, the steel couplings are plated to resist rust).

To avoid scratching or marring decks, rubber crutch tips are slipped on over the bottom end of each leg or rib frame—unless the bottom end of that rib or frame is clamped onto a stanchion. Scrap pieces of carpet should be tied around the clamps where the canvas will be lying against them to avoid chafing, and the entire framework should be lashed down to the hull to avoid lifting in strong winds.

Kover Klamps are sold in cartons of eight. A single carton or set (of eight) sells for $29.95, and will generally be adequate for boats up to about 20' in length. Two cartons (16 clamps) will cost $59.90 and will be enough for a 25' outboard, while three sets ($89.95) will be adequate for a 25' cabin cruiser. A kit consisting of six cartons (48 clamps) will cost $179.70 and will be enough to erect a framework over a 40' cabin cruiser.

In addition to the clamps, the only other materials you will need are enough lengths of the thin-wall conduit tubing to form your framework (about $25 for ten 10' lengths) and the rubber crutch tips for the bottom of each leg that rests on the deck (all hardware stores and marine supply outlets sell these).

As far as tools are concerned, all you will need is a tubing cutter, which usually costs under $5, and perhaps a tubing bender (about $10) if you will be forming many curved ribs or frames. These tools are sold in most hardware stores, as well as in the same electrical supply houses that sell the tubing.

Pointers on Winter Covering

A properly covered boat will be protected against the elements (wood boats against rot and peeling paint; fiberglass boats against fading and deterioration of the gel coat), but it is important that you do the job properly if you don't want to do more harm than good. Here are some points you should keep in mind:

(1) Make sure the canvas cover is in good repair. Small tears are certain to get bigger, and worn sections are certain to rip or shred when the winds blow.

(2) If possible, give the inside of the boat a good cleaning *before* you cover it. This will not only make it easier to get it back in shape in the spring, it will also lower the chances of mildew developing. Mildew is a fungus that thrives on dirt and dampness, and dirty surfaces stay damp longer.

(3) Make sure the frame is designed so that the cover won't form pockets that trap and hold great pools of water or wet snow. If necessary, add more ribs or braces, or move them closer together. Additional longitudinal poles or a second ridgepole might be required.

(4) Every cover should be vented so that there will be an ample flow of air through the boat and under the cover. Failure to have vents sewn into the canvas, and to allow for openings along the bottom as well as at the bow, is certain to lead to mildew and condensation—and may actually add to the danger of rot developing.

(5) As part of the need for adequate ventilation, make sure your cover doesn't fit like a glove. It should not be "skin tight" over the cabin tops or sides, or along the transom. It is even a good idea not to have the cover tight against the side of the hull in many places. To keep the cover off the transom, try hanging a number of small fenders or strips of dockside bumper material under the bottom edges of the cover to hold it away.

(6) Use plenty of tie-down lines to hold the cover secure in high winds and under heavy snow and water loads. Add more grommets if needed so lines can be spaced closer together. And remember these lines will take plenty of chafing along the bottom where they pass under the keel, so make sure you use stout *line*, not bargain twine or string.

(7) The cover should have zippers or flaps so you can get on board when it is on—either to get some chores done or to inspect the inside during the winter. Arrange your tie-down lines to provide for this so you won't have to cut lines and retie the whole thing every time you get under the cover.

(8) After the cover is on and secured, make sure you leave all doors, cabinets, windows, and lockers slightly open to help air circulate easily and to help prevent the development of musty odors and mildew.

(9) Don't be stingy with padding where the cover will be lying against or rubbing against metal or wood parts of the frame. Use scraps of old carpet, pieces of sponge rubber, or anything else, but use plenty and tie each piece on securely.

Checklists for Winter Engine Lay-up

Even if you prefer to let your boatyard or dealer do the winterizing, it is still important that *you* know what should be done, and how—and that you double-check the list with your dealer to make certain everything has been attended to. Even the best of yards has mechanics who may get careless or forget something in the hectic rush of winterizing a large number of boats in a few short weeks.

Here is a checklist that applies to most inboard gasoline engines.

——1. Sometime before the boat is hauled, spend an hour or two in the engine compartment with a flashlight, screwdriver, and a set of wrenches. Check all hose clamps to make sure they are tight, replace any that are rusted, then spray one of the moisture-displacing lubricants on each to prevent corrosion and seizing-up. Check mounting bolts and straps that hold cables and other controls in place, and be sure to lubricate wherever there are pivotal or sliding joints that must move freely.

——2. When the time comes for actual winterizing, run the engine until it's good and warm—better yet, take the boat out for a good ride—then shut down the engine and drain out all of the oil while it's still hot (on some engines you can remove a plug on the bottom of the pan; on others you have to pump it out through the dipstick tube). It's important you do this while the oil is still warm because sludge and metal particles will still be in suspension and will be drained out with the oil. Refill the crankcase with fresh oil, using the type specified for your engine.

——3. Replace oil-filter cartridges with new ones.

——4. If the engine is freshwater cooled and has a heat exchanger, check the amount of antifreeze in the coolant and add more if needed to protect the engine down to the coldest temperatures that can be expected, plus about a 20 percent safety margin. Remember that in most cases there should be at least 35 percent antifreeze mixed with the water to protect the engine against corrosion during the winter months, even if weather in your area doesn't get below the freezing point. Of course, if you do have freezing temperatures, it is best to do more than drain the block of fresh water. Some run the motor intermittently, after hauling, until heat dries out all water-jacket areas. Others use antifreeze. See your engine manual.

——5. After adding antifreeze (if needed) run the engine until warm, then check coolant and oil levels. Top up as necessary.

——6. While the engine is running at a fast idle, remove the flame arrester and slowly pour about one cupful of rust-preventive oil in through the carburetor to "fog" the insides of the cylinders with a light film of oil. If possible, stall the engine near the end by pouring the last couple of ounces into the carburetor rapidly.

——7. Clean the flame arrester according to the recommendation in your owner's manual, then replace it on the carburetor.

——8. Shut off the fuel valve at the tank, then remove the fuel filters and clean out the sediment bowls. Then install fresh cartridges and replace the filters. Remember that on many inboard installations

there are two filters—a large primary mounted on one of the bulkheads near the engine, and a secondary one on the engine itself (the primary filter is installed by the boat builder, so it probably won't be mentioned in your manual).

——9. If possible, drain all fuel out of the carburetor and out of the fuel lines leading to it, then remove each of the spark plugs and squirt a little rust-preventive or valve-top oil (about an ounce) into each cylinder.

——10. With the plugs still out, crank the engine over a few times with the starter motor, or by hand, to spread the oil around on the inside. Then replace the plugs.

——11. Remove all drain plugs and drain all the raw cooling water from the engine. Remember, if your engine has a freshwater cooling system with heat exchanger, drain just the raw (salt) water, not the freshwater coolant. As you remove each drain plug, check to see that water flows out easily—if not, clean the opening by probing through the hole with a piece of coat-hanger wire. Before replacing the plugs, dab a little grease over the threads to keep them from seizing up or rusting in place.

——12. Shut off the sea cocks at the cooling water intakes, then disconnect the hoses just above them so the water will be drained out completely. Loosen the cover plate on the water pump to make sure all water is drained out of that housing also.

——13. Remove the batteries and arrange to store them at home or have the yard store them. They should be in a place where they will be protected against freezing and where a trickle charge can be applied.

——14. Loosen the tension on alternator and water-pump drive belts, then spray all electrical con-

nections with WD-40, LPS I, or similar lubricant. Don't forget grounding cable connections, distributor caps, and other places where moisture should be kept out. Squirt a little inside the distributor, the cam, and breaker points.

——15. After the boat has been hauled, bung the exhaust openings in the stern with oily rags, and disconnect the propeller-shaft coupling where it joins the engine transmission to avoid undue stress on this connection when the boat is sitting on blocks. Wipe the shaft and coupling surfaces with oily rags to protect against corrosion.

Most authorities now agree that fuel tanks should be filled, with an additive fuel conditioner, such as Stor 'n' Start, included.

Outboard Motors

——1. Outboards that are run normally in salt water should be flushed out with fresh water. Depending on the size and weight of the engine and on facilities available, this can be done by running it in a test tank or by using one of the various flushing attachments that permit hooking the water intake to a dockside hose.

——2. While the engine is still running at idle speed, remove the cowl and shut off the fuel valve. Immediately squirt some rust-preventive oil into the carburetor intake. Use the oil recommended by your motor manufacturer and remember that the higher horsepower models have more than one carburetor. As the fuel in the carburetor(s) is about to be used up, squirt in an extra large dose of the oil to stall the motor.

——3. Take the motor out of the water and hold it vertical until all water drains out of the drive-shaft housing. Then remove the drain plugs to let the rest of the water run out. Crank it once or twice by hand or with the electric starter to force water out of the water-pump housing. Remember that the smallest amount of water trapped on the inside can freeze and crack a gear housing or water-pump case.

——4. Drain the fuel tank and all the fuel lines going from the tank to carburetor.

——5. Remove each spark plug, then squirt a few drops of preservative oil in through the openings, and crank the engine over a couple of times to spread this oil around on the inside of each cylinder. Replace the spark plugs after checking them to see if they need cleaning or replacement.

——6. Use an oil can to lubricate all parts of the steering and tilt mechanisms, the throttle linkage, swivel pins, and all other parts that move or slide. Wipe unpainted metal surfaces with an oily rag, and touch up painted areas where the paint has cracked or peeled, or where signs of rust are showing through.

——7 Check lubricant level in the lowest part of the drive unit, following directions in your owner's manual, and add grease if necessary. Inject the grease through the filler hole at the bottom until it starts to flow out the air-vent hole at the top. Then replace the plugs.

——8. Remove the propeller and inspect for nicks, dents, or scratches, and send out for reconditioning if necessary. Clean the shaft with bronze wool, coat with a light film of grease, then replace the wheel.

——9. Remove the storage battery (if the motor has electric starting) and store it at home where it will be safe from freezing and where you can check its charge periodically—or let your dealer check it for you.

——10. If you are storing the motor at home, keep it where it

will remain clean and dry; it doesn't have to be kept warm, however. A piece of canvas or cloth thrown over it will help keep out dust, but don't cover it tightly with plastic as this may lead to the formation of condensation inside the power head.

Stern-Drive Engines

Since these engines are basically hybrids where a standard inboard engine is married to an outboard stern drive not unlike that of a conventional outboard motor, most of the winterizing steps are already described under the lists given for "Inboard Engines" and "Outboard Motors."

Start by following the first fourteen steps for inboard engines, and then with the boat out of water and propped slightly bow-high (so that the engine is level or tilted slightly aft so that all water will drain out of the block), winterize the drive unit as follows:

——1. Lower the drive to the full-down position, but make sure it does not touch the ground. Remove drain and flushing plugs and allow all the water to run out. If the boat normally operates in salt water, flush with fresh water, following the directions in your owner's manual. When done, leave the petcocks open or the drain plugs out (place plugs in a plastic bag and tie firmly in place on the unit).

——2. Check oil level in the upper gear chamber or drive-shaft housing, and add lubricant as needed. Then do the same with the lower gear housing. It is important that both these chambers be full of grease during lay-up to minimize the possibility of water damage.

——3. Lubricate steering linkage, using the grease or oil recommended by the manufacturer, in-

cluding the gimbal-housing pivot pins.

——4. Remove and inspect the propeller to see if repairs or replacement are necessary. Coat the shaft with grease and reinstall the propeller. If your shaft has a zinc ring behind the propeller, check its condition; replace if necessary before the prop is reinstalled.

Diesel Engines

Modern marine diesels are generally simpler to winterize than gasoline models because they have no ignition system or carburetors. Also, diesel fuel does not tend to gum up the way gasoline does over a few months of storage, so there is no need to drain fuel lines.

Make sure you fill your tank completely before storing, as condensation is bound to cause bacterial growth when combined with any air present. Further, it may be useful to put a quart of fuel conditioner (MDR makes one called Stor 'n' Start) in the tank to insure against sludge formation.

Diesel Lay-up Checklist
—by Ed Dennis

Each fall, thousands of owners of diesel-powered boats have to prepare their engines for hibernation. Since your diesel engine is the most expensive piece of equipment on your boat, I suggest you take care of it and winterize it properly.

Here is a checklist of steps you should take to combat the ill effects that a long period of inactivity can have on your engine:

Cooling

• Drain and thoroughly flush the closed cooling system with soft, clean water. Then refill the system with more of the same, adding the correct amount of rust inhibitor and antifreeze (after first checking your service manual or asking your engine dealer).

- If the cooling system is to remain empty all winter, a tag or sign attached to the engine should so state.
- If necessary, check and adjust your injectors, spray nozzles or, as Perkins calls them, atomizers, to make sure they will be ready to operate when you start up in the spring.
- Start up your engine and gradually increase its rpm's to slightly above its high idle speed and to about 160° to 185° F. (85° C.) to completely circulate the new coolant into all the crevices of your engine and to get your lube oil up to operating temperature.

Lube Oil

- Stop your diesel and either pump out or drain completely the hot lube oil from the oil pan (use caution, as hot oil can burn your hands). When completely drained, replace and snug the oil plug tight with a new gasket.
- Remove and replace the lube-oil filters, draining the excess old oil into a heavy plastic bag or a bucket.
- Fill the oil pan to the full mark on the dipstick with SAE 30 or 40 weight preservative lube oil, such as Esso Rust Ban 623, Shell 66202, Texaco preservative oil #30, MIL-L-21260, or their equivalent.

Marine Transmissions

- Drain your marine transmission case completely and refill with new lube oil of the same recommended grade, viscosity, and type.

- Remove and replace the filters and clean any strainers.

Fuel Oil

- When a preservative fuel is to be used, drain the fuel tank completely (if possible) and refill with enough fuel treated with a rust-inhibitor fuel additive to permit your diesel to run fifteen to twenty minutes. Check with your engine dealer for a brand name.
- Drain and disassemble fuel filters, strainers and fuel/water separators. Discard used elements and gaskets.
- Wash the shells and parts in clean preservative fuel and insert new elements. Fill the cavity between the elements, etc., to their full mark with the same rust-preservative fuel compound as used in the fuel tanks. Then install them on the engine with new gaskets.
- If spin-on fuel filters and strainers are used, discard the old cartridges, fill the new cartridges with the same fuel, and install them on the engines.
- If you are unable to drain off your fuel tanks, then close their fuel valves and disconnect both the inlet and return fuel lines. Put the fuel pump suction line into a 10 or 15 gallon container of rust-inhibitor fuel oil, and do the same for the hot return line in an empty container.

    Start up and operate your engine at high idle for about five to ten minutes on the preservative fuel oil while engaging the gears alternately back and forth to circulate the new lube oil all around the case to give all the internal moving parts a good coating of oil.

    Stop your diesel and reconnect the fuel lines to their proper connections. If you were not able to completely drain your fuel tanks, then, after your boat is fully sup-

ported on shore, try topping off the tanks.
- As temperature changes can cause condensation to form and microbiological organisms to grow in your tank, I suggest you add a proper amount of fuel stabilizer and biocide to your fuel. Here are a few I have run across: Racor RX300, Kanacide, Nalco, J.B., Biobar M.F.
- Water accumulation can sometimes be controlled by mixing isopropyl alcohol into the fuel oil at the rate of one pint per 125 gallons of fuel.

Turbos

- Detroit Diesel suggests that since turbocharger bearings are pressure lubricated through external oil lines leading from the engine while the engine is operating, no further attention is needed. However, the turbos' air inlet and outlet connections should be sealed tightly with moisture-resistant tape.
- Remove your engine's valve covers and spray all the mechanisms with a good film of rust-preventive lube oil and reinstall the covers tightly.

Outdrives

- On Volvo's outdrives, loosen the oil drain plug at the bottom of the outdrive and drain the old oil. Then refill to the proper oil level.
- Remove the prop and coat the shaft with a preservative oil or grease.
- Clean the stern drive and wash with fresh water and paint with a light preservative oil. Grease all fittings.

Seawater

- Close the sea cock and drain all the raw water from it and the strainer. Then spray both with a heavy coating of WD40, CRC, or similar fluid.

- Remove all drain and zinc plugs. Then drain any raw or salt-water cooled components. Sacrificial zincs should be reinstalled for protection from any galvanic corrosion.

Electrical

Don't neglect to spend a few minutes winterizing the electrical elements—any extended lay-up period can be extremely hard on your engine's electrical systems. Disuse, dampness, salt water, as well as dirt invite corrosion.

- Remove, clean, and then store your batteries in a warm, dry place (and off concrete flooring). Many marinas have a battery storage room with an automatically regulated trickle charger to keep them up to full charge.
- Clean and spray all electrical connections and switches with WD40 or similar fluid. Cover the engine's starter, alternator, and any electrical motors with a plastic or canvas covering, but be sure each has sufficient ventilation.

Miscellaneous

- Loosen all belts and insert heavy strips of paper between the pulleys and belts to take the strain off them and prevent any sticking.
- Seal all engine openings, including exhaust outlets, crankcase, and transmission breathers and air inlets, with moisture-resistant canvas, tape, plywood, or metal covers. All materials used must be water and vapor proof, and possess sufficient strength to resist puncture or damage from expansion of entrapped interior engine air.
- Clean and protect all external,

unpainted surfaces with a suitable nonflammable preservative, such as Esso-Seracote or Shell Ensis fluid.

- Position all controls for minimum exposure, then coat them, as well as all shafts, flanges, etc., with grease.
- Place several small bags of silica gel around the engine and transmission. Then cover the engine and adjacent machinery lightly with a canvas or plastic dustcover for protection against any overhead or deck leaks.
- Make some kind of sign indicating just what precautions you have taken and warning that the engine should not be turned over until it is dewinterized.
- If possible, eyeball your engine compartment and its machinery every month or so during its long winter hibernation.

Fall Lay-up—Gas Engines —by Tim Banse

One of the most important duties a boatman performs is laying up his engine for the winter. It's during frigid winter months that water in gearcases and engine blocks freezes, expands, and then cracks expensive housings. Winter is when gasoline separates into gum and varnish, plugging up carburetor passages, and when batteries slip into a state of sulphation and discharge, dying forever. An experienced boatman avoids that kind of grief by following methodical guidelines for engine lay-up. Here's how to do it:

- With the boat still in the water, crank up the engine. While waiting for it to reach operating temperature, add stabilizer to the

fuel tanks. You may wish to check with your insurance company regarding storage of the boat with drained or topped-off tanks. The stabilizer will keep the gasoline from separating. Directions on the can tell how many ounces to add depending on fuel capacity and how many months it needs to be preserved. It is important to add the stabilizer while the engine is running. Otherwise, the fuel in the tanks will be protected, but fuel left inside the carburetor will not. For this reason it is a good idea to add the stabilizer during the last warm-up, just prior to changing the oil. When you shut down the engine, all the vital jets and passages will be stabilized. An alternate method would be to close off the fuel line at the tank, start the engine, and run all the fuel out of the carburetor.

- Drain the engine oil hot with all the acids and corrosive elements churned up in the crankcase solution. That way they drain out with the old oil instead of doing a termite number on vital ring and bearing surfaces during the long winter months.
- Always replace the filter with an oil change, lest that quart of contaminated oil dirty up the clean oil when the engine is started. Before screwing the new filter on finger tight, fill it with oil (it takes a patient hand, as the oil seeps very slowly into the element). Prefilling the filter means bearings won't have to wait for the oil pump to first fill the filter, then fill the galleries, and finally provide bearing lubrication. Also, remember to dab a fingerful of oil around the filter gasket to help it seal against the block. With the new filter in place and the oil-level topped off, start the engine.
- Immediately check the filter base

for leaks, and tighten as necessary.

- Scrutinize all the hose-clamps and tighten as necessary.
- Squeeze the cooling system hoses. Bulges or soft spots indicate weakness that should be corrected.
- Go over the engine block for rust streaks around freeze plugs where coolant may be trickling out.
- There are two acceptable techniques for rust-proofing an engine. The first technique involves running an engine almost, but not quite, out of gasoline. Just as it starts to die (you have to have a good ear for the engine and a quick pair of hands), squirt fogging oil down the carburetor throat. During those last few revs, flood the engine with fogging oil. This method runs all the gasoline out of the carburetor, protecting it from gumming up, and also rust-protects the cylinder walls.

The second approach involves removing the spark plugs and dumping an ounce of fogging oil into each cylinder, being careful not to let any crud drop in. Replace the plugs and crank the engine for fifteen seconds in order to thoroughly coat the cylinder walls with oil. Naturally, the high-tension lead should be removed from the ignition coil to preclude engine start-up during the procedure.

- With the boat out of the water, backwash the cooling system with a garden hose adaptor to flush out salt, sediment, and rust flakes. Seawater impellers should be removed. Heat exchange tubes need removal and cleaning about every other year.
- Remove the drain plugs from the engine block. If possible, tip the bow higher than the stern to facilitate draining the low spots in the engine. Consider storing the drain plugs in a plastic bag along with the keys. This works well if you are absentminded and liable to crank up the powerplant *sans* drain plugs.
- Inspect, then loosen drive belts. During a lay-up tension can stretch belts and strain bearings and hydraulic pump rotors. Verify the lift unit pump's oil level; it should be filled to the bottom of the threads in the fill hole.
- Now for the dirty work: the battery. Will the cables and terminals stand up to the rigors of another season? If so, remove the terminals and neutralize the inevitable buildup of green crud with a solution of baking soda and water. Wire-brush clean, inside and out. Likewise, clean the top of the battery with the baking soda and water solution, taking care not to let any of the solution seep into the electrolyte in any of the cells. The baking soda and water is good medicine for the connecters but is poison for the electrolyte. Clean the lead posts with a wire brush or sandpaper until they have a dull leaden shine. Top off each cell with distilled water. Coat the terminals with grease, Vaseline, or spray protectant. Trickle-charge until the specific gravity reaches 1.260. Hydrometers are cheap. Never recharge the battery in excess of 6 amps. Take the battery home, or at least indoors where it won't be exposed to the elements. Store in a warm dry space, preferably off the floor.
- Spray the electrical system with moisture-displacing lubricant. Shoot the works on instrument bulb sockets, terminal blocks, and fuse panels. Check the connections for corrosion and looseness.
- Grease the steering linkage, shift cable, tilt mechanisms, and swivel points. Scout out stray lube fittings that may be starved for attention. Let them eat grease. Replace any of the fittings that won't take lube.
- Remove the carburetor flame arrestor. Lubricate the carburetor linkage. Soak the flame arrestor in kerosene, air dry, and then reinstall; seal the opening with waterproof tape. Remove the fuel filter. Clean the sediment bowl and replace the filter. Coat the sediment-bowl gasket with a fingerful of oil before replacing.
- Don't be tempted to skip the lower unit chores until spring, as any water that might have seeped into the gear case may freeze and crack the housing. Inspect the lower unit, beginning with the lubricant. Crack the bottom drain plug with a big-handled screwdriver. Let the old oil drip out. A gallon plastic milk jug laid open is a good drain pan. Scrutinize the oil closely for bits of broken gear teeth and shavings from worn bronze bushings. Sniff the oil. Does it have the ominous aroma of burned bearings? Water can be a bad omen. If there is more than an ounce, a seal may have gone belly-up. Once satisfied the gear case is tight, refill with the proper lube. Don't forget to check and refill the upper gear chamber. Check the boot and rubber seal at the transom. Look for cracks and for brittleness.
- Remove the prop nut by blocking the blades with a chunk of wood to prevent it from turning. Spark-plug wires are removed when working on a lower unit to prevent accidental starting. Slip off the prop. Check the prop-shaft seal for monofilament. When the prop picks up fishline, it spins onto the shaft. Often, it keeps right on going, worming its way into the seal and cutting it. That's

one way that lower unit oil leaks out and water leaks in. Pay special attention to the propeller. Bent blades vibrate and wear out engine bearings and shafts. Out-of-true wheels also waste fuel and cut top speed. Gently tap out minor dings with a rawhide mallet. File the nicks smooth. Replace any propeller that's been badly abused by rocks and stumps. Before installing, coat the shaft with antiseize compound to keep the prop from corroding in place.

- Replace the anticorrosion sacrifice bars that have been eaten away to less than one-half their original size. Make sure they have good metal-to-metal contact or they won't work. When replacing the zincs, clean the marine growth off the lower unit with a wire brush. Paint any bare metal to stave off corrosion.
- With the engine cover up and out of the way, rid the bilge compartment of debris that settled in over the season. Next, combine a bucket of hot water and your favorite brand of laundry detergent. Scrub out the bilge with this solution and a long-handled, stiff-bristled brush. Rinse the bilge, and then air dry.

Exhaust Covers

One essential step in the proper lay-up of any boat with an inboard engine is covering and sealing the exhaust opening (or openings) in the transom in order to keep dampness out of the engine's exhaust system and internal openings.

A popular method for doing this is to stuff the exhaust opening with several heavy rags. However, since the rags can become saturated with water and do not always create a reasonably airtight seal, an improvement over this is to cut the bottom end off a plastic soft-drink bottle of the right diameter, then slip this "cap" over the opening. To seal and hold it in place, wrap the edges with some strips of duct tape around the outside.

Many different products are packaged in bottles of this kind, so it shouldn't be hard to find one or two that are about the right size to fit neatly.

Lay-up Tip for Sailboats

High winds, which often accompany fall and winter storms and which can knock down trees, power lines, and cranes, can also knock over sailboats that are stored on land with their masts and rigging fully in place. Some sailboat owners (and yards) may consider such an accident an act of God, but it requires a complete lack of understanding to make it possible. Storing a sailboat with its mast(s) in place greatly increases the risks of its being blown over on its side during a storm.

In addition to this danger, there are also two other significant reasons why a boat should not be stored with masts and rigging in place:

(1) A fully rigged mast cannot be adequately inspected for the condition of the fastenings and various fittings, or for potential failure points. All uninspected masts will eventually fail—it is only a question of when. A cursory inspection made by someone in a bosun's chair does not afford adequate protection against this potential danger.

(2) Masts, rigging, chain plates, mast steps, and even the hull itself, were not designed to withstand the severe forces exerted by a wind-driven mast and its rigging when the hull is firmly fixed in place. A floating hull has give and thus helps to ease the shock so the system can bend with unusual loads.

Frugality and a lack of knowledge on the part of the boatowner, combined with a lack of forcefulness from yard owners who know better and do not stand up for, or speak out on, what they know is proper—even if more costly—can result in disaster for the boatowner and the yard owner alike. Sailboats should not be stored on land with their masts stepped.

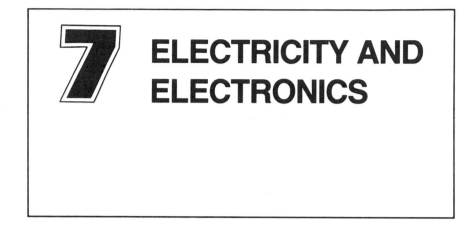

7 ELECTRICITY AND ELECTRONICS

Guide to Color-Coded Wiring

Troubleshooting your boat's electrical system can be fairly simple if all wiring is color-coded according to the American Boat and Yacht Council standard (E-3)—and if you know the code. If you are rewiring an older boat, or adding electrical equipment to one now wired in accordance with the code, following the recommended practices will be a help to you when it's necessary to track down a malfunction.

Under the standard, it should be possible to tell at a glance what circuit a given wire serves, particularly in the DC system fed by the boat's battery. Wiring for AC is color-coded to the extent that bonding wires, grounded current-carrying wires, and the ungrounded (hot) wires can be identified as such. Bare wiring used as grounding and bonding conductors is not color-coded, of course. All other wiring on the boat must be insulated.

In AC circuits, white always is used for the grounded current-carrying conductors, with red and black used for the other two conductors in a three-wire system; and

red, black, and blue for the current-carrying conductors in a four-wire system. The grounded, white, current-carrying conductor in an AC system is considered the neutral conductor, and it is connected to the side of the AC source that is maintained at ground potential. It is *not* a bonding conductor. Where bonding conductors are part of the wiring, they are used to connect exposed metal enclosures of electrical equipment to ground in order to minimize shock hazard to the crew in case of a short in the equipment. These bonding conductors are always green.

Green is also used for insulated bonding wires in DC systems, and, as in AC circuits, this type of wiring does not normally carry current. Bonding wires in a DC system must not be confused with the negative (return) wires that run from the negative terminals of electrical equipment back to the common ground point for the electrical system. Unlike automotive practice, where the entire vehicle is used as "ground," and only a "hot" wire runs to each electrical component, a boat is wired with both positive and negative leads. All negative leads return to a com-

mon ground point, usually on the engine block. These negative leads may be either white or black, but, whichever color is used, it is to be maintained throughout the system to the exclusion of the other color.

Red is used in DC systems for the main leads from the battery to the starter, and thence to the starter/ignition switch, and to the ammeter. These lines generally are not fused. Fused circuits are those protected by fuses or circuit breakers.

Beyond the ignition switch and ammeter, ten basic colors are specified for individual circuits, and some of these can serve more than one type of circuit. In these cases, one use is associated with the engine while the others have non-engine functions, which help to provide separation. Also, ABYC allows for addition of stripe to the basic colors as an aid in identification.

One of the basic colors does include a stripe to begin with: the yellow wire with red stripe that runs from the starter switch to the starter solenoid. This combination is used for no other purpose.

Yellow wiring is to be used between the generator or alternator field terminal and the field terminal on the voltage regulator. It is also the color for wiring from a fuse or switch to bilge blowers.

Dark gray wires should run from a tachometer sender to the gauge itself; this is also the color for navigation-light wiring, running between the fuse or switch to the lights.

Brown is used for the lead running from a generator armature to the ground terminal of a voltage regulator, and for wires from the generator or the alternator auxiliary terminal to a charge light—the little "idiot" light that goes on when insufficient current is being generated—and thence to the voltage regulator. Brown wires are also used for leads running from fuses or switches to bilge pumps.

Orange is the accessory-feed wire color for lines that run from the ammeter to a fuse or switch panel. It is also the color for the lead running from the ammeter to the generator or alternator output terminal.

Purple wiring should run from the ignition switch to the coil, and from the ignition switch to the distribution panel for electrical instruments, and from the panel to the instruments themselves.

Dark blue is the color for instrument and cabin lights, running from fuses or switches to the lights. Light blue wiring should run from the engine's oil-pressure sender to the oil-pressure gauge. As in the case of all other instruments, there may be three wires attached: the purple "feed" line, the white or black negative-return line, and, in this case, a light blue line that leads to the sensor.

Tan is used between the water-temperature sender and its gauge, and pink wiring runs from the fuel-gauge sender to the dial of its instrument.

If this color code is followed, the ABYC feels that a wiring diagram need not be supplied by the boat manufacturer. If some other means of identification is used, such as a different color code or numeral system, the proposed standard states that a wiring diagram should be provided that indicates the method of identification. In the case of another color code, the grounded return conductor must still be either white (preferred) or black (permitted).

It is possible, under the proposed standard, to use a single color for all wiring if colored sleeving or some other permanent means of applying color is used at all terminal points. Where numerals, letters, color coding, or other identification is applied in the form of tape wrapped around a conductor, the tape should be at least 3/16" wide and long enough to make at least two complete wraps around the wire. It should be visible near each terminal that the wire serves.

Where an electrical device has leads requiring polarized or selective connections, these leads should also be color-coded in accordance with the proposed standard.

The ABYC standard calls for AC conductors to be loomed or jacketed separately from DC conductors when they must be run together in a common trough, tube or raceway.

Note that wiring size should be in accordance with ABYC Standards E-8 (AC Electrical Systems) and E-9 (DC Wiring Systems Under 50 Volts). In any rewiring work or installation of new equipment, these standards should also be followed in regard to circuit protection, load distribution, and all other safety factors.

Checking Your Batteries

Electrolyte nominal specific gravity varies slightly in different makes and designs of marine batteries. However, most manufacturers specify about 1.260 as the value for a fully charged cell. Specific gravity decreases as the battery discharges; increases as it charges. Consequently, its value is an approximate indicator of the battery's state. Between full charge and discharge state, a typical battery will evidence a gravity drop of 125 points: Full-charge gravity is 1.260, half charge 1.197, and discharged 1.135.

Standard electrolyte temperature for hydrometer readings of specific gravity is 77°F., made when electrolyte level is above the plates. In order to get accurate gravity readings, the hydrometer float indication must be corrected for temperature and electrolyte level. The corrections are applied as follows:

(1) Add one gravity point for each 3°F. above 77°F.; alternately, subtract one point of gravity for each 3°F. below 77°F.

(2) Subtract 15 points for each 1/2" below normal level; alternately, add 15 points for each 1/2" above normal.

From the above, it is apparent that a battery having electrolyte level 1/2" above normal, and with temperature 107°F., will require plus 25 points correction. Thus, if the hydrometer reads 1.235, corrected value is 1.260, indicating the battery is fully charged.

Specific gravity is never tested immediately after water is added to the cells because the fresh water on top of the cells will make the reading much too low. Time must be allowed, and the battery used, to thoroughly mix the liquids. Battery manufacturers also say that age alters the normal gravity reading, pointing out that a decrease of several points a year is normal.

In order to split battery or AC power into fairly even loads for each branch circuit, you can compute to the total load for each circuit and make adjustments as necessary.

Circuit Loads

In AC circuits, appliance and bulb loads are expressed in terms of *watts*. Watts are the product of voltage times current draw (amperes), and indicate power required for the time. Bulb sizes range from 40 watts to 100 watts for most lighting requirements (note that fluorescent lights give much more light than incandescent bulbs of the same wattages). Electronic gear and appliances may require anything from about 25 watts to 1,500 watts, with units that have heating elements (stoves, cabin heaters, hair dryers) at the high end. Wattages are stamped on bulbs, and on manufacturer appliance plates. Total the wattage on a circuit, divide by voltage (usually 115/120 volts AC), and you have the amperes drawn on the circuit with everything turned on.

In DC circuits, bulbs are marked according to current draw (amperes), and equipment may be marked in watts (particularly those with heating elements) or amperes, but total circuit load can be determined in terms of amperage.

In either case, if you determine that some circuits are carrying loads considerably heavier than others, it would be wise to rewire in such a manner as to balance the loads. Of course, heavy-duty appliances may require separate circuits for themselves.

Voltmeter Readings

A voltmeter indicates the potential power supplied to a circuit; the "electromotive force" (EMF) available from the battery. A battery cell of any type has a potential of a bit more than 1.5 volts when fully charged, no matter the battery size or type. Of course, the larger the cell, the more *current* can be drawn from it over a longer period of time before the charge level becomes inadequate. Cells hooked together in series make up marine batteries of 6 volts, 12 volts, etc. Voltmeters can be used to check the potential of individual cells as well as total battery voltage, and can give a quick indication of battery condition.

Ammeter Readings

An ammeter indicates *rate* of current flow *from* a battery (discharge) or *to* it (charge) while the engine is operating. If a battery is used for lighting direct-current accessories, and it is not hooked into the charging circuit, an ammeter will indicate a current draw that depends on the number and wattage of lights or other units being operated.

If the ammeter in the engine-charging circuit indicates a constant discharge while the engine is running, the generator or alternator may not be putting out enough current to compensate for the load on the entire system. An ammeter cannot indicate battery condition.

Solving an AC Grounding Problem

Much has been written on the subject of marine alternating-current systems and their adverse effects on underwater metals—especially on metal-hulled craft and wood or fiberglass boats with outdrives.

My boat is a 28′ fiberglass Bayliner with twin 888 Mercruiser drives. She is kept at a slip in Chesapeake Bay and came with builder-installed AC shore power. All receptacles and appliances, including the shore power inlet, contain the green grounding wire, the ends of which converge at a lug in the main distribution (breaker) panel, which is, in turn, connected to the land ground. There is *no* connection, at any point, of this wire to any part of the DC ground, or to the through-hull bonding system. All equipment that uses AC power, such as the battery charger and hot-water heater, is grounded to the shore via the green wire, but not to any metal with continuity to the water or to the DC ground. This insures against any corrosion or shock hazard, since any short would bleed to ground via the shore-power cable and green wire.

However, a year ago I installed an Onan 3-kw gasoline generator with transfer switch and related hardware. The generator is the typical two-wire 115-volt sort, so for safety's sake, I ran a grounding wire between the generator frame and the green-wire lug on the distribution panel. Unfortunately, with the shore power plugged in, I now had continuity between the earth ground and the water ground—my generator-to-panel wire providing the path. Immediately, my protective zincs began eroding at an alarming rate.

Various solutions came to mind:

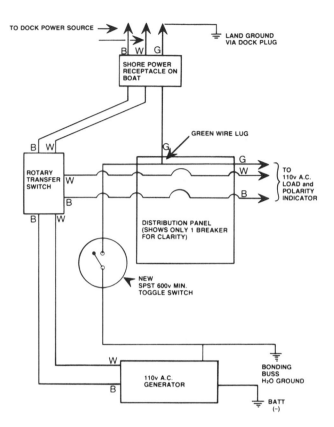

TO DOCK POWER SOURCE →

LAND GROUND
VIA DOCK PLUG

B W G

SHORE POWER
RECEPTACLE ON
BOAT

GREEN WIRE LUG

B W

ROTARY
TRANSFER
SWITCH

W

B

B W

G

G
W

TO
110v A.C.
LOAD and
POLARITY
INDICATOR

B

DISTRIBUTION PANEL
(SHOWS ONLY 1 BREAKER
FOR CLARITY)

NEW
SPST 600v MIN.
TOGGLE SWITCH

W

B

110v A.C.
GENERATOR

BONDING
BUSS
H₂O GROUND

BATT
(–)

Single-pole, single-throw switch is used to break generator-to-
distribution panel ground.

(1) Eliminate the green wire at the dock—very unsafe. (2) Use an isolation transformer—effective but very expensive. (3) Use of a green-wire isolator, such as the Quicksilver Isolator—also expensive. (4) Mechanically break the generator-to-distribution-panel ground when plugged into the dock with a switch.

I chose the fourth solution for simplicity and reliability, not to mention cost. Adjacent to the shore power-generator transfer switch I installed a heavy-duty, weatherproof SPST toggle switch. To one pole on this switch I attached a #10 wire terminating at the other end at a lug on the generator's frame. From the second pole of the switch I ran another #10 wire to the green-wire lug on the distribution panel. Now when plug- ged into dockside AC power I need only open the new toggle switch to effectively isolate the water-source ground from the land ground. When using the generator, the switch is closed to provide a safe path for stray current arising from any equipment failure or internal short. Notice, however, that there is *no* switch or breaker of any sort between the green wire at the shore-power receptacle on the boat to the distribution-panel lug, or from the distribution-panel lug to any 110-volt outlet or appliance. A polarity indicator plugged into a receptacle near the transfer switch reminds one to close the toggle when operating on generator power. (It would definitely be unsafe to run the generator with the new toggle switch open, so a prominent warning sign, or perhaps a warning light of some kind, should also be installed right next to the generator-start switch or transfer switch—Ed.)

This setup will not work on a boat where battery charger, water heater, or other AC appliances have their frames grounded to any part of the ship's DC system or bonding system, so check this with an ohmmeter first. Nor will it help on a metal hull with continuity between all AC devices and the hull. An isolator would be in order here.

A final note: Make a complete survey to make certain all through-hull fittings are effectively bonded. Determine that correct polarity exists from the dock plug and generator to each and every receptacle and permanently connected electrical appliance. Replace household-type SPST breakers with marine-rated DPST types, and check all connections to insure lack of corrosion or looseness at every junction. Lag all 110-volt conductors well away from wet areas, especially in the bilge, and last but most important, disconnect all sources of power when using your ohmmeter or making connections.

Suppress Radio-Frequency Interference

The best marine radiotelephone can be almost useless if your boat's engine is creating so much static interference the radio signals can't be heard. One of the easiest, least expensive, and most rewarding projects is to remove ignition-caused radio-frequency interference. The information here is based on material supplied by electrical engineer Lou Heiner.

Radio-frequency interference is caused by sparking at the plugs, distributor cap, points, generator (or alternator), and voltage reg-

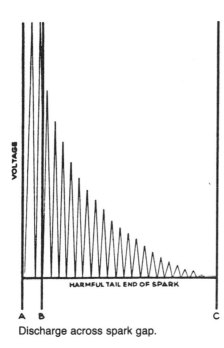

Discharge across spark gap.

ulator. The drawing above shows the wave pattern of the spark at the plug of a typical ignition system. The useful part of the spark is the portion between A and B; the rest is "hash" that's picked up by the radiotelephone.

By flattening out the wave between B and C, the noise from this source is reduced materially; in many cases completely eliminated. This wave train is "damped" by adding resistance into the high-tension circuit, which can be done in four ways:

(1) Place a 10,000 ohm resistor (Erie type L7VR-1OME or equivalent) in the center tower of the distributor, and a 5,000 ohm resistor (Erie type L7VR-5ME or equivalent) in each cable tower.

(2) Use resistance-type spark-plug cable.

(3) Use resistor-type spark plugs.

(4) Use a combination of any two of the above, but *not* all three.

The sketch to the right illustrates the combination of resistor-type plugs and resistor cables, and re-sistor plugs with resistors in the distributor-cap towers. Note that some ignition systems incorporate a resistor in the distributor's rotor, which acts the same as an internal resistor-suppressor in the central tower.

The standard resistor-type plug is also shown, and it is this type that usually is used in marine applications. The shielded type is more expensive, but it is waterproof and explosion proof. The drawing below shows how the resistor plug flattens out the useless part of the spark discharge.

Resistor cables use a resistance center instead of a metallic conductor. They may be identified simply as "radio" or "radio resistance" cables, but present-day standards specify two types: HTLR (High Tension Low Resistance—3,000 to 7,000 ohms per foot); and HTHR (High Tension High Resistance—6,000 to 12,000 ohms per foot). Normally, these cables are purchased in sets with cables precut to proper lengths for the particular engine, and with the proper terminals at each end.

Note that care must be used in handling these cables. Never pull on the cable itself when removing it from a plug or the distributor cap! Pull on the boot or the terminal. Never cut resistor cable to attach a screw-on suppressor, and never try to repair an end terminal. Replace the entire cable—and preferably the entire set.

If you have no marine telephone, but you're picking up engine static on your broadcast-band receiver, resistor-type plugs, or resistor cable, will generally be all that's needed to eliminate the interference. For radiotelephones, however, use of the resistors in the distributor towers in conjunction with standard cable and resistor-type plugs is recommended.

As a high-tension spark is generated between the rotor tip and the

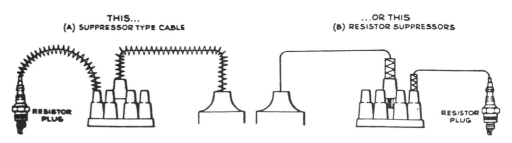

You can generally choose either (A) resistor plugs with suppression cable, or (B) resistor plugs with a 10,000 ohm resistor suppressor in the center of the distributor, and a 5,000 ohm suppressor in each of the towers. Many operators of heavy-duty boats prefer (B). It is not recommended that these two alternatives be combined.

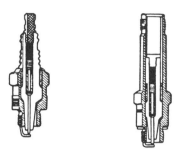

Left: cross section of typical unshielded resistor spark plug. Right: typical shielded resistor plug.

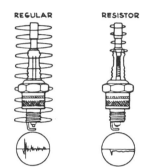

Radio interference characteristics from plugs.

cable inserts within the distributor cap, it is also a source of interference. The best prevention here is a clean, new rotor and cap, as the most noise is caused by dirty, worn components. Don't try to file away corrosion on a rotor tip; replace it!

Breaker point "bounce" at high engine speed creates high-frequency interference over the entire radio spectrum. Clean, properly adjusted points reduce this—and improve engine performance.

Next install a 0.1 MFD feed-through coaxial capacitor (Sprague 48-P-9 or JN-17-907 or equivalent) as close to the coil primary terminal as possible, between the primary terminal and the ignition switch. This is shown in a drawing. At the time you do this, remove the coil mounting bracket, clean any paint away from it and the engine block where they make contact, and reinstall it.

If your engine has a generator, a

worn commutator can generate interference that's heard as a high-pitched whine. If the commutator appears to be rough and uneven, or if the brushes are worn to half or more of their original length, the generator is due for an overhaul.

When the generator is in good condition, remove the factory-installed bypass capacitor and install a 0.5 MFD coaxial capacitor (Sprague 48-P-18, rated at 40 amperes, or JN-17-965, or equivalent). The second drawing to the right shows how this is to be grounded to the generator frame under the screw provided for the original bypass capacitor. The wire that goes to the Armature terminal on the generator is removed and reconnected to one end of the coaxial capacitor. The other side of the coaxial capacitor is connected with a short (3″ or less) length of #10 gauge wire to the Armature terminal, as shown.

Most, if not all, new engines have an alternator, rather than a generator. It has no commutator, and brushes ride on smooth slip rings. However, worn or rough slip rings can cause a whine on the radiotelephone. Have them "trued up" on a lathe by a specialist.

The diode rectifier of an alternator system should be completely noiseless, but a defective diode can cause noise. In this case, a 0.5 MFD capacitor (JN-17-965 or equivalent) should be connected to the alternator output terminal as shown at right. Do not connect any capacitor to the alternator Field terminal!

In some cases, to completely eliminate alternator interference, it may be necessary to use shielded wire between the alternator and regular terminals. Be sure to ground both ends of the metallic shield.

If your voltage regulator is causing interference, it's heard as an er-

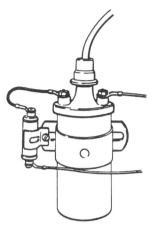

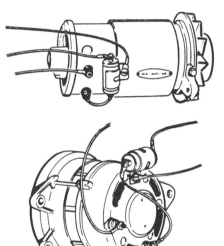

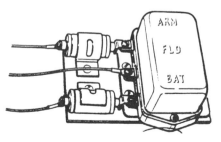

Connection points for noise suppression capacitors are shown (top to bottom) for the distributor, a generator, an alternator, and voltage regulator.

ratic popping that changes only slightly with engine speed. If your engine has a generator, mount two coaxial 0.5 MFD capacitors (Sprague 48-P-18 or JN-17-965 or equivalent), rated at 40 amperes, in series with the battery lead and the regular BAT terminal and the generator armature lead and the regulator ARM terminal. This is shown at right. Shielded wire from the generator armature and field terminals to the corresponding terminals on the regulator also helps.

An alternator regulator is similar to that used with a generator, except that it may be a single control or a double control system. Install a 0.5 MFD coaxial capacitor (Sprague 48-P-18 or JN-17-965 or equivalent) at the Ignition (I) terminal of a single unit regulator. On a double unit regulator, install the same type of capacitor on the battery terminal. Be sure the case of the capacitor is grounded.

Watertight Deck Connector

When plug-type connectors are used to bring wires through the deck, they are seldom if ever really watertight. Either they allow water to come through the deck into the cabin, or they are subject to corrosion and oxidation due to the dampness.

Instead, I have worked out a waterproof and noncorrosive inlet for the wires that come down from my mast (including the coaxial VHF antenna cable). It is made out of two PVC pipe elbows that are joined together and glued, as shown in the drawing.

Available in most plumbing supply outlets for use with PVC pipe, these elbows come in various sizes, so you can select the size that will best handle the number of wires to

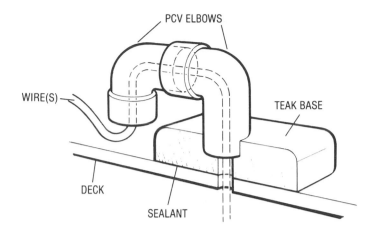

Pipe elbows on a wood base make a watertight housing through which wiring can be led.

be passed through. I used ¾" elbows (inside diameter) to take care of two #14 wires plus the coax antenna cable. If it is necessary to cut the elbows shorter, trim off the male end with a hacksaw.

The two elbows are joined together with PVC cement or a silicone rubber sealant, then one end fits snugly into a hole drilled through a teak block, as shown, sealing this joint with silicone rubber sealant. The block of teak should be about 1" thick and can be any convenient size and shape.

A hole is drilled through the deck to accept the number of wires to be passed through, then the teak block is fastened down with its opening centered over the hole in the deck so the wires can be passed through from above. Use stainless screws to fasten the block down, and use sealant under it to serve as a bedding compound that will keep water out.

Installing a Dual Battery System

—by Tim Banse

Ever been stranded because all the electronic goodies on board

drained the battery so low it wouldn't crank the engine? That frustrating situation can be avoided by installing a second battery and a selector switch. With this setup, storage batteries can be dialed-up individually, or together. Usually, one battery will be selected to power ship-to-shore radio, trolling motors, and onboard electronics, while the other, fully charged, is held in reserve for engine starts. Once underway, the selector switch can route recharging voltage to either or both batteries.

To make this installation, first decide on where to locate that extra battery. Just like the original battery, it should be a marine-grade, deep-cycle battery. An automotive battery will not do. A deep-cycle battery is built to withstand up to 200 charges and discharges, while a no-maintenance car battery will only last from 20 to 50. The no-maintenance, marine grade, deep-cycle batteries are made with gelled electrolyte.

Since batteries are rather weighty, they should be located close to the keel and as low as possible. In order to keep voltage drop to a minimum, they should be located as close to the engine as possible. The shorter the battery cables, the less voltage loss. How-

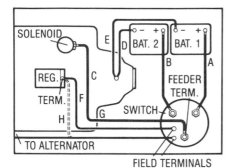

Typical dual battery installation.

ever, right next to the engine is no good—all that heat will kill the battery.

Fresh air is a necessity. A battery under charge gives off explosive hydrogen fumes. Never set a loose battery down in the bilge. Instead, locate it in a securely mounted, acid-tight box. Allow at least a foot of clearance around the box for air to circulate. The lids on these boxes are vented, so even when strapped down, they breathe. Make sure that leaks and spray are not getting to your batteries. Salt water splashing on a battery creates toxic and explosive chlorine gas.

With the battery mounts secured, disconnect the existing battery. Route the cables from the main and auxiliary battery to the selector switch. Again, since cable length determines voltage drop, the distance from the batteries to the switch and back again, should be as short as possible. Naturally, a compromise must be established between length and convenient access to the switch. Most are mounted so they are easily accessible when raising the engine cover.

The cables should be stranded, insulated copper. Single-wire cable is prone to fatigue and breakage. When routing wires through bulkheads, fit them with a grommet to prevent the sharp-edged fiberglass from cutting through the insulation. It's also helpful to color code the wire—red for positive, black for negative. Wire size is also important: The higher the number, the smaller the wire.

Typically, the selector switch will have three large terminals and two smaller ones. One of the large ones will be marked BATTERY #1, and another, BATTERY #2. Connect one cable to terminal #1 and route it to the main battery. Do not connect the battery. Connect the cable on terminal #2 to the auxiliary battery. The remaining large terminal is the common feed line. It's polarity is positive, and connects to the starter solenoid. Use wire ties to band the new cables to the existing wire harness.

Those two small terminals provide a circuit that automatically disconnects the alternator when both batteries are switched off while the engine is running. This prevents voltage surge from burning out the alternator.

To connect the alternator cutoff circuit, locate the voltage regulator's field terminal. It's usually marked "F" or "FLD." Loosen the screw and remove the wire. Replace it with one of the two small wires running from the selector switch. Snip off the terminal lug from the disconnected field wire. Strip off ½″ of insulation. Likewise, strip the second small wire from the selector switch. Splice the two together.

Now you are ready to mount the switch. Cut an oblong piece of ¾″ marine plywood to fit. Use the switch as a template. Lay it on the piece of plywood and center punch the mounting holes. Remove the switch and drill those holes. Wood screws are usually provided with battery switch kits. Fasten the switch to its backing plate and then lay the backing plate against the hull. Drill three or four more holes to attach the backing plate to the hull. A dab of fiberglass or epoxy glue on the threads will keep the screws from vibrating loose.

The last step is to turn the selector switch to OFF and connect the cables to the batteries. Naturally, the battery posts and terminals need to be squeaky clean and coated with corrosion-resistant protectant. To test the new electrical system, flick on the running lights. Rotate the switch through all its positions. The lights should stay lit on all three battery choices, but douse on OFF.

An Oil-Pressure Alert You Cannot Ignore

Loss of oil pressure, if undetected for even a few moments, can put an inboard engine—gas or diesel—out of commission for keeps. The oil pressure warning light should tell immediately of the impending catastrophe, but idiot lights are often easy to ignore. I've found an audible alarm more consistent with the severity of the problem, and more likely to prompt quick action.

To convert your low-oil-pressure warning light to an instant audible alarm, just buy a 12-volt Mallory Sonalert, or similar piezoelectric signaling device, and wire it into the electrical line from the oil-pressure sensor. The sensor is a threaded plug with an insulated screw terminal located low on the engine block. To check that you have the right wire, turn the engine switch ON, but do not start the engine. Disconnect the wire and the oil-pressure warning light should go out. It is not necessary to remove the warning light from the circuit since the Sonalert draws only a few milliamperes and will operate with the light in the circuit. (With the Sonalert in the circuit, the light will no longer go on, but then you can't have everything.)

Mount the Sonalert securely to a bulkhead of the engine compartment. A block of wood with a 1⅜" hole drilled into it will work nicely. It may be necessary to extend the length of the wire; use a piece of plastic-coated wire of about the same gauge and crimp-type connectors. The Sonalert is available at most fair-sized electronics stores for about seven bucks. A suitable model is the SC-12; it will operate on 12 volts. The Sonalert is a polarized device—it has a positive and a negative terminal. After you install it you may have to reverse the leads to get it to work. Radio Shack and others also make similar piezoelectric signaling devices, but my experience had been with the Sonalert.

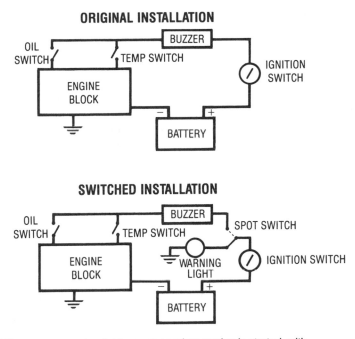

ORIGINAL INSTALLATION

SWITCHED INSTALLATION

Oil-pressure warning light comes on when engine is started, with buzzer disconnected, as a reminder to reactivate buzzer once the engine is running.

Switch to Silence Alarms

To update my boat I recently had a warning buzzer installed that sounds off if the engine overheats or if the oil pressure drops. Like most such systems, the buzzer sounds every time I start the engine, which can be very annoying—particularly if the engine does not start quickly.

I solved this annoying problem with a simple switch. It is a single-pole, double-throw switch that is cut into the positive or "hot" wire leading to the buzzer (between it and the ignition switch) by connecting the hot wire from the ignition switch to the common position on the new switch. One side of this switch is then connected to the buzzer as it was before, while the other side of the switch goes to a newly installed warning light that is mounted on the control panel and grounded to a common ground on the panel.

Now when I turn on the ignition switch to start the engine the buzzer sounds as usual. I flip the new switch to shut it off—but this turns the warning light *on*. After the engine is running, the warning light is still on and reminds me to throw the switch back the other way—activating the buzzer again so it can warn me if the engine overheats or loses oil pressure.

Electrical System Preventive Maintenance

Of the many calls the Coast Guard receives for assistance each season, a large majority are attributed to battery failure. Most of these could have been prevented by routine maintenance. Here are ways to insure your electrical system is working smoothly.

The Battery

Remove the battery by first disengaging the *negative* terminal. (If the wrench slips on the positive terminal and contacts the engine block, there will be a nasty and dangerous flash-arc. Disengaging the negative terminal first will prevent such a short circuit.) After loosening the clamp bolt, work the terminal clamp loose by tapping lightly with a wood mallet. Better yet, use a terminal puller. Battery terminals are easily damaged because they are fabricated of soft metal. If it won't come off easily, insert a screwdriver blade between the ends of the clamp to spread its jaws. Tuck the negative cable out of the way and then remove the positive clamp. If it isn't already marked, use a screwdriver blade to tap a plus sign into the soft metal so you won't mix up the cables.

If the battery is in a proper box or is clamped into position (as it should be), release the hold-down clamps and lift the battery out of the engine compartment or box. Using a proper lifting strap will make the job easier, but you should still cover the battery with an old towel or rag so that battery acid will not get on your clothes.

If possible, take the battery completely out of the boat, then wash the outside thoroughly to remove the oil, salt deposits, dirt from deck and bilge areas, and acid deposits. These all allow minute amounts of current to leak from one terminal to the other. Over a period of time (one weekend to another) these leakage paths can "empty" a marginally charged battery.

Wash the battery with fresh water and a small amount of detergent soap, taking pains not to get the water into the filler-cap areas. Rinse with plain water. Burnish the terminals with a terminal cleaning brush (a cheap but effective combination tool sold in all automotive parts stores) or use sandpaper or steel wool. Brush metal chips and terminal crud from the top of the battery.

Remove each of the cell caps and check the vent holes with a straw to make sure they are clean. Consider replacing the filler caps with the new catalytic caps that recombine the battery gases back into water as the battery nears the end of its charge cycle. (These caps are available from, among others, Surrette Marine Battery Co. of Salem, Massachusetts.)

Inspect the level of the electrolyte (mix of water and sulphuric acid) in each cell to make sure there is at least enough to cover the plates. If the plates are exposed to air they will oxidize. Check the specific gravity of each cell with an inexpensive floating-ball hydrometer. The charge in the cells should be nearly identical. Skippers who are really serious about battery preventive maintenance use a regular hydrometer. Take a reading of each cell, compensate for temperature, and then record the result in the engine log. This practice predicts an "incipient malfunction."

Top off the battery (if the electrolyte is low) with distilled water purchased in any drug store. If this seems a bit much, catch rainwater and save this for battery water. (Tap water has dissolved iron, salts, chlorine, limestone, etc., which will shorten the life of the battery.)

Terminals

If it is accessible (and it rarely is) remove the retaining nut from the stud on top of the starter-motor solenoid and then the end of the positive battery cable. Take some care as this is often used as a main tie point for several electrical leads in small craft. Clean and burnish every one of the terminals using a wire brush, a terminal cleaner, or some sandpaper. This terminal and its feed cable must carry a lot of current, and cleanliness is essential to conductivity. Reattach each lead to the solenoid terminal using a flat washer, a lock washer, and a burnished nut. Dress the leads well clear of any grounding metal. Finish by spraying the entire terminal area with a moisture-displacing spray such as LPS, WD-40, or CRC, or apply Vaseline or a light coating of grease. The idea is to keep air and moisture away from the metal terminals so that current-inhibiting oxides will not form.

Replace the battery and make sure it cannot move when the boat rolls.

Use the terminal-cleaning tool to burnish the inside of the cable clamps. If the clamps are extra cruddy, wash them with a dilute solution of baking soda and water; then rinse and dry. It is a good idea also to purchase and install terminal corrosion-inhibiting pads, available in most auto supply stores.

After the clamps are back on and tightened, spray LPS, WD-40, or CRC, or coat with Vaseline.

The following applies to both inboards and outboards. Remove, inspect, burnish, and clean each of the wires connected to the back of the alternator. In the case of an inboard engine this may involve the removal of insulating rubber boots. If the boots have been in place, the terminals may be clean and bright—if so, just check the tightness of the clamp nuts. With an outboard the alternator is often part of the flywheel, and the field and output leads may not be easily accessible. Spray the terminals before replacing the rubber insulating boots.

Inspect the alternator drive belt next. Look for cracks on the inside by bending and stretching any suspicious areas, and look for frays and shiny burned spots. Replace the belt if there is the least suspicion it won't make it through the season. To do this loosen the alternator tension adjustment bracket and slip the new belt on after taking the old one off. Set up belt tension by prying down on the alternator with a stick or tool handle while you tighten the mounting bolt. Test belt tension by pushing down on the belt with your thumb. The belt should depress about ½". Do not overtension the drive belt as this can cause alternator bearings to wear out. If your drive belts are in pairs, DO NOT replace only a single belt—always replace both belts with a matched pair. Don't pry the belts on or off with a screwdriver; loosen the alternator bracket so that the belts can slip loosely over all pulleys. After installation and tensioning, note how deep the belt sets in the pulley grooves. If the belt is flush with the edges of the pulley groove it is either worn and has taken a set, or it is too tight.

The Charging System

Check the voltage regulator (or an alternator) by turning the ignition key to ON, but do not start the engine. Hold the shank of a steel screwdriver close to the back of the alternator. You should feel a faint but definite magnetic attraction. This simple test tells you that the rotor (field winding) of the machine is ready to work. One basic weakness of the alternator is that it will not charge a completely dead battery. It must have a trickle of current to energize the field winding.

Further checks. First, the abomination, the idiot light. When you turned the ignition key to ON the charge light should have come on. Start the engine, let it warm up, then set to a fast idle. Note that the idiot light goes out. If you have a charge/discharge ammeter, note that the indicating needle swings into the charge area of the meter. In each case, all might be well. But since both instruments are often unreliable, you may have to check further.

To check out the alternator and the voltage regulator when the alternator does not appear to be charging, connect a jumper wire *momentarily* between the output terminal and the field winding. If the charging light goes out, or if the ammeter swings into the charge region all at once, you have a bad voltage regulator and it must be replaced (if it's one of the electronic sealed units). On many inboard boats a heavy fuse is hidden, wrapped in rubber tape, between the alternator output terminal and the control panel. Use a cheap but very effective test lamp made up of a 12-volt lamp, some zip cord, and

a pair of alligator clips to test this. Ground one clip of the test lamp to the engine block, and touch the other clip to the output terminal of the alternator. The lamp should light. Check both sides of the fuse by unwrapping the tape. The lamp should light on both sides. Check both terminals of the ammeter with the test lamp connecting one clip of the lamp to any convenient negative return and the other clip to each of the meter terminals. The lamp should light in each case.

The lamp should light with the same brilliance it does when connected directly across the battery. In almost all cases if it doesn't, the trouble will be found to be a broken or dirty connection. In the worst case it will be traced to a faulty voltage regulator.

While almost all voltage regulators today are fully transistorized and molded into plastic cases, a few of the older electro-mechanical relay-type regulators still exist. Unlike a DC generator, an alternator does not require a current-limiting relay since the alternator is self-limiting. As a result no relay will be seen inside the voltage regulator box. Nor does the alternator require a cutout relay since the rectifying diodes block back current from the battery when the engine is shut down. All that remains is a black metal box with one or two relays inside.

One of the relays is always the voltage-controlling relay, and the other (if present) energizes when the ignition key is turned on to supply field current to the alternator. A very few voltage-control relays can be adjusted to set the output voltage of the alternator to the specified amount set by the engine maker. This task should be turned over to an experienced mechanic/electrician as it requires special tools and instruments.

Voltmeter

Perhaps one of the best preventive maintenance tasks that the do-it-yourself skipper can do is to junk the idiot light and install one of the inexpensive (low-voltage reading) DC voltmeters sold in most electronic hobby shops for $10 to $15. These are easily dash-mounted and connected with short leads to the cold side of the ignition switch and the normal negative return near the instrument panel.

When the ignition switch is turned on the unloaded battery voltage will be displayed. As the starter key is activated the heaviest load possible is placed on the battery. Should the voltage drop to below 9 volts there's trouble a-brewin' in electric city. A dirty corroded terminal, low water, or a bad cell is indicated. (Neither an ammeter nor an idiot light will give you this information.) After the engine has started and the alternator has taken over the boat's electric load the charging voltage will be displayed on the voltmeter (13 or more volts). Once the battery is up to full charge the displayed voltage will drop back to 12 volts or thereabouts. Anything less and the charging system is not working properly.

Many small craft are equipped with automotive-type batteries. These batteries are designed to provide a very short spurt of high current to start the engine. Once this task is accomplished they give up the load to the alternator. For a boat, the automotive surface-charge battery is poor at best. At anchor, the radio, stereo, lights, pumps, etc., all run from the small surface charge of the car battery, and when it is time to start the engine the battery might be dead. That's why you need a marine-service-rated battery with lots of cold crank power and a deep reserve rating. Still better, install a dual battery system with a vaporproof transfer switch so that one battery is always held in reserve and does nothing else but start the engine.

Floating Transducer

The installation instructions for my new depth sounder suggested I mount the transducer inside the hull using a silicone adhesive. (I would have preferred a transom mount, but my 27′ deep-V has both an outdrive and trim tabs, leaving little room.)

However, I found the return signal to be quite weak—it apparently had trouble penetrating both the hull and the adhesive. After much further experimentation, I tried letting the transducer float freely in the few inches of water in my shower sump. It worked flawlessly! The water provides a perfect coupling between the hull and the transducer.

Tips on Choosing and Installing Knotmeters

Racing sailors have long recognized the value of a knotmeter, but cruising yachtsmen—especially powerboatmen—have been slow to add one of these valuable instruments. Besides speed, knotmeters also provide distance traveled, either by means of an attached log or a simple speed/time calculation. In conjunction with calculations for current, the knotmeter offers boatmen the best instrument available for simple dead-reckoning.

It is for these reasons that more and more powerboat owners are installing knotmeters (usually with a log) and why practically every sailboat owner considers a knotmeter of some kind almost as essential as a set of sails.

Fortunately, there are many good units available in a wide range of different prices, and in styles that are suitable for all different kinds of boats—power or sail. Prices start at about $250 to $300 for the recognized brands, which is comparable to that of other marine instruments, but the more sophisticated digital units, which can measure speeds to the nearest 1/100th of a knot and indicate a trend of acceleration or deceleration (important to racing sailors), can cost as much as $1,000 or more.

According to one of the largest electronic marine equipment dealers on the East Coast, Griffith Marine Navigation Inc., of New Rochelle, NY, the most popular units are those that sell for between $350 and $600, so chances are that this is about what you will be likely to spend for a reliable unit. But even this is not bad when compared with some of the more sophisticated pieces of electronic gear that yachtsmen are currently ordering faster than most manufacturers can produce them.

When shopping for a knotmeter (also called a marine speedometer) there are a number of questions you will have to decide on in order to select the brand or style that will best meet your particular needs (and budget).

First, do you want a model that gives a digital readout, or one of the less expensive analog models that have a dial or meter to indicate speed? The digital models generally give a readout in tenths of a knot (below 10 knots only in many models), so they are more precise at slow speeds. With an analog or dial-type model, you will have to interpolate the reading yourself to determine whether the needle is one third, one quarter, or halfway between two whole-knot readings.

The second question you will have to answer is whether or not you want a log included. With some knotmeters a log can be added later on, but with others you cannot, so check before you buy. Also, some logs are mechanical, which means the reading will remain even after the power is shut off. Digital models, on the other hand, may have only an electronic memory that turns the unit back to

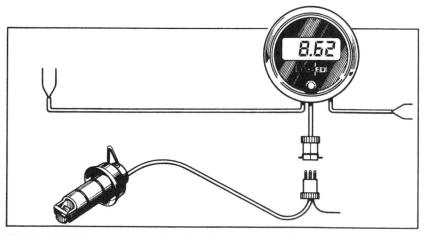

This digital knot meter has a paddle-wheel transducer and a hookup for a second display unit. Wire at top right goes to the power source; black wire off the three-pronged plug goes to ground.

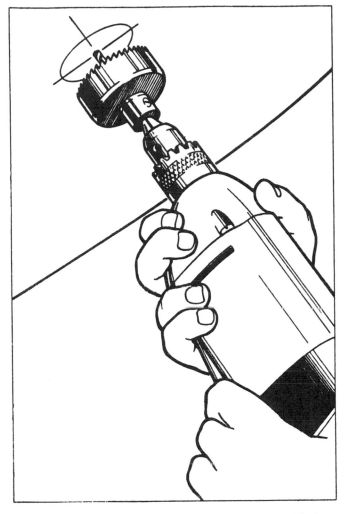

Cut hole for transducer in a location accessible from inside the boat.

knotmeter/log, is not an especially difficult job. Any reasonably handy boatowner should have no trouble tackling the installation himself. The hardest part for some will be installing the through-hull fitting for the transducer, so you may prefer to have the yard handle this while the boat is still out of the water. On some boats the most time-consuming part will be snaking the necessary wires and cables from transducer to indicator, or from power supply to the indicator or control box, but with patience none of this should be a serious problem.

Although installation manuals supplied are supposed to tell you just what to do, some are quite sketchy, and many leave out a number of important pointers. To save you the trouble of finding these out the hard way, here are a few guidelines that should be followed, and some things that should be kept in mind when installing any type of knotmeter.

(1) The indicator should be installed where it will be reasonably well protected from the weather if it will be mounted on top of an existing panel or helm station in its own housing—most external meter housings offer only marginal protection from rain and spray. If you must mount it in an exposed location, buy one of the units that are made for recessed mounting in the panel or in a cockpit bulkhead; these have a waterproof facing to protect the instrument.

(2) If you want more than one station to be able to read the knotmeter, make sure the unit you select has the capability to drive more than one indicator or dial (even if you don't want the remote station now, you may want to add it later on). On a powerboat with a flying bridge you may want the bridge station to have a panel-

zero when the power is shut off at the end of the day, or when there is a sudden power failure. Logs also differ in that some go up to as high as 999.9 miles before automatically starting at zero again, while others may only read as high as 19.9 miles before resetting themselves to zero.

The third question you will have to answer is the type of transducer you want—the transducer being the part that sticks down below the hull to sense the speed through the water. Actually, this question is more or less answered for you by the type of boat you have—or rather by the maximum speed readings you will need.

There are two types of trans-

ducers currently in widespread use: the paddle-wheel transducer, and the turbine-type transducer. Paddle wheels are by far the most popular according to most dealers, and according to John Schebendach of Griffith Marine, they are also more accurate at slower speeds (up to about 20 knots). At higher speeds, however, paddle wheels may be affected by excessive turbulence and cavitation, so most high-speed knotmeters use turbine-type sensors. Though less affected by turbulence, these are more prone to fouling by weeds, grass and other drifting material that tends to get wrapped around the spiral-shaped turbine drive.

Installing any knotmeter, or

mounted, waterproof indicator, while you can use a separate bracket-mounted unit below.

(3) Plan the location of your through-hull fitting very carefully. You have to be sure the transducer's paddle wheel or turbine will project down into undisturbed water where readings will not be affected by undue turbulence when underway. Generally speaking, a spot that is about one third or less the length of the waterline aft, starting from the bow, is preferable. It should also be near enough to the centerline so that the transducer will never come out of the water when the boat heels to either port or starboard. In sailboats, the location should be forward of the keel, if possible, and in all boats it should be forward of the widest part of the hull.

(4) Selecting a location for the transducer is complicated by the fact that it must also be easily accessible from the inside while the boat is in the water. This is because all paddle wheels and turbines get fouled at times, and the only way

to free them up (short of hauling the boat or calling in a diver) is to pull the transducer out from inside. All are designed with an auxiliary plug or cap that permits you to quickly cap the through-hull from the inside when the transducer is pulled for inspection or cleaning. You will also need a minimum of 6″ to 8″ of clearance above it—water will be gushing in, so you will want to get the cap or plug in fast after the unit is pulled.

(5) These units all use very little power—less than 1 amp in most cases—but the power supply should not be "tapped off" an ignition switch, ammeter, radio, or other instrument or piece of electronic equipment. Power should be drawn directly from the battery, or from a buss bar or panel that is connected directly to the battery. Hooking up to any "hot" terminal is merely looking for trouble as the sensing unit might then pick up stray impulses that will affect the accuracy of its reading. If a log is included as a separate instrument, then it may need its own power

supply. The installation manual furnished with the unit will spell this out clearly.

As a rule, the actual installation usually begins with the through-hull fitting while the boat is out of the water—all other work can then be done after the boat is launched. After selecting the location for the through-hull, you will need a hole saw of the proper diameter to cut the needed hole in the bottom. No fairing blocks will be needed as a rule, but some of the fittings are designed so that you will have to make a slight recess or countersink to permit the flange or rim of the through-hull fitting to fit flush.

Use plenty of good bedding compound, such as one of the silicone rubber compounds, to install the fitting, and make sure you line it up properly fore and aft before tightening it into place (there will be an arrow or some similar mark on the housing). For this part of the job you will need someone to give you a hand tightening the

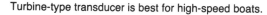

A paddle wheel, the most popular transducer type.

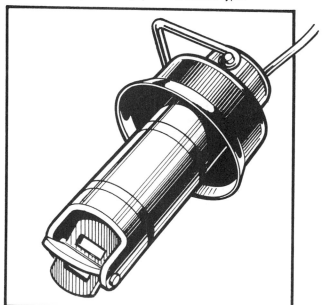

Turbine-type transducer is best for high-speed boats.

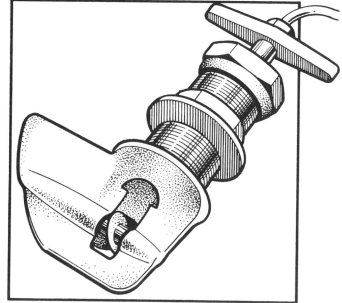

locknut on the inside while you hold the outside.

When running the transducer cable up to the indicating unit, avoid having any splices or connections located where they will be in the bilge water, or where they will frequently get wet. The original cable supplied by the manufacturer is usually the safest thing to use (without cutting or splicing), so if the one supplied is not long enough, order one with a longer cable, or have the dealer make up an extension for you.

The indicator or display should be installed at a convenient location in or near the helm station where you can see it easily, and where you can also reach the back without removing it. The unit will have to be calibrated after the boat is launched (to correct for minor variations from boat to boat), and in most cases the calibration adjustments are located on the back of the indicator or the control panel, so keep this in mind when installing it—leave plenty of room for easy access. Use bedding compound to seal around a recessed, panel-type unit.

If you have purchased a unit with a log that must be mounted separately in its own housing, then make sure you pick a location where both indicators can be close together so you can see both simultaneously. Also, remember the log must be within easy reach to permit resetting to zero when desired.

Another factor that may have to be considered is the relative location of the unit with respect to the ship's compass. Some models have small magnets inside that could affect the compass if too close, so test for this by holding the indicator next to the compass before you actually install it.

Remote indicators, if planned, are installed in much the same way, though they may not need

their own power supply. However, you will have to snake a cable from the first indicator to the second in order to wire the two in series so they will respond to signals from the same transducer.

If you want to get maximum results with your knotmeter, be sure you follow the manufacturer's instructions on calibrating the instrument. This involves an hour or two of running back and forth over a known distance (a measured mile is ideal), but the extra time spent will be worth the effort and will insure your getting truly accurate readings from your newly installed knotmeter.

Through-Deck Fitting for Heavy Wires

After installing an electric anchor winch on the bow of my boat, I found myself faced with an unexpected problem. I had to bring two heavy (#6) wires up through the deck near the winch for power, and the problem was to find a waterproof through-hull fitting for the wires where they passed through the deck.

Most marine outlets do sell waterproof fittings that are designed for passing wires through, but all those I could find would only accept wires up to about ¼" in diameter (they are used primarily for passing antenna wires through the side of a bridge or cabin). No one had a waterproof fitting that would take the large wires I had to install, particularly since the surface they had to go through was horizontal.

I finally solved the problem with a different type of fitting entirely. I bought a water inlet fitting that is designed for hooking up to dockside water (the one I used is made by Perko). This comes with a threaded female collar for accept-

ing the male end of a standard garden hose fitting. I then ran the electric wires through a piece of ¾" clear plastic hose, and to the end of this hose I attached a male garden hose fitting (widely sold for repairing hoses when the original fitting needs replacing).

After drilling the necessary hole through the deck, I then was able to run my heavy wires through the plastic hose and down through the water inlet fitting, which was well bedded and firmly screwed down to the deck as illustrated. The end of the hose, with the male fitting attached and the wires inside, was then screwed into the deck fitting, which has a standard hose washer inside. This makes a watertight connection at the deck. The clear plastic hose enclosing the wires is long enough to reach the winch housing, where a seal was formed by use of a thick bead of silicone rubber so that water could not enter from that end.

Portable Electronics Mount

When we bought our new trawler one problem we faced was where to mount the depthfinder and VHF radio—both on the flying bridge and at the lower station. Flush mounting the electronics meant cutting large holes in the fiberglass bulkhead on the bridge; below, it meant cutting into the beautiful teak in the saloon.

We thought about mounting the electronics on brackets, but it was hard to decide where each bracket should go, so we finally struck upon a solution that is simple yet completely flexible. All units were mounted with their regular bracket on a solid board with rubber suction cups on the bottom—making the whole package completely portable.

We can use the instruments at either the upper or the lower station by means of two separate cable harnesses—one going up to the bridge, and the other coming up through the teak bulkhead in the saloon. The package is stowed out of sight in a locker when not in use, thus protecting it from the weather as well as from thieves.

For the board we used a ready-made mahogany bookshelf, which we finished with several coats of varnish. The suction cups are the kind sold in auto accessory stores for use under top-carrier racks, and these are fastened in place with stainless screws after drilling holes through the board near each corner.

We originally thought this would be a temporary setup until we decided on a more permanent mount, but the suction cup mounting has worked so well—it doesn't move even in rough seas—that we now think of it as a permanent arrangement.

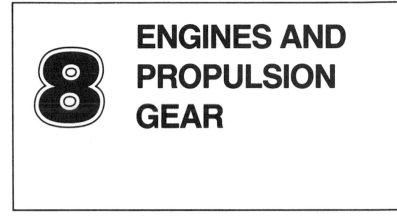

ENGINES AND PROPULSION GEAR

When Your Gas Inboard Engine Won't Start

In a marine environment, the usual cause of an engine's failure to start is moisture—either wet wiring that shorts out the electrical system, or water in the fuel supply. Your first step in troubleshooting is to eliminate these possibilities, then to follow a logical sequence that will lead to the fault with little fuss and no need for special equipment. You eliminate guesswork and unproductive random checks.

Begin by spraying all wiring with a moisture-displacing compound such as CRC or WD-40. Remove and clean spark plugs; wet, dirty porcelain on the exterior provides a low-resistance path to ground for the high-tension voltage that otherwise would jump the spark gap. If the engine was spun a few times by the starter, plug tips should be damp with gasoline—an indication that the fuel system is okay; troubleshooting procedures under this heading should not be necessary.

However, if plug tips are wet with water, there's water in the fuel system. Drain and clean fuel filters; remove and drain the car-buretor float bowl; disconnect and drain fuel lines from fuel pump to carburetor, and from tank to fuel pump. If there's any reason to suspect water in the fuel tank, this should be drained and fresh fuel added. When working with the fuel system, be sure to observe all safety precautions: No smoking on the boat or in its vicinity; use of proper containers for drained fuel and proper disposal of these ashore, along with rags used to wipe up any spills. Ventilate and use the blower before trying again to start the engine.

Very few starting failures are caused by faults in the fuel system under normal circumstances, and the above procedures practically eliminate this system as a source of the trouble. However, if the engine still fails to kick over while it is being spun by the starter, make sure there's fuel in the tank (a gauge reading may be misleading, so try with a dipstick), and that the fuel shutoff valve at the tank is in the open position.

Battery and Starter

Now check out the electrical system. Note that each step presents an either/or situation, so the steps are presented in outline form for the sake of clarity. Start by turning on the ignition switch.

I Ammeter needle doesn't move, or telltale "idiot" light doesn't glow: Battery is dead, or connection is broken between battery and ignition switch. Charge or replace battery as necessary; clean and tighten all connections; replace worn or frayed cables.

II Ammeter shows slight discharge, or telltale light glows: Current is flowing. Operate the starter.

  A. Starter action is sluggish: Battery is defective or partially discharged; loose, corroded, or dirty battery terminals; mechanical failure in starter; defective starter switch or starter drive. Turn on a cabin light supplied by starter-battery voltage, that you can watch as you operate the starter again.

    1. Light goes dim, or out completely: Trouble is in the battery or its connections or cables. Voltme-

ter readings should be 1.5 volts for each battery cell; hydrometer reading should show specific gravity of 1.250 or better.

    a. Low voltage or low specific gravity: Recharge or replace battery as necessary.

    b. Proper voltage and specific gravity: Clean and tighten battery connections and cable terminals. Replace any cable that appears worn or frayed.

2. Cabin light remains bright: Trouble is between battery and starter, or starter or its switch is defective.

    a. Make sure all cable connections are clean and tight.

    b. Have starter switch or starter itself repaired or replaced, as necessary.

Ignition Primary Circuit

B. Starter spins engine easily. Trouble is in ignition system. Make visual inspection to check for broken, worn, or disconnected wires. Remove distributor cap, block points open with a piece of cardboard, and use a voltmeter or test bulb to check for voltage at the terminal on the distributor.

1. No current present: There's a break in the circuit leading back to the ignition switch, or the condenser has an internal short to ground. Disconnect condenser from the distributor plate so that its outside shell is not grounded; test again for voltage at the distributor terminal.

    a. Current is indicated: Condenser is faulty; replace it.

    b. No current shown: Check wiring connections at distributor; work back, checking for voltage at each connection, to the ignition switch. This will locate the faulty wiring or connection. Replace wiring or tighten connections as necessary.

2. Voltage is present at distributor: Trouble within the distributor, most likely burned or dirty breaker points. Remove the piece of cardboard and rotate engine until points are closed. Check for current again at the distributor terminal.

    a. Current present: Points are defective; replace them. In an emergency, points can be cleaned by using the sanded side of a match box, a knife blade, or the sharp edge of a screwdriver to scrape scale from the points. After cleaning, the points can be gapped to about .020″ by using 4 layers of newspaper as a feeler gauge.

    b. Current not present: Causes include a weak or broken breaker-arm spring, distorted or bent breaker arm, or nonconductive dirt on the points. Inspect and replace as necessary.

Transistorized Ignition Systems

If a capacitor-discharge ignition system is used that incorporates the standard breaker points, the procedures outlined for testing a standard ignition primary circuit can be followed to some extent. If possible, disconnect the transistorized unit (or on some models, such as the Heath unit, simply switch to "standard") and rewire to the standard mode. If the engine runs, the transistorized unit is at fault.

With other units, particularly breakerless systems, special equipment and procedures may be required. Check your manual.

Ignition Secondary Circuit

If the ignition primary circuit checks out okay and the engine still fails to start, test the secondary circuit. Remove the high-tension lead from a spark plug and hold its end about ¼″ away from the block while the engine is being cranked by the starter.

I. No spark, or weak spark: Remove high-tension lead from the center of the distributor cap (the lead from the coil) and hold it about ¼″ from the block while the engine is cranked by the starter.

    A. No spark, or weak spark: Faulty secondary-coil winding; replace the coil.

    B. Good spark: Coil is okay; distributor cap or rotor are faulty. Inspect and replace as necessary.

II. Good spark from spark plug lead: Ignition secondary circuit is good. Inspect spark plugs; clean and regap them, or replace as necessary. An emergency feeler gauge for the plug cap can be made by folding a piece of newspaper 5 times (this results in 32 layers of paper). When changing the gap be sure to bend only the side electrode and never the center one, as there is danger of breaking the porcelain.

SPARK PLUG NOTE: If you are used to looking at your spark plugs closely whenever you remove or change one, you should know what a normal plug looks like. If it's brown, light brown, or gray, it's probably okay. If it's black and wet, it's saturated with fuel and oil. If it's loaded with carbon deposits, it can be cleaned or replaced. (Since you always carry spares, you can replace when in doubt.) A plug that's been overheating shows an eroded electrode, blistered insulator, or glazing of the insulator. These are symptoms—wrong type plug, engine overheating, or other problems. Replacing will help temporarily, but you should correct the cause at the first opportunity.

Automotive books, such as *Basic Car Care*, show you in color pictures what spark plugs look like under normal and abnormal conditions. Or get a mechanic to explain how he judges plugs by inspection.

Fuel System

If for any reason you did not check for water in the fuel system, and there is no fault on the electrical side, the trouble must be in the gasoline feed. Remove the flame arrester and make sure it is clean. Look down into the carburetor throat while operating the throttle linkage; the accelerating pump should push gas through the pump jet, which you can see.

I. Gas spurts from pump jet when linkage is operated: Choke action is probably defective. With a cold engine, the choke valve should be closed.
   A. Choke is closed. Engine is probably flooded with gas-oline. Replace flame arrester, open throttle all the way and crank engine with starter until it starts. (However, do not run starter more than 25 seconds at a time. Let it cool down.)
   B. Choke is open. Place the palm of your hand over carburetor throat as starter is operated; engine should start.

II. Gasoline does not spurt from pump jet: Fuel is not reaching the carburetor. Check fuel-pump operation by disconnecting the line from it to the carburetor, and hold a container under the open end of the line. When the engine is cranked, fuel should pulsate out of the line. Be sure to take all safety precautions while working with the fuel system: no smoking on board or in the vicinity of the boat; wipe up spilled gasoline and dispose of rags properly ashore; dispose of any contaminated fuel properly ashore; ventilate and use blower before trying to start engine.
   A. Gas spurts from fuel pump: Carburetor float valve may be stuck, or float may be damaged so that its valve is jammed closed. Replace valve or float as necessary.
   B. No fuel spurts from pump: Make sure fuel shutoff valve at tank is in the open position. At the fuel pump, disconnect the line from the tank, and if possible, blow back through it while someone listens at the tank (it may be necessary to disconnect each section of fuel line and blow through it individually to make sure it is not clogged).
      1. Bubbles are heard gurgling up into the tank as you blow through the line: Fuel line is clear; the trouble is in the fuel pump itself. Remove the sediment bowl and screen; clean and replace, making sure there's an airtight fit. If the pump still does not function, it must be replaced.
      2. Bubbles are not heard at the tank: Line is clogged. Remove each section of line and blow through it individually to clear it; replace any line that you can't clear by blowing through. Since a clogged line indicates foreign matter in the tank, it is best to have the tank drained or pumped out and fresh fuel taken on after lines have been cleared or replaced. It's advisable also to add a heavy-duty filter and water-separator unit at the tank end of the line to remove any substances not drained with the old fuel.

Mechanical Failures

The above procedures should locate the problem in almost all cases, particularly on an engine no more than a few years old. However, if the engine is getting a good spark at the plugs, and a fuel/air mix is reaching the cylinders, and it still fails to start, the problem must be a mechanical one. Most often this is a case of improper timing; the distributor housing has slipped on its shaft. Some engine manuals provide instructions for static timing, or a strobe timing light, if available, can be used while the engine is being cranked.

On an older engine, particularly

one that has gone for a long period without an overhaul, burned and worn valves may cause lack of compression in the cylinders; a compression check will reveal this.

If you don't have the information or equipment needed to check and adjust timing and compression, it's time to call in your marine mechanic.

A vacuum gauge is a useful diagnostic tool; readings and their meanings are shown in the table below.

VACUUM GAUGE READINGS

Engine Operation	Reaction of Needle (In. Hg.)	Meaning of Reaction
Slow idle	Steady at 17-21	Engine okay
Open and close accelerator rapidly	Bounces from 2 to 25	Engine okay
Slow idle	Steady at 17 to 21; occasional drops of 1 to 5	Exhaust or intake valve sticking; sparkplug misfiring
Accelerate gradually	Bounces between 17-21; drops several inches at regular intervals	Burned exhaust or intake valve
Slow idle; then open and close accelerator rapidly	At slow idle, steady between 3 and 5 below normal; as accelerator opens and closes, needle bounces between 0 and 22	Piston rings or cylinder walls may be worn
Slow idle	Steady at 13-16	Ignition timing off
Slow idle	Steady between 8-14	Valve timing off due to worn camshaft lobe of timing gear
Fast idle	Steady between 5-12	Intake manifold gasket, carburetor gasket or PCV hose leaking
Fast idle	Drifts slowly between 14-16	Sparkplug or breaker point gap out of adjustment; damaged plug, high-tension cable, distributor
Fast idle	Floats slowly between 12-16	Carburetor out of tune
Slow idle: accelerate gradually	Steady when engine starts; slowly drops to 0 at idle; slowly rises at acceleration	Exhaust-system restriction may exist
Slow idle: accelerate gradually	Swings widely at all engine speeds	Head gasket leaking
Slow idle: accelerate gradually	Vib.ates rapidly between 14-19	Valve guides may be worn

Midseason Checklist

—by Tim Banse

Midseason checklists couldn't come at a worse time of year—when you'd rather be out on the water enjoying the boat rather than under the engine cover wrestling with wrenches. Thankfully though, if the maintenance performed during spring commissioning was adequate, little needs to be done besides checking for problem areas and heading them off before serious malfunctions occur.

Here's how to get the job done in ten quick and easy steps:

(1) Mark the spark-plug cables with masking tape at the boot end 1, 2, 3, 4, and so on. This is to insure they will be reinstalled in their proper firing order and you won't have to rely on your memory. It is, however, also considered fair play to simply remove, inspect, gap, and replace one plug at a time. Whichever method you decide on, be sure to pull off the cables by the boot, don't just grab and yank them by the wire. Clean and regap the spark plugs. How many hours running time have the plugs logged? New plugs have the advantage of low cost, lower fuel consumption, easier starting, and smoother running. Improved reliability is their chief asset, so, if in doubt about the plugs, replace them. Don't replace the wires just yet. Wait for the engine test run.

(2) On the carburetor, remove the flame arrester. Open and close the throttle once. The choke plate should open with slight finger pressure. If it needs adjustment, check the owner's manual for details. Both the fuel filter and gasket should also be changed. Consider adding gasoline deicer to the tank(s) to absorb any moisture.

(3) Check the battery. A dirty surface allows voltage leakage. Baking soda is good for cleaning that surface since it neutralizes the battery acid, but don't let any drip into the cells. Are any of the cells low on water? If so, top off with distilled water. A hydrometer reading should indicate a specific gravity of 1.250 to 1.260 after a day's

running. All cable connections should be cleaned and protected with a light coat of grease. Are any instrument panel fuses blown?

(4) Check the alternator V-belt. Adjust the tension if slack, replace if frayed. Lubricate all the grease fittings on steering and shifting cables. Spray some lube on the carburetor and magneto linkage as well. With a flashlight and screwdriver, check hose clamps to make sure they are tight. Give the connector threads a shot of spray lubricant. If the engine is freshwater-cooled and has a heat exchanger, check the level of the onboard coolant. Beside the obvious benefits, antifreeze will provide antirust protection.

(5) Drain the gear case. Scrutinize the fluid. Be on the lookout for water, broken gear teeth, or bits of bronze bushing. Refill with fresh oil.

(6) Remove the prop. Straighten the dings. File smooth any nicks. Double-check the diameter and pitch. Is it right for your boat? The correct wheel will put a well-tuned motor in the middle to upper half of its recommended operating range. Does the zinc block on the drive or hull need replacing? If it is eaten away to less than half its original size, replace it. Check the prop-shaft seal for monofilament fish line. Coat the prop shaft with antiseize compound and replace the prop.

(7) Check the trim/tilt/lift-unit oil level. Top off as necessary. If it's very low, have a certified marine mechanic look at it. Tighten the lines running to the lift ram if they've worked loose.

(8) Start the engine. Once it's warmed up, adjust the idle speed and mixture. Rev up the engine a couple of times. Listen to it run. Is the engine in tune? Last time out on the water, did she perform like a thoroughbred or cough, woof,

and gag like a dying beast? Sick engines waste gas. Economy fuel tips include: Installing a dash-mounted vacuum gauge to monitor and optimize fuel consumption. Watching the readings encourages the pilot to go easier on the throttle bending. It's all right to accelerate crisply, but not like a hydroplane racer. Consider installing trim tabs and an economy pitched propeller. TIP: Don't idle the engine more than a minute at a time. Longer than that, and it costs more in fuel to run the engine than to shut it down and restart. The best fuel-miser of all is to keep the engine in tune.

(9) Get out the flashlight and inspect the block for water leaking out of freeze plugs or blown gaskets.

(10) Shut down the engine and change oil and filter. Draining the old crankcase oil is made more civilized by one of the drill-driven pumps. It also makes for a cleaner bilge and engine compartment. Filters should be filled with oil before replacing. A fingerful of oil smeared around the rubber filter gasket makes for a tighter seal.

Prefilling the filter prevents a dry start-up while the oil pump first fills the filter, then the galleys and bearings with oil. Check the dipstick to make sure it is up to level, then restart the engine. Look for leaks around the base of the filter. Tighten as necessary.

With everything in order, you deserve a shake-down cruise.

Rust-proofing the Starter

Clunk, clunk, clunk. That sound, at engine start-up, has ruined many a boating weekend. What is the source of this ominous noise if it isn't the battery? It is more than

likely an oxidized (rusted) starter Bendix.

In over fifteen years of servicing boats, I have found that 70 percent of boats dead in the water at dockside have had problems with battery or starting motor. A weak or discharged battery can be put back in commission by a quick battery charge or by use of jumper cables. An oxidized Bendix, however, is something else. The starter will then have to come out, and on some of the boats manufactured today this is no easy task. It's down there somewhere, close to the bilge, on one side of the engine or the other. Have you looked to see where yours is located? Sometimes just finding it is difficult; if it goes bad it has to be removed, and the real work begins.

We all know that a well-protected metal surface stands a far better chance of surviving exposure to the elements than does a bare one. This is the case with the starter motor. The outer housing is painted—protected, more or less, from the splashing of bilge water—but the Bendix end isn't and is susceptible to rust.

When there are a couple of gallons of water in the bilge, each wave or wake that your boat bounces over causes this water to be sloshed, splashed, whipped, and sprayed into every opening on the lower part of the engine. The starter usually takes a bath. With the engine running, a slight vacuum is sometimes created in the bell housing. The spinning flywheel acts much like a big fan and sucks bilge water in. As this spray inside the bell housing condenses, it drips down and settles in the bottom of the bell housing. As the flywheel rotates, the starter ring-gear teeth—located on the outer edge of the flywheel—pick up this water and sling it at high speed into the unprotected starter Bendix. It doesn't take too many of these exposures before the Bendix rusts to the starter motor shaft. The result is that clunk, clunk.

It is impossible to keep the bilge as dry as the Mojave desert in mid-July, so the solution must come in the form of rust-proofing for the starter Bendix. Here's how to do it:

Furnishing yourself with an electric-drill motor and a ½″ drill bit, first locate where the starter is and where the Bendix extends into the bell housing. Drill a hole above the Bendix in this area. If you coat the bit with heavy grease before you drill the hole, it will pick up any metal shavings that might fall inside. Find a suitable neoprene or wooden plug for the hole. The plug should be something that you can easily remove since you will be removing it every time you have water sloshing in the bilge. Once the Bendix is located, the hole drilled, and a plug found, you now have a way to service the Bendix. Spray or pour some CRC, WD-40, or other rust-preventive into the hole. Two or three ounces will do. Install the plug and start the engine. You can now be sure that the starter is safe from rust for a while.

During my first few years in the marine-engine repair business, I replaced something like three starters a week, usually as a result of starter-Bendix corrosion. The old adage, "An ounce of prevention is worth a pound of cure," led me to the technique described here, and changed three starter replacements a week to only three a month. Needless to say, my customers were delighted to find that they need not spend $50 or $60 for a starter; I was able to eliminate the problem before it developed by providing a simple lubrication system.

If your boat is more than a year old, or approaching its first birthday, I highly recommend that you perform the drilling operation. It will save you time, trouble, and money.

Tune-up in a Can
—by Tim Banse

Thanks to recent advances in ignition systems, most of them will keep an engine running very well, or not at all. If an engine is running poorly, chances are that what's gone wrong is either the spark plugs or the combustion chamber. In both cases, carbon fouling is the culprit causing the hard starting and the bad fuel economy.

Never fear. There is an inexpensive cure that is simple to use. Some folks around the marine circuit have dubbed it "Tune-up in a can." Both MerCruiser and OMC market spray cans of the stuff, calling it "Internal Engine Cleaner." It works equally well on outboards and inboards. It even helps smooth out ragged-running lawn mowers.

To use it, start the engine and run it until the dash gauge indicates operating temperature. The only tool you'll need is an open-end wrench to remove the flame arrester for a straight shot down the throat of the carburetor. Rev the engine to about 1,800 rpm. Then shoot some of the cleaner into the intake. Wash the throttle plates and venturi cluster. Use the little strawlike nozzle to shoot deep into the throat. Really load the engine

Squirt engine cleaner directly into throat of carburetor.

with great gobs of the stuff. You'll see clouds of white smoke billow out the exhaust. Ignore the disapproving stares of the passersby. Keep squirting. The engine will threaten to conk out. Keep it running just a little longer. Now bog the engine down with the cleaner until it dies.

Click off the ignition key and walk away for an hour or so. During that time the chemicals will be doing their dirty work, loosening up the carbon and other fouling deposits from the pistons and combustion chambers. After the hour is up, crank the engine. It will probably cough and wheez before it starts. Initial running will be rough. Expect sputtering for a minute or two as it coughs out all the junk that's been choking its fuel efficiency. Soon the old power plant should be purring like a well-oiled wheel.

If the engine is hard starting, pull the spark plugs. Kick the engine over a few revolutions to blow the excess cleaner out of the cylinders. One by one, dry the plug insulators with compressed air or a towel, then install. Now the engine will start.

While internal engine cleaner may seem like an unsophisticated method for problem solving, one thing's for sure: It works.

Fuel Filters: The Necessary Option

There are those among us who remember straining gasoline through a chamois cloth (actually a lamb skin used to wash and polish the family car) that we folded into a large metal funnel. I rather doubt the effectiveness of this old idea, but it enjoyed such reputation that Lindberg refused to try his trip across the Atlantic until the gas

had received such treatment. We were sure that it completely removed all water and impurities.

In those days much of our fuel was stored in steel tanks or drums and was full of all sorts of dirt, rust, and water. The situation today is much improved—many marina gas pumps have quite effective filters built right into the nozzle. Tanks also are of much higher-quality materials, and distribution systems are cleaner and better maintained—yet we still have horror stories of contaminated fuel. And with fuel prices going up, the possibility of bad fuel is less remote all the time. In fact, watered fuel is increasingly common. And if you cruise the Bahamas, you're familiar with the problem.

Diesel engines are particularly sensitive to water in the fuel and have quite sophisticated systems for its removal, but our interest in this article is directed to their gasoline cousins. For fifty years or so we depended upon the automotive system of a glass "sediment" bowl, with the later addition of a screen or ceramic insert to remove unwanted particles. The operation was simple—liquid fuel entered near the top of the device, filled the bowl, and exited from the top. Water, being heavier than gas, dropped to the bottom and was dumped out. The screen or ceramic strained out larger lumps of trash and was cleaned when the bowl was emptied. As we became more safety-conscious we got rid of the glass bowl (would you believe that I never saw a broken bowl in all my years?) and replaced it with thin metal. Oddly enough this was occasionally eaten through by highly contaminated water and caused some explosions.

Modern Filtering

There is excellent, reasonably priced filtering equipment available

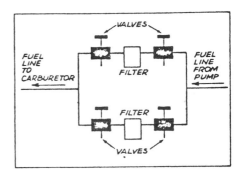

Above: Dual filters allow servicing of one. Below: A coalescing filter.

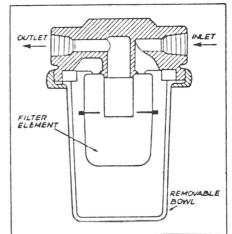

today and the smart boatowner will make use of it. You will hear "micron" used regularly—it is one-millionth of a meter. A human hair is about 50 microns and adequate gasoline filtering is about 40 microns. There are three devices available: strainers that remove trash particles down to 150 microns; separators that remove most water; and filters that remove particles down to 40 microns. Remember that diesel filters will work with gasoline except that you may have to replace the clear bowl with metal, and you must replace the drain petcocks with pipe plugs. Filter material ranges from screen, ceramic, cotton, paper, and thin metal plates to a combination of these. Water separation can be accomplished by a centrifugal system, but is done usually by "coalescing," which means passing fuel through chemically treated paper that causes little particles of water to form into large drops. These are then separated from gasoline by gravity.

My suggestions are not identical to many writers. I think that on a well-found inboard you should have at least a separator and filter. They should be strongly mounted to remove all strain from the fuel line, should be readily accessible for service, and you should check and drain them at least every twenty-five hours. The modern units are replaceable "cans" or feature cheaper elements that are installed into take-apart housings. Some mechanics suggest the filter be installed between the fuel pump and carburetor, but I prefer that both filter and separator be on the suction side of the pump. Automotive "in line" can-type filters are stock equipment on some engines, and while they may be okay for outboards, they aren't if placed in the bilge. You are generally safe if you use the filters that are furnished by the engine builder, since they should comply with current Coast Guard and ABYC standards.

Dirt particles can jam the carb float valve, causing flooding and even an explosion, and water, of course, completely kills your engine. A fuel filter system can prevent all this—provided it is properly installed and well maintained. Be sure that you use marine components, that they are approved by a respected testing lab, and you will be taking another long step toward hassel-free cruising.

Remote Engine Start/Stop Switch

When making adjustments to, or tuning up your engine, one of the most tiresome chores is climbing in and out of the hatch to start and stop the engine. The hand-held combination starter switch and kill switch shown here will eliminate that problem by enabling you to start or stop the engine from your working position in the bilge.

Two switches are needed: an inexpensive automobile-type momentary contact starter switch, and a single-pole, single-throw (SPST) toggle switch. You will also need four alligator clamps, two red and two black, four lengths of wire, each about 4′ to 5′ in length, and a rubber bicycle handle grip. The two pieces of wire connected to the starter switch should be #12 gauge, but the two pieces going to the "kill" (toggle) switch can be #18 wire.

Attach the 12-gauge wires to one pair of alligator clamps and attach the other end of each wire to the terminals on the starter switch, as shown here. Now do the same with the two 18-gauge wires, attaching one end of each to the toggle switch. Solder these connections to insure solid contact.

Now slit the rubber handle grip lengthwise on the side opposite the molded finger grips, and make a hole in the end to fit the body of the push-button starter switch. Cut another hole near the other end for the toggle switch. Spread the handle grip apart along the slit, then push the two switches in place in their openings. Close the grip along the slit and wrap tightly with tape to hold everything in place.

To use, you snap the alligator clips from the starter switch (they are connected to the heavier wires) onto the starter terminals—red to positive and black to negative. Then snap one of the other two clips onto the terminal on the coil that leads to the distributor. The other clip is clamped to any accessible engine block ground.

Now all you have to do is leave the ignition key turned on. With the toggle switch in the OFF position you can push the starter button to start the engine. To stop the

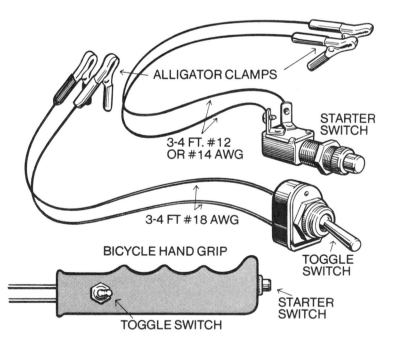

Remote starting switch is built into a bicycle handgrip.

ALLIGATOR CLAMPS

STARTER SWITCH

3-4 FT. #12 OR #14 AWG

3-4 FT #18 AWG

BICYCLE HAND GRIP

TOGGLE SWITCH

TOGGLE SWITCH

STARTER SWITCH

engine, flip the toggle switch to the ON position (this shorts out the current going to the distributor and stops the engine).

How to Start Your Engine with Two Flashlights and a Radio

What do you do when your motorboat is stalled because of a dead storage battery and you're stranded in a remote anchorage on the Hudson River?

If you happen to be as resourceful as boatmen-engineers Charles Moran and Robert Velleman, you might be able to think yourself out of a predicament of this kind. They did just that on a cruise this past summer up the Hudson, thanks to some offbeat engineering.

Here's how Charles Moran describes the adventure.

"We anchored the boat—a 21′ Grady White powered by a 100-hp Evinrude engine—about thirty miles south of Albany at a place called Rattlesnake Island. While setting the anchor forward, it is necessary to put the boat in reverse to insure a good firm grip. At the same time, we threw the aft anchor to prevent the boat from swinging in the wind.

"As the bow anchor took hold, the engine stalled as it was running at a low rpm. After the ten seconds required to carry out this operation, the ignition switch was inadvertently left on causing the storage battery to drain. By the next morning, when we were prepared to take off, the battery was stone dead.

"After evaluating various possibilities, Bob suggested that we try using the Duracell dry-cell batteries in the radio and flashlights. The radio, incidentally, had also been left on all night with the re-

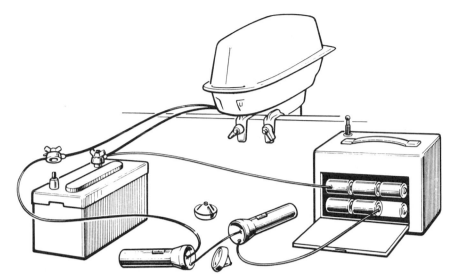

Flashlight and radio dry cells in series provide 13.5 volts for emergency starting power.

sult that its batteries were not up to their maximum supply capability.

"As it turned out, there was no problem with the dry cells. Nine of the "D"-size Duracells were hooked up in series to provide a 13.5-volt power supply sufficient to aid us in manually starting the motor. After three tries, the motor turned over and we were back in business.

"It was an interesting experience, something that the average boat owner might not anticipate. We were lucky to have the Mallory dry cells on board, otherwise we might have been in real trouble with little chance of getting the engine started."

EDITOR'S NOTE: Of course, you don't always have a couple of guys like Velleman and Moran on board, both of whom are graduate engineers, when you're faced with battery failure in the boondocks. Velleman received his E.E. degree from Lehigh and a Masters Degree in Systems Engineering from West Coast University. Moran has a Mechanical Engineering degree from Fairleigh Dickinson. For the bene-

fit of less technical boatmen who may find themselves similarly stranded on some future cruise, the diagram shows how the Duracells were connected with odd bits of wire. The storage battery had been disconnected and the wiring hooked directly to the dry-cell battery leads, which in turn were hooked to the coil. Batteries in the radio were isolated from the radio itself by inserting small pieces of cardboard. This was done to protect the radio from possible voltage overload during the series connection. In total, the voltage supply to the coil was 13.5 volts, sufficient to aid in manually starting the motor. The dry cells employed in the hook-up were nine Mallory "D"-size 1.5-volt Duracell alkaline batteries.

Emergency Point Replacement

—by Tim Banse

Carrying a spare set of ignition points can save an uncomfortable night drifting at sea. But even if you do have a spare set in the on-board inventory, how do you install them without a fancy timing light? The answer: The same way grandfather used to set the points on his old clunkers underneath the shade tree—with a scrap of paper.

To do so, bump the starter, or turn the crankshaft over with a wrench, until the marks etched on the pulley line up with the marks on the timing cover. Six to 10° of advance will work if you're not sure. Then remove the distributor cap. Is the rotor lined up to fire number 1 cylinder? If not, rotate the engine one full turn until it is.

Remove the old points and clean off the distributor cam, then dab on a tiny amount of the lube that comes in the little red pill along with the new points.

With the new points set, and the crank lined up to its timing marks, loosen the distributor hold-down bolt enough to allow free rotation. Gently pry open the points with a screwdriver and slip in a piece of paper. Let the points close. Never let the paper drag against the points or the scratches will spell an early death for them.

Rotate the distributor in the opposite direction the rotor usually turns while holding the scrap of paper between two fingers. The instant the paper seems to give is when the points are just starting to break. It's at this point that the engine sparks, firing number one cylinder.

Break the points a couple of times to get the feel for the procedure. With the crankshaft lined up against its timing marks and the points just breaking, the engine will be relatively accurately timed. It is a crude method, but it will get you back to port.

NOTE: This method does not work with an old set of points be-cause surface corrosion will grab at the paper.

How to Save a Cooling Pump from Itself

After long use or after standing unused for long periods of time, rubber impellers for cooling pumps tend to "shed" their vanes. Where do these vanes go?

A few years ago my trawler yacht (*Minnie McCoy*) developed an engine overheating problem. Examination of the freshwater circulating pump disclosed that the hub was stripped of all but two of its impeller blades. I took a new impeller out of my spares locker and replaced the stripped unit.

Although this repair got me back to my dock, it was obvious that I still had a problem. Where *had* all those little bits of rubber gone?

I spent that night—till 3 A.M.—with my eyes propped open cataloging all the downstream places those rubber parts could have lodged to restrict my cooling system's operation. There was the transmission-oil heat exchanger. There was the thermostat. There were all those little passages cast in the manifold, the head, and the block. There was a tricky little by-pass pipe between the block and the head. And finally there was the main seawater/freshwater heat exchanger.

The following morning found me down on the dock with a high-pressure dockside bilge pump with flexible pressure and discharge lines running into *Minnie's* engine hold. Sure enough, two hours of reverse flushing of the cooling system yielded a small pile of bits of rubber at the end of the discharge line. I was a little uneasy since the pile of rubber did not look as though it was big enough to account for all the missing vanes. Unfortunately, my concern was well founded.

My spare time in the following weeks was occupied by tearing down the entire cooling system, taking apart the heat exchangers, and "rodding" all the tubes to push out the little pieces of rubber. More back flushing of the individual parts of the system and the "yield" finally convinced me that I was back in operation again with a clean system. However, I never wanted to go through *that* hassle again!

I started to canvass the marine hardware stores for a downstream strainer to install on the output of my freshwater pump. No luck!

All the available strainers were designed to attach to the suction side of the pump—to protect the pump from damage because of crud in the water. I wanted to protect my engine's heat-exchange system from pump parts. Suction strainers could not stand the pressure that would be built up in them if they were on the discharge side and became plugged with impeller rubber—if enough impeller-vane material remained on the hub to build up discharge pressure.

My solution was to abandon the marine hardware people and go to a boiler equipment supply store. I was able to purchase a 1¼″ boiler feedwater strainer for less than $20 that would withstand 125 pounds per square inch. It was cast iron, but it would be used in fresh water, and its strainer element was 64-mesh stainless steel. This strainer was designed to offer very little restriction to the water flow; its strainer element being a cylinder over 1″ in diameter and about 3″ long. This strainer was installed in the discharge pipe of my freshwater pump.

After two years of trouble-free cruising, I again noticed an increase in engine heat. Checking the freshwater pump impeller once more, I found it stripped again. Opening the clean-out port in the strainer yielded a pile of rubber from the disintegrated impeller that had collected.

Replacement of the impeller this time was a ten-minute job, and I could have perfect confidence that I still had a clean cooling system.

No-Mess Oil Drain

To do a neat job of draining the oil from a hard-to-reach drain plug without spilling or dripping it all over the bilge, try the simple trick shown here. Take an empty soup can and cut out the bottom and the top. Then fasten an empty plastic trash bag around the middle with several wraps of a heavy rubber band so that the open end of the bag is securely tied to the end of the can, as shown.

Run the engine long enough to heat up the oil thoroughly, then stop the engine and remove the drain plug while holding the open (uncovered) end of the can under the drain-plug opening. This will form an oversize, but flexible funnel that will catch and hold the oil as it runs into the bag.

Fire, the Uninvited Guest —by Ed Dennis

Every powerboat, whether it be diesel or gasoline, has some kind of an electrical system on board. And every boatowner should be able to cope with electrical hazards in order to avoid a potential fire at sea.

As a marine engineer, I can say there is no such thing as a small fire. It is just a big one getting started.

A fire develops in several stages. First, there is the incipient stage where heat and a combination of particles called aerosols are formed with no visible smoke. As these particles increase, they become visible as smoke. Ignition then occurs, giving off infrared and ultraviolet energy in the flame stage. Finally, large amounts of heat and flame develop rapidly as toxic gases form.

While a diesel engine's electrical system will rarely provide the sole fuel for a fire, it sometimes can cause one. A short-circuited wire in a wiring harness or in an electrical cable can cause the wire or cable to heat up and melt and ignite its insulation or some adjacent combustible material.

As a safety precaution, all marine electrical wiring should be fitted with some kind of fuse or circuit-breaker system that will blow long before any high-danger point is reached. When a fuse blows or a circuit breaker kicks out, they're trying to tell you something is wrong. And you should check into it immediately. Fuses and circuit breakers are your first line of defense against an electrical fire.

There are two basic reasons why a fuse will blow. Either the fuse has been overloaded or there is a short circuit somewhere in the line.

Flexible funnel prevents oil change spills.

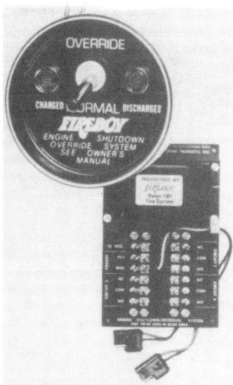

A discharge system such as this provides both an audible and a visual alert in the event of an extinguisher discharge. Installation requires only a small hole for the unit and a three-wire hookup.

Replacing a 15-amp fuse with a 30-amp fuse will only make matters worse. Don't do it!

I've been on board when an electrical short caused a diesel engine to stop dead in its wake by shorting out its fuel shut-off solenoid valve. Another time, a shorted wire energized the starting motor's solenoid, cranking the engine continuously till we pulled the terminal off the battery.

Make sure all electrical connections are clean and tight, all the wires are clean, of the correct capacity, size, and not overloaded. Avoid all wire-routing where there might be an excess of vibration, heat, or contact with metal. It is also very important to route all wires away from the bilge area.

I still remember the tragic explosion on the *Hildanoring*. The mechanic, after working on the starter, forgot to put the starter's band back on. The next morning, sparks from the poor contact the brushes were making against the rough surface of the commutator ignited the accumulated fuel fumes in the bilge, and within minutes the entire boat was engulfed in flames.

Make sure your changeover, shore-on-board's electric current switch is in the right position. It would be disastrous if you neglected this and both currents attempted to work on the same lines.

The U.S. Coast Guard says, "Batteries can explode." They should always be kept in a well-ventilated place to prevent the accumulation of explosive hydrogen gas. One small spark from a bad wire could cause your battery to explode into fire on board your vessel.

Excessive charging of your batteries will also release large amounts of dangerous hydrogen gases into your engine compartment. Remember to disconnect the charger when connecting or disconnecting a battery; and all terminals should be clean and tight.

Ventilation

Engine-room-compartment temperatures should always be kept as low as possible. Large cowl vents to provide sufficient amounts of air to enter your engine compartment are a must aboard any inboard pleasure boat.

Power blowers in the engine room or generating-set compartment can be wired to operate whenever machinery in the compartment is running. Blowers can be hooked up to operate automatically whenever the electric generating set is running by wiring them to the generator output or control; or they can be operated by a remote switch located at the helm station.

Avoid making any electrical adjustments with the generator engine running. If you must work around the generator while it is running, stand on a dry surface or a rubber mat to reduce shock and fire hazard.

Fuel Lines

Here is a list of precautions for fuel-system safety:

- Use seamless, annealed fuel lines approved for marine installation and double-flared connections.
- Run fuel lines at the top level of fuel tanks to a point as close to your diesel engine as possible to reduce danger of fuel siphoning out of tank if the line should break.
- Keep fuel lines away from your hot engine or exhaust piping.
- Make fuel lines long enough to prevent binding or stretching due to engine vibration or movement.
- Install only Coast Guard approved flexible, nonmetallic, nonorganic fuel oil lines between your solid fuel lines and diesel engine to absorb any vibration.
- Use nonferrous metal straps without sharp edges to secure fuel lines.
- Quick shut-off valves must be installed at both the tank outlet and at your diesel engine.

Know Your Diesel Fuel Filters —by Ed Dennis

You've serviced them or watched them being serviced, but are you aware of the exact function and makeup of your engine's filters?

Filters protect your diesel engine from harmful impurities; therefore, an improperly maintained or an incorrect filter can sometimes be as bad as no filter at all.

Since a filter is designed and engineered to do a specific job for a specific engine, it is foolish to substitute filters because they look alike. Type of fluid, viscosity, gpm, pressure flow, operating temperature, and type of material are the key factors in choosing the proper filter for your diesel engine.

The primary fuel strainer screens out most of your fuel oil contaminants. The strainer works much like a sponge, in that it absorbs the fuel into its element and holds back the contaminants while still permitting the diesel fuel to flow through. Detroit Diesel says that to provide good filtration, your diesel oil strainer should contain a high-quality, nonwoven, cotton element with a filtering efficiency of at least 30 microns. The element must be able to strain out and hold water, gum, varnish, emulsions, and dirt without matting, cracking, or rapidly becoming plugged up. And since the fuel strainer is almost always located on

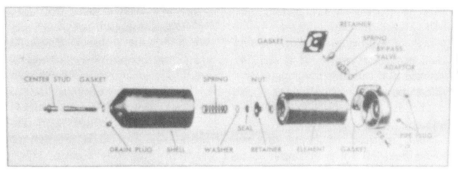

Full-flow lube oil filters like this one must be changed regularly.

the inlet or suction side of the fuel pump, the strainer element should create only a very low rate of restriction to the full flow.

Engineers and maintenance mechanics say that the single greatest cause of injector pump and injector nozzle failure is water in the fuel system. Water erodes injector tips and the microsmooth surfaces inside high-pressure fuel pumps. Today, almost all diesel installations include a water/fuel separator between the fuel tank and the primary filter or transfer pump. It's a must, especially in the tropics.

The secondary fuel strainer cleans the fuel oil a second time, before it moves on to the high-pressure pump or to the injectors. It is usually installed in the fuel line after the low pressure transfer pump. Today's spin-on filters usually contain a surface-type pleated paper element that cleans the fuel by passing it through the microscopic pores of the paper medium.

This fuel-filter element should have a filtering efficiency of at least 10 microns and be able to withstand a pressure of up to 75 psi.

Lube Oil Filters

The primary function of your diesel engine's lube oil filters is to help maintain the engine's oil in a clean condition by removing any dirt, carbon, or other contaminants or foreign matter from the oil.

Full-flow lubricating oil filters, either element or spin-on type, are standard accessories on most of today's production-line-produced diesel engines.

When should you change your lube oil and filter? The answer is obvious. You should change them before any additive depletion and contaminants begin to affect engine performance and life. How soon this happens depends on numerous variables, such as your engine's general condition and how you have maintained it, plus the area in which your boat operates.

Generally speaking, 100 to 200 hours of operation is the norm. But play it safe and check your service manual or your engine dealer. I also highly recommend a lube oil analysis every oil change or two.

Air Filters

The importance of good air intake filter maintenance cannot be over-emphasized. Remember, dirt and diesels don't mix. Few diesel owners realize that today's average diesel needs about 12,500 gallons of fresh air for every gallon of diesel fuel it consumes. While the average marine diesel is not subject to a lot of dust like a land-based engine, abrasive materials have a way of being absorbed into its air intake, and a periodic air filter cleaning and replacement is a necessity.

Water Filters

Using a coolant spin-on filter and a water conditioner in the closed freshwater cooling system of your diesel engine is just as important as its fuel, lube oil, and air-filtering systems.

Coolant filters and chemical inhibitor additives must be checked regularly to maintain their efficiency. Failure to do so may cause internal damage or even engine failure when you need your engine the most.

Fuel Filter/Water Separators —by Ed Dennis

Just how clean and dry is your fuel oil? Chances are that you are buying a lot more water and gook than you think. A diesel engine's worst enemy is water in its fuel, and every single droplet is dangerous. Condensation inevitably forms in all fuel tanks, along with dirt, sludge, and algae. The older the tank, the more contamination is likely.

Almost all diesel-powered pleasure boats will at some time take on water contaminated fuel oil (I have). This almost unavoidable occurrence is most prevalent in out-of-the-way, tropical, or sub-tropical marinas where fuel storage tanks are exposed to high humidity and high temperatures.

Since you don't have much control over the quality of the diesel fuel you buy, the best bet is to control the one basic area you can—the cleanliness of the fuel flowing from your boat's fuel tanks to its diesel engine.

Your diesel may be one tough baby, but it does not take kindly to water. Water is unique among the many contaminants found in fuel tanks because water is incompressible and will crack or break whatever is trying to compress it. It is most dangerous in a diesel's fuel pumps and injectors, where the microfitted tolerances are sometimes measured in thousandths of a millimeter. Under pressure, water can become a liquid abrasive. It can erode injector tips causing enlargement of the spray holes and destruction of the fuel-spray pattern. It can also lead to "popping" the end off an injector tip.

Your diesel engine's extra high temperature can also add to its water-contaminated fuel problems. Any water reaching the injector could instantly be turned into steam. This violent action occurring just before combustion of the diesel fuel can also contribute to "blowing" your injector tips.

The next cause of serious damage to fuel-injection pumps and nozzles are solid particles in the 5 to 10 micron range. That's two to three times smaller than a human hair. These minute particles are not always stopped by some of today's popular paper spin-on filters.

I had an incident once off the North Carolina coast, in the dead of night, when water and gook plugged an injector on the only diesel engine in the boat. The only quick way to remedy the situation was to replace the bad injector and do it in a damn big hurry, as we were dead in the water.

Considering the fact that over 50 percent of diesel engine failures can be traced to faulty fuel systems, and that the most common cause of failure in injector pumps and nozzles is water, it is easy to realize that the best investment any diesel-powered boatowner can make is a first-rate fuel-filtering system.

One method of being assured clean fuel oil to your diesel is to pass the fuel through a combination fuel filter/water separator before it goes to your engine. This double-filtering system removes both water and solid contaminants right on down to the 1 or 2 micron mark.

Basically, almost all fuel/water separators work in the same manner (see diagram)—a three-stage process. They are usually composed of a filter, a series of baffles, and a clear bowl sump at the base. When contaminated fuel enters the separator, the solids are filtered out. Then, through a coalescing action, the heavier contaminated beads of water eventually fall to the bowl sump to be drained off periodically. The lighter clean fuel rises to the top to be drawn into the main fuel-flow stream. These filters/separators should always be installed between the fuel tank and the primary filter.

An alternative fuel/water precaution I also strongly recommend is a duplex fuel/water separator. This is a dual filter with a swing-over hand lever that takes only a split second to switch over from a clogging filter to a clean filter.

Always remember to check, change, or clean your fuel filter as

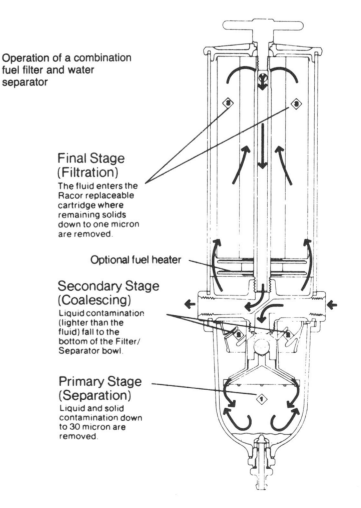

Operation of a combination fuel filter and water separator

Final Stage (Filtration)
The fluid enters the Racor replaceable cartridge where remaining solids down to one micron are removed.

Optional fuel heater

Secondary Stage (Coalescing)
Liquid contamination (lighter than the fluid) fall to the bottom of the Filter/Separator bowl.

Primary Stage (Separation)
Liquid and solid contamination down to 30 micron are removed.

soon as the normal fuel pressure on your fuel-pressure gauge starts to drop, signaling the element or separator is clogging up. Don't wait until the last minute—it may be too late then.

If you don't have one of these diesel fuel filter/water separators in your engine's fuel system, I strongly recommend you check into installing one. Here is a list of manufacturers:

CR Industries, Dept. MB&S, 900 N. State, Elgin, IL 60120.
Dahl Mfg. Inc., Dept. MB&S, 2521 Railroad Ave., P.O. Box No. 5, Ceres, CA 95307.
Fram Automotive Div., Dept. MB&S, 105 Pawtucket Ave., E. Providence, RI 02916.
Fleetguard, Inc., Dept. MB&S, 1340 River Bend Drive, Dallas, TX 75247.
Racor Ind., Inc., Dept. MB&S, Box 3208, Modesto, CA 95351.

Tools for Engine Repairs Under Way

—by Ed Dennis

Remembering that not all boatowners are mechanical wizards and that some would probably go bananas trying to fix junior's bicycle prompted me to write about tools and spare parts.

After handling mechanical tools all my life, I can say "don't splurge." But when you do purchase tools always buy quality, not quantity. Then, add to your toolbox as you widen your knowledge.

The most important tools you should have onboard are your "service manuals," and I suggest you stow them in a plastic gadget bag to keep dampness away from them. My "must emergency survival kit" would consist of an 8″ crescent

wrench, a 6″ or 8″ screwdriver, slip-joint pliers, a small ball peen hammer, and a good sharp Boy Scout knife. Next, add a roll of plastic tape and roll of bailing wire plus a can of spray lubricant.

To this you may care to add an electrical jumper wire or two, a small can of all-purpose grease, a pump-type oil can, and a small moisture-proof can of washers, cotter pins, etc. Some small nuts and bolts might come in handy along with a few fuses and hose clamps.

Also, remember that every boatowner should have a couple of good watertight flashlights on board.

Next, secure a good strong wood or fiberglass toolbox with brass or stainless steel hardware. Then fit a thick piece of oily felt cloth to the total inside bottom plus another for the inside cover to help keep out any salt moisture.

These additional tools you will probably accumulate as necessity demands (but not necessarily in this order): a set of combination box-open wrenches, and a pair of vise grips. Screwdrivers come in all designs, such as common and Phillips head, etc. Obtain ones with square shanks, so you can use a 6″ crescent wrench with them. Pliers come in a variety of sizes and styles; they're useful for crimping and bending metal, and let's not forget "old reliable," 8″ diagonal cutting pliers called "dikes."

Some sort of a pry bar will always come in handy for tightening or adjusting belts, etc. And some day you may need a hacksaw with a few extra blades along with a couple of bastard and smooth files. To this list my colleagues have added a 14″ or 16″ pipe wrench.

If any special tools such as injector cutout, removal, or adjusting tools are needed for your particular diesel, then they obviously belong in that toolbox, too.

And, as most engine manufacturers are going metric, check and see if you need American standard or metric sizes.

A few basic spare parts should always be carried on board. I suggest you first speak to your engine dealer about what is appropriate.

Several diesel engine manufacturers have come up with on-board repair kits. Packaged in water-resistant containers, the kits usually contain such items as belts, injectors, filters, pumps, etc., along with your engine's service manual.

I understand Perkins has made up kits for both minor and major repairs. Lehman Power Corp. (Ford, etc.) calls its kits "Limited Cruising" and "Extended Cruising Range Kits," and I have heard Johnson and Towers is offering spare-parts kits for its line of General Motors Detroit Diesel Allisons.

Adding further, you should have a spare set of fuel and lube oil filters *wrapped* and *preserved* for *emergency use only*; also a few cans of lube oil.

Speaking from experience, most emergency repairs can be made with what you carry on board. With a little imagination, the average boatowner can jury-rig enough to get back to port.

Tools and Spare Parts for Troubleshooting

Every spring I am besieged with questions about the right tools and spare parts for troubleshooting. There is no pat answer because there are too many variables. But here's a sampling of what you might need.

The first question to ask yourself is what are your skills around machinery? I have an optometrist friend who refuses to carry even a pair of pliers. He can't fix anything and knows he would ruin something that is working if he barely touched it. However, he has one foolproof tool—a loaf of stale bread. If trouble comes his way, he starts tossing bread overboard. In minutes every gull in the river is over his spot—all other boats know that gulls mean breaking fish, and in minutes he has plenty of company. He also thinks a good two-way radio is the world's best troubleshooting tool. He is the type to carry no tools and no spare parts; but he does have a stout eye through the stem of his boat for efficient towing. That is the first "must" item.

Next, where do you cruise? If you never leave the dock, all you need is a good ice crusher and a bottle opener; if you are on a world cruise, you will need quite an assortment of parts and tools, as well as skill. How about the size of your boat? A small outboard needs a minimum of tools and spare parts, but a well-found 70' cruiser is another problem entirely.

But let's start at the beginning. The prime need is the operating manual for your power plant, which always carries troubleshooting information and instructions. If you can't find your original manual, there are several good books on the market. The absolutely minimum tool kit, for any boat, is a pair of pliers, screwdriver, hammer, adjustable wrench (5" to 7"), a hank of wire, and a roll of elec-

trical tape. Spray them with oil or silicone to control rust and wrap them in a piece of stout cloth.

Tools are merely extensions of your hands and you can do some things without tools, but not without parts. For basic parts on a gas engine I start my inventory with those that were replaced at tune-up time. They worked then and should have enough life to get you back home after a breakdown. These include spark plugs, ignition points, condensors, and rotors—all wrapped in plastic sandwich bags. As skill improves, you will add an ignition coil, distributor cap, a complete set of V-belts, an extra water pump impeller and gasket, and a set of fuel-bowl gaskets, or material out of which they may be cut. Many engine builders sell excellent "on board" spare parts kits, and if you are cruising any distance you should have a spare everything. It is also wise to have some knowledge of the parts and services available at marinas and dealers along your cruising route. Remember, V-belts disable you completely. There is no excuse for not carrying spares because they are cheap, easy to store, easy to change, and good insurance against breakdowns.

Tools seem to accumulate automatically as skill improves. If you have a special need, such as an Allen wrench for the shaft-collar set screw, then buy it. Your tools will usually be bought in this order: after skinning a knuckle you will

buy sized wrenches. The first is usually a set of open ends, next is box wrenches, which fit completely around the nut, and then there are combinations with one of each on opposite ends of the handle. These are the "turning" tools, but the ultimate turning tool is a good set of socket wrenches. "Cutting" tools start with a good folding pocket knife and progress through hacksaws, cutting pliers, and compound handle snips. "Gripping" tools include pliers, especially the opening-up type which can turn a stuffing box nut, water pump pliers and vise grips.

The tools of a troubleshooter are those least likely to be used by a skilled mechanic—but favored by the handy man. Some sort of storage box is also needed; a galvanized metal one is good, but I prefer a wood one that will fit into one special place on the boat and not bang around. The trademark of a troubleshooter is his "junk can." It may either be a jar or a plastic box, but it is sure to contain all sorts of old copper nuts, fuel fittings, hairpins, fuses, and all sorts of goodies "I'll need some day." No boat is complete without a junk can, and even department stores sell them.

A FEW TIPS: As soon as the rig quits, anchor, unless you find yourself drifting toward home. Look for the obvious, such as a broken part, steam coming from the cooling system, or a V-belt hanging from a pulley. Get the manual out, check to see if you have fuel, and start from the source of everything to where it is ultimately used (fuel, water, electricity). And 'n't be afraid to try something because it might work. Oh yes—if you get in over your head, don't be too proud to pick up the radio and ask others for assistance. Chances are, the same thing has happened to them.

Diesel Engine Troubleshooting

—by Ed Dennis

Because diesel engines do not have electric ignition systems or carburetors—the two most frequent sources of trouble in a gasoline marine engine—they not only require less maintenance than a typical gasoline engine, but are also more trouble-free in normal operation.

However, this does not mean that the owner of a diesel-powered boat never has engine trouble. Instead of a carburetor and ignition system, the diesel has sensitive injectors and a complex fuel-injection system that must not only be properly adjusted and timed, but must also be fed a steady flow of clean fuel that is not contaminated by the slightest amount of water or air in the lines. Air trapped in a diesel engine's fuel line, or water mixed in with the fuel, can result in all kinds of problems—a lack of power, misfiring of one or more cylinders, stalling, rough running, hard starting, or complete stopping of the engine.

Water is kept out of the fuel system by buying clean fuel from reliable sources when possible, by making certain deck filler pipes and caps are watertight, and by passing fuel through adequately sized multiple filters (which should be checked regularly) before it reaches the injection pump.

Air is kept out by making certain that all connections in the system, from the fuel tanks to each of the injectors, are good and tight. If a connection does work loose (these too should be checked regularly), then air bubbles will slip into the system and bleeding it to get rid of the air is the only solution. This involves opening a series of vent plugs located on top of each filter, as well as at various other points in the system, then manually pumping or forcing fuel through the lines until bubble-free fuel flows out of each opening (you open and then close one at a time, usually starting with the highest one on the engine).

Most diesel engines have built-in priming or pumping levers to facilitate this, and the owner's manual should give detailed instructions outlining the sequence to be followed. However, if you are in doubt about how this should be done, then you should contact the manufacturer or an authorized service depot for more details about the procedure. You can't always find an experienced diesel mechanic when you need one.

In addition to keeping air and water out of the fuel system, there is one other important point to remember: All diesel engines require large volumes of air while running. This means you have to make certain the engine room has adequately sized air scoops or vent openings for air intake into the engine room; and the air filters on the engine must be checked regularly to make certain they are not dirty or clogged, thereby restricting the amount of air that is actually reaching the cylinders. Your engine manual will tell you where these air filters are and how they can be cleaned or replaced when dirty.

By keeping these points in mind, and by consulting the troubleshooting information appearing on these pages, owners of diesel powerboats or diesel-powered auxiliaries should be able to track down the most likely sources of trouble when their engines fail to start or when they "act up" by not running smoothly.

Careful attention to procedural details plus patient checks of all potential trouble spots is probably the best investment any boatowner can make toward prolonging the life of his engine(s), and toward minimizing the likelihood of breakdowns.

Probably the single most important thing to do is to study the owner's manual before getting started. If you don't have the manual that came with your engine, order one from the manufacturer.

Although some manuals are sketchy in this department, the better ones will include illustrations that show you where all the drain plugs are for the cooling and lubrication systems, where the fuel and oil filters are located, how they are removed, and what kind of cartridges they need.

The manual will also include specifications giving the amount of coolant required, the number of quarts of oil the crankcase holds, the type of oil recommended, and other important data you should be familiar with.

Simple Preventive Maintenance for Diesels

—by Ed Dennis

With today's mechanic's labor charges pushing the $40 to $50 an hour mark, it is highly advantageous for the average boatowner to do some of his own engine maintenance work.

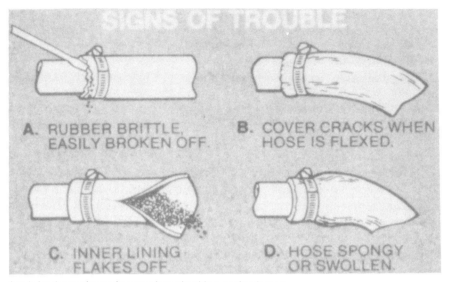

Look for these signs of wear when checking engine hoses.

With a good, simple preventive maintenance program, you can almost always be assured of a safe return from that special fishing trip. So fix the little things before they become big ones.

Here are a few simple jobs that you as a boatowner can do yourself with just an 8″ screwdriver, a couple of box/open-end wrenches, and a pair of pliers:

Belts and Pulleys

Since the proper care and maintenance of drive belts and belt pulleys plays an important part in your diesel engine's cooling and electrical systems, it is vital that you check them frequently.

While V-belts and V-belt drives do not require alignment to as close a tolerance as most other types of drives, it is a good idea to "eyeball" them every so often. Unless the belts enter and leave the pulleys' grooves in a comparatively straight line, the belts' wear will be accelerated.

Look at both frictional surfaces for signs of wear, cracks, or breaks. Normal wear can be recognized as even wear on both surfaces of the belt and the pulleys'

grooves. Inspection of a V-belt is largely a matter of first looking and then listening when the diesel is running. The slapping of belts is usually caused by loose belts or excessive vibration. Squealing belts are usually caused by poorly tensioned belts or by foreign matter in the pulley grooves.

To properly carry their full load, drive belts must grip the entire area of contact with the pulley. Belts that are too loose can slip, heat, burn, grip, or snap. When belts are tightened too much, they can damage your diesel by causing side loading of the crank-shaft bearings and accessory drive units. Hot accessory (alternator, etc.) drive bearings can be caused by belts that are either too tight *or* too loose.

Always check the condition of your diesel engine's pulleys before replacing belts. Inspect the pulleys' grooves for chips, cracks, rust, salt build-up, or bent side walls. Clean off any grease or oil accumulation and dress down any burrs with a small #6 Swiss (fine mill) file. Badly worn grooves can shorten a belt's life by causing tensional differences between matched sets of

belts, and eventual bottoming and slipping.

If your pulley is worn, out of round, or loose enough to wobble, the only safe procedure is to replace it. And always replace belts in matched sets from the same manufacturer. New belts will stretch after the first few hours of operation. After installing them, run the engine slowly for a few seconds to seat the belts properly. Then, after a few hours of operation, stop your diesel and check and re-tension them if necessary.

Adjust a belt's tension so that a firm push with your thumb at a point midway between the two pulleys will depress the belt about ½″ to ¾″. If a belt tension gauge is available, so much the better. It is always advisable to have a complete set of spare belts on board at all times, just in case of an emergency.

Belt dressing? Some engine people say yes, and some say no, so you had better check with your engine distributor.

Hoses and Clamps

Many a pleasure boat has sunk because of a faulty hose or a rusty clamp. Hoses harden and crack with heat and age causing engine-coolant leaks and high engine temperatures. They can also transmit engine vibration and a rocking action, putting stress on connections and components.

Carefully check all your engine's hoses and clamps every six months or so, first while your diesel is under normal operating pressures and then again after it has cooled down. Use caution around moving parts.

Squeeze all hoses to test for brittle, cracked, bulging or soft spots, which indicate a need for replacement. Hose clamps may become loose occasionally. If so, retighten as needed. Use caution: any over- or under-tightening of clamps may result in leaks, cuts, or seepage.

Any leaks on the suction side of your pump increase the chances of air and corrosion in your engine's enclosed cooling system. External leaks are usually easy to spot, as antifreeze and inhibitors leave stains at the hose connections. These leaks most commonly occur at water-pump hose connections, seals, zinc plugs, and at cylinder head and other gasket spots. You might need a flashlight or a drop-light to see some of the out-of-the-way spots clearly; but don't neglect them.

Remember, water under pressure coming from your engine's through-hull-fitting hose connections can flood your bilge in an alarmingly short time, so inspect these areas slowly and carefully. Through-hull cooling systems usually have a sea cock, gate, or globe intake valve for any emergency shutoff should a hose or clamp fail and water begin to rush in

Make sure support brackets are solid and there is nothing chafing or rubbing against the hose that will cause wear. Particles of deteriorated hose insides can be carried through the cooling system and clog or restrict small passages in your heat exchanger, lube oil cooler, or pump.

Use good silicone rubber hoses. Silicone rubber contains both natural and synthetic materials that combine chemically to produce a substance that is capable of withstanding extreme heat and cold.

Replace hose clamps that look rusty with stainless steel clamps that have positive worm gear drives. Remember, by using two stainless steel clamps, you increase your safety percentage significantly.

Heat is usually the culprit for lube and fuel oil-hose failure. The high temperature from these two circulating oils tends to harden hoses by continuing the curing process of the rubber or composition makeup. Engineers say that for every 20°F. increase in fluid (oil or coolant) temperature above optimum levels, you cut the life of your engine's hoses in half.

As there is no known cure for this form of oil-hose hardening, the problem can be minimized by using good-quality high-temperature and high-pressure hoses in these two oil systems. Then, periodically check for flexibility, tightness, and temperature. A leak or rupture in these two oil systems can cause a loss of oil pressure, engine overheating, seizure, or a fire.

Alarms and Safeties for Diesels
—by Ed Dennis

If you don't have any safety alarms on your boat, you should consider installing some. You may never really need them, but just having them on board may ease your mind a bit and may save you some money on your insurance bill as well.

A broken water-pump belt on a diesel engine is easy to repair, providing the engine was stopped before it started to overheat. The same goes for a plastic bag or some other sea debris sucked into and blocking the seawater inlet on your cooling system. A cracked or broken lube or fuel oil line is a cinch to repair, provided you stopped your diesel before it caused a fire in your engine compartment.

A runaway or uncontrollable engine can be extremely hazardous at sea. A leaking stuffing box combined with a malfunctioning bilge pump is no fun either.

Practically all diesel engine malfunctions give some warning to the operator. But sometimes a delay of only a few seconds can mean the difference between a ruined engine or one with only a slight malfunc-

Diesel alarm systems, like this Aqualarm cooling water-flow detector, can protect your engine against such hazards as overheating. Other alarms can protect against fire, low oil pressure, flooding, etc.

tion. Push that stop button as fast as you can if the safety alarm goes off on your boat.

Alarms and safety devices come in all sizes and shapes. Some boat instrument panels have red warning lights that flash on and off to attract the boat operator's eye. But, as an additional precaution on board any powerboat, an audio warning system is also important. It helps relieve the boat operator of the constant pressure of "gauge watching," and sounds off loud and clear in the event of a malfunction below the hatch.

Almost all diesel engine manufacturers equip their marine engines for the installation of four basic monitoring instruments: (1) Lubricating oil pressure; (2) Water temperature; (3) An ammeter; (4) A mechanical tachometer.

But few of today's small pleasure boats come equipped with engine or engine-compartment safety systems. This means that the boatowner must buy and install any sensing and alarm devices he deems necessary. So, before you order your next diesel-powered boat or before you repower with a diesel engine, think about protecting your investment with an alarm system and perhaps some other safety devices.

Here are a few safety and alarm devices I have run across recently:

Aqualarm has a unique and easily installed six-way automatic early warning alarm system for the average pleasure craft. This multi-alarm system can protect your engine and boat against any loss or damage due to fire, bilge flooding, low lube oil pressure, or engine overheating. Its red warning lights give the captain a visual warning; if that doesn't draw enough attention, its high-pitched alarm will make any boat operator sit up and take notice in a hurry.

The Aqualarm cooling water-flow detector is a plastic tubing device with a small interior gate. When placed in your engine's cooling water inlet system, it monitors the flow of seawater passing from your boat's seacock to your engine's cooling system. As long as the gate is open, the alarm is silent. When the water flow drops below 5 gpm, the alarm will sound off loud and clear. It will also sound an alarm if the engine's water pump or heat exchanger should develop a malfunction.

A Murphy "Swichgage" has some very interesting audio-visual alarm devices too. One that is particularly appealing is their differential-pressure "Swichgage." It is designed to monitor pressure changes across filters used in lubricating oil or cooling water systems. As the difference in the filter input pressure and the filter output pressure gradually reaches a critical preset ratio (usually due to a contaminated filter), a pointer activates a visual and audible signal and alerts the boat captain that a dangerous situation is approaching that needs his attention.

One of the wisest installations a powerboat owner can make on his boat is a "fumes-in-the-bilge alarm." There are several makes on the market. If you install one, don't forget to test it whenever you board your vessel.

Insta/Sniff makes one that prevents you from starting your diesel if the fumes are above its calibrated level. Odor Sniffer is another reliable bilge fumes detector.

Another wise decision to make would be the installation of a flooding-in-the-bilge alarm. The kit generally consists of a water-level sensor and an alarm bell. My approach would be to locate one in the engine compartment near the engine's starting batteries to insure an alarm warning in case the bilge water gets too high and threatens the battery's terminals.

Heat and fire detectors and alarms are another item that the safety-minded boatowner should consider. From personal experience I can attest that there is nothing more frightening and disastrous than a fire at sea.

Borg-Warner makes transmission alarm kits that alert the boat operator to any unsafe transmission oil temperatures, and Kysor-Cadillac also makes a series of heat alarms and engine protection systems.

A word of caution: Check your alarm system periodically and always be sure to run your engine compartment blowers before starting up your engine to circulate the air in the bilge and engine compartment. And, if you do decide to make a few safety improvements on your boat, be sure to comply with Coast Guard regulations on the installation of your new alarm system.

Cold-Weather Starting of Diesels
—by Ed Dennis

When diesel fuel (#2) approaches freezing temperatures, its free flow is adversely affected. Waxing and ice crystal formation combine to create starting and running problems.

Basically, the problem arises from the diesel principle itself, which is "ignition is by heat of compression." Thus, it is essential that the temperature of the air in the combustion chamber at the moment of injection be high enough to ignite the fuel-and-air mixture.

In warm weather, the ambient

temperature of the air and that of the metal parts of the diesel are favorable to high enough temperature for prompt ignition, but in extreme cold weather the opposite is true.

To assist in starting a diesel in extreme low-temperature conditions, several cold weather "helpers" are available.

Simplest of these auxiliary starting aids is the fixed ether cartridge, by which a measured charge of ether is injected into the air intake at the moment of cranking. This highly volatile gas ignites at extremely low temperature, so that even though the air in the combustion chamber is well below ignition temperature, the ether will ignite and kindle the charge of diesel fuel.

Once firing commences by this method, sufficient heat will be imparted to the combustion chamber walls, piston crown, valves, etc., to support continued diesel operation.

When employing a small spray can of starting fluid or ether, use caution: Read and follow the manufacturer's instructions on the can, then open the engine compartment wide for total ventilation and safety, then spray a small amount of the fluid directly into the intake air filter on your diesel while cranking the engine over.

Use extreme caution when using either method. The old expression of a little more won't hurt is not true here. Ether is an explosive gas. If too much is used, it could cause an uncontrolled explosion resulting in cracked pistons, bent rods, and other engine damage.

Several diesel engine manufacturers, such as Volvo, Perkins, Lehman-Ford, and DDA, have mechanical devices, methods, and tips for cold-weather starting too numerous to mention here. I suggest you check your engine's man-

ual or speak with your engine's distributor.

Any safe means of warming your engine, its fuel lines, and filters will help to eliminate some of these problems. This includes the use of electric blankets, heat lamps, strip heaters, and even piped hot water.

In Cleveland, Ohio, on Lake Erie, some boatowners have set up an electric heater attached to a long shore-powered extension cord close to the diesel's air intake for easier starting. And if they had plenty of time, they would heat up the whole engine room or compartment with several heaters an hour or two before attempting to start.

Racor makes a fuel-heater element for their filter/separators. This solid-state heating unit fits into the base of most of their filter/separators and is gradually turned on by an internal, automatically controlled, electronic thermostat. The preset temperature is maintained by the automatic operation for easier starting, and even in the coldest of weather waxing and icing are eliminated.

Almost any electric or fuel-fired coolant heaters are excellent during the starting-up and warming-up periods. They will help in creating a more satisfactory running condition by reducing cylinder and cranking drag and wear occasioned by the cold, and will help in the complete combustion of the fuel oil.

Preventing Electrical Problems
—by Ed Dennis

One very simple way to keep electrical problems from ruining your next fishing or cruising trip is to check your diesel engine's cable

and wiring systems periodically and correct any potential problems you come across. Starting hang-ups are often the result of faulty cable or wire maintenance.

Full engine electrical maintenance is beyond the scope of this column, and generally speaking, it is beyond the scope of the average pleasure boatowner. However, any boatowner can check and correct, if necessary, his engine's electrical wiring system.

Generally, if electrical equipment is kept dry, not overloaded, abused, or subjected to extremely high temperatures, it will give you years of trouble-free service. It is important, however, to periodically inspect, clean, tighten, or replace any cables, wires, terminals, or connections that may have become frayed, loose, broken, or corroded.

Insulation cracks in cables and wires can lead to problems when the cracks fill up with dirt and salt moisture. Either replace them or clean and tape them and then spray with WD40. If you do need to replace any wires or cables, replace them one at a time and don't forget to color code or number them for easy future identification.

Also, while you are checking for any broken or cracked strands of wire, feel along each one of them separately (while they are being worked, if possible) for any rise in temperature. Electrical wires become warm when their current-carrying capacity is being exceeded or hampered through any resistance. This type of problem could cause a fire in your engine compartment if not corrected.

Marine diesel engine starting and electrical systems differ very little from those of any heavy-duty truck or most other diesel installations. Most of today's diesel engines have two electrical systems. The one for starting generally uses either a 12-

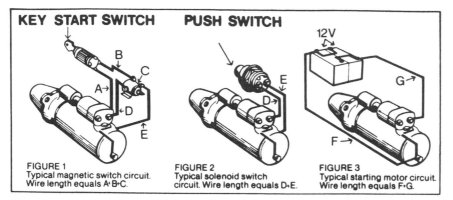

KEY START SWITCH   **PUSH SWITCH**

FIGURE 1
Typical magnetic switch circuit.
Wire length equals A+B+C.

FIGURE 2
Typical solenoid switch
circuit. Wire length equals D+E.

FIGURE 3
Typical starting motor circuit.
Wire length equals F+G.

Measure wiring length based on type of circuit, above, and use table below to determine the proper wire size needed.

STARTING MOTOR WIRE SIZE RECOMMENDATIONS						
	Magnetic Switch or Series Parallel Switch Circuit Figure 1 Reference Wires A, B, C		Solenoid Switch Circuit Figure 2 Reference Wires D & E		Starting Motor Circuit Figure 3 Reference Wires F & G	
	Length in Inches	Wire Size	Length in Inches	Wire Size	Length in Inches	Wire Size
12V System	Less than 125	No. 16	Less than 66	No. 10	Less than 114	No. 0
	126-195	No. 14	67-107	No. 8	115-145	No. 00
	196-300	No. 12	108-214	No. 6	146-187	No. 000
					188-238	No. 0000
24V System	Less than 250	No. 16	Less than 196	No. 12	Less than 199	No. 0
	251-400	No. 14	197-309	No. 10	200-249	No. 00
			310-490	No. 8	250-321	No. 000
					322-410	No. 0000
32V System	Less than 310	No. 16	Less than 449	No. 12	Less than 199	No. 0
	311-490	No. 14	450-719	No. 10	200-249	No. 00
			720-1120	No. 8	250-321	No. 000
					322-410	No. 0000

Courtesy of Detroit Diesel Allison

or a 24-volt system. However, some engines need 32 volts for starting purposes. A 12-volt system is generally used on board for lights, navigational equipment, and other electric accessories.

Electric starting is a matter of each component contributing its total capacity and energy to bring the diesel up to the necessary rpm for starting. Most diesel engines will start at a cranking speed of around 250–300 rpm if they are in good shape.

Many starter problems are the result of not having the correct size battery-to-starter cable or connections, thus hindering the adequate passage of voltage and amperage (see chart).

Having the correct size wires and cables is very important. An insufficient size cable will create high re-sistance to an adequate flow and volume of electricity to the starting motor's circuit. This, in turn, will reduce the efficiency of the cranking motor's capability to overcome the diesel's high cylinder-compression ratio (18 to 1) and will cause a hard-starting problem.

Solenoids

The average piggyback-type sole-noid—mounted on top of the cranking motor—is actually an electric switch used to energize the starting motor and put it in motion. As the solenoid is normally ener-gized by a simple pushbutton usu-ally located some distance away, a relatively heavy-gauge wire is gen-erally required to transmit the needed amperage to the solenoid relay and solenoid.

Using a small-gauge wire can re-sult in insufficient current reaching the starter, overheating the wires, insufficient travel of starter pinion, and failure of engine to start. Re-member, the solenoid-to-starter ca-ble or connector also has to be of heavy gauge. We're thus insuring proper voltage.

Terminals

Just as cables provide the vital electrical link-up between the bat-tery and the cranking motor, ade-quate clamps and connections should always be used. Crimp-on terminals without solder are the source of many electrical head-aches. From experience, I have found these quick and easy crimp-ons loosen or corrode after a short while, especially around salt water.

Since resistance-causing corro-sion and looseness will help rob the starter and other accessories of electrical energy, all terminals must be adequate and kept tight. When a battery terminal connection be-comes loose, corrosion usually sets in between the battery post and the clamp, and the terminal's current-carrying capacity suffers.

Whether old or new cables are used, the cable ends should always be clean, bright, and tinned. The terminals should then be crimped onto the cables and the assembly dip soldered, or the junction com-pletely filled with solder in order to insure a solid, low-resistance elec-trical connection.

Routing

Cable and wire routing is a matter of good judgment. Here are a few basic guidelines:

(1) Runs should not be too loose or too tight.
(2) Strain relief should be pro-vided a short distance from battery

terminals to help prevent battery terminal failures.

(3) Support all cables and wires every 18″ to 24″ with plastic ties or tape wrap.

(4) Try to avoid spots where excess heat, vibration, or abrasion might damage the cable or wires.

Keep a wary eye open for green corrosion. Just like vibration, corrosion aboard a boat is hard to avoid, particularly if you're a saltwater yachtsman. To protect exposed wires and terminals, an application of light grease (like Lubriplate or Dow-Corning #4) or oil (WD40) usually does the trick.

Run an occasional voltage-drop test on cables or wires that are not entirely visible due to harnesses or looms. You can check your battery-to-starter cable with a draw meter—they're very simple to use and inexpensive to buy.

Poor cables and wires promise nothing but trouble and aggravation for diesel owners. Check yours periodically to prevent problems.

Diesel Engine Thermostats —by Ed Dennis

Often called the diesel engine's watchdog, a thermostat is the nerve center of your diesel engine. A remarkably compact device, it senses liquid temperatures and modulates your diesel's coolant flow as the engine approaches its correct operating temperature.

This silent, unseen, but reliable engine part bears the responsibility for maintaining engine operating temperatures within the prescribed narrow limits (about 170° to 190°F.) required for maximum engine efficiency.

When engine coolant temperature is below 160°F., the bel-

lows in your thermostat is contracted and its valve is in a closed position, thereby cutting off the circulation of the coolant to your engine's heat exchanger. When your engine starts to warm up and reaches its designed "thermostat start to open" temperature, the thermostat allows coolant to flow through the heat exchanger until the valve is fully open (185° to 190°F.) and your diesel engine is operating at its correct temperature. When you shut down, the thermostat valve will close when the temperature of your diesel's coolant drops below the 160°F. mark (or whatever degree it was designed for).

Thermostats in today's diesel engines are normally located in the coolant flow passage near the "engine-out" connection. This is where the coolant leaves the engine block on its way to the heat exchanger.

Detroit's diesel engine thermostats consist of a brass cup filled with a heat-expansive, waxlike material (see diagram). This compound is sealed within the cup by an elastomeric boot that extends into the cup to form a core. A lubricated, tapered-end, stainless steel piston fits into the core. The

valve is attached to the top of this piston and is held in the closed position by a stainless steel spring.

As the engine heats up, the wax-like material expands. As the coolant temperature reaches the calibrated "start to open" thermostat setting, the force of the expanding wax on the boot and piston exceeds the closing force of the spring and the valve begins to open. As the coolant temperature continues to increase, the waxlike material continues to expand and the valve opens further until it reaches its maximum.

When the temperature of your engine's coolant drops, cooling of the wax causes it to contract and allows the spring to draw the valve back toward its seat and close the thermostat and water passageway. Detroit's marine diesel engines have a thermostat "start to open" to "full open" temperature heat range of 170° to 190°F.

Volvo uses two thermostats on its popular TMD40 and three on its TAMD120A. On both engines, the thermostats work in series to help prevent a sudden rush of cool water to the engine. Volvo's new TAMD40 also has two thermostats, one is set at 158°F. and the other as 168°F. Volvo believes that

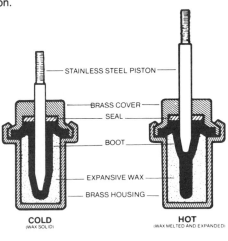

Expansion and contraction of wax operates thermostat piston.

STAINLESS STEEL PISTON
BRASS COVER
SEAL
BOOT
EXPANSIVE WAX
BRASS HOUSING

COLD
(WAX SOLID)

HOT
(WAX MELTED AND EXPANDED)

the gradual cooling allowed by a series of thermostats helps maintain the highest engine efficiency.

On Caterpillar's 3208 diesels, space considerations favored two small thermostats rather than one large one. If one thermostat fails to operate correctly, the other thermostat will give some operating capability since they are connected in parallel.

Cat's regulators, as Caterpillar calls them, are set for 165° to 190°F.; and both are located in the same housing—near the expansion tank and heat exchanger.

On Detroit's new 8.2 fuel-pincher diesel, the temperature of the engine is controlled by two 180°F. thermostats located in the water-pump body mounted on the front cover.

Thermostats frequently become corroded, bent, or broken, or develop a malfunction. A thermostat stuck in the closed position will result in rapid overheating. If stuck in the open position, it will result in slow engine warm-up and will accelerate engine wear. Overcooling can also cause considerably higher fuel consumption.

Detroit Diesel cautions that when replacing a thermostat, always check the new one and its temperature range with the specs in your service manual, and make sure it is fully seated in the housing counterbore. Also, always use a new gasket.

Easy Air Bleed

Tightening diesel fuel-line fittings, after bleeding air from the system, can easily strip threads in the soft-metal filter housing, whether the wrench is in the hand of the owner or a marina mechanic. Each new filter housing costs about $20 and the boat may be laid up until the new part arrives. I solved this problem permanently on a Perkins and an Albin by adding an air bleed-off valve at a high point on the filter housing. Air that enters the fuel system when (1) the filter is changed, (2) a fuel line is replaced, or (3) the water is drained from a separator filter is quickly hand-pumped through the new valve. The valve closes tight with two fingers. Fuel-line fittings, once sealed, are never disturbed.

Diesel Fuel Can Attack Engines
—by Ed Dennis

The high sulfur content in today's fuel oil can be deadly for your diesel engine, reports the research department at Caterpillar's Engine Division. Diesel fuel with excessive sulfur can damage engines rapidly and silently. Unlike other types of engine wear, sulfur damage gives no advance warning. Your engine will run normally with little change in start-up time or output power. Suddenly, your engine is worn out. Piston rings stick. Rings and cylinder liners are worn thin, causing excessive blow-by and oil consumption. Acids, resulting from use of high-sulfur fuel, contaminate the lubricating oil and quietly destroy your engine.

This happens during combustion. The sulfur in the fuel forms sulfur oxide, which combines with moisture in the intake air to produce sulfuric acid. Suspended in the lubricating oil, this acid chemically attacks cylinder liners, piston rings, exhaust-valve guides, and other vital engine parts.

This problem is becoming more severe for several reasons:

(1) There is an increasing amount of sulfur in today's imported crude oil supply, and refiners cannot remove enough to meet the criteria for "low sulfur" fuel.

(2) Many users are neglecting to adjust their lube oil change intervals to compensate for this change in fuel sulfur content.

(3) Fast running with heavier loads increases fuel consumption and therefore increases sulfur intake.

(4) Lower than normal engine operating temperatures increase moisture condensation. This depletes the oil additives and combines with the sulfur in the fuel to make more acid.

(5) High humidity aggravates fuel sulfur wear. This cannot be controlled, but you should be aware that your diesel will suffer more from fuel sulfur wear in a coastal area than in a hot desert climate.

The symptoms of fuel sulfur wear only occur after the damage is done. These symptoms are similar to those of normal engine wear, but occur much earlier. The following early-wear indications should alert you to the possibility of problems:

- Increased oil consumption.
- Increased crankcase blow-by.
- Vapor visible in the crankcase blow-by.
- Blue exhaust smoke.
- Increased iron and chromium reading in SOS samples.
- Oil analysis showing increase in sulfur products and decrease in alkalinity.

To minimize fuel sulfur wear, always use the best fuel available. If you must use fuels with more than 0.4 percent sulfur content, the following practices can help minimize the damage:

(1) Know the sulfur content of the fuel you use. Check with your

fuel supplier. Or, use the Caterpillar publication, "Fuels for Caterpillar Diesel Engines, Form SEHS7076," which lists fuel standards. If none of the standards apply, assume you're using a 1 percent fuel sulfur. Or, contact the refineries. If possible have a private laboratory make a test for fuel sulfur. The laboratory should use test procedures ASTM D1552, or D1266, or D129. Fuel sulfur cannot be measured with litmus paper or any simple process.

(2) Use CD oil. Oils with CD classification are alkaline and tend to neutralize some of the acids.

(3) Adjust oil-change intervals to compensate for the increased sulfur content of the fuel. Use the normal oil-change interval for your engine application when fuel sulfur content is less than 0.4 percent. When fuel sulfur content is 0.4 percent to 1.0 percent, oil should be changed at *one half* the normal interval. When fuel sulfur content is above 1.0 percent, oil should be changed at ONE FOURTH the normal interval.

(4) Change oil filters when oil is changed for best results.

(5) When operating, make sure the engine temperature is within a normal range.

How to Purge Your Fuel System
—by Ed Dennis

Anything that can be drawn into your engine's fuel system more easily than its diesel oil will eventually displace the fuel. When that happens, you have a dead engine on your hands.

The presence of air (or water) will be indicated during your diesel's operation by one or maybe several of the following symptoms:

(1) Engine turns over but won't start.
(2) Rough running and misfiring.
(3) Stalls at low rpm.
(4) Sudden changes in engine rpm.
(5) Not enough power.

Several of these symptoms overlap and are both air- and water-related troubles.

Learning to purge trapped air from your engine's fuel system is simple and quick, providing you follow these simple instructions or the ones in your engine's service manual.

Most pleasure boat diesel fuel systems are tailored to each boat and engine, but in general the average installation will consist of the fuel tanks, a primary filter or filter/water separator, a fuel-transfer pump, a secondary filter, a high-pressure injection pump, and then the injectors. If you have a GM with unit injectors, you eliminate the high-pressure pump.

Always make sure the fuel shutoff valve is OPEN all the way, you have plenty of fuel in your tank, and a fully charged heavy-duty battery or two.

CAUTION: Always put a heavy-duty rag over any connections you are cracking open, as the fuel oil will be under pressure and could possibly blind you.

Air can enter your fuel system:

(1) From any suction leak at loose or cracked connections, usually but not always before the fuel-transfer pump.
(2) You ran out of fuel in one tank and sucked in air before you had a chance to change over to another.
(3) You changed or cleaned a filter or a fuel line and forgot to refill it before you installed it.
(4) A faulty fuel-transfer pump.

If you find air bubbles after your transfer or high-pressure pump, you are sucking in air. So check and tighten all fuel-line connections and the gaskets around your filters right up to your injectors.

Then, starting at the beginning of your fuel line, open bleed valves or plugs, one at a time, turn the engine over a few rpm with the starter, or use, if available, the hand primer on the fuel-transfer pump. Pump until no air bubbles show in the fuel, then close that valve and go to the next fitting or purge plug.

Bleeding a diesel's fuel system of air is slightly different with each make of diesel. On Cat's 3208 Diesel: (1) Stop engine; (2) loosen the air-vent valve on the injection-pump housing; (3) operate the hand-priming pump located on top of the final fuel filter until the flow of fuel from the filter is free of bubbles; (4) tighten the vent valve; (5) start the engine. If engine continues to misfire, CAUTIOUSLY loosen the first fuel-injection line nut and allow the fuel to flow till it is free of air bubbles; (6) if necessary, do the same to the other injectors.

Volvo says on D40s: (1) open venting screw on top of first fuel filter a few turns with a 10 mm wrench; (2) pump fuel using the hand-primer lever on the transfer pump until the fuel flows free of air; (3) then tighten venting screw. If that doesn't do the job, (4) crack each injector's delivery-pipe nut a few turns and crank engine over ten or fifteen seconds till the fuel is free of air bubbles; (5) tighten all nuts.

On Renaults, Perkins, and Lehman-Ford engines, the procedure is pretty much the same. Start at the discharge side of the transfer pump; hand pump or crank the engine over a few rpm. After it's open, bleed and tighten at each air-vent point up to the injectors.

Then, if it is necessary, you can crack open and back off a turn or two on each fuel-line nut, and crank the engine over till solid fuel flows out.

On Cummin's 902 and 555 models, you crack open the fuel-line nut leading from the last filter (at the bottom of the PT fuel pump) and crank the engine over several times till the fuel flows solid. These engines have internal fuel lines leading to the injectors, and there is no way to purge air at the injectors.

On GM engines, open the air-vent plug on the first filter after the transfer pump and crank the engine over till it is free of air; then tighten. If necessary, open the fuel-inlet nut at each injector, one at a time, crank engine over a few rpm's till fuel flows free of air, tighten, and go on to the next injector, etc.

Detroit's new 8.2 liter, 4-cycle diesel engine has internal fuel-injector feed lines. Check for loose or faulty external connections. Any faulty fuel lines, or any connections around the filters, could cause the pump to draw in air on engines that have screw-on fuel filters.

I suggest you crack open the nut on the filter's discharge line till you get clear fuel flowing, then tighten and go on to the next air-purging point.

In addition to air in the fuel system, faulty operation can also be caused by water in the system and by inadequate fuel pressure.

Know Your Diesel's Cooling System
—by Ed Dennis

New engineering developments in metallurgy and flow design in today's high-speed/low-weight-to-

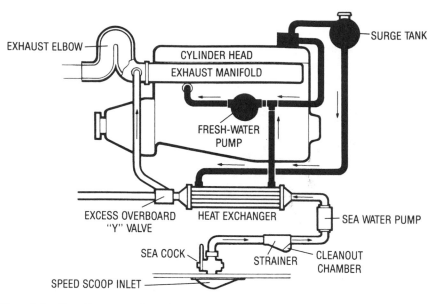

Closed-circuit cooling system based on a heat exchanger. Note that seawater is diverted to the exhaust elbow.

horsepower marine diesel engines have led to vast improvements and greater stability in their cooling systems. But, along with these improvements have come critical performance criteria that make your diesel engine's cooling system one of the most important service items to be checked regularly.

Cooling systems for today's diesel engines still perform the same basic function they did for the very first marine diesel engine back in 1902 on the Seine River in France, and that is circulating a coolant around the engine's cylinder head and jacketed blocks to remove its excess heat to the atmosphere.

In general, there are three types of marine cooling. Direct or seawater cooling, keel cooling, and the most efficient and popular kind, the "enclosed" type.

The enclosed type with its heat exchanger emerged in the 1930s. It is probably the single most important improvement made to marine diesel engines. Without it, today's small, high-speed, lightweight diesel engine would not have been possible. Controlling engine temperatures with this system, how-

ever, is a cinch. And one of its major advantages—the elimination of saltwater corrosion internally—is crucial when aluminum turbocharger housings are used.

The system provides for the continuous recirculation of treated coolant in a closed circuit. It consists of a circulating pump that forces the coolant around the engine's head, cylinder water jackets, oil coolers, and in some cases the turbocharger, before passing through the heat exchanger for cooling and recirculation. A second water pump circulates cool raw seawater through the heat exchanger and then discharges the hot water overboard, usually through the transom.

Adequate engine heat removal is not accomplished by the liquid cooling system alone. Interrelated engine systems also form part of the cooling team. Involved in this heat-removal job is the lube oil system, the exhaust system, and to a lesser degree your engine's surface radiation. As a general rule, today's diesel engine cooling systems are designed to handle 2,000 to 2,500 BTU's per hour of brake horsepower if the engine is turbocharged, and 2,500 to 3,000 BTU's if naturally aspirated.

Normal engine operating temperatures for most pleasure boat diesel engines usually range from 170° to 190°F. (check your manual) or a jacket water temperature differential of about 15° to 20°F., measured across the engine at full rpm. Some engines go higher, depending on ambient air temperature and water temperature, but thermostats are generally set around the 200°F. mark. The size of the water pumps, raw and fresh, and hence the volume of cooling water, is the key to versatile operation in a variety of conditions. Pathfinder, for instance, has just informed me they dropped their thermostat settings on new engines from 220° to between 200° and 205°F.

It is very important to remember that the proper heat range be maintained or your diesel engine's performance will be adversely affected. The amount of heat being dissipated must, within a few degrees, equal the amount of heat being generated or else a heat imbalance will occur.

If a heat-to-cold-dissipation (BTU's per minute) lag occurs and it persists, your diesel's coolant will boil, its overheated parts will distort, and the engine's lube oil will break down, resulting possibly in engine seizure.

An overcooling imbalance can also occur if the BTU's are dissipated too fast. When this happens, your diesel will run too cold and very erratically.

Overcooling, although less sudden in effect than overheating, can in most cases be equally detrimental to your diesel. Long idling or low operating temperatures, especially in cold, damp weather, result in excessive fuel consumption, the unburned raw diesel fuel washing down your cylinder walls and being added to your lube oil, as well as formation of oil sludge and acids from condensation within the oil pan.

Remember for good diesel (heat ignition) efficiency, your engine must operate within its designed heat range, neither too hot nor too cold.

Electric transducers or capillary tubes are generally used to monitor water temperatures. Measurements are usually taken at the freshwater (coolant) manifold outlet to the heat exchanger.

High temperatures may be caused by: (1) a clogged sea cock, filter, or hull strainer; (2) low water level in heat exchanger tank; (3) loose water pump belts; (4) collapsed water hoses; (5) faulty water pump; (6) a faulty thermostat or temperature gauge; (7) or a clogged heat exchanger.

And while you're overboard removing sea gook from around your inlet screen, check for barnacles and weeds—they may have insinuated themselves farther inside your inlet cooling system.

Excessively low temperatures can generally be traced to a stuck-open thermostat, the inlet raw or seawater being too cold, or operation of your diesel at too low an rpm for too long a period of time.

A coolant additive should always be used with today's closed freshwater cooling systems. The additive should prevent two things: (1) corrosion within the system, which is often accelerated by the chlorides and/or sulfides in the water; and (2) scale deposits, which build up on the walls of the cooling system from concentrations of magnesium and calcium in the water. As these deposits thicken, they dramatically reduce the rate of heat transfer by insulating the metal.

Since the first oil embargo, a new culprit has joined the cooling scenario, and it takes effect when the engine is run cold continuously for a while. The culprit is the sulfur content—.8 to 1.1 percent—in today's diesel fuel.

When you run with a low temperature reading, less than full out for long periods of time, or in a humid area, the humidity in your engine's air intake, along with the water vapor produced in your engine combine with the extra-high sulfur in today's fuel. These conditions can, during combustion, cause sulfuric acid to form within your diesel engine.

This acid accumulates in your engine's lube oil system where it chemically attacks the internal moving parts. Most unfortunate, there is no advance warning. Acid destroys engine metals without the boatowner being aware of it.

Temporarily, you can cope with this situation with higher thermostat (heat) settings, more oil changes, and if you can get it, a fuel oil with a lower (5 percent or less) sulfur content.

Preventing Diesel Engine Corrosion
—by Ed Dennis

You cannot escape Mother Nature's tendency to corrode the metal in and around your diesel engine, but you can help to retard it by having some knowledge about the "whys" and "hows" of corrosion and electrolysis, along with their effective counter measure, zinc.

Webster defines corrosion as the gradual eating or wearing away of a metal substance. Marine engineering manuals say electrolysis is the decomposition of metals into "ions" caused by the action of small electrical currents, and that

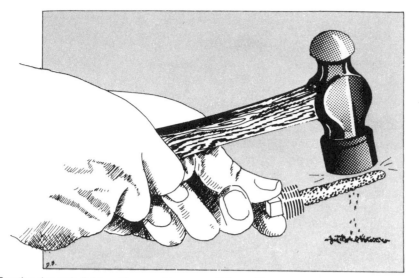

Tap the zinc rods lightly with a small hammer. If the rod has deteriorated, or flakes, install a new zinc electrode.

zinc, the counter measure, is used as a protection against these erosions.

Because corrosion and electrolysis are such vast subjects, we will confine this column to the nitty-gritty of just your diesel engine and try to view the problem in some perspective.

Simple corrosion—rust—occurs because moisture in the air oxidizes the metal. In salt air the salt accelerates the process. Your engine should be already thoroughly protected against oxidation by means of paint or plating. However, the internal passages of your heat exchanger are prone to oxidation, and you should be sure your heat-exchanger tank is free of trapped air.

Galvanic corrosion (electrolysis) occurs in your engine when salt water (electrolyte) is circulated through two or more dissimilar metals that are part of the makeup of your engine.

Your diesel probably hosts a variety of metals (copper, brass, aluminum, iron, etc.) in combination with one another; keep these diverse metals dry and you're okay, but put them in contact with an electrolyte (salt water) and you have trouble.

When this condition occurs, a reaction very similar to that which occurs in your storage battery takes place. The most chemically active metal of the union will decompose.

The union of dissimilar metals can be eliminated to a vast degree by using a single type of material such as stainless steel, monel, copper, or brass, or by separating dissimilar metals in the raw-water piping system with an insulator such as a piece of common rubber hose.

Electrolysis that is caused by two dissimilar metals not in contact with one another, but in contact with an electrolyte (salt water) often can be almost completely eliminated by providing a common ground throughout your boat and by connecting every exposed metallic component to that ground.

Today's marine diesel engines usually come equipped with zinc electrodes in or near your engine's heat exchanger, raw-water pump, and other parts of your engine. These sacrificial zinc plugs, being lower in the galvanic series than other engine metals, will gradually decompose and protect the vital parts of your diesel engine. Some diesels have zinc plugs in both the saltwater and freshwater systems—and some in only the saltwater system.

The popular method of protection to other vital parts, such as propeller shafts, rudders, and struts, is with sacrificial zinc collars and rudder zincs. These are attached near or directly to the part to be protected; being lower in the galvanic series, the zinc is sacrificed by gradually disappearing.

And now for the nitty-gritty of what you can do to help combat this problem on your boat.

Inspect your engine's zinc electrodes periodically (at least every six months). Your engine's manual should tell you where they are.

If it doesn't, they are usually located at or near the suction side of the raw-water pump and near the heat exchanger. However, Cat 3208 diesels have them in the heat-exchanger bonnet and in each of the raw-water-cooled exhaust risers. Some diesel engines also have zincs in the oil cooler, the after cooler, and in the marine gear cooler.

First, close any water valves as necessary, otherwise you will flood your bilge. Then: (1) Move your battery disconnect switch to its OFF position. (2) Screw out the zinc plugs and brush or scrape off any powdery deposits. Tap the rod lightly with a small hammer. If the rod has deteriorated more than 50 percent or flakes when tapped, deep-six it and install a new zinc electrode. If, for some reason, one or more of the electrodes has not been attacked by corrosion, then check for a poor contact between the electrode and engine (plug hole). Then scrape the surfaces clean and install again, making sure there is a good tight metal-to-metal contact.

Periodically, inspect the rudder, propeller shaft, and any special outdrive zincs such as Volvo's Aquamatic drive, where you check the zinc ring on the inside of the propeller and the zinc plate under the transom shield.

While you are looking around, take a good look at your through-hull fittings and also at all the bonding-system contacts for any green deposits. If you find them, remove, clean, and resecure them tightly.

In closing, corrosion and electrolysis can be retarded or stopped by using the prescribed freshwater (coolant) treatment, by inspecting and replacing all zinc anodes when necessary, and keeping the heat-exchanger tank free of any trapped air.

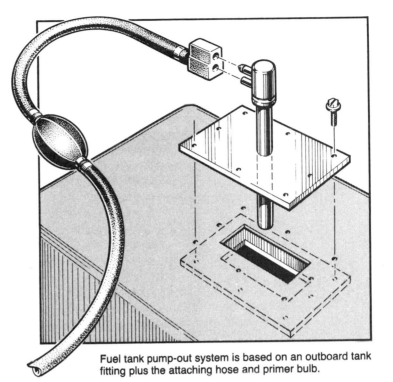

Fuel tank pump-out system is based on an outboard tank fitting plus the attaching hose and primer bulb.

Pump-out Method for Water in Your Fuel Tank

Most of us have been reminded all too often that water does not mix with fuel. Some of us have experienced the sudden shutdown of our power plant followed by annoying hours in the hot hole cleaning the water out of carburetors or injectors and replacing filters. There are water-separating filters available that do a commendable job of keeping water from passing into the engine, and one should be included in your fuel system. However, water is introduced into the fuel tank on a regular basis both by refilling the tank and by drawing humid air through the tank vent as fuel is being consumed. Because of this, there must be a constantly nagging question of how much water is in the tank and when will it cause a problem?

Most tanks are constructed with baffles to prevent sloshing, and it is extremely difficult to feed a rubber hose down through the filler neck and past these baffles in an attempt to draw water from the lowest part of the tank.

A positive and permanent solution to this problem can be achieved by borrowing from the technology of the outboard remote tank fuel system. Parts are available from your local marine store or any one of the discount houses. The parts required are an outboard tank fuel fitting, a length of the attaching hose with primer bulb, and a 6″ or 8″ inspection deck plate. The remaining pieces can be purchased at a hardware and a sheet metal shop or industrial surplus store.

First, gain access to the top of the fuel tank in the general vicinity of the present fuel "out" line. If the tank is located under the cockpit sole or under a built-in berth or seat, locate the fuel out line and cut an access hole to the tank slightly to one side of this outlet. This hole should be about 1″ in diameter for a starter to assure that it is located properly. With this assurance, the hole can be enlarged for installation of the standpipe system. If the tank is in the engine compartment, its top may be readily accessible. Some tanks have inspection/clean-out ports which are ideal for installing this water remover.

First cut a rectangular hole 1″ × 3″ in the top of the tank. *Please make sure the tank is purged of absolutely all liquid and fumes before doing any cutting.* Make two plates 3″ × 5″ from ½″ aluminum. Cut a 1″ × 3″ hole in one plate to match the hole in the tank. Clamp the two pieces together and drill eight equally spaced holes around the perimeter ½″ from the edge using a #21 drill. Tap holes in the lower plate for 10-32 machine screws; redrill the holes in the upper plate to accept them. Put the upper plate in place as a template and drill the eight holes in the tank.

Now slip the lower plate into the

tank diagonally and clamp temporarily in place. To affix the plate permanently, drill two ⅛″ holes through the tank and plate, for securing with pop rivets.

Drill and tap a hole in the center of the upper plate. This hole must be sized for the particular outboard tank fitting you've purchased. Press, or better, solder a length of copper tubing of appropriate diameter, then cut the tubing to reach within ¼″ of the lowest part of the tank. Install this assembly over a gasket thick enough to account for the two pop rivet heads, insert the screws with lock washers, and tighten until leakproof.

When you want to draw off water, merely attach the hose fitting to the assembly and pump into a container until you get only clean fuel.

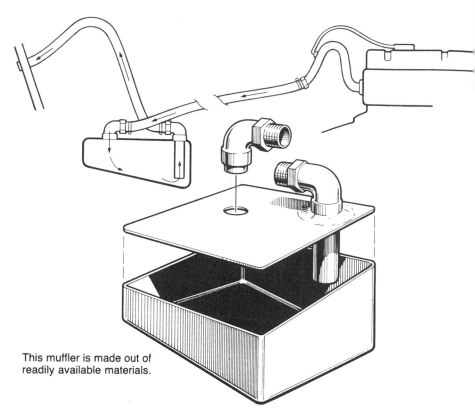

This muffler is made out of readily available materials.

Custom-built Water-Lift Muffler

When I replaced the gasoline engine in my sailboat with a compact new diesel, I found that the diesel engine came equipped with flexible, vibration-absorbing mounts instead of the rigid mounts used on my old gasoline engine. This meant that I could not use the original rigid exhaust system—at least not without extensive modifications. I decided to replace it entirely, using the popular water-lift muffler.

To minimize exhaust noise, a water-lift muffler should be lower than the exhaust outlet on the engine. This permits injecting the engine cooling water through a mixing elbow into the exhaust gases at the earliest possible moment, while also cooling the exhaust and reducing its volume. Rubber exhaust hose, which is flexible, can be used to connect the en-

gine to the muffler and the muffler to the overboard discharge opening.

When the engine is running, water comes into the muffler along with the exhaust gases until enough water accumulates to cover the bottom of the open discharge tube. Incoming exhaust gas then builds up enough pressure on the water to force some of the gas (and water) up into the discharge line and over the loop, as shown in the drawing. The whole system is quite simple and temperatures are low enough to allow safe use of fiberglass and resin for making the muffler.

The vertical leg of the discharge hose is always full of water, so when the engine stops this water will drain back into the muffler. Therefore, the muffler must be large enough to hold at least this volume of water and prevent it from flowing back into the engine, even when the boat is heeled.

None of the commercially avail-

able water-lift mufflers were small enough and of the right shape to fit in the space I had in mind in my boat, so I decided to make my own. It has a rectangular shape with a level top, and the bottom is shaped to fit the contour of my hull. Because I wanted to make the muffler as small as possible, I made sure the hose connections in the top would be as close to the centerline of the hull as possible— again to eliminate any possibility of water draining back to the engine when the boat was fully heeled.

The first step in actually building the muffler is constructing a model out of cardboard and masking tape. This is then used as a plug (a mold over which the fiberglass and resin can be formed). The model is covered with waxed paper (to keep the resin from sticking to it), then alternate layers of fiberglass cloth and resin are applied to the sides and bottom until a thickness of approximately ³⁄₃₂″ is built up. This forms a sturdy box that is open at the top.

When the resin is cured the plug (cardboard model) is removed, and the top edges are leveled and smoothed off. Next, an oversized flat cover is made by laying up fiberglass and resin on a flat surface (covered with waxed paper) to a similar thickness. When this cures hard the cover is trimmed to fit the top of the box.

From a local plumbing supply house you then buy the appropriate size ABS plastic pipe fittings to make the needed connections for the discharge hose and the inlet hose from the engine. Cut the two holes needed in the cover for these fittings.

After sanding the surface of each ABS fitting, use chopped-up fiberglass and resin to glue the fittings in place on the cover, then join the cover to the body of the muffler with more resin and fiberglass. Allow this to set up for at least twenty-four hours, then plug one opening and pressure test the assembled muffler to see if there are any leaks. Leaks that are found can be easily repaired with a little more resin and a strip of fiberglass.

Mounting the muffler in the boat is simple. You can either use some type of wood clamp to hold it down, or you can cement it down with silicone adhesive and then add a few hose clamps or stainless steel straps to secure everything. Rubber exhaust hose is used to connect the muffler to the engine and to the discharge opening in the hull.

Removing a Drive Shaft

If you work on your own boat, sooner or later you will have to remove a shaft from an inboard engine. While this can be an arduous

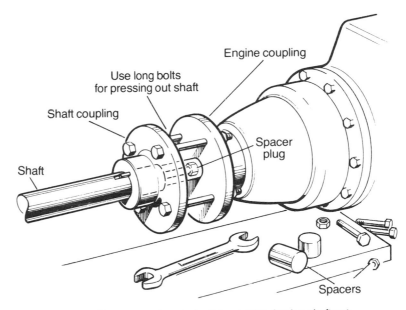

Spacer seen inserted within coupler, forcing shaft out

task, I offer this simple procedure.

While the boat is stored on land, spray the coupling and bolts on the coupling with a penetrating fluid, such as CRC, to loosen any rust or corrosion. After any rust or corrosion is loosened, remove any set screws on the shaft coupling and remove the coupling bolts themselves.

Move the shaft back away from the engine coupling. Find four or five old bolts to use as spacers between the shaft coupling and the engine coupling. Using the first bolt, which should be shorter than the coupling bolts, place it in the shaft coupling in the center of the shaft. Move the shaft back up to the engine coupling while keeping the bolt spacer centered on the shaft. Install the coupling bolts and tighten them equally until the two couplings draw together.

Care should be taken to tighten the coupling bolts evenly to ensure that the couplings will not be warped. After the couplings draw together, you should notice the shaft starting to be pressed out of the coupling. Remove the coupling

bolts again and install a slightly longer spacer and repeat the procedure.

Repeat the procedure using successively longer spacers until the shaft is free of its coupling. Once free, the shaft can be removed from the boat without the use of any special tools.

Silencing the Engine Alarm While Starting

Engine alarm buzzers that warn the skipper when the engine overheats or when oil pressure drops to a dangerous level are a great safety feature. But the buzzer always goes off when you are trying to start the engine, because during the starting cycle there is obviously no oil pressure. Since the oil-pressure sensing switch is a "normally closed" type, it sets off the buzzer as soon as the ignition switch is turned on. The buzzer keeps sounding until the engine revs up enough to build up the oil pressure; then the sensing switch opens and shuts off the buzzer.

The trouble with this system—aside from the annoying noise—is that on some boats when you start the engine (or engines) from the flying bridge the buzzer makes so much noise that you cannot hear if the engine has actually started, so you sometimes crank the engine longer than you should.

To get around this problem there is a simple change I have made that can be made on most other inboard engines: I installed a "normally open" vacuum switch and wired this into the engine alarm system so that it is in series with the buzzer on its ground side.

With this in the circuit, here is what happens: When you turn on the ignition switch the vacuum switch is in its "normally open" position, so even though the oil-pressure switch is in its "normally closed" position (indicating no oil pressure) the alarm does *not*

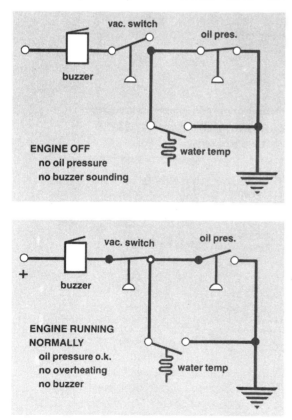

ENGINE OFF
no oil pressure
no buzzer sounding

ENGINE RUNNING NORMALLY
oil pressure o.k.
no overheating
no buzzer

Vacuum switch keeps oil-pressure buzzer disconnected until the engine has started.

sound. Cranking the engine with the starter will not create enough vacuum to close the vacuum switch, so the buzzer won't sound while you are trying to start the engine.

However, once the engine starts, there will be enough vacuum to close the switch. Then if the oil pressure is not fully up, the buzzer will sound; if the oil pressure comes up to normal, the buzzer won't sound.

None of this affects the operation of the heat sensor. Since it is normally open it will only sound the buzzer when the engine overheats—it never sounds when you are merely starting the engine.

The vacuum switch can be a standard unit available from any auto parts store, such as the Cole-Hersee #92007 or equivalent. Since all marine engines are actually marinized auto or truck engines, all have several vacuum sources already drilled and tapped, though they are capped or sealed with plugs. The distributor vacuum advance hole (not used in boats) is one possibility. Another would be the hole for the PVC valve hose nipple on the manifold of most V8s. Also, many carburetors have a vacuum break linked to the choke, and the hose leading to this can be cut so that a small T can be inserted. One leg can then go to the choke, while the other is used for the vacuum switch.

As shown in the accompanying diagram, the ground wire going from the buzzer to the two sensor switches (oil pressure and water temperature) is cut and connected to one side of the vacuum switch. Then the other side of the vacuum switch continues on as it was in the original wiring—going to both the oil-pressure sensing switch and the water-temperature sensor. Therefore, no new wiring is required, except perhaps an extra length of wire from the buzzer to the newly installed vacuum switch.

SHORTCUTS TO SAVE TIME AND MONEY

Easy Way to Snake Flexible Hose

Because rubber and plastic hoses are both quite flexible, passing a length through a small hole can be aggravating, especially if the destination is far away or not in a line of sight.

A trick I learned for this procedure is to run a guide of heavy wire through first, than push the hose along the wire. First, bend a loop in one end smaller than the inside diameter of the hose. In the other end bend a short length (an inch or two) at a right angle. This bent end will provide a handle for maneuvering the wire, if necessary.

Push the wire through the openings and spaces until the loop emerges. Have someone hold the bent end, and begin feeding the hose over the looped end. If the hose sticks, the person at the bent end will have to twist the wire to shake the hose free.

If you figure the hose will get stuck, say where it must pass through a second bulkhead at an angle, fit a tapered wood plug with a ¼" hole drilled into its nose into the leading end of the hose. Wrap the shoulder of the hose with tape to create a smooth surface, then shove the hose along as described above.

How to Take Off Curved Outlines

There are many projects a boat-owner tackles that involve cutting pieces of wood so they will form a snug fit against a curved or irregular contour—for example, when cutting the end pieces for a strum box.

One method is to make a continuing series of smaller cuts until the piece fits close enough to permit final shaping with sandpaper or a rasp. Another is to make paper or cardboard patterns. Both methods can work, but the first method involves a lot of trial cutting and fitting, while the second method often results in errors when the outline is transferred from pattern to wood.

There is a much easier way—a method that is standard with experienced carpenters and cabinet-makers. They use an ordinary child's compass or a pair of dividers to scribe the exact outline onto the wood.

As illustrated, hold the piece of wood to be cut against the curved surface so that it just touches at one point. The wood should be held firmly in the same position in which it will be installed. Open the

The key to this simple method is to hold the compass in the same attitude while the line is drawn.

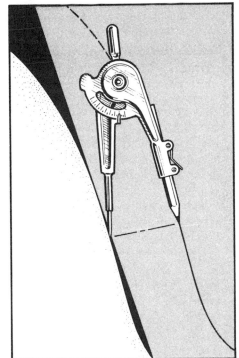

compass or dividers so that the point on one leg just touches the contour to be matched (the side of the hull, for example) while the other leg with the pencil point touches the piece of wood at the place where the wood is farthest away.

Without shifting the setting of the two legs on the compass or dividers, and without changing the horizontal plane of the compass, move it slowly along the contour of the surface. The point will follow the contour of the hull while the pencil is tracing the same curves onto the surface of the wood.

Wood Plug Removal

To extract a wood plug without damaging the surrounding wood, drill a ⅛″ pilot hole in the center of the plug, then insert a #8 wood screw, the point of which has been slightly blunted with a file. As you turn the screw down, the plug will be forced up and out.

Sanding Curved Moldings

You can't use a sanding block as a backing for your sandpaper when you are sanding curved moldings the way you can on flat surfaces. This usually means holding the sandpaper clutched between your fingertips, and can result in your picking up lots of splinters. It also makes it hard to get the sandpaper to follow the contours of the surface—in many cases you will wind up rounding off edges you didn't intend to.

A simple way to avoid all this is to use the edge of a deck of cards as a "sanding block." As you press the sandpaper-covered edge of the deck against the curved surface, the cards will slide in and out to create a matching contour. You can then hold the sandpaper in place and sand as hard as you want. As the sandpaper wears, slide it over to expose a fresh surface.

Diver's Trick Helps Find Overboard Items

When something is accidentally dropped overboard, even a trained diver can often have trouble finding it because the exact spot where the item went over is not always known—especially if several hours go by before the diver actually goes down to look. This is particularly true if the bottom is muddy or if the water is murky so that vision is limited. Nothing is more frustrating than knowing where something went over, but not being able to find it.

A friend and former Navy diver helped me solve this problem once when I accidentally dropped something overboard. The item dropped was a spring for which I had no replacement, yet without it the jam cleat for my main sheet was virtually useless—and I was leaving on a trip across open water with high winds expected. I definitely would need that jam cleat.

My friend told me to immediately drop a weight of some kind overboard in the exact same spot, but to tie a length of heavy white nylon cord to the weight. Allow the weight to fall freely, and then take the slack out of the line and hold onto it.

When the diver went overboard to look for it, all he had to do was follow the white line down to the bottom, then search the area around it. The spring I was looking for was within about a foot of where the weight was resting on the bottom, so it was quickly found. It's best to use a fairly heavy weight so it will stay put when it falls. In most cases the weight will be within a foot or two of the object you are looking for.

Long-Reach Lighter

I have a gimballed alcohol two-burner stove on my boat, and lighting it requires a foot-long match, or one of those long-reach butane or piezoelectric devices that are designed to permit lighting a burner from a distance. Sinced these devices are expensive and often hard to find, and since they often fail to work at a critical time when they are most needed (especially the piezoelectric device when the vapor pressure is low on cold

Alligator clip on rod extends reach of lighted match.

days), I finally assembled my own device which solves the trouble inexpensively and uses ordinary wooden matches.

All you need is an inexpensive metal alligator clip (sold in hardware stores and electronic supply stores), a scrap piece of wire coat hanger, and a little quick-drying epoxy. Attach the alligator clip to the end of the wire coat hanger with the quick-setting epoxy as shown in the drawing, then use its jaws to hold an ordinary wood or paper match so that you can reach in easily to the farthest burner.

Barbecue Bellows

Getting a good barbecue fire going when there is no wind to add needed draft can be a problem. Dangerous starting fluids have no place on a boat. A safe and simple solution, for those who carry or tow an inflatable dinghy, is to use the foot pump as a bellows. Set this up near the barbecue then give the pump a few strokes while holding its hose aimed at the base of the fire. You'll have the coals glowing in a few short minutes.

Tender Launch and Recovery

No one will argue that a tender is an extremely useful device on a cruising boat. But, whether you stow the dinghy on deck or tow it, there will still be occasions where you will need to either raise the dinghy on board or lower it into the water.

While I don't offer any suggestions for dinghies stowed on the deck of a powerboat (unless a trawler with spar), there are sev-

Spread bridle with whisker pole to flip the dinghy, above. Below: Steadying lines fore and aft allow a one-man job.

eral methods that may be employed on a sailboat to make this operation relatively easy. These range from the strong-arm method (not recommended unless you happen to be a close relative to a gorilla) to the employment of halyards, winches, and other equipment. It is this latter approach which I propose to address.

We had been using a 35-pound Sea Snark for several years. This was satisfactory until our family started to grow. It wasn't long before we found ourselves buying a new, larger, heavier dinghy that would hold all of us. It immediately became obvious that the strong-arm method of launch or recovery was no longer practical.

The first approach that came to mind was to use the mainsail halyard attached to the painter of the dinghy and the main halyard winch to raise the bow of the dinghy while someone (read "I") lifted the stern by brute force to raise it to the deck, lower it to the water, and turn it over. This worked fairly well except for the awkward part where the dinghy was between the gunnel of the big boat and the water. In this stage, you usually ended up banging the dinghy against the hull or found yourself leaning well outboard, off-balance, and inviting a sprained back.

After a few tries with the above operation, a simple modification was employed. We swung the boom well outboard and held it in that position with a line run forward. In addition to the painter-fastened halyard, a line from the stern of the dinghy through the end of the boom to a jib sheet winch solved the problem of turning the dinghy over and kept it from banging the hull as it was raised or lowered. It also reduced the likelihood of generating back problems or inviting an impromptu swim.

However, it still required two people to operate; one to work the halyard winch and an octopus to work the jib winch, turn the dinghy over and support the stern until the line from the boom became usable.

The procedure was still a nuisance and took time. Then, serendipity! A whisker pole we store on deck came to my attention. By running a line the same length as the dinghy painter from the stern of the dinghy to the main halyard shackle and taking up the slack in the halyard, it became possible to simply insert the whisker pole between the painter and the stern line, spreading these lines apart far enough to raise the dinghy, move it to one side, and spin it over. The whisker pole was then removed and the dinghy pushed outboard and lowered away. By cleating the halyard when the whisker pole is inserted or removed, and effective use of the halyard winch, it is relatively easy for one person to lower the dinghy to the water. While it is possible to push on the dinghy gunnel with one hand while letting the halyard slip with the other, it is simpler to insert the whisker pole in the halyard shackle and use it to push the dinghy outboard. The process is reversed to raise the dinghy. However, a second person is required to crank the winch unless you want to go to the trouble of

rigging fore and aft lines on the dinghy and fastening the inboard end of the whisker pole to a part of the boat. In either case, the amount of strength and effort involved was insignificant.

There are, of course, more refinements that can simplify this technique. For instance, knots in the dinghy painter and stern line to keep the whisker pole from sliding or, if the design of the dinghy allows, dispensing with the whisker pole altogether. It still remains the easiest way, short of installing davits, to raise or lower a dinghy to or from the deck of my sailboat.

Easy Anchor Retrieval

After spending a pleasant afternoon at anchor in a small boat, taking the anchor in means going forward to haul in the line. If the water is by then a bit choppy, walking forward on the narrow deck of my cruiser, and then hauling in on the anchor line while trying to balance myself on the small bow-deck area can get a bit chancy—especially for a senior citizen like myself.

To get around this problem, especially when I am alone, I attach a retriever line to a cleat in the

Retrieval line pulls anchor rode aft, where it can be handled from the cockpit.

cockpit with the other end attached to a brass or stainless-steel ring that has been previously slid over my anchor line as shown in the illustration.

From the cockpit I can pull on the retriever line until I can take hold of the anchor line—then I can pull in on the anchor from the safety of my cockpit.

Anchor Saver

My major concern when anchoring, aside from dragging, is the possibility of fouling my expensive anchor and its ⅜" chain so badly I can't retrieve it.

My solution is to attach a trip line with its own buoy to the anchor so I can work on it from another angle. I've found ⅜" polypropylene works best—it's readily available in bright colors and it floats, which reduces the possibility of it becoming entangled in the flukes. The diameter is about the minimum for comfortable handling.

Shock cord around the wood block holds trip line to desired length.

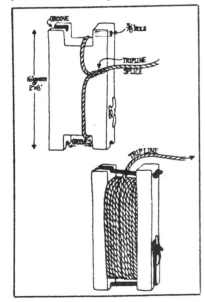

The buoy system evolved from a bleach bottle into the more elaborate wood construction, as shown. First, I wanted to be able to use the float to pull on the line. Second, I wanted to be able to adjust the length of the line to match the depth of the water.

The float is made from a 16" piece of 2" × 8" lumber cut to the shape shown. The ends are notched to hold the trip line neatly. The wrapped line is held in place by an adjustable length of shock cord—I cut grooves in the ends of three of the tabs to hold the shock cord, and drilled a hole in the fourth to dead-end the cord. The cleat allows me to wrap or unwrap the trip line and to adjust the shock cord. I painted my float white, but any visible color will do.

Rode Stowage

A nylon ice bag, obtainable at most marine supply outlets, makes a handy container for your anchor rode. Starting with the inboard end of the rode, feed it into the bag. Stowed thus, the rode won't twist, tangle, or hockle, as sometimes happens when you coil it. Dump the chain on top and attach the shackle loosely to one of the handles. A piece of line tied around one of the handles will allow you to secure the bag on the foredeck.

Baffles for Drawers

Any large flat drawer can easily be divided off into small civilized areas by using either ⅛"-wide plywood baffles or ready-made plastic trays. The latter have many advantages over the plywood and should be used in places where

things may be spilled or leaked, like in the head and galley. Cleanup can then be effected by removing and rinsing one tray only, without the need to unpack the entire drawer. The plastic trays couple nicely together with molded grooves and tongues so they will not shift and slide about.

If you use plywood baffles, cut them ½" lower than the sides of the drawer. Each piece should be cut at half its height where it intersects with another piece. In plywood of ⅛" thickness, any radial arm or table-saw blade will be enough to make the cut. Assemble without any glue or permanent cleats. If well measured and cut, the baffles will have enough tension to hold themselves in place and still be easily dismantled and removed for cleaning or modification.

Mercury-Switch Burglar Alarm

Mr. Zadig's mercury switch bilge-water alarm (August 1980 "Boatkeeper") brought to mind my own use for a mercury switch—a boat-trailer alarm. I've had the following device on my trailable boat for some time, and wouldn't be without it. It activates the boat's horn when the trailer is raised or lowered more than a couple of inches, and the noise would be more than enough to discourage a boat thief.

Parts needed are as follows: A 1"-diameter dowel 6" long; a miniature mercury glass bulb switch; a toggle switch (for deactivating the alarm); wiring consistent with the wiring used for the boat's horn; and a bolt with nut, the length of which is determined by the thickness of the bulkhead where the device is fastened.

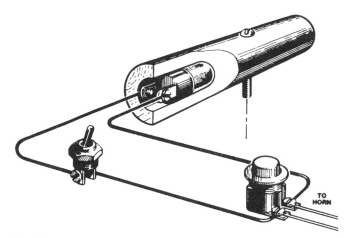

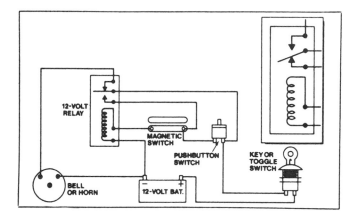

Dowel containing mercury switch is mounted inside boat; it sounds boat horn when trailer is tilted more than a few inches. Wiring diagram is shown below.

Drill two holes in the dowel—one in the end to hold the mercury switch (the switch should fit snugly, then glue it to be sure), and the second hole through the center of the dowel. Mount the dowel parallel to the centerline of the boat in some out-of-the-way spot, preferably near the horn so as little wire as possible is needed. Wire the mercury switch and the toggle switch as shown.

The dowel is adjustable, making the alarm useful at whatever angle you stand the boat and trailer. But play with it a bit—you might find that you want more sensitivity, and if so, simply cant the dowel slightly.

Power Failure Alert

Every boat that is plugged into dockside 110-volt power has at one time or another found that the dockside power goes off and they don't realize it—often until hours afterward. If there is a refrigerator or freezer on board, this can mean spoiled food. In other cases it can mean the inconvenience of having light timers and similar devices go off without your being aware of it. On my boat I use an inexpensive and very handy gadget that simply plugs into any outlet in the boat and sounds a loud buzzer when the dockside power goes off. It's par-

ticularly valuable when cruising and we plug into outlets on a strange dock.

Called the Dark Blazer, and made by Nicholl Brothers (1204 West 27th St., Kansas City, MO 64108), the device is sold in many local hardware and houseware stores. It also serves as a small emergency flashlight—it comes on automatically when the power goes off so you can see your way around the cabin.

You leave it plugged in all the time in any convenient outlet. A red diode on the front glows to tell you the power is on. When the power fails a built-in rechargeable battery (which is always fully charged) causes it to sound a loud buzzer and turn the light on in the dome at the top. You can then unplug it and use it as a small portable flashlight or chartlight. Separate switches enable you to turn the rechargeable light on or off, and to deactivate the buzzer.

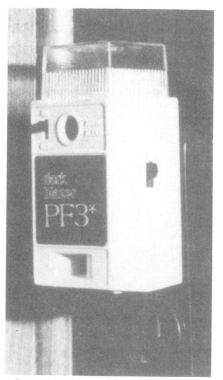

Dark Blazer plugged in

Identifying Fuses More Easily

All too often when a fuse blows in your 12-volt system—or in one of your pieces of electronic gear—and you pull it out for replacement, you just can't seem to make out the markings on the metal end (the markings that tell you what size fuse it is so you will know what size replacement you need). This is especially true when you are working in dim light, or have crawled in behind, a panel where there isn't enough light to see what you're doing, or the fuse is scratched.

By the same token, when you go through your spare-parts box and want to make certain you have all the fuses you need, how many times have you found that even in normal interior room light, reading the markings on the end of the fuse is all but impossible?

One simple way to eliminate this headache is to pull out each fuse and wipe it dry and clean. Then, after checking the markings with a bright light, use a waterproof marking pen to clearly mark the fuse size on the glass, or on the metal end cap. Then you will be able to read the marking even when in a hurry and in dim light.

Removing Rounded Nuts

Anyone who owns a set of both metric and fractional-inch-sized socket wrenches, and has occasionally mixed them up, has probably noticed that most metric wrenches are either a drop too big or a drop too small to fit most standard nuts in fractional-inch sizes.

When it became necessary to remove the exhaust manifolds on my boat, I discovered that the nuts on the manifold had become badly rusted and partially rounded off. As a result, the normal 9/16″ socket wrench that should have fit kept slipping. The nuts were set in deep pockets in the casting so that I couldn't get at them with Vise Grips or a similar tool. It seemed as though drilling and chiseling out the nuts would be my only recourse.

Then I stumbled on the idea of using a 13mm, 12-point metric socket wrench over the rounded nut. I placed this on top of the nut and firmly pounded it down on the nut as far as it would go, using a small hammer. I found that I was able to remove the balkiest of these nuts without too much difficulty. I also discovered (when the nut was taken out of the socket) that hammering the socket down had created a splinelike fitting between the wrench and the nut.

Frozen Nuts and Bolts

The following five steps, used in turn, are guaranteed to free those corroded nuts and bolts that are inevitable on marine fittings and machinery.

- STEP 1 (*Extreme Confidence*) Penetrating oil liberally applied to the stubborn nut or bolt will generally free it after letting it soak a few minutes. Use only box, socket, or end wrenches, never pliers or adjustable wrenches. If this does not loosen the stubborn nut proceed to . . .
- STEP 2 (*Quiet Confidence*) Apply penetrating oil liberally once again. Use a ball-peen hammer tap on the flat part of the nut or bolt to crack the rust seal. Try the box or socket wrench again. Switch to the open end and apply pressure while tapping the exposed flats. Still no luck? Then proceed to . . .
- STEP 3 (*Determination*) Now heat the S.O.B. with a portable propane torch. Be careful and keep a fully charged fire extinguisher nearby. Try Steps 1 and 2 again. No give? Well, take a break. Go down to the local dime store or raid junior's toy box for a bit of modeling clay. Now build a dam around the nut or bolt with the clay after thoroughly cleaning the

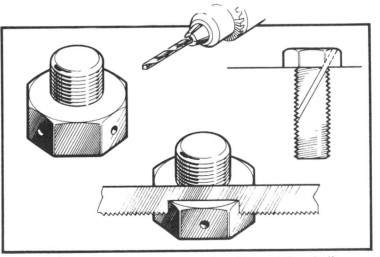

Holes drilled in nuts and bolts allow penetrating oil to reach threads. If necessary, cut two sides off nut and peel the remainder away from stud.

area of oil and dirt (perhaps a little blood and skin also). Fill with penetrating oil and let it soak overnight. Then with renewed vigor try again all the preceding steps. Still the #%° holds. Now proceed to . . .

- STEP 4 (*Inspired Desperation*) Carefully measure the distance across the nut to the stud. Using a small drill with a wood stop, drill holes on four sides of the nut just to the stud. Drill at a slight downward angle to permit holding the penetrating oil. Repeat the preceding steps. Still the S.O.B.##%°!!! hasn't broken. Now . . .
- STEP 5 (*Absolute Desperation*) This works! Simply hacksaw the nut on two sides parallel to the stud. Be careful not to damage the stud. Then simply peel the nut carcass away.

The above steps can be applied to bolts except Step 5. Holes can be carefully drilled on an angle through the bolt head to permit the penetrating oil to reach the threads. For bolts (Step 5), drill holes straight in for a screw extractor or cut off the head. Drill out and retap the hole. Be careful not to hit the water jacket in the case of cylinder heads.

Oil Access

Use a thin wire to lead lubricating oil down to inaccessible oil holes by placing the base of the wire in the hole and letting drops of oil flow along it.

Soundproofing Mats

Decorative mats placed around turning blocks on deck prevent the deck from becoming scarred, and also make life a little more peaceful for the watch below. The mat shown is a simple, circular weave using three ropes.

Solo Man Overboard System

Probably the greatest danger to any single-handed sailor offshore is that of falling overboard, or getting thrown overboard, when no one is around to lend a hand. This potential danger has actually been increased in recent years by dependable self-steering devices that make it a simple matter for the single-handed sailor to get away from the helm whenever he wants, while insuring that the boat will keep sailing away in a straight line.

Needless to say, every prudent sailor should be wearing a safety harness that is securely attached to something solid on the boat, but even so, hauling yourself back aboard while the boat is making speed could be an extremely difficult—if not impossible—task in rough seas and high winds.

Eric Hollerbach, winner of the 1980 Port Huron to Mackinac Single-handed Race, started thinking about this one hairy night in the middle of Lake Huron. His safety harness was on, but could he ever get back aboard with the boat making tracks? He decided to rig up something that would help to slow the boat down if he ever did fall overboard, and make it easier for him to climb back aboard.

The main component he recommends is a large canvas sea anchor with a standard yoke across the front. To this yoke he attached a 20' length of doubled ½" line. At 2' intervals along this doubled line he tied large half hitches, then attached the bitter end of this knotted line to a large stern cleat.

The whole length of line was then coiled inside the sea anchor, and the assembly then fastened to the outside of the stern pulpit with a few narrow strips of duct tape. The idea is to use only enough tape so that the sea anchor is just being held in place, yet can be easily yanked off by a pull from behind.

The next step is attaching a 20' length of ¼" line to the back of the sea anchor. This line is allowed to trail behind the boat at all times when underway. Before the start of a race or single-handed cruise, Eric rigs jacklines from bow to stern, outside the lifelines, so that no matter where he went over he would eventually wind up astern. Then he could easily grab the trailing ¼" line and give it a sharp jerk to tear the sea anchor loose. Once in the water, the sea anchor would

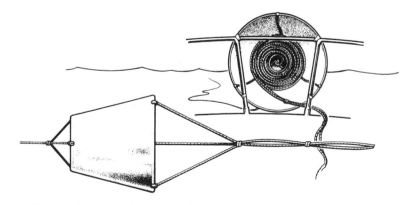

Man overboard can free sea anchor by a sharp pull on line trailed from it.

slow the boat down enough to allow him to haul himself along the knotted double line. He could then use the doubled rope as a ladder to haul himself back aboard.

A Better Cotter Pin

Cotter pins or rings are not only easily lost, they are a nuisance to take out and replace.

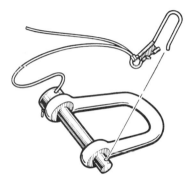

Stainless-steel snap replaces standard cotter pin.

A simple substitute that works as well but is much easier to handle is a stainless steel fisherman's snap used to join the monofilament to leader or lure. It comes in several sizes, and will fit a variety of clevis pins. It locks like a safety pin and is designed not to open accidentally. For convenience, tie a short piece of line between the snap and either the shackle or the clevis pin.

Emergency Fender

Those large plastic 1½-liter soft-drink bottles that we all use so many of during the summer can serve as an emergency fender when one of your regular fenders gets lost or damaged on a weekend—or when you don't want to use your regular fenders when tying up next

Soft-drink bottle makes emergency fender.

to a dirty or greasy piling or dock. All you do is make sure the cap is screwed on tight, then tie the end of a length of ¼″ line around the neck, just under the lip. When no longer serviceable, the "fender" can be simply thrown away and replaced the next time you have another one of these empty bottles.

Save Ice by Plugging Icebox Drain

The common method of draining an icebox is to allow water from the melted ice to drain directly into the bilge through a length of hose attached to a hole in the bottom of the box. But this also allows the cold air inside the box to escape in the same manner, greatly shortening the life of the ice inside the box—especially on hot days.

We developed a very simple solution to this problem that anyone can use to help prolong the life of the ice inside the box. Insert a snug fitting cork in the end of the hose to keep the cold air from "falling" out. In warm weather this cork must be removed at least once a day to let the water drain out, but at the same time you can drain the water directly into a bucket and thus eliminate the need for pumping out the bilge as often. This is a

real bonus for those who don't have electric bilge pumps.

Quick and Easy Rust Removal

To remove rust flecks from electronic panel bezels and screws, fishing gear, and other delicate surfaces, use a lead pencil. Rub the graphite point on the affected area, knocking off rust and other corrosion. The graphite film will offer some protection until a more permanent remedy can be applied. Once back in port, lightly buff off the lead sheen and paint the surface with zinc-chromate or clear fingernail polish.

Catalyst Caution

When using a catalyst-activated mending compound, use a separate scoop to transfer the fresh compound from the container to the mixing surface. If you use the spreader you've been applying the activated compound with, you may introduce catalyst into the container of fresh compound.

Salt Solution

After a rough passage or a day sail in a windy bay, saving your gear and deck shoes from being ruined by salt can be a problem. To eliminate stains, soak the shoes or clothing thoroughly in a vinegar-and-water solution (1:2), then set them out in the sun to dry. The smell of vinegar will evaporate with heat, and your gear should be soft and flexible. If the shoes are stiff, apply some saddle soap.

The Jerry-Can Lift Trick

When somebody has to go up the mast, it's obviously better and easier if there's someone around to winch you up; and better yet if there's someone handy, and lighter, who's willing to go aloft while you stay below with the winch handle. Sooner or later, however, the chances are fairly good that the day will come when you're alone and something has to be done at the spreaders or masthead. If so, take advantage of the fact that a gallon of water weighs about eight pounds, and that most cruising sailboats often carry a jerry can or two.

The classic solution for a single-hander with a problem at the masthead is to rig a four-part tackle, hoist it to the masthead, and then pull himself up in a bosun's chair. The problem here is that many tackles are rigged as boom vangs or preventers, with relatively short lines, and using them means the existing line has to be unreeved and a longer line substituted.

A better solution is to fill two or three jerry cans with water, lash them together, and bend them to a halyard, clipping the whole thing to a forestay. Winch the jerry cans up the mast, make the bosun's chair fast to the halyard, and climb the mast with the jerry cans as counterweight. Two jerry cans will reduce the climbing weight of a 160-pound man to something a bit less than 80 pounds, while three will make it less than 40. (Be sure to keep in mind the weight of the halyard, masthead to deck, or your perch may be permanent.) Once at the top, either clip the bosun's chair to a convenient fitting, or make fast to the mast with a rolling hitch.

The jerry-can system of going aloft works best with the new canvas sling-type bosun's chairs, but is perfectly feasible, though slightly more difficult, with the old-fashioned plank type. If you use the latter, it's helpful to rig an extra line at lap level across the front of the chair and another across the small of your back, so that the chair doesn't slide.

Sailbag Tip

In the interests of efficiency and reducing fatigue, a cruising skipper should routinely instruct his sailmaker to provide him with sailbags 50 percent larger than normal for offshore sailing. Stuffing stiff sails into too-tight bags on a heaving foredeck makes an unpleasant job much tougher. Time saved in this area may be accidents prevented. Ask, also, for loops to which you can attach tie-down lanyards.

Filling the Gap

Many boats have a large gap between the hatch cover and the removable boards—a space that provides welcome ventilation in warm weather but allows cold drafts through in fall and spring.

Towels and sweaters stuffed in the gap provide some relief. However, there is a simple and much more effective solution. Foam rubber cut in the proper shape is easy to snap into place and forms an excellent insulator.

We used left-over open-cell foam, since our companionway is protected from rain by a dodger. Closed-cell foam (foam that is impervious to moisture) would be a better choice if the companionway is exposed to weather. Either is available at most discount stores, or scraps may be bought from an upholsterer or a sailmaker who does upholstery.

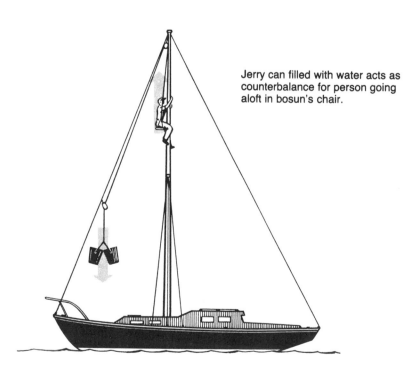

Jerry can filled with water acts as counterbalance for person going aloft in bosun's chair.

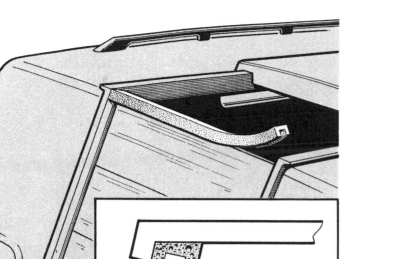

Foam filler strips eliminate drafts at companionway hatch.

The foam may be cut with a large, sharp butcher knife. However, an electric carving knife is much easier to use and provides a neater cut. Since the foam is compressible, it should be measured slightly oversize to assure a tight fit.

If the foam is to be used only when you are inside the boat, it should be U-shaped, and overlap both sides of the boards. If the foam is to be applied from either inside or outside the hatch, for example when the boat is left for a period of time, an L shape is easier to use. In both cases, the hatch cover is first closed, then the filler snugged into place.

Foam is easily marked using a ballpoint pen. To cut a vertical groove, make two cuts—one slightly deeper than the other. With the deeper cut facing you, fold over the loose flap and carefully cut the bottom of the groove.

The result will be a nice square cut.

Our foam filler kept us snug and draft-free through two Maine winters. When it gets sufficiently dog-eared, we'll toss it out and make another.

Easy Clothes Dryer

Many's the time I've done some laundry offshore, only to discover my last clothespin had been blown away in the last breeze. So anything I draped over the lifelines would immediately take to the wind and never be seen again.

However, there is a very easy way to hang clothes securely on deck and not have them blown away. All it takes is two lengths of line.

I use ⅛″ nylon braided line, the kind every boat has a few spare hanks of. I use about 50′, with a loop in the middle so it becomes two lines in parallel. I slip the loop

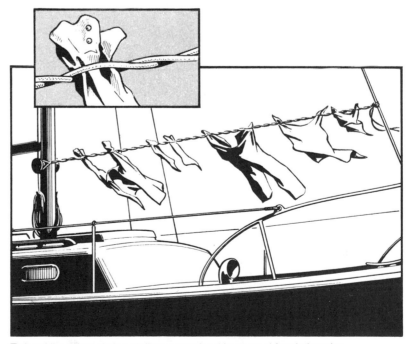

Twisted line holds drying clothes securely without need for clothespins.

over a mast halyard winch, or some other convenient fitting, then twist the two lines around each other for their entire length (however long you need). At the end I usually attach them to my forestay, leaving about 25′ of twisted line.

To hang the clothes, simply pull apart one of the twists, pop in a tail of the shirt, pants, or cut-offs, and let the line contract. They'll stay better than with clothespins, even in a pretty stiff wind.

Steadying Sail

Sitting at a mooring or while at anchor, a ketch or yawl with a set mizzen will weathercock into the wind. However, the modern fin-keel spade-rudder sloop often sails around its mooring, requiring an inordinate amount of sea room and risks dragging in a heavy blow.

The solution is simple: a small steadying sail, rigged off the backstay. On our C&C 40, we have a 35-square-foot sail made of heavy dacron. Its leach is hanked onto the backstay, the clew attached by a line to the backstay turnbuckle, the tack secured to the mainsheet traveler by our boom vang, and the halyard sets the sail up tight.

In a pinch, this sail can double as a backup storm jib.

Hi-Tech Whipping

Here's a quick, simple, and inexpensive way to whip line ends. Pay a visit to your local electronic supply store and pick up some shrink tubing. It comes in various diameter sizes. Find some approximately the size of the line you wish to whip. Work the shrink tubing up over the line approximately 1″, and cut it off as close to the end of the line as you can. Then hold a match, lighter, or even a hair dryer under the tubing and roll it over the heat. The tube will constrict around the line and "whip" it.

Working with Plastic Tubing

When plastic tubing is used to replace a water line in the boat's plumbing system, or to add a line to an existing one by means of a T fitting, the tubing is often a tight fit over the end of a piece of metal pipe or fitting of some kind—which is as it should be. However, all too often trying to slip the tubing on or off becomes a major job (especially when working in tight quarters) because the tubing is just a bit *too* tight.

A simple solution lies in using hot water to soften the tubing and make it more pliable, thus making it easier to slip on or off. If you are trying to remove the tubing from a fitting, wrap with heavy cloths, then pour hot water on and wait about a minute for the heat to work. If you are trying to slide a piece of tubing onto a fitting, dip its end in some hot water and let it soak for a minute—then slide it on.

Connections are further secured by using small hose clamps, but don't tighten until after the plastic tubing has cooled completely.

Anchor Wash Down

After we have anchored in mud or clay washing the anchor and its chain becomes a necessary evil. In the past, this always meant laboriously hauling buckets of seawater up from the rail and refilling the bucket repeatedly while we also scrubbed the links clean with a small brush.

My husband, Dave, solved this neatly with a simple length of plastic hose which we hook onto the end of our saltwater spigot next to the galley sink. We attach the hose to the spigot with a hose clamp and attach a nozzle to the other end. Then we pass this through the aft companionway and take it forward. A crew member stands there and hoses off the chain as it comes in while the saltwater pressure system pumps away. He then finishes the job by hosing off the anchor and the decks before stowing the hose down below.

Bernie Gladstone's Boatyard: Readers' Questions Answered

Q: I own a 30′ boat that was purchased new in 1977. It has two 50-gallon water tanks made of polyethylene, and for about eighteen months I have been having a problem with a smell much like rotten eggs from the tap water. The problem seems to be worse after the boat has been sitting unused for a couple of weeks and I turn on the faucets for the first time. Is there something I should add to the water in the tanks to stop this problem?

A: Since the smell is worst when the faucets are first opened, I am inclined to think that the trouble is not in the tanks at all, but in the water out of the pipes or hoses. Try flushing the whole system out with baking soda—mix this in with the water in the tanks, run part out through the faucets to make sure the solution is in all the pipes, then let this sit for a few days before flushing it all out and replacing with fresh, clean water. If this doesn't help, your best solution may be to replace the hoses or pipes.

Q: My 17′ fiberglass boat has a transom that consists of a core of plywood. I realized that the core was gone when the motor bracket cut through the outer layer of fiberglass when tightened—apparently the wood was all rotted. I used a wire tool to scrape out all of the deteriorated wood, then repaired the hole in the transom and installed two layers of cloth across the entire transom, with three extra layers of cloth where the motor clamps on. How should I go about installing a new solid-wood core?

A: This should have been done before you did all that fiberglassing. If a wood core is needed for the strength of the transom, and to provide a solid grip for the motor bracket, then the only way is to cut the fiberglass out (on the inside would be simpler now), then glass in the piece of wood, and cover with additional layers of glass and resin on the inside.

Q: The aluminum spars on my new sailboat were coated with linear polyurethane by the manufacturer, but after about one year the paint began blistering wherever stainless steel screws and hardware were attached. The spars have all been recoated by the manufacturer, since they also showed signs of corrosion where the stainless steel was attached. It seems as though aluminum and stainless steel are not good company, according to the galvanic series of metals. Yet most aluminum masts do use stainless hardware. What do you think is the problem?

A: Stainless hardware is universally used on aluminum masts and spars, but you must remember that there are many varieties of stainless, and these are rated differently on the list of metals more prone to electrolytic problems—if indeed that is your problem. The best type for use around a marine environment is one of the 300-series, such as type 316. There is another possibility for the paint breaking down around the hardware—these items may not have been cleaned or properly primed before the paint was applied over them.

Q: My boat is a 41′ fiberglass trawler with a deep keel and skeg-to-rudder-post design enclosing its single screw. The keel is hollow and about 2″ wide on the inside. This hollow keel has taken some inexcusable bumps on Bahamas coral without the least sign of trouble. However, I am still worried about the hollow keel. Should it be filled for extra strength in cases of grounding, and if so, with what?

A: There are undoubtedly hundreds of boats such as yours that have the same type of hollow keel, and which are having no problems. I doubt if you have to worry about filling it. However, if you are really worried about it, I suggest you contact the designer or builder and get his suggestions.

Q: I have a boat with a Philippine mahogany hull. I plan to store this boat out of the water for about four years. Is there anything special I should do to prevent damage from this long storage—for example, should I remove the cover to prevent excessive heat buildup?

A: Keeping a wood boat out of the water for as long as four years is bound to result in excessive drying out of the planking, and will certainly call for some careful recaulking and attention to seams when the boat is finally launched again. There is no way anyone can tell you how bad the condition will be because there are too many variables involved. However, I would make certain that when the boat is securely covered it is also well ventilated under the cover. It might be a good idea to remove the cover occasionally during nice weather. At that time clean the boat thoroughly, inside and out, and touch up any paint or varnish that shows signs of cracking or peeling. Also, pay extra attention to cradling and proper blocking to make sure there are no stresses that could cause distortion of the hull.

Q: I have a well-known brand of inflatable dinghy that has a hole about 1½″ by 3″ in one side (chewed by mice). I have tried to apply a patch with tire cement, but it doesn't seem to hold. I have pieces of the material to make the patch—it is a type of fabric coated with neoprene rubber—but I need an adhesive to hold it in place. Do you know what I can use?

A: Your best bet is to get the adhesive you need from the manufacturer of your dinghy. A dealer who sells that brand of inflatable may also have some of the adhesive you need. However, remember that this cement ages, and in time becomes useless, so make sure it has not been lying around for years.

Q: I have a 17′ speedboat with an 85-horsepower outboard mounted on it. There is a crack in the engine mount on the transom, and several people have told me to reinforce this by using metal plates and bolts. However, there is no place for me to mount these plates. Would a fiberglass filler be strong enough to fill the crack and keep it from getting worse?

A: Metal plates to reinforce the outboard mount probably refer to plates that are large enough to bridge the entire area and thus tie to the solid parts of the transom on each side. The bolts should then go clear through. I would suggest, however, that you try to contact the manufacturer of your boat first. He knows best how it was built, and what would be needed to reinforce the cracked area. If this is not practical, speak to a knowledgeable yard in your area. I don't think just filling the crack with fiberglass or resin would help strengthen it enough.

Q: I own a 1964 powerboat and have been troubled with a white saltlike deposit that continually keeps forming around the bronze screws that hold down the bronze plate housing the shaft log. I have cleaned this area repeatedly, and it keeps coming back. Can you suggest a solution?

A: This is probably oxidation or corrosion—not uncommon around some types of bronze alloy when continuously exposed to salt water. Or it may simply be crystallized salt from the water that seeps in around the shaft log then evaporates. Either way, I would scrub the metal surfaces clean once more, then spray with a moisture-displacing spray such as LPS or WD-40. Then smear a liberal layer of waterproof grease over the entire area to keep moisture from attacking the metal.

Q: I have a 1977 sailboat that has developed large numbers of half-dollar-size blisters in the gel coat on the underwater portions of the hull. I have had varying opinions as to just how serious this is, and as to what should be done about it. One person with a surveyor's background said that each blister should be stripped off and the area ground out to form a shallow pocket that can then be filled with epoxy resin and fiberglass mat. I have noticed that the blisters ooze a sticky brown substance from a pin-sized hole in the center when they are exposed to the sun, and there seems to be water inside the fiberglass. However, following the surveyor's recommendations would make for a very time-consuming job, and I am afraid it would weaken the hull because of the many potholes that would have to be dug out and filled. Do you think this is really serious, and if so, do you have any recommendations?

A: This type of gel-coat blistering is, unfortunately, not uncommon. The brown oozing means water is getting behind the gel coat and being absorbed into the fiberglass mat or cloth—and that is not good. The first thing I would do is contact the manufacturer of your boat. The company may be willing to do something about the problem, or it may at least be able to give you some sound advice. If not, the advice you got from the surveyor was basically sound—all blisters should be ground out and then filled. However, unless they are larger than you say you don't need to use any cloth or mat. Epoxy resin alone should do the trick. The job is time-consuming, but a small hand grinder (the kind used by modelmakers) will speed up the removal of the blisters, and without applying mat or cloth the job should not take as long as you think. Anyway, unless you get the work done you could wind up with a still more serious problem.

Q: My 26′ fiberglass sailboat is moored on an inland lake, and I was planning to leave my boat in the water all year round. However, several of my fellow sailors in this area tell me that this is not a good idea because our lake has a high calcium content, and when boats are not hauled occasionally this calcium content causes blisters and peeling to develop in the gel coat. I have never heard of such a problem and wonder if you know if there is anything to this warning?

A: As you can see from reading the previous letter, there is a problem that sometimes occurs with gel-coat blistering—but I have never heard this problem blamed on a body of water that has high calcium content. There is a fair amount of research being done on this by manufacturers of boats and finishing products, and as far as I know, there is no basis for blaming the chemical content of the water in which the boat is moored. It is apparently due to inherent prob-

lems with the gel coat or the resins used in manufacturing the boat. In other words, if your boat is going to have this kind of problem, the water is probably not to blame.

Q: I own a 33′ sailboat, and the original light blue deck color is badly faded and wearing to the point where white is showing through from underneath. I would now like to paint it with one of the new two-part polyurethanes on the market for do-it-yourselfers. However, the decks have a nonskid texture apparently molded into them, and I am wondering if painting them would fill this texture in and make them dangerously slippery. I have called the manufacturer of the boat, and a large paint manufacturer, but they cannot give me an answer. Can you help?

A: Chances are that if you paint the decks you *will* fill in the nonskid pattern to some extent—depends on how deep the texture is now, and on how heavily the paint is applied. I would suggest you put the paint on this area with a roller instead of a brush. A roller is less likely to fill in the low spots if you don't load it up too much. When the job is done see how it looks and feels when you walk on it. If it does seem slippery, all is not lost. You can still paint over this area with a product like 3M's Liquid Carpet. It creates a good nonskid surface and can be neatly applied if you outline the areas to be coated with masking tape.

Q: It recently became necessary to replace the gasoline tanks in my cabin cruiser. After the job was done the original cockpit sole was replaced with ¾″ marine plywood that was then covered with fiberglass. I have on hand a quantity of ⅓″-thick teak marine plywood and was wondering what chance of success I would have if I wanted to

cement down 2″-wide strips of this teak on top of the fiberglass. Also, what adhesive and what filler compound should I use?

A: You would have better luck with solid wood because of the possibility of the plywood delaminating in time. If you use the plywood, you would also have better luck with large sheets and less seams. However, if you want to go ahead with your idea, your best bet would be to cement the strips down with an epoxy, then fill the joints in afterward with the black polysulfide or thiokol-type sealant. It's best to seal the teak strips on the underside with a teak primer first to help insure a good bond with the epoxy. Teak is an oily wood and getting a bond is sometimes a problem. Or, instead of using a primer, sand the undersides with fine-grit paper before laying them, then wipe each off with acetone before you put it down on the bed of epoxy. The acetone will remove the surface oils so the epoxy will bond better.

Q: Several years ago you ran an article in "Boatkeeper" about using polybutylene plastic pipe and fittings for water lines and plumbing inside the boat. This sounds like a great idea for a couple of jobs I am now planning, including the installation of a new holding tank and some new water lines. But my problem is that none of the local marine supply outlets in this area seem to carry this pipe. Any idea where I can buy it?

A: I normally don't answer "where do I buy" letters in this column, but since I wrote that article so many readers have written in with the same question you ask that I decided to let you in on the secret. Plastic pipe and plumbing fittings may not be available in your local marine supply outlets, but it is widely available in most regular plumbing supply outlets, as well as in many large hardware stores and "home centers" or "do-it-yourself" stores. If you still can't find it nearby, write to one of these manufacturers: Qest Products, Inc., 1900 W. Hively, Elkhart, IN 46515; Genova, Inc., 7034 E. Court St., Davison, MI 48423; and Chicago Specialty Manufacturing Co., Skokie, IL 60076.

Q: We recently acquired a six-year-old 23′ sailboat that has a keel centerboard. What is the easiest way for me to get antifouling bottom paint on this centerboard and on the inside of the centerboard trunk?

A: If you can possibly take the centerboard out without doing too much damage, then your best bet is to take it out and paint it separately. Then, to paint the inside of the trunk in which this board rides, get a stick that is long enough to reach down the full length of the enclosure and nail a small square of plywood to the end. Then staple some scrap pieces of carpet to each side of this plywood to form a sort of painting pad. Dip the carpet into the paint and drag this up and down on the inside of the center-board well to coat both sides. If you can't get the centerboard out, you will have to lower it as far as it will go, then paint as much as you can from the bottom (while the boat is hauled and blocked, of course). The well can be painted as described above by reaching up from the bottom to get those sections that you can't get when reaching down from the top.

Q: I recently bought an inexpensive small sailboat with a Styrofoam plastic hull (it was originally offered as a premium). Now I would like to apply something to the foam hull to make it more durable and provide better resistance to penetration of water. Can you suggest anything that would be suitable?

A: About the only thing that would work, and that would do much of a job of protecting the soft plastic against damage, would be to cover the hull with fiberglass or with one of the other laminating cloths. An epoxy resin would probably be better than a polyester resin for this, but it would cost more. However, you may have no choice because some types of foam may not be compatible with polyester resin, though will not be attacked by epoxy. To play safe, you should check this with your dealer, and even then, experiment on a small area—ideally a spot located in a noncritical area—before you go ahead with the whole job.

Q: My single-screw express cruiser came equipped with a 12-volt system that has only one battery. I would now like to add a second battery that can be used for engine starting in an emergency, as well as to handle the extra electrical accessories that have been added to the boat. What is the proper way to do this?

A: In addition to the second battery, which should be a deep-discharge marine-type storage battery, you will also want a vapor-proof master battery switch—the kind that has settings that allow you to connect the load to battery #1, battery #2, or both. There will also be an OFF position which is a good way to insure against unauthorized use or accidental battery drain when you leave the boat. Install this second battery close to the first one, then run heavy battery cables from each battery to the new switch, and from there to your starter and the rest of the 12-volt system. (Instructions supplied with the switch will show how to hook it up.) Once installed, this switch will enable you to select either battery, or to hook both in parallel temporarily when extra power is needed (or while charging). Generally, you designate one battery for starting only; switch to the other battery when at anchor or dockside so that you do not drain the starting battery—and thus have one always ready to go. Use the battery switch to keep both batteries fully charged when underway.

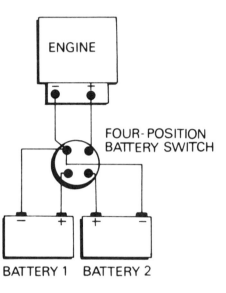

Two-battery installation

Q: I have a 17′ boat that I keep on a trailer. The boat is five years old and the outside looks fine, but the carpet inside the cockpit is faded and stained. Using a carpet cleaner on it did not seem to help very much, so I am planning to remove the old carpet and install new carpet. Can you tell me what sort of carpet I should buy, and what type of adhesive?

A: For an open boat the best type of carpet to use is the indoor/outdoor carpet sold for use around swimming pools and on patios, terraces, or other outdoor surfaces.

The cheapest grades have no backing or a foam-type resilient plastic backing. Most dealers also sell a mastic adhesive that is made for cementing it down. However, my suggestion is not to cement the carpet down at all. With a rubber backing it will pretty much stay put without adhesive, especially if you cut it to a fairly snug fit on all sides. You can then take it out at any time to give it a good scrubbing. If you do decide that you want it cemented down, then I suggest using a silicone rubber cement or sealant. Apply this in strips near the edges and in just a few places in the center.

Q: My 27′ wood cruiser is kept on a freshwater lake of pretty good quality. I plan to leave it in the water from the spring to the fall each year, although up till now it has always been trailered. Can you tell me if it is necessary to paint this boat with bottom paint every year—or even if it is necessary to use bottom paint at all?

A: Theoretically, when a boat is used only in fresh water it should not need an antifouling bottom paint—at least not for barnacles and similar growth. However, as a practical matter these days most bodies of fresh water (lakes and rivers) are at least moderately polluted, so if nothing else, there is almost always a problem with slime or "grass" growing on the bottom. Antifouling paint will prevent this. One of the best ways to decide on what, if anything, is needed is to check with some of the other boatowners or with one of the reliable boatyards in the area. Find out what their experience has been and whether or not they have found it advisable to use bottom paint on their boats.

Q: The centerboard on my 1971 30′ sailboat had the bottom 8″ or 10″ broken off, and I don't know whether the centerboard is solid fiberglass, glass over wood, or metal. Some people have advised me to merely finish off the rough, broken end and leave it as is, but others have advised me to get the centerboard repaired to its original specifications. What do you think?

A: In a well-designed centerboard boat there is a safety margin built in that permits using less than the full depth of the centerboard in most situations, while still providing adequate lateral resistance—even when well heeled over in a stiff breeze. However, exactly how much "extra" was included in the design of your sailboat I cannot say. Also, it depends on what percentage of the board is actually missing. I would advise contacting the manufacturer to get his advice. If this is impractical, then I would talk to a local naval architect or designer, or consult a local yard that specializes in sailboats. My own suggestion would be to replace the centerboard entirely—it would probably be difficult to rebuild it back to its original size.

Q: I have read and heard from many sources that teak is a wood that will stand up to the elements without needing any protective coating, so after I bought my new boat a couple of years ago I left the teak as is and just scrubbed it regularly. Now I find that the teak looks scruffy and, worse yet, it is starting to crack, split, and check in a few places. Local yards and other "experts" now tell me that the reason is because I never took care of the teak by oiling it or by using a sealer of any kind. Is this right?

A: Yes and no. Teak can stand up to the elements almost indefinitely without protection as far as rot is concerned (as long as fresh water is not trapped underneath or inside the wood), but this does not mean it will not split or check and crack—or that it will not get dirty and scruffy looking. That is why most boatowners prefer to use an oil or sealer of some kind. Also, much of the teak used on boats in the last few years is not properly seasoned the way it used to be (some is not even really teak, I've been told), so it tends to check and split more than it should. As a rule, if the teak is even of reasonable quality, some checking will take place when the teak is not protected, but this should not affect its structural strength. However, if you're worried about further checking, apply an oil or sealer.

Q: On my 25′ twin-screw inboard I have a continual problem with an excessive amount of barnacle growth on the two shafts. This growth greatly cuts down on my speed and causes considerable shaft vibration after a couple of months in the water. I install zinc collars on each shaft at the beginning of the season, but this doesn't solve the problem. My boatyard has warned against painting the shafts as this would cause an electrolysis problem. I am considering applying a special coating that is supposed to make bottoms so slick that barnacles won't hold on it. Can you tell me if this will work, or is there another method that will solve my problem?

A: Painting your shafts will not result in an electrolysis problem if you use one of the vinyl-base bottom paints, not a metallic-base bottom paint such as one containing copper. Unfortunately, however, most boatowners who have tried this still find that it doesn't really help much—the paint wears off the shaft very quickly due to the friction created by high-speed rotation, especially in a power boat. I have also tried painting props, and this doesn't help either for the same reason (one day's run and the paint is just about gone). I cannot answer your question about the special coating you are talking about because I have honestly never heard of it, but I have serious doubts. I know of no one who has found a solution to this, and if a solution were found, word would spread very quickly.

Q: I am having a problem with caulking that won't stick to the teak trim where the trim meets the fiberglass. I am using a well-known top grade of marine caulking, but after a few months you can peel it off the wood easily. Any suggestions?

A: Teak is an oily wood that does give problems with varnish, paint, and sealants. That is why most companies make a primer that should be used on teak first. It is a clear, fast-drying sealer that you brush on first and allow to dry before applying the caulking—you will find that the caulking then sticks a lot better.

Q: We have recently completed an extensive painting and remodeling job around the inside and outside of our boat. We are now finished but are having one problem: We used lots of masking tape and didn't bother to start taking any of it off until after we had finished. The tape on the windows and the fiberglass just doesn't seem to want to peel off. What can you suggest?

A: There are several things that will help. One is to use rubber cement thinner on those places where the tape is mostly removed but there is still a sticky residue left on the surface. The thinner will also help soften old tape, and generally will not harm most finishes or gel coats. In places where the tape is

really stuck tight and won't budge at all, mild heat will generally soften it up enough to simplify removal. Don't use a torch; use a heat lamp or similar mild source of heat.

Q: I have a wood sailboat at least thirty years old that is now stored out of the water each winter (it spent the first half of its life always in the water). I would now like to fiberglass the bottom, but I am getting conflicting opinions on this. Some say it will encourage dry rot in the wood of the hull. What is your opinion?

A: There have been many old boats that had their bottoms fiberglassed, and I have never yet heard of a problem with dry rot on the wood inside the glass sheathing—if anything, testimony seems to indicate that there is much less rot than would otherwise have occurred. However, all this assumes that the job is done right with proper precautions for preparing the old wood so that the resin will bond properly. The old paint must *all* be removed by scraping and sanding. Don't use remover as the chemicals will soak in and prevent a proper bond. Don't use a torch as you may scorch the wood and again there will be trouble with a bond. Some experts also recommend stapling or nailing the first coat of fiberglass to the wood to insure against delamination—and be sure you build up enough layers to insure adequate strength. An epoxy resin will cost more than polyester, but most agree that it will also be stronger and more waterproof.

Q: I am going to do some interior work joining teak. Is ordinary waterproof wood glue okay to use with teak, or is there a special glue that I must use?

A: A regular plastic resin wood

glue (which is quite waterproof and should be adequate for use inside a boat) can be used, but since teak is an oily wood you should take a little extra care to make sure the surface is clean. After sanding the wood, wipe the surfaces to be joined with acetone or lacquer thinner to remove surface oils, then glue as usual. Just make sure the joints fit snugly (this type of glue does not fill voids very well) and make sure joints are clamped till the glue sets. If clamping is impractical, you might try using a new type of glue called Depend (made by Woodhill Chemical, and sold under the Duro brand line). This is a two-part "instant" acrylic that will bond to oily or greasy surfaces, and it is almost as strong, and just about as waterproof, as an epoxy.

Q: The sides of the cockpit on my cabin cruiser are finished with perforated Masonite, and the paint is continually flaking off. Can you suggest a solution to this problem?

A: Since your letter does not mention anything about the Masonite delaminating, even though it is exposed to the weather and to dampness, I assume that an exterior-grade perforated hardboard was used originally. This has a very smooth, hard surface that is sometimes a problem when ordinary paint is applied. What you need is a primer or first coat that will bond to the slick surface, after which your regular marine paint can be applied over it. The best type of primer I know of for this purpose is a pigmented, shellac-base primer and sealer that dries to a flat white finish. It has exceptional bonding power due to the fact that shellac has very strong adhesive qualities. The two most widely sold brands are Enamelac and BIN. You will find them in regular paint and hardware stores, especially those that cater to professional painters. Incidentally, you will find it easier to paint the perforated hardboard if you use a roller rather than a brush.

Q: I bought my sixteen-year-old fiberglass runabout about five years ago, and it was in excellent condition. For the past three years we have stored it over the winter in one of Missouri's limestone caves. There was a little mildew on the boat each time, but this washed off quite easily in the spring. However, this year there were also a number of small blisters in the gel coat. These blisters do not seem to compress easily when pressed with a finger. Can you tell me how to remove them, and are they caused by being stored in a cave?

A: There is no way to remove the blisters without damaging the gel coat, since the blisters are in the gel coat—in other words, the gel coat is already damaged. To fix them you will have cut each one out, or grind it out with a small abrasive bit in a hand power tool. Then fill with an epoxy resin patching compound and sand smooth. You can also use one of the gel-coat repair kits. Some are also available with coloring materials that enable you to tint the patching material so it will blend in more uniformly with the color of your gel coat.

It is hard to say for sure whether or not storing the boat in a cave caused the problem, but I doubt it. However, the fact that you have mildew each year means that the cave is quite damp, and dampness certainly won't help the condition (often due to moisture being absorbed through porous sections of gel coat, or because of a breakdown of the gel coat in the underwater portions of the hull).

Q: All the articles I have read about using zincs to correct galvanic action gave me the idea that these zincs, to be effective, must be placed against the metal to be protected, and must be in solid contact with the metal—for example, the steel shafts, the trim tabs, or the rudder. Yet, in spite of this every marine catalogue I look at carries the zinc "mermaid" or "guppy" that is fastened to the stern rail by a cable and is then said to "protect the entire boat from damage." Do these, in fact, eliminate the need for diving down two or three times a year to replace the zincs on the underwater shaft by simply hanging in the water off the stern?

A: To be effective, zincs must be in solid *electrical* contact with the metal parts they are designed to protect. But they do not have to be physically touching the bare metal; they can be connected to it by a heavy piece of wire or similar good conductor of electricity. That is the principle behind master-bonding systems on most larger boats—they have one or two large zincs mounted underwater, and all other underwater metal parts are connected to this by a heavy copper cable or length of copper strapping. The hanging zinc you describe can help when there is a problem—if it is connected to the shaft or engine or similar major grounding point, and if everything that needs protection is properly bonded together. Fastening it to the stern rail is merely a means of suspending it in the water; there is then an electrical cable that has to go to a master grounding point aboard the boat (such as the engine or shaft).

It is, however, possible to over protect with zincs, causing deposits to form on underwater metals and wood burn around fittings through wood hulls. Whether you use guppies or fixed zincs, make sure you use little enough to show significant deterioration over the course of a season.

Q: I have a 27' sailboat that has an ice box which measures about three cubic feet on the inside. The problem is that this ice box is nothing more than a fiberglass shell with a ¾"-thick plywood lid that sits in a slight recess in the counter top so that its top surface is level with the rest of the countertop. The trouble is that both the lid and the box are uninsulated, so keeping anything cold for several days is almost impossible. I have installed some ⅝"-thick Styrofoam of good density by taping pieces of this to the sides and bottom of the ice box, and while this has helped it still doesn't give me the insulating qualities I want. The outboard and rear sides are not very accessible, so building a mold and using a foam spray would not be practical. Also, I know that the lid must be insulated to improve cold-keeping qualities. What can you suggest?

A: You need more than ⅝"-thick foam—at least twice, and preferably triple, that thickness would be more like what is recommended. You say that the foam board you put in was taped to the sides and bottom, but if you cut pieces for a really snug fit they should have been force fit and would need no taping. Further, no part of the bottom or sides would be exposed, so you should not be able to tape to these surfaces (unless you used double-stick or double-faced tape).

As far as using a pressurized insulating foam, you can erect a shell or liner of waterproof plywood inside the existing box by cutting pieces to fit, then assembling them on the inside with strips of tape to hold them in place. Coat these pieces of plywood with an epoxy paint to make it easier to keep them clean later on. You erect this inner shell so it leaves a space of about 2″ between it and the inner sides and bottom of the box, and drill a ¾″ hole in the center of each of these side pieces, as well as the bottom piece. This hole will be used to pump pressurized insulating foam (sold in marine supply outlets) into the spaces between the inner shell and the original box. When the foam hardens you cut away the part that oozes out of the holes (some will), and you can then remove the tape that holds the pieces of plywood—the foam will bond them permanently in place. The lid can be insulated by gluing a piece of 1″-thick Styrofoam to the bottom, making it smaller than the overall size of the lid so that it does not cover the lip around the edge where it has to rest in the recess cut into the counter top.

Q: The stuffing box or packing gland around the rudder post of my sailboat has been leaking steadily, but I cannot seem to tighten it down enough to stop the leak. The large packing nut is in a tight spot in the stern of my boat so that I cannot seem to get at it with a large wrench. The yard where I keep my boat says the only cure is to haul the boat and pull the rudder post, but I keep the boat in the water all year round and hadn't planned to have it hauled for some time yet. Do you know of anything I can do to tighten the large packing nut without hauling the boat?

A: A trick that the pros often resort to when they cannot get at a stuffing box or packing nut with a wrench is to use a hammer and a punch of some kind—a large nailset or even a blunt cold chisel. The idea is to tap the end of the punch against one flat on the side of the large nut, near its corner where it angles off to form the next flat. Place the punch firmly against the nut, then rap it sharply with your hammer a few times. This will turn it enough to expose the next flat section on the nut. You can repeat this action until the nut is as tight as you want it. If it becomes necessary to loosen the packing nut (you may have to replace the packing), then simply reverse the process until it is loose enough to turn by hand.

Q: I have a 30′ fiberglass powerboat that is used only in Lake Michigan. The bottom has been painted each year for the past seven years. When the boat is hauled the bottom is washed clean with a water-pressure sprayer before the boat is stored. Then in the spring the bottom is painted and launched. I have never sanded down to the bare fiberglass—just painted a new coat on over the existing bottom paint each time. Do I have to remove all of the old bottom paint before the next paint job, and if so, is there an easier method than sanding it all off?

A: If you have gotten away with applying a fresh coat of bottom paint without sanding for seven years, then you are really lucky. However, if you look closely you will probably find that the bottom is now pretty rough and its surface quite pockmarked, because that is how bottom paint tends to wear, and each succeeding coat adds to the unevenness as the layers build up. That is why at least some sanding is required each year, not so much to remove all of the old bottom paint but to smooth it down (and remove the sections that are blistering or peeling and flaking). You may be able to get by with just scraping off the bad spots and then sanding the surface smooth before you apply your next coat, if most of the old paint is still bonding well.

However, if there are signs of it coming off in places, then you would be better off removing it all and starting from scratch. Sanding and scraping is the usual method, but sandblasting is becoming increasingly popular because it is faster and much easier. If your yard is not equipped to do this, you may be able to have a private contractor come in to do the job, or you can rent a paint sprayer for sandblasting (with a special gun) and do the job yourself.

Q: My new fiberglass center console boat is supposed to have all stainless steel deck hardware on it. However, after one month of use along the Jersey shore, and in spite of hosing it off with fresh water after every trip, rust stains began to appear on the fiberglass around the cleats and around some of the other deck-mounted hardware. The streaks were removed, although they did not come off very easily, but they keep coming back. Can real stainless hardware actually leave rust stains on fiberglass?

A: It all depends on the quality of the hardware and on the kind of stainless used (there are a number of different alloys on the market). Also, when stainless is machined, fine particles of steel are sometimes left on the surface by the tools used to machine the metal, and these particles rust later on. The hardware is supposed to be treated with a special wash to get rid of these microscopic steel particles, but some manufacturers are not very diligent about doing this. Another possibility is that the metal bolts or screws that were used to secure the deck fittings are rusting, rather than the actual deck fitting. Even if stainless bolts or screws were used, the threading and machining process may leave metal particles that will permit some corrosion to develop in the threads or on the surface, especially if a poor-quality stainless was used in making the bolts or nuts. This rust then "weeps" out and "bleeds" into the fiberglass around it.

So what can you do? First, replace any bolts, nuts, or screws that seem to be showing signs of corrosion. Second, squirt a little moisture-displacing penetrating oil (such as WD-40, LPS, or CRC) around all bolt heads and screw heads, as well as around all nuts. This will help to keep moisture out, and will leave a protective film that will help prevent corrosion. And third, keep the hardware coated with a good boat wax as a further deterrent to corrosion. Renew the wax a couple of times each season.

Q: I would like to mount a navigational chart onto a piece of Masonite so that I can frame it and then hang it on the wall of my recreation room at home. I have asked different people about this and have gotten conflicting opinions as to how to avoid bubbles, wrinkles, etc. Can you give me any advice on this?

A: The best way to do this is to use one of the vinyl adhesives sold in paint and wallpaper stores for use in hanging vinyl-type wallcoverings. These come in a powdered form that you mix with water, or in a ready-mixed liquid form that may or may not need thinning with additional water. The ready-mixed liquid is stronger and costs more, but I think the powdered type will be adequate. Just be sure you mix it thoroughly and break up all lumps. I would prime the Masonite with a shellac-based sealer such as BIN or Enamelac (sold in most paint and hardware stores). Let this dry, then mix the paste and apply it to the back of the chart with a small roller. Make sure you cover every square inch of the paper and do not skip any spots; otherwise blisters will result. Apply the paste uniformly, but not too heavily—just enough to cover evenly. Then flip the chart over and smooth it onto the Masonite immediately, rubbing over the entire surface with the palms of your hands, a long straight edge, or a hard roller of some kind. Wipe off any paste that oozes out around the edges before it has a chance to dry.

Q: I have a new sport fisherman bought this past year which has a light yellow hull. Around the transom door, exhaust pipes, and transom corners the gel coat has faded a great deal (the first season) to where it is now almost white in places. Cleaning and rubbing with compounds does not seem to help, so I am convinced it is a defect in the gel coat. I would like to have the entire transom redone this spring, but my dealer says I would be making a big mistake. He says that there is too great a risk of improper color match between the new and the old, and that I would be better off just learning to live with the condition. My question is: If I hire a reputable fiberglass man who is experienced in working with gel coat, are the risks as great as he says so that I would be sorry I started?

A: About the only one that could answer this question with any degree of certainty is the man who would actually be doing the work. There is no doubt about the fact that matching gel coat colors is tough, but if you are doing the whole transom, not just sections, a very slight difference between that area and the nearby hull sides would probably not be very noticeable. However, I am a bit confused about why only the transom would have faded—if the gel-coat color was defective (as you seem to think) why wouldn't fading also take place elsewhere on the hull? They apply all the gel coat at one time. I would advise contacting the manufacturer of the boat before you go further, at any rate—perhaps he has a suggestion. Also, before going ahead with refinishing, I would see if this is not something that can be compounded off; perhaps it is a surface stain caused by exhaust fumes.

Q: The entire deck of my 30′ fiberglass sloop needs to be painted. I have already painted the topsides with a well-known brand of epoxy and am satisfied with the results but haven't painted the deck or the cockpit sole the same way because of the molded-in nonskid areas on these surfaces. I am afraid if I paint these the paint will run into the valleys and will quickly wear off the peaks, reducing the effectiveness of the nonskid. If I leave them unpainted, they will not be slippery, but they will look awful. Have you any suggestions?

A: It is always tough to paint these nonskid molded surfaces without destroying their effectiveness—but it can be done with a reasonable amount of success if you use a roller rather than a brush, and if you take reasonable care in applying the material. Don't thin the paint any more than you absolutely have to so that it will tend to "stay put" better without sagging, and keep the roller well loaded with paint all the time (don't let it run dry). Don't flood the paint on in one heavy coat—put on two thinner coats, and move the roller back and forth in two or more directions over each section. When preparing the surface, make sure it is absolutely clean and dry, and after you are finished allow about two or three times the usual drying time before anyone walks on the painted surface (to make sure it is completely hard).

Q: I have a 33′ utility boat that has an unusual feature I have never come across before—a "backing rudder" that is mounted *forward* of the propeller and the last supporting strut. It is much smaller than the regular rudder (which is located aft of the propeller in the usual location) and is supposed to help steering when in reverse. However, I see no special improvement in control when backing this boat, and because of the extra linkage required, mechanical steering is stiffer than it should be. In addition, I believe the extra rudder may be causing water-flow interference for the propeller—and there is an extra through-hull fitting to worry about. Because of all this, I would like to remove this unit. Do you know of any reason why I shouldn't?

A: I have personally never seen a boat with this extra rudder, so I asked some old-timers in the business about it. One or two have heard of and even used boats with this extra rudder setup—apparently in utility boats that had to spend almost as much time traveling in reverse as in forward. One claimed it helped a bit with the steering, the other agreed with you that it was of little, if any, use. If you want to take it off, I see nothing wrong with doing this—just be sure you do a proper job of plugging the old through-hull opening and disconnecting the linkage on the inside.

Q: I unwisely left a metal toolbox standing on my fiberglass deck, and now there is a rust stain that I cannot seem to remove. The fiberglass is a buff color. Do you have any suggestions as to what I can try?

A: In many cases this type of stain can be removed with one of the hull cleaners that are sold for getting yellow oxide stains off fiberglass hulls. Two brands I know that are widely available are FSR and Y-10. These are wiped on and allowed to soak for about three minutes, then you scrub with a brush and flush away with lots of water. If this doesn't work, then the next thing I would try is a regular rust remover such as Naval Jelly—again rubbing it on lightly and then allowing it to stand for about five minutes. Then rub with a stiff brush and flush away with water. If both these measures fail, then your last hope is an abrasive-type fiberglass cleaning compound—the kind sold for restoring badly weathered fiberglass. You can rub this on by hand, but you will have to rub hard and for quite a while, so if possible use a power buffer instead.

Q: I own a 1966 open skiff that is in excellent condition except for the topsides which are vinyl. This vinyl is showing cracks and I am afraid that I may be getting water between the deck and the vinyl. Can this vinyl be painted, or am I better off taking it off and replacing it with new vinyl?

A: When you speak of the topsides being covered with vinyl, I assume you are actually referring to the decks, as this is where vinyl is often used on wood boats of this type. You can paint over the vinyl with a regular deck paint—after you scrub the surface thoroughly—and then apply a coat of primer as a base coat. But frankly, I would not advise it if the vinyl is cracked and shows signs of aging. All of these vinyls have to be taken off eventually, just as the old-time canvas covering did—and if you have painted over it, the job of getting the old material off will be harder than ever. In fact, at that point you would be better off putting a new deck of plywood over the old material. For now, I would advise ripping the old material off and replacing it with new vinyl. Most large marine supply outlets sell vinyl decking and the special adhesive used to put it down, and the manufacturers supply detailed instructions.

Q: I have a 1968 52′ motor yacht and every two months the speed decreases (and the fuel consumption increases) due to the growth of barnacles on underwater shafts, struts, rudders, props, and trim tabs. I have tried painting these underwater metal parts with copper bottom paint, but this doesn't seem to help much. I keep my boat in the lower Chesapeake Bay and all my yachting friends seem to be having the same problem—we have to haul our boats or hire a diver every two months to scrape the barnacles off these metal parts. What good is the development of those new long-lasting bottom paints (some claim up to two years) if the metal parts need attention every couple of months?

A: Marine growth on props, rudders, etc. can certainly slow a fast boat, and can add to fuel costs; but the loss in speed and fuel efficiency would be even greater if the entire bottom also had this kind of growth on it—so you are still better off with a bottom paint that lasts longer. You can always clean off the metal parts by diving underwater, but you cannot put new bottom paint on without hauling.

As far as painting the metal is concerned, paint will not stand up for long on props and rudders, but painting the struts and the trim tabs with a good grade of vinyl bottom paint should help slow the growth during the first couple of months. Some boatyards have reported good protection for the metal by coating props and rudders with a layer of WGL's Teflon grease. I tried this on my own props and rudders late last summer (when my boat was hauled), and it did seem to help quite a bit when I dived down to look about a month later—but this is still too short a time to be sure. I will know better when the boat is hauled again this summer.

Q: The teak decks on my boat have rubber caulking between the strips of teak. I believe this teak was laid over fiberglass-covered plywood. I am having a problem with water leaking through to the cabin below. The leaks seem to occur where the forward and aft slopes of the deck meet, creating a low point where water tends to stand after a rain. Can you suggest any way to correct this or fix the leak?

A: The leaks are probably due to water getting through the fiberglass under the teak—probably dripping through the holes in which the screws go, holes that apparently penetrate the fiberglass. Sometimes a leak of this kind can be cured by digging out the black neoprene caulking in the suspected areas, then replacing it with new material. To do this, run a knife along the edges of the caulking next to each teak plank: then pry the caulking out with the point of the knife. You will be able to almost peel it out in one long strip. Make sure the wood is dry, then apply a coat of teak sealer and let this dry before applying new caulking. Use a black polysulfide caulking (such as black Boatlife or similar material made for use on teak decks). The sealer (made by the same company that makes the caulking) is important on the exposed teak edges to ensure a good bond with the caulking.

If this fails to stop the leak, then you may have to also remove and then replace the screws that hold the teak planks down. This means first digging out the wood plugs that cover the screws, then carefully backing out the screws with a large-blade screwdriver. After the screws are out, pump some caulking into the hole, then replace and retighten the screws, but replace any that are chewed up or look bent.

Q: My 25′ sailboat has a light gray epoxy paint on the deck. I wrote the company that makes the boat and ordered a quart of the paint to redo the deck. After I received the paint I followed instructions and mixed four ounces of the hardening agent in with the quart before applying it. In five minutes the paint hardened like plaster and was unusable. I ordered another quart, and this time added only four drops of the hardener to the quart. The paint worked fine, but this time it took about two weeks to dry hard. Is there any other kind of paint I can use over this two-part epoxy that will not require mixing anything in with it?

A: You really went from one extreme to another. Even though the four ounces recommended may have been too much for the temperature that particular day, you went too far in cutting back to just four drops. Something like three ounces, or even two ounces, would have made more sense and probably would have worked fine. But, to answer your question, you can apply a regular one-part alkyd or polyurethane marine paint over the epoxy paint without difficulty—it just won't last as long in many cases.

Q: My 26′ cruiser has an aluminum deck tank, and I recently installed fuel shut-offs on the lines leading to the engines. I replaced the aluminum antisiphon fittings and shutoff valves with brass fittings, but now a friend tells me that I may have a problem after a time because there are different metals in contact with each other. What is your opinion on this?

A: It is generally not a good idea to have different metals in contact with each other due to the possibility of a chemical reaction similar to electrolysis or galvanic corrosion. However, this is not often a problem between aluminum and brass when these metals are used in fuel lines; it is more a problem when the metals are in direct contact with salt water. Nevertheless, if you can get fittings of aluminum—fittings that would also be reasonably resistant to a salt water environment—I would suggest installing these in place of the brass ones.

Q: My 29′ trawler has fiberglass diesel-fuel tanks molded into the hull—one 30-gallon tank on each side. One of these tanks started "weeping" after the boat was delivered (it was trucked cross-country with each tank half full), so we only used the tank on the other side when cruising. However, to maintain trim it became necessary to fill the leaking tank with water—the water doesn't leak out the way diesel fuel does. Is there any liquid I can pour into this tank to seal it without having to go through an expensive repair job?

A: If there is, I am not familiar with it. I have seen some products advertised for use in portable metal fuel tanks (you have to turn the tank over and from side to side so the liquid can coat all sides), but I don't know how well these work, or even whether or not they will work on fiberglass tanks.

Q: The bottom of my 21′ sailboat is completely covered with blisters approximately ½″ across. The local boat dealer says this is the paint that is blistering. The local auto body shop says it is the gel coat. A friend says to sandblast the bottom, then apply a liquid silicone. The auto body man says sandblasting would set the fiberglass afire, and he never heard of liquid silicone. Have you any thought on this?

A: That's quite a collection of misinformation you have been gathering. First, the blistering could be either the paint or the gel coat. To check, all you have to do is scrape some of the blisters off to see if it is only the paint that is blistered, or if the gel coat under the paint is blistered. I'm sure the gel coat and the paint are not the same color so you should have no trouble in telling which is blistering.

Second, I have never heard of a liquid silicone for use on boats; there are a couple of types that are used in the building industry and around homes, but I have never heard of using these on boats and see no advantage in using one of these products instead of one of the coatings that are made specifically for marine use.

Third, if sandblasting sets fiberglass on fire, then there will be hundreds of boats burned up each year. It is a technique widely used to clean old paint off boat bottoms (I have had it done to my own boat), and I have never heard of any of these boats catching fire from the sandblasting.

Q: I am an avid reader of your magazine and was very interested in the "Boatkeeper" article on fiberglass repairs (April 1982). I have a 1963 31′ powerboat that has extensive fine crazing on the bow, the flying bridge, and in some places along the sides. I am trying to decide which method would be best to cover all this crazing and feel that complete refinishing with one of the two-part urethane finishes would be the best solution. There is only one yard in this area that does this kind of work, so I was wondering if any of these are brushable and suitable for application on the outside. If I do the job myself, can I make the boat look like it had just come off the factory assembly line?

A: In the "Boatkeeper" section of March 1982 (see pages 11–14), and in a "Boatkeeper" section two years earlier (March 1980), I described two-part urethanes now on the market that are designed for brush or roller application by the boatowner who has to work outdoors. Needless to say, you have to pick your days carefully to make sure you get favorable weather, and you have to follow instructions exactly. Experience indicates that most people get the smoothest job by using both a brush and a roller to put these paints on. Use a sponge-type roller cover to put these paints on, then smooth off immediately with a top-quality, soft bristle brush (make sure you buy the kind that will withstand these solvents; some sponge roller covers will disintegrate when used with such powerful solvents).

You should get a beautiful job if you are careful, but don't expect it to look like it came off an assembly line. No brush-on or roll-on paint job that is applied to an old boat while it is sitting outside will match an original top-quality factory gel coat job, but if applied with skill, the paint job will make the boat look *almost* as good as new.

Brightwork Spots

Your June 1981 article about brightwork ("The Clear Urethane Solution") describes the problem of white spots appearing in the wood due to a break in the coating, or due to water finding its way under the film.

The solution to this problem lies in finding a highly penetrating oil that will provide a good sealer between the wood and the urethane finish, and will darken the white color. Varnish is not a good penetrant, but I have found that Deks Olje #1 is. When first treating the wood I apply the #1 oil until a full finish is obtained, then allow it to dry for about two days before applying the first coat of urethane on top. I have yet to have any breakdown of the surface coats.

On areas that were not pretreated in this manner, when a white spot does appear I use a stiff bristle brush to work the oil in over the white spot. As the oil penetrates the tiny break in the film (there is almost always a microscopic crack in the film), it penetrates and darkens the wood underneath, until it practically disappears. If the white spot does not change, I use a small pocket knife to pierce the surface very carefully, then apply the oil again. Allow this to dry for at least one day, then apply another coat of the urethane over the surface. Allow to dry, then sand and apply a second coat the following day.

Both of these techniques result in a very beautiful and long-lasting finish.

Q: My boat has a homemade steering pedestal that is made entirely of brass, except the chain and sprocket—those parts are made of plain steel. Is there any type of compass I can buy that will work properly on this pedestal?

A: It is possible that a conventional magnetic compass could be used if the steel is at least 3′ to 4′ away, and if the compass can be compensated to eliminate any deviation. If this is not possible (you really won't know till you try), then there are remote reading compasses you can buy. These have an indicating unit that you can mount on your pedestal, but the actual magnetic compass can be almost anywhere else in the boat. The indicator is connected to this electrically and gives you a reading of what the compass indicates.

Q: My present cabin sole is fiberglass over plywood, and I want to put a new wood sole down on top of the fiberglass. I want to use 2½"-wide strips separated by ½" strips, all about ⅜" thick to avoid losing cabin height. I want to use adhesive to avoid mechanical fasteners of any kind, except perhaps around the hatch cutouts, and I don't want to use teak because it is too expensive. What kind of wood and adhesive would you recommend?

A: Mahogany would be my second choice if you are not going to use teak, but it will require more maintenance to keep it looking good. If mahogany gets wet and stays damp, it turns black; teak is more forgiving in this respect. Teak is also more resistant to rot under most circumstances. As for the adhesive to use, I think a two-part epoxy adhesive would probably be your best bet, but remember, once you put it down with this, getting it up again (if you ever want to) will be quite a job.

Q: My 36' trawler has an internal bonding system that links all underwater metal parts—all the through-hulls, stuffing box, rudder, shaft, tanks, etc.—to two large zince plates positioned on the transom. When the vessel was hauled last fall I noticed that the two zinc plates looked almost like new, while the rudder and shaft zincs had deteriorated quite a bit. Does this lack of deterioration on the big transom plates indicate they are not functioning properly, and if so, what can I do to remedy the problem?

A: Chances are there is nothing wrong. It is not unusual for local zincs of shafts and rudders to go completely in a few months; in fact, that is natural since the smaller units that are closer to the metal and totally underwater are bound to go first (both are protecting the same shafts and rudders).

However, to play it safe I would make sure that the zincs are clean (not painted or coated with grease or other foreign material that can interfere with the electrolytic action) and see if they are under water when the boat is actually in the water at rest and also under way. Sometimes transom-mounted zincs are out of the water most of the time, so they really cannot do their job.

And finally, why not take an hour or so and go over the whole bonding system? Make sure there is good electrical contact between the zinc plates and the wires and bolts connecting to them, then follow the wire back through the boat's innards to see if it is really connected at all points where it should be. During construction, one of the wires may have been broken, or a careless workman may even have forgotten to make one or two critical connections. As you check each connection, make sure there is no corrosion interfering with good electrical contact at all the junction points.

Q: In your article on converting to a shore-supplied water system ("Boatkeeper," May 1982) you explained how this involves replacing the old hand-operated, pump-type faucet with an electric pump. Wouldn't it be sensible to leave the hand-operated spigot or faucet in place as a backup in case of a failure of the electric water pump? That way you will still be able to get water out of the tank if the electric pump fails or the battery goes dead.

A: The idea is basically sound, but it would involve running a separate water line from the tank, or at least from before the electric pump, to the hand-operated sink faucet. If you tried to use a pump-type faucet on the line coming from the electric water pump, it would not be able to draw water from the tank (it would be difficult to draw water through the stationary pump if it was not operating). That's why you either have to run a separate water line, or build in a bypass at the pump with manual valves so that you can cut out the pump (by manually switching valves) when the pump fails.

Q: I have a 1971 35' sloop which was built by a company that is no longer in business. The boat has an iron keel bolted to channel section floors. I want to know if there is any way to check these bolts to see if they are still sound without actually loosening or removing them. Also, would it be feasible to fiberglass over the whole keel and the joint formed with the fiberglass bottom to avoid the necessity for caulking the joint each spring, and for scraping and priming the metal keel each year before the bottom paint can be applied over it?

A: Assuming that there is no sign of excessive play between the keel and the bottom of the hull, and there is no sign of extensive corrosion seeping through, I know of no simple way to check the condition of the bolts without taking them out so you can physically inspect them. As far as fiberglassing over the whole keel, there is nothing wrong with this—in fact, it has often been done by others. Just make certain you get the metal absolutely clean and bright before you brush on the first coat of resin; and use a waterproof resin that is made to stand up under constant immersion—probably an epoxy resin, rather than polyester. Fill in and fair out the joints and rough spots by using an epoxy putty before you start.

Q: I have an 8-volt battery in my 22′ boat and wish to get a new battery charger. I cannot locate an 8-volt charger, and have been told to use a 12-volt charger. Do you agree?

A: I don't agree. Chances are that if you used it very carefully, and kept a continual watch on the battery and the charger, you might be able to get away with it for a short charge. However, I have checked with a manufacturer of batteries and their expert agrees that using a charger with a higher rated voltage than the battery could be dangerous—you could damage the battery or the charger, or both, or you could even cause an explosion due to a buildup of gases. (Normally 8-volt batteries are used in series with three or four connected together to put out 24 or 32 volts—you can get chargers for these voltages.) I would recommend checking with some manufacturers of battery chargers to see if they can come up with a charger of suitable voltage, or with some type of transformer or resistor that could be used to reduce the voltage on a 12-volt charger. Otherwise, maybe you should consider changing to a 6-volt or 12-volt battery.

Q: The aluminum water tank in my boat, which holds about a hundred gallons of water, has accumulated a calcium scale on the inside. This apparently happened when I had the boat in lower Florida for about six months. I was not aware of any problem until recently when the coating or "sludge" started to break down (water in my home port is rather soft, so we do not have this problem). The "sludge" does not seem to affect the quality of the water, but it is having a devastating effect on the water-pressure pump. It has been suggested that I put some sulphanic acid (not sulphuric acid) into the tank, but no one seems able to tell me how much—or whether or not it will harm the tank.

A: My first suggestion is that since the only problem is the ongoing damage to the pressure water pump, why not install a filter in the water line leading from the water tank? This will keep the sediment from reaching the pump and damaging it. If you want to try something that will dissolve the calcium buildup (assuming you are right and that is what the problem is), then I would suggest trying some vinegar in the tank. It is a mild acid and certainly isn't poisonous. Can't say how much you should add, but experiment with various quantities poured into the tank when it is about half full and then allowed to stand for a week. Flush out thoroughly when you return, then add more water and see if there are still particles coming out. If so, repeat with a stronger solution.

Q: I find every issue of your magazine to be most enjoyable and informative and would appreciate your advice on the following: I am thinking of buying a wood sailboat in the 50′ range but would like to know what the problems would be with fiberglassing over the hull and keel. Would the wood under the fiberglass tend to rot, and would the addition of this fiberglass sheathing adversely affect the balance and performance of the boat?

A: There have been many cases where old wood hulls were successfully covered with fiberglass; and I have never heard of one where this has led to wood rot on the inside. I have also spoken to various experts in the field, and they too say that this seldom, if ever, happens. The few instances where rot has been a problem were almost always due to faulty workmanship—either the layers of resin and glass did not bond properly to the wood underneath, or the layup job was poorly done, and as a result the fiberglass sheathing cracked and allowed water to enter. Most experts agree that for best results the first layer of cloth should be mechanically fastened to the wood with rustproof staples. Also, all of the old paint must be thoroughly cleaned off to insure a solid bond with the resin, and the wood must be completely dry and clean before you start.

As far as the question of whether or not fiberglassing will affect the performance of the boat—only a naval architect or experienced boatbuilder who is familiar with that particular design could answer that. Chances are it won't, but you will be adding weight, so there is a slight chance that this might affect performance. However, I doubt if it would affect the balance or stability of the boat.

Q: We have a 1973 fiberglass motor yacht with all-copper plumbing in the water system. I think we have a fiberglass water tank built under the aft deck. Our problem is a musty taste in the water. What can you recommend to get rid of this taste?

A: The taste is most likely coming from the water tank, although I cannot be sure. I would start by locating the tank and then seeing if there is any simple way to flush it out—or possibly to remove it and have it steam-cleaned. If this is not practical, try adding some fresh Clorox to the water tank—about one tablespoon for each gallon of water it holds; then fill the tank with water and go out for a ride, preferably on a choppy day.

When you come back, or on the way in, empty the tank by pumping all the water out. Then refill with fresh water and see if this helps. I would also advise installing a taste-and-odor water filter in the system after the water pump—or at least just before the sink where you draw drinking and cooking water. These filters use replaceable cartridges which you can change as needed (usually once a season will do).

Q: I have tried using acetone to remove the black stain that eventually seems to accumulate on all my white rubber fenders. It removes the stains, but it leaves a sticky residue on the surface of the rubber. What chemical would you suggest for cleaning these fenders?

A: If you are talking about black dirt stains and abrasion stains that occur from normal rubbing against docks, then here is what I have found works best: If the stains are not too severe, I use a strong detergent such as Spray Nine, Fantastik, etc. I use it straight, but scrub it on with an abrasive pad such as Scotch Brite or something similar. Scrub a section at a time, then rinse off with water before it gets a chance to dry.

If this doesn't get the stains off, then the only solvent I have found that does not attack the rubber or leave it sticky is one of the non-flammable dry cleaning or degreasing solvents which are sold in all hardware stores and in many marine supply outlets. This is the type of solvent that is now sold in place

of carbon tetrachloride (carbon tet is now banned). Paint thinner also works, but not as well, and it is inflammable.

If the dark stains are left by tar or creosote, with which many pilings and some docks are impregnated, then the best you can do is lighten them—you will never get them out completely. At least I have never heard of anything that works. The quicker you get to work on the stains the better your chances of getting them out. I get the black residue off with one of the solvents that I have mentioned above. But there is always a light, rust-colored stain that remains embedded in the surface, and nothing seems to get that out.

Q: I have a twin-screw diesel trawler with a flying bridge, and I almost always run it from the bridge. However, I am having trouble getting the engines synchronized properly. When they are not in synch there is a lot more vibration, which I'm afraid will harm the boat in time. There was an engine-synchronization indicator on the boat when I bought it, but I did not find it very reliable or dependable. I have since installed a different model synchronizer which seems to work better, but the engines still drift out of synch after an hour or so and often won't stay in synch in rough seas. Although I can detect this when I am running from below, just by listening, on the bridge I can't hear the engines as well so it is tough to synchronize by the way they sound.

I understand that there is a synchronizer that will synchronize the engines automatically, and that this will also help save on fuel costs—in addition to cutting down on wear and tear on the engines, struts, mounts, etc. Is this so, and if so, is this something I can install myself?

A: In a past issue of *MB&S* I de-

scribed the installation of a device that will solve all synchronization problems—the Glendinning Synchronizer. This device automatically keeps both engines in synch by continuously making one follow the other. In other words, you move only one throttle; the other engine's throttle control becomes a "slave" and follows automatically—and exactly. This eliminates all vibration and "rumble" when underway, so it will result in some small fuel savings in most cases. But it is the savings in wear and tear—on the skipper, as well as on the boat—that are the greatest benefits.

Installation is not very difficult if the direction manual is carefully followed. But installing the Glendinning Synchronizer is not a job for the man who is "all thumbs." However, Mr. Glendinning is most cooperative in answering questions and giving advice to customers who contact him when they run into a problem while installing one of these units.

Q: I have recently purchased a 1963, 57', flush-deck motor yacht, and after inspecting the engines I noticed that three of the mounts on the starboard engine were loose. I am sure that the engine and shaft are out of alignment, but in an attempt to correct this, I ran into a problem. When I uncoupled the plate attached to the shaft from the plate attached to the engine, I discovered that the shaft has no support close to the engine. The nearest support is the stuffing box, which is about 5' away. When uncoupled, the weight of the shaft is enough to cause it to sag several inches, and I can move it as much as 4" to 6" from side to side. How can I determine where the shaft should be for correct alignment, and when the engine is in alignment?

A: Aligning an engine coupling with the shaft coupling is a task that calls for some experience, and, among other tools, a set of feeler gauges. When you tighten the coupler bolts to draw the plates flat up against each other there should only be a minimal air gap between the two at any point (usually about .002″ is the maximum allowed). The shafts should then be uncoupled and the prop shaft rotated 90° while the motor plate and shaft are held in the same position, then the plates brought together again and tested once more with the feeler gauge. This is repeated till the shaft has been rotated through 360° (four times in all).

Actually, this is only the first test a skilled professional will make. If problems are found, the test is repeated with the prop shaft held in one position while the motor plate is rotated through 90° increments as just described. In each case minor adjustments may have to be made to the engine mounts. But even this may not solve the problem. There is also a possibility that the shaft is bent—in which case it will have to be pulled and sent to a machine shop for straightening—or the possibility of improper clearances in the way the pilot (between couplers) was bored, or in the strut alignment. All in all, this is generally not a job for the amateur. Proper engine and shaft alignment really calls for the services of a competent professional. He would know which of the many variables—engine mounts, struts, bent shafts, etc.—could be causing the problem and would best know what additional steps, if any, will be required to correct the condition.

Q: Two seasons ago I removed all the varnish from the mahogany cabin and toe rails on my 1959 boat. Then I saturated this wood, as well as my teak decks, with multiple coats of Deks Olje #1. This solved problems I had with the deck swelling and shrinking excessively, but I am very disappointed that the golden-brown color I originally had has now changed to a dirty, dark-looking, ugly brown. Spots where the surfaces were covered with canvas and the vertical surfaces on the cabin have not changed much, however. What can I do about the unsightly appearance?

A: You can blame your problem on the sun, and on the water that accumulates on horizontal surfaces. Vertical surfaces (as well as those under canvas) don't get as much direct sun, hence the wood doesn't suffer as much. However, you must remember that no teak sealer or finish will last two full seasons, and you really should have been keeping after the finish before it got so bad. Additional coats are usually needed each spring and at least once more during the late summer. Now your only solution is stripping all the sealer off and then cleaning the teak and starting over.

Q: I am interested in restoring the finish on my 31′ fiberglass sloop. The gel coat has lost most of its sheen, but the estimate I received of about $2,000 for having it professionally sprayed with a two-part polyurethane paint puts that job way out of my reach. I have a portable air compressor and a spray gun, but the problem of toxicity and providing a clean environment for painting has me stumped. Can you give us do-it-yourselfers any tips on spraying to get a good job, and can these two-part paints be applied with one of the better quality "airless" spray-gun outfits?

A: The best suggestion I can give any do-it-yourselfer about spraying his boat with one of the two-part polyurethane paints is DON'T! This is really a job for a professional shop that can do the job indoors under controlled conditions. The shop must be equipped with the necessary ventilating equipment to do this kind of work safely, and they must have the kind of experienced help that is familiar with this type of painting to give you a really good job. However, a careful do-it-yourself can get a good result with the brushable polyurethanes, especially if you first put them on with a foam roller, then lay them out with a top-quality brush (preferably badger hair). This technique was described here in "Boatkeeper" in the March 1982 issue. It is safe, and gives beautiful results if properly handled—I know because I've done it.

As for using an airless sprayer—that would really be a disaster! Those sprayers are fine for painting a fence or the outside of a house, but they are not suitable for any really smooth finishing jobs such as the painting of a boat or an automobile.

Q: The cockpit rails on my 25′ cruiser are teak. A few years ago I was advised to apply seven or more coats of Deks Olje #2 to seal the oily wood, so I did—and the appearance was indeed beautiful. It looked like well-varnished, light mahogany. But now all the rails look as though they have been painted black. What went wrong, and what corrective measures can I take now?

A: The advice you received was only partially correct. The instructions for the product you used tell you to apply multiple coats of the company's #1 oil first, then apply several coats of the #2. The #2 is something like a light-bodied varnish, but the wood should have been sealed with their oil (#1) first. Even if you had done everything right, the finish still needs annual maintenance—you can't expect any clear varnish or sealer to last for several years.

What you have to do now is use a varnish remover to strip off all of the existing finish down to the bare wood. Then use a teak cleaner and a brightener or bleach to clean and lighten the wood (these are sold in all marine supply stores). Wait until the wood dries, then refinish— but this time follow directions and remember that you will have to maintain the finish by applying additional coats at least once or twice a year, depending on wear and exposure.

Q: I have a 1965, 44' carvel-planked wood boat. The previous owner used surfacing putty in all the seams above the water line, and as a result many of these seams are opening and the putty is cracking out in places. I want to remove all this hardened putty so that I can recaulk the seams with one of the newer flexible seam compounds. What kind of compound or tool can I use to remove the putty without damaging the planking?

A: I don't think there is any chemical compound you can use that will work satisfactorily. Seams of this kind are usually dug out in one of two ways: by hand or with power tools. To do the job by hand you will need a tool that most people make up themselves. You heat the tang of an old file and then bend it to form a sort of right-angle hook or curve at the end. Then grind the end of this hook to a chisel-like edge so you can use it to dig out the compound by raking it hard along each seam. Make the "blade" or hooked end the width of the groove you want to dig out.

To do the job with power tools you can use a portable circular saw with the blade set to no more than the depth you want the groove to be (usually ¼" to ½"). Some people

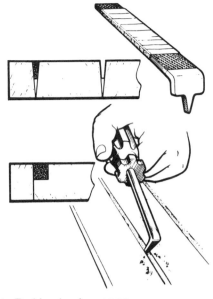

Tool for cleaning seams

prefer a portable router with a bit that cuts a groove of the width and depth required. Using power tools makes the job go much faster, of course, but both saw and router require *very careful* control if you don't want to gouge the planking unnecessarily. Rigging up a long board to act as a guide for each joint or seam will help a lot.

Q: I recently purchased a 36' Chris-Craft with twin gasoline V8s. The boat has a waterline length of 31' and weighs approximately 15,000 pounds. It was designed as a planing hull with some V forward but pretty flat aft. My plan is to replace the gas engines with either two small diesels or one bigger diesel. Would you recommend the conversion? If so, which would you select—single or twin?

A: The underlying questions involved in any engine swap are: How much in the way of hull and engine-mount modifications will be necessary to make the change? And, once the carpentry is finished, how well will the new engine combination perform?

Switching from dual engines to single is not easy, but it can be done. It's more a question of bottom configuration than anything else. Repowering from dual to single obviously means the rudders have to be changed. And what kind of keel does the boat have? Can a shaft be cut into the center? These kinds of determinations are best made after a "hands-on" survey by a repower specialist.

Regarding engine horsepower, if you are not looking for planing speeds and would be happy with displacement hull operation, smaller engines will work.

Q: My boat is eight years old and has been hauled and painted each year. Now it looks like it is time to remove all the bottom paint and start over. I was thinking of sandblasting and wonder if this is an acceptable method for removing bottom paint. A local bottom-cleaning service uses an underwater power brush to scrub the bottom, and they suggest doing this every few months. They claim there will be some repellent to carry me through from one brushing to the next— until they finally get down to the gel coat. Then the boat would be hauled and painted. With eight coats to go through, this could take a year or more, saving me the cost of at least one haul-out. What do you think of this idea?

A: I'm not sold. Even though the boat has been painted eight times, you don't have eight coats of bottom paint; much of each coat was worn off before you repainted. And I assume you did some sanding between coats—which took more off. Also, at the end of a full year, much of the toxic material is gone—it leaches out of the paint continuously when in the water— so there is little of this left for following years. If it were my boat, I would go with sandblasting and starting from scratch. Sandblasting is a highly effective way of removing bottom paint—but it should be done by someone who has the equipment to do it right, and the experience to get the job done without damaging the fiberglass or gel coat.

Incidentally, if you do start from scratch, you might want to look into using one of the new copolymer bottom paints such as the ones made by Pettit and Interlux (see pages 15–18 for the full story on this). These bottom paints will last more than one year, so they do make it possible to save on hauling jobs.

Q: Two years ago I installed a knotmeter and log on my 35′ sloop, but I keep having trouble with the underwater impeller. It gets clogged every time the boat sits in the water without moving for a week. I have tried coating the impeller with an antifouling paint, but that didn't help. Even after I take the impeller out and clean it, then spin it by hand to make sure it works, I can never count on it working for long. I have contacted the manufacturer, but they say that's the way it goes. Is there a knotmeter that has no moving parts sticking through the hull—or is there any other cure you can suggest?

A: Every knotmeter I have ever heard of has some kind of sensor—an impeller, a paddle wheel, or some type of small rotating propeller—sticking through the hull, because this is the only way the instrument can sense the movement of the water past the hull (Kenyon used to make a model that had only a "wand" sticking down which did not rotate—it sensed water pressure as it was pushed through the water—but this type is no longer made). The only other way to measure speed would be with Loran C; it tells you the speed over bottom, not the speed through the water.

However, knotmeters do vary in design and some are apparently more prone to fouling than others. For example, some have a narrower opening for the wheel or prop. So they are easily blocked by grass or a small growth. Also, the design of the movable paddle wheel or propeller itself varies from one brand to the other—again with some being more prone to fouling than others. Also, some are more prone to snagging underwater grass and other debris.

Antifouling paint does help if the fouling is due to growth, but it won't help if floating debris is catching on the impeller. Your brand is probably one of those that fouls more easily. If you decide to get another one, consult a reliable marine electronics dealer first, and ask others about the experiences they have had with their particular brands.

Q: My outdrives have stainless steel clamping bands on them that I have to change frequently because the worm screw that tightens the band rusts badly. Yet the clamping bands are labeled "all stainless steel." I tested with a magnet, and sure enough the screw part tested magnetic just like regular steel. When I complained to the manufacturer, the explanation I got was: "Turning the screw in the lathe when the screw was manufactured rendered it magnetic from contact with the ferrous turning tools used." Is this just a glib excuse to cover up poor quality in an overpriced "marine" item, or is this information accurate and thus describes a condition I must live with?

A: There is some truth to the "excuse," in that machining does tend to make some types of stainless steel more prone to rusting—if they are not properly formulated and are not "passivated" afterward (a process of treating with a special acid to remove the ferrous particles). I have found over the years that some stainless steel clamps have the problem you describe with the worm screw rusting, while others do not. My suggestion is to shop around for a different brand if you can—maybe it will stand up better. I have one other precaution that I always follow: Get in the habit of regularly spraying the worm screw on each clamp with a heavy duty rust-preventive penetrating oil such as LPS-2 or LPS-3. This kind of protection will prevent rusting for years if you renew the spray often enough.

Index